Believers Church
Bible Commentary

Douglas B. Miller and Loren L. Johns, Editors

BELIEVERS CHURCH BIBLE COMMENTARY

Old Testament
Genesis, by Eugene F. Roop, 1987
Exodus, by Waldemar Janzen, 2000
Joshua, by Gordon H. Matties, 2012
Judges, by Terry L. Brensinger, 1999
Ruth, Jonah, Esther, by Eugene F. Roop, 2002
Psalms, by James H. Waltner, 2006
Proverbs, by John W. Miller, 2004
Ecclesiastes, by Douglas B. Miller, 2010
Isaiah, by Ivan D. Friesen, 2009
Jeremiah, by Elmer A. Martens, 1986
Lamentations, Song of Songs, by Wilma Ann Bailey, Christina Bucher, 2015
Ezekiel, by Millard C. Lind, 1996
Daniel, by Paul M. Lederach, 1994
Hosea, Amos, by Allen R. Guenther, 1998

New Testament
Matthew, by Richard B. Gardner, 1991
Mark, by Timothy J. Geddert, 2001
John by Willard M. Swartley, 2013
Acts, by Chalmer E. Faw, 1993
Romans, by John E. Toews, 2004
2 Corinthians, by V. George Shillington, 1998
Galatians, by George R. Brunk III, 2015
Ephesians, by Thomas R. Yoder Neufeld, 2002
Colossians, Philemon, by Ernest D. Martin, 1993
1-2 Thessalonians, by Jacob W. Elias, 1995
1-2 Timothy, Titus, by Paul M. Zehr, 2010
1-2 Peter, Jude, by Erland Waltner, J. Daryl Charles, 1999
1, 2, 3 John, by J. E. McDermond, 2011
Revelation, by John R. Yeatts, 2003

Old Testament Editors
Elmer A. Martens, Mennonite Brethren Biblical Seminary, Fresno, Calif.
Douglas B. Miller, Tabor College, Hillsboro, Kan.

New Testament Editors
Willard M. Swartley, Anabaptist Mennonite Biblical Seminary, Elkhart, Ind.
Loren L. Johns, Anabaptist Mennonite Biblical Seminary, Elkhart, Ind.

Editorial Council
David W. Baker, Brethren Church
W. Derek Suderman, Mennonite Church Canada
Christina Bucher, Church of the Brethren
John R. Yeatts, Brethren in Christ Church
Gordon H. Matties (chair), Mennonite Brethren Church
Jo-Ann A. Brant, Mennonite Church USA

Believers Church
Bible Commentary

Galatians

George R. Brunk III

HERALD PRESS
Harrisonburg, Virginia
Kitchener, Ontario

Library of Congress Cataloging-in-Publication Data
Brunk, George Rowland, 1939-
  Galatians / George R. Brunk III.
    pages cm. -- (Believers church Bible commentary ; 27)
  ISBN 978-0-8361-9860-7 (pbk. : alk. paper) 1. Bible. Galatians--Commentaries.
I. Title.
  BS2685.53.B78 2015
  227'.407--dc23
                                    2014042112

Copyright © 2015 by Herald Press, Harrisonburg, Virginia 22802
Released simultaneously in Canada by Herald Press,
Kitchener, Ontario N2G 3R1. All rights reserved.
Library of Congress Control Number: 2014042112
International Standard Book Number: 978-0-8361-9860-7
Printed in the United States of America
Cover and interior design by Merrill Miller

To order or request information, please call 1-800-245-7894 or visit www.heraldpress.com.

19 18 17 16 15   10 9 8 7 6 5 4 3 2

To Erma Hess

and

Ruthann Miller

Abbreviations

*	The Text in Biblical Context
+	The Text in the Life of the Church
AT	author's translation
BCE	before the Common Era (= BC, before Christ)
CE	Common Era (= AD, *anno Domini*, in the year of the Lord)
cf.	*confer*, compare
ch./chs.	chapter/chapters
e.g.	*exempli gratia*, for example
esp.	especially
et al.	et alia, and others
etc.	et cetera, and the rest
i.e.	*id est*, that is
KJV	King James Version of the Bible
lit.	literally
NIV	New International Version (2011)
NIV 1984	New International Version (1984)
NLT	New Living Translation
NRSV	New Revised Standard Version of the Bible (1989)
NT	New Testament
OT	Old Testament
RSV	Revised Standard Version
TBC	Text in Biblical Context, in the commentary
TLC	Text in the Life of the Church, in the commentary
v./vv.	verse/verses

Contents

Series Foreword

The Believers Church Bible Commentary Series makes available a new tool for basic Bible study. It is published for all who seek more fully to understand the original message of Scripture and its meaning for today—Sunday school teachers, members of Bible study groups, students, pastors, and others. The series is based on the conviction that God is still speaking to all who will listen, and that the Holy Spirit makes the Word a living and authoritative guide for all who want to know and do God's will.

The desire to help as wide a range of readers as possible has determined the approach of the writers. Since no blocks of biblical text are provided, readers may continue to use the translation with which they are most familiar. The writers of the series use the *New Revised Standard Version* and the *New International Version* on a comparative basis. They indicate which text they follow most closely and where they make their own translations. The writers have not worked alone, but in consultation with select counselors, the series' editors, and the Editorial Council.

Every volume illuminates the Scriptures; provides necessary theological, sociological, and ethical meanings; and in general makes "the rough places plain." Critical issues are not avoided, but neither are they moved into the foreground as debates among scholars. Each section offers explanatory notes, followed by focused articles, "The Text in Biblical Context" and "The Text in the Life of the Church." This commentary aids the interpretive process but does not try to supersede the authority of the Word and Spirit as discerned in the gathered church.

The term *believers church* has often been used in the history of the church. Since the sixteenth century, it has frequently been applied to the Anabaptists and later the Mennonites, as well as to the Church of the Brethren and similar groups. As a descriptive term, it includes more than Mennonites and Brethren. *Believers church* now represents specific theological understandings, such as believers baptism, commitment to the Rule of Christ in Matthew 18:15-20 as crucial for church membership, belief in the power of love in all relationships, and willingness to follow Christ in the way of the cross. The writers chosen for the series stand in this tradition.

Believers church people have always been known for their emphasis on obedience to the simple meaning of Scripture. Because of this, they do not have a long history of deep historical-critical biblical scholarship. This series attempts to be faithful to the Scriptures while also taking archaeology and current biblical studies seriously. Doing this means that at many points the writers will not differ greatly from interpretations that can be found in many other good commentaries. Yet these writers share basic convictions about Christ, the church and its mission, God and history, human nature, the Christian life, and other doctrines. These presuppositions do shape a writer's interpretation of Scripture. Thus this series, like all other commentaries, stands within a specific historical church tradition.

Many in this stream of the church have expressed a need for help in Bible study. This is justification enough to produce the Believers Church Bible Commentary. Nevertheless, the Holy Spirit is not bound to any tradition. May this series be an instrument in breaking down walls between Christians in North America and around the world, bringing new joy in obedience through a fuller understanding of the Word.

—*The Editorial Council*

Author's Preface

Paul's letter to the Galatians has been a special focus over my entire teaching career, during which I regularly taught a course in Greek exegesis of Galatians. The writing of this commentary on Galatians has taken place over a considerable span of time. Most of the work on the manuscript was done during two sabbaticals from teaching and administrative duties at Eastern Mennonite Seminary and in the rare occasions of spare time amid more pressing duties. The disadvantage of this delay in publication is the lack of access to a key New Testament document for the readership of this commentary series. The advantage, on the other hand, is that the commentary thus benefits from developments in the study of Paul during a particularly creative period of new insights and perspectives.

Even though I have deliberately kept citations to a minimum, I gladly acknowledge extensive dependency on the wide range of literature on Galatians and on Pauline theology. The primary conversation partners in this project were the commentaries of Longenecker, Dunn, and Witherington. Especially helpful was the massive commentary in the Italian language by A. Marcello Buscemi, with its careful analysis of the Greek grammar. I also regularly consulted the commentaries of Betz, Bruce, Burton, Lightfoot, and Martyn. I have found the writings of Michael Gorman on Paul particularly stimulating. I hammered out much of my perspective on Galatians with seminary students in Greek exegesis classes. I express my gratitude to all of them as colearners at the feet of Paul. Finally, I acknowledge with appreciation the critical assistance of Jacob Elias, my peer reader for this project and colleague over many years in theological education.

I especially acknowledge the support of my first wife, Erma Hess, who, before her death, faithfully and graciously encouraged me in the first stage of writing. Heartfelt thanks go to my present spouse, Ruthann Miller, for standing with me in the final stages of this work. To them I dedicate this volume with deepest appreciation.

—*George R. Brunk III*
Harrisonburg, Virginia

Introduction to Galatians

The study of the apostle Paul's writings in the New Testament has experienced a new spurt of energy in recent decades. So much so, in fact, that it is common among scholars to refer to the New Perspective on Paul. Because of this fresh interest in the study of Paul and his writings, a spate of commentaries on Paul's letter to the Galatians has appeared, many of them from leading New Testament scholars of our time. Most of these commentaries are for specialists in historical and theological study. The present commentary focuses in another direction. While building on and drawing from the full range of current Galatians interpretation, it has the practical purpose of serving the church and confessional interests as it seeks to gain from and contribute new insight to a particular faith tradition in its conversation with the canonical letter of Galatians.

The purpose of this commentary, and its rationale, is twofold. First, reflecting the purpose of this commentary series, it deliberately brings the perspective of a certain theological tradition into the conversation on the significant theological and ethical issues treated in Galatians. That tradition is clearly acknowledged in the commentary series title as that of the believers church (rooted in the Anabaptist stream of the Radical Reformation). I am aware of only one commentary in this tradition—a small volume by the Dutch preacher Fritz Kuiper, which relates the Galatian theme of freedom to the Dutch context of World War II (see bibliography). Consequently, the commentary unapologetically reflects a particular faith tradition. However, in another sense it represents a kind of correction, given the fact that Galatians has had a somewhat marginal place in this tradition (see below).

Second, the commentary has as its audience the leaders in church life who use Scripture in teaching, preaching, and pastoral care. Therefore, I am making an effort to bridge the gap from the text in its original context, to the context of the church today—to point a way from exegesis to application. This approach inevitably gives the commentary a more context-specific character, determined by the context of the author and the faith tradition for which it is written. I hope that a wider audience will find even this particularity useful. Indeed, the challenge of our time, more than ever, is for all traditions to listen to one another's distinctive perspectives, learning from them even as they evaluate them. Within the commentary itself I have attempted to engage in such conversations.

In light of the intended audience, the commentary does not go far in reviewing the history of interpretation and responses to it. For the same reason, I avoid providing extensive documentation of scholarship. I cite sources for highly original views and, of course, for direct quotations. And I typically note possible options in understanding the text to assist readers in arriving at their own judgments on the issues. At the same time I usually offer and defend a specific position. Readers wanting more detailed information can consult the more technical commentaries listed in the bibliography.

The Historical Influence of Galatians

By most any reckoning, Paul's letter to the Galatians is one of most important documents in Christian history. It has exercised a major influence in the history of the Christian church and in the experience of individual believers. At crucial turning points in history, this short but forceful writing has played a central role. Galatians is a document with life-changing and history-changing power—a kind of revolutionary manifesto.

Galatians played a central role in the momentous shift in Christianity from being a messianic sect within Judaism to becoming a Gentile-dominated religious movement that would eventually come to be seen as an *alternative* to Judaism. Paul is the key figure in the founding of Gentile churches that did not embrace the Jewish observance of the Law (circumcision, for example) as a requirement in becoming a follower of Jesus. Galatians is the oldest witness we have that reflects the debate among early believers in Jesus on the relation of the new in Jesus Christ to the old in Moses, and the relation of Jew and Gentile. It defends a new direction by laying out the case for a faith that, while affirming the unity of God's purposes in history, takes Jesus and the Spirit as the final authority rather than the Law of Moses. The debate around this issue is reflected at numerous places in the New Testament, but Galatians represents the earliest and most intense version of this debate that we possess.

Another major point in history where Galatians figures prominently is the sixteenth-century Reformation. Paul's letters to the Romans and to the Galatians were the source for Martin Luther's breakthrough understanding of right standing with God by faith apart from human achievement (thus justification by faith alone) and then his critique of the contemporary church's theology and practice. Galatians was a favorite part of Scripture on which he often lectured. The entire family of Protestant churches, including those in the Anabaptist tradition, thus depends to one extent or another on this rediscovery of the spiritual power of Galatians.

Within the Reformation scene, the Anabaptist movement was ambivalent toward Luther's rediscovery of justification. The Anabaptists accepted its basic point as essential but criticized the lack of a clear bridge to moral transformation of life. This ambivalence is reflected in the limited use of Galatians in their writings. In the polarities of debate of the sixteenth century, the Anabaptists highlighted what they perceived to be neglected: the parts of the New Testament writings that teach a new way of life, which they referred to as discipleship. Galatians did not contradict their understandings; its emphases simply did not have priority in their context. Interestingly, references to Galatians in the extant Anabaptist writings reveal a significant usage of Paul's appeal to divine curse on his opponents (Gal 1:8-9). This surely reflects the intensely polemical style of debate in that time. Paul's equally intense debate style appeared to give them scriptural warrant.

More recently, Galatians has had an impact on social questions in church life and on the broader society. Paul's thesis that in Christ there is *not male and female* (Gal 3:28 AT) has been a major leverage point in the effort to dismantle patriarchy, the male-dominated church life that marked the church's longer history. In an earlier era, this same Galatians text undermined human slavery, based on the assertion that in Christ there is *neither slave nor free* (NIV). As these cases illustrate, this writing has proved its ability to critique oppressive social constructions and accommodations by pointing to the radical essence of a Christ-centered gospel.

Along with Galatians' world-changing power we sense its deeply personal power. In writing Galatians, Paul did not disguise his personal experience of the gospel. In fact, he used it as a persuasive strategy to appeal to his readers. This same quality speaks to any believer who desires a close relationship with the God of biblical revelation. A passage like Galatians 2:19-20 (*I have been crucified with Christ; and it is no longer I who live, but it is Christ who lives in me*) is a spiritual classic readily and frequently cited in testimony to life in Christ. Other similar references are 4:4-6, 9, 19; and 5:22. So the transforming power of this text operates at both the personal and the social levels of life, as well as the devotional and ethical levels.

Since the Reformation, the interpretation of Galatians has largely been dominated by mainline Protestant perspectives. The doctrine of justification by faith has been seen as the central and nearly exclusive theme, with justification understood as an alternative to human attempts to gain good standing with God by doing good works. Until recent decades, even groups whose theological stance and emphases differ from the mainline Protestant genre have generally accepted this way of understanding the letter. One such group is the Anabaptists and their heirs. Within this group (and others where holiness of life or sanctification is stressed) the commitment to following Christ in all of life makes ethics (good works) essential. They have tended to find the teaching of Jesus, as in the Sermon on the Mount, more congenial than the teaching of Paul—at least as understood by the dominant interpretation.

Unfortunately this bias against Paul has resulted in the relative neglect of Galatians in such circles, apart from a few isolated favorite verses. With some confidence we can say "unfortunately" because more recent interpretation has opened up new understandings of our letter and of Pauline theology generally. These understandings see justification not in fundamental contrast to good works. Rather, justification is fully consistent with and actually elicits a new life of godliness and righteous, or just, living. In this view, Paul opposes a certain understanding of works, not works as such. The present commentary offers an interpretation that draws (critically) on these new understandings of Paul (known as the New Perspective on Paul) and depends (also critically) on the theological insights and life experience of the Anabaptist tradition.

Author, Audience, Date

Because of the particular purpose of this commentary series, only modest attention will be given to the introductory questions of authorship, audience, and date. There are ample resources in other commentaries and Bible reference works on these matters. An overview is offered here as a ready source for the reader to the introductory questions and as a summary of the assumptions informing the interpretation of the letter.

Authorship

That Paul is the author of Galatians is one of the points of greatest consensus in New Testament studies. The letter makes that specific claim in the introduction (salutation). The conclusion was originally written in Paul's own hand in order to authenticate the writing as coming from the one whose writing style was recognizable. The strong autobiographical component in the body (and argument) of the letter, especially in chapters 1 and 4, makes it possible to pinpoint times, places, and relationships that ring true with all we know of the wider history of the times and of the early Christian movement in particular. Moreover, the firsthand immediacy of the writing and the depth of passion evident throughout the letter reduces the possibility of someone writing under an assumed name or creatively constructing a narrative. For these reasons Galatians is considered by the vast majority of scholars as the best starting point for reconstructing the life and thought of Paul and the history of the first-generation church.

Original Audience

The opening of Galatians names the recipients of the letter as the *churches of Galatia.* So the letter is in some sense a district letter, meant for multiple churches (probably house churches), having in common the description—*of Galatia.* To what exactly does that geographical term refer? The term was used in New Testament times for two locations, and this ambiguity leads to a major debate. Galatians first named the Gallic or Celtic people who migrated from Europe into the north-central part of Asia Minor, south of the Black Sea. The territory where they settled was called Galatia. However, at the time of Paul's mission, Galatia was also a province of the Roman Empire, created out of the earlier ethnic territory plus other parts of Asia Minor farther south. So the question is whether Paul uses Galatia to refer to a territory or to a province. Both areas are part of modern-day Turkey.

According to the book of Acts, Paul evangelized in the southern part of the province of Galatia during his first missionary journey (Acts 13–14) without using the provincial name. This included the cities of Antioch of Pisidia, Iconium, Lystra, and Derbe. Acts 16:6 and

18:23 explicitly mention visits of Paul to Galatia in later missionary trips. Many take these to refer to a time of ministry in ethnic Galatia in the north, which Acts does not recount in detail. As a result, students of the Galatian letter are divided as to whether the persons addressed were in north Galatia (North Galatian theory) or in south Galatia (South Galatian theory). The majority opinion throughout church history has favored the North Galatian view. Recent scholarship, however, is more evenly divided. This commentary finds the south Galatian view more persuasive but avoids interpretations based solely on one particular view (see below).

Date

Understandably, the date for Galatians is dependent on the previous point of who the Galatian people are and on the related question of when in Paul's career he is likely to have written the letter. The latter point depends on how we understand the chronology of Paul's life and ministry. Of particular interest in our case is the question of how to correlate Paul's visits to Jerusalem in Acts with the visits recounted in Galatians. A central question in that regard is whether the visit of Galatians 2:1-10 is the same as the Jerusalem Council in Acts 15:1-30, or whether the former visit occurs earlier, perhaps at the same time as the famine relief visit in Acts 11:30; 12:25.

If the Jerusalem visit in Galatians 2:1-10 (and the Antioch incident in 2:11-15) comes before the Jerusalem Council of Acts 15, then the letter could be dated as early as 48–49 CE. In that case Galatians would be one of the earliest writings of the New Testament, perhaps the earliest. If Galatians 2:1-10 and Acts 15 are the same visit, then the date for Galatians could be in the early 50s with the South Galatian view, or some years later with the North Galatian view.

The question of the chronology of Paul's life has never found solid resolution, due largely to differences between Acts and Galatians. No dating of the events in Galatians or of its writing has been completely satisfying. The dominant view from the early centuries to the present is that Paul wrote the letter to churches in the northern territory of Galatia and that the Jerusalem visit of Galatians 2 is the same occasion as Acts 15. In this view, the date of writing is in the mid-50s. This dominance is hardly surprising. The Roman province of Galatia was soon reorganized and renamed, so even early interpreters of Galatians likely knew only of the territory, not of the province. Moreover, the association of the meetings of Acts 15 and Galatians 2:1-10 is natural since they are the only narratives of a similar event and they have some common features.

However, this commentary prefers the earlier date for Galatians and the South Galatia destination. This would mean that Paul wrote the letter before the Jerusalem Council of Acts 15. The meeting with Jerusalem leaders in Galatians 2 is then a different occasion, focused more broadly on the legitimacy of Paul's Gentile mission and not specifically on circumcision. A major consideration is the fact that neither the visit to Jerusalem nor the Antioch incident (Gal 2), in Paul's recounting, refer to a definitive decision on the question of circumcision, which is the focus of both the Galatians letter and the Jerusalem Council (Acts 15). If such a clear decision was made before Paul wrote Galatians, then the lack of any refer-ence to it in the Antioch incident (Gal 2:11-15) or any appeal to it in Paul's argument against the Galatian opposition seems astonishing and incomprehensible. Even then, many still prefer the option that Acts 15 and Galatians refer to the same meeting, but that Luke has made something different of its purpose and outcome and focuses more on an agreement about circumcision. Some further discussion of these questions is found in the main part of the commentary, but the interpretation of the central theological claims of Galatians does not depend on these questions of dates and chronology.

The Literary Type and Structure of Galatians

Galatians is in the form of a letter, or epistle. It displays the standard features of the Hellenistic letter of its time. The opening and closing parts of the letter show the formal features that parallel those in common letter writing in the Greco-Roman society. All of Paul's writings in the New Testament possess these features, with a high degree of uniformity. Within the uniformity is variation to fit the specific needs of a given letter or Paul's creative impulse.

Clearly then, Galatians reflects a standard literary form or genre. Letters served a broad social function. That function was simply the communication of an author with a distant audience, for whom oral discourse was impossible. Within the letter form a great variety of specific interests or purposes could be served, such as friendship, recommendation, admonition, praise (or blame), information, busi-ness, and official communication. Leaders in the early Christian movement used the letter as a means of contact with the scattered believers. In this way they could continue their spiritual guidance to many congregations while absent.

Traditionally, the letter of Galatians has been seen as structured into three sections: autobiographical narrative (chs. 1–2); theologi-cal argument (chs. 3–4); practical teaching (chs. 5–6). The dividing point between the theological and practical sections has, however, been debated. (Does it come at 4:12; 4:31; 5:1; or 5:13?) This outline does justice to the general character of each part, but it also has its problems. Parts of the "theological" section are more practical or personal—3:1-5; 4:12-20. The allegory of Hagar and Sarah seems to be an afterthought, disconnected from other scriptural arguments in the middle section. Moreover, certain portions of the "practical" section are actually theological argument—5:2-6, 13-24. This unfortunate distinction between theology and practical teaching (ethics) has led many interpreters to see chapters 5 and 6 as unrelated to the main purpose of Galatians. They think Paul was merely following his conventional practice in letter writing by adding some practical admonitions appropriate to any religious audience. In fact, however, these chapters continue the main theme of the letter and bring it to a climax.

We do greater justice to the letter by taking our basic clue to the structure from the rebuke/request feature clearly discernible in the letter. Such a feature reflects a standard form of Greek letters *[Literary and Rhetorical Features of Galatians, p. 314]*. In Galatians the rebuke section runs from 1:6 to 4:11 and the request section from 4:12 to 6:10, the latter being clearly distinguished by the heavy use of imperative verbs. This structure recognizes the general movement from (1) making a case against the error in Galatia to (2) pointing toward correct action, though even this is not absolute, as the reprimanding tone of 5:2-7 shows. It gives full recognition to the freedom with which Paul interweaves autobiographical, theological, and practical elements. Each part of the letter contributes directly to Paul's case for a way of life that is faith-based rather than law-based.

In achieving his purpose, Paul employs the full range of the means of persuasion known in his time (and still today). The philosopher Aristotle explained that the modes of persuasion (rhetoric) are essentially three: appeal to the character or integrity of the speaker (ethos); appeal to logic (logos); and appeal to the emotions of the hearer (pathos). These three are all conspicuous in Galatians. Throughout the letter, Paul moves from one mode to the other. Appeal to his own character predominates in chapters 1 and 2, yet also appears elsewhere (e.g., 4:12-16). Appeal to logic or reason is strongest in chapters 3 and 4 but is not limited to that part. The appeal to emotion is distributed throughout, as in 1:6, 8-9; 2:5; 3:1; 4:19-20; 5:12; 6:17.

In the effort to achieve his purpose, Paul draws not only on

Hellenistic letter-writing types, but also on Greco-Roman rhetorical forms. In recent years, Galatians has been the object of careful comparison to the standard rhetorical forms in the Greco-Roman culture. There are clear traces of the judicial or apologetic form, used in legal defense in the courtroom setting. Paul is mounting a defense of himself and his gospel. But there is also evidence of the deliberative form of rhetoric, which has the purpose of exhortation and correction. Most commentators now suggest that Galatians is primarily a deliberative letter in which Paul uses certain elements of the apologetic form [*Literary and Rhetorical Features of Galatians, p. 314*].

In the end, one must recognize that the writer of Galatians does not rigidly follow literary conventions or rules of argumentation. Behind Paul's rhetoric are both the issue itself and Paul's passion to effect change in the reader. As a man of Hellenistic and Jewish culture, Paul draws more or less spontaneously on the literary and oratorical usages of his day to promote the gospel.

Identifying the rhetoric of Galatians is important for interpreting the letter. All readers recognize the intense feeling and conviction reflected in the writing. This state of mind and heart on the part of Paul, along with his strong desire to bring change in the Galatian believers, prompts him to use every linguistic means of persuasion. We can therefore expect an author to use overstatement and even one-sided argument in order to make the point more forceful. The interpreter of Galatians will want to be alert to this possibility without falling prey to one's own overreaction to the rhetoric. Fortunately, Paul wrote other texts on similar topics but in other states of mind. With them we can test our understanding. This is especially true of the letter to the Romans, which treats many of the same themes in a less polemical situation and at a more mature point of Paul's ministry.

Contemporary Significance of Galatians

That Paul's letter to the Galatians is significant for the contemporary church is already suggested by our brief review of the letter's influence earlier in this introduction. That this writing transcends the particular occasion that precipitated its composition is evidenced by the history of its influence.

In Galatians, Paul is seeking the ultimate ground of true life. He is trying to identify the essence of life before God. Paul's convictions in this regard are what help him sort out the practical issues that he must address in the Galatian congregations. His writings in general—and certainly Galatians in particular—show the strategy of thinking through every question from foundational truths to their consistent expression in life practices. In Galatians, that leads Paul on a search for the essence of the gospel, from which alone can there be authenticity and coherence in life.

In Galatians this central passion appears explicitly in 3:1-5, where Paul appeals to his readers to remain attached to the essential spiritual reality with which their faith began. Anything that does not sustain that central reality is inauthentic and constitutes a threat to the truth of the gospel. Another way this search for essence appears in Paul's writings is in the terse summary statements that help him and his readers to keep the basics clearly in view. A beautiful example in Galatians is found in 5:5, a formulation that manages to summarize the entire thrust of the letter: *For through the Spirit, by faith, we eagerly wait for the hope of righteousness.*

Paul already knew, as church history and individual experience have confirmed since then, that we easily major on secondary matters and rely on material means to achieve spiritual ends. The good obscures the essential. The superstructure loses contact with the foundation. The form is present, but the spirit is absent.

Paul leaves no doubt about the essentials of faith as he understands them. Galatians is a sustained defense of Jesus Christ as the center of faith, from whom flows true life and to whom all of life must conform. Paul reasons and argues his case in Galatians in many ways, some even appearing strained to contemporary ways of reasoning. But what seems to drive every argument is the key question: What is consistent with the person of Christ? At the center is a person, not an idea. Paul wants his understanding of the gospel to be judged by that standard.

Alongside this central role of Christ is the role of the Spirit. This emphasis on the Spirit in Galatians has traditionally been eclipsed by other themes, such as justification and freedom. That it ranks right along with Christ at the heart of Paul's gospel is nicely reflected in 4:4-6. God's redeeming work for the world is based on two parallel actions: the sending out of the Son (Christ) and the sending out of the Spirit of the Son. The theme of the Spirit is prominent from chapter 3 onward. For Paul, the key to authentic experience of faith is an intimate relationship with the Spirit, who teaches us the language of fellowship in God's family (4:6) and who empowers believers to achieve what mere human potential cannot.

In light of this passion for the heart of the matter, we can understand Paul's concern for truth—*the truth of the gospel* (2:5, 14). Truth is a matter of both right understanding and right conduct. Paul is concerned about rational coherence (right ideas), but not as an end in itself. The goal of truth is coherent living where we walk truthfully in life. The understanding of truth and the expression of truth in life are dependent on each other. Paul's concern for truth therefore parallels his concern to move coherently from essence to existence.

Galatians keeps before us the challenge of seeking truth and confessing truth even in an age of postmodern skepticism about truth claims. Paul would no doubt agree with that skeptical view of human claims to truth, but in agreement with the gospel of John, he would find optimism and courage in the promise of Spirit guidance into the truth (cf. John 14:26; 16:13).

Growing out of this central concern are several practical truths that Paul applied to the Galatian situation and that are of universal relevance. To confess the fullness of truth in Christ leads necessarily to acknowledge the full unity of the people who identify with Christ. While the immediate concern in Galatians is the unity of Jew and Gentile, this concern for unity crosses every natural human distinction (3:28). A close corollary to unity is the theme of equality. Those who relate on an equal basis to the one Christ must relate equally to one another. It is in this unity and equality grounded in Christ that, according to Paul, true freedom is found. Freedom is being released from every enslavement or submission that is not coherent with identification with Christ. Within that identity, freedom involves both submission to Christ and submission in love to other followers of Christ (5:13).

Neither in Paul's day nor in all subsequent church history has the grand vision of the gospel glimpsed in Galatians seen complete and consistent realization. But before there can be reality, there must be vision. The enduring function of the letter to the Galatians is to provide us such a vision. And precisely because it articulates so high a vision, it retains through time the power to inspire ever new and higher reaches of realization of that vision.

Features of this Commentary

The primary translation used in the commentary is the New Revised Standard Version. Any departure from this usage is noted. A major topic in Galatians is law. The reader should be aware that the commentary distinguishes between "Law" as the Law of Moses (the OT's Pentateuch, or Torah) and "law" in a generic sense, although the word *law* is actually more complex than the two senses allow. References to the Christian confessional tradition reflected in this commentary (and its series) can vary. The following terms are used interchangeably: *believers church*, *Radical Reformation*, and *Anabaptist*.

At several points in this commentary I refer to the Second Temple period and to Second Temple Judaism, terms with which the reader may not immediately be familiar. These terms refer to the time the Second Temple stood—from the time it was rebuilt after the Babylonian exile, from about 520 to 515 BCE, until it was destroyed by the Romans in 70 CE. *Late* Second Temple Judaism covers the final century or two before the Common Era and then up to 70 CE. Paul wrote Galatians near the end of the late Second Temple period. This somewhat longer phrase helps to clarify that the Judaism with which Paul identified and with which he was interacting in this letter was not the same Judaism that developed after the destruction of the temple, known as rabbinic Judaism. The literature of late Second Temple Judaism includes Daniel, the Old Testament Pseudepigrapha, Josephus (even though, technically, he wrote *after* the destruction of the temple), Philo, the Dead Sea Scrolls, the Apocrypha, and the letters of Paul.

The reader is particularly encouraged to compare the viewpoint of this commentary with the volume on Romans in the Believers Church Bible Commentary series. There are many points of agreement but also differences in perspective that will stimulate more informed and critical reflection. The perceptive reader will notice that I have a somewhat different take on Paul's theology than John Toews has, and that the present commentary thus serves as a conversation partner with the one on Romans in this series. In particular, I disagree with Toews's understanding of *pistis Christou* (faith in Christ versus faith of Christ), and my own embrace of the New Perspective in Pauline studies is more moderated than his fuller embrace [*The Faith of Jesus Christ, p. 305*]. Nevertheless, because the essays in Toews's volume cover a wide range of Pauline vocabulary and concepts, many of them relate directly to the themes of Galatians and are thus a helpful resource.

Galatians 1:1-5

The Letter Opening

PREVIEW

Galatians is in the form of a letter, or epistle—the ordinary form for written correspondence in the Greco-Roman world. The modern reader can identify parts of this form with ease because they have persisted as features of written correspondence up to the present time. The formal opening identifies the sender and receiver(s) of the letter and establishes a personal relationship by means of a formula of greeting. The formal closing may contain several elements, but there is always an expression of well-wishes.

While the early Christian writers respect the standard forms, they also freely adapt the language to their faith (see comments on 1:3). Moreover, Paul expands on the basic structure to make even these formal parts of the letter serve the purposes of the body of the letter. In Galatians, the expansion serves to establish the tone of the letter and to alert the readers to the author's agenda. In a typical letter of the time, the introductory material includes a thanksgiving for something associated with the recipients. Paul normally observed this practice. It helped to build relationships. However, in Galatians the thanksgiving is conspicuously missing. This certainly is a deliberate move to strengthen the effect of the disappointment and rebuke that Paul expresses later in the main body of the letter.

OUTLINE

Author, 1:1-2a
Addressees, 1:2b
Greeting, 1:3-5

EXPLANATORY NOTES

Author 1:1-2a

The letter identifies multiple senders—*Paul . . . and all the members of God's family who are with me*. By placing himself first and apart from the others, Paul indicates that he is the principal author. This is supported by the first-person singular (*I*) that predominates throughout the letter and by the reference in the closing to his own handwriting (6:11). Other persons associated with the sending of the letter show that there is a community of support for the viewpoint defended in the letter. Since Paul's authority as an apostle is a crucial factor in the letter, it is all the more significant that others are mentioned. Paul exercises apostleship and its authority from a base in the wider community of faith (see also on 2:2). The presence of the word *all* strengthens the point by implying a solid backing of Paul's stance. The accountability process at work in the letter is one of community (the company of believers with Paul) to community (the Galatian churches) as well as one of individual (apostolic leader) to community (cf. 1 Cor 11:16; 14:33b).

Paul is the Greek name for the man whose Jewish name was Saul (Acts 13:9). Generally Paul uses the title of apostle in introducing his letters. This is understandable because the letters we have are part of Paul's ministry of guiding young churches. Reference to his role enhances the significance of what he writes in the eyes of the reader. The word *apostle* is related to the Greek verb "to send." In the New Testament the noun is used for persons who are sent with a commission on behalf of someone else. Paul's life and message, as apostle to the Gentiles (2:7-8), reflects Paul's powerful self-awareness of being under commission from God. This status gives authority to his ministry, including his pastoral guidance in letter form.

Now Paul expands on the title with an extended comment, carefully worded. His explanation has to do with the ground of his apostleship, and he therefore is establishing his credibility as author. Paul's claim to apostolic standing by divine commission is supported first by a negative assertion and then by a positive one. He is an apostle *neither by human commission nor from human authorities*, or more precisely translated, *not from human source nor through human*

mediation (1:1a AT). The emphasis is on the two differing prepositions *from* and *through*. Paul's intent is to exclude humans both as
the originating cause and as the intermediate means through whom
another agent acted (God, in this case). It is not likely that Paul
expects the Galatian believers to associate these statements with
specific persons or occasions. The language is too general even to
allude to specific things in the past.

While the human factor is eliminated, the divine ground for
Paul's apostleship is asserted—*but through Jesus Christ and God the
Father* (1:1b). Surprisingly Paul does not say *through Jesus Christ and
from God the Father* in exact (but contrasting) parallel with the prepositions *from* and *through* of the previous clause. That is common in
the New Testament: in achieving divine purposes, God (the Father)
is the source, and Jesus Christ is the agent. Such is, in fact, the
underlying thought here. However, the particular form of the
expression appears to be determined by the fact that in early
Christianity, apostleship is linked directly to a commission of the
risen Jesus (and such was Paul's conviction, based on his own experience). Therefore Jesus Christ is mentioned first. But Paul wants to
acknowledge the ultimate source as *God the Father, who raised [Jesus]
from the dead* (1:1c). His apostleship has its ultimate cause in God the
Father and its intermediate cause in Jesus Christ. Paul may also want
to express the unity of Father and Son (Christ) with one preposition
(cf. the same pattern in 1:3).

The reference to resurrection is, therefore, not a mere formality of the letter's opening. As near as we can tell, the term *apostle*
was normally used for someone who had received an appearance
of the resurrected Jesus. The commission as an apostle came as
part of the appearance of the risen Lord. A mutual dependence
exists between the resurrection and apostleship. The resurrection
needs the witness of the apostle for its proclamation and verifica-
tion. An apostle requires the authorizing of the resurrected Jesus.
It follows that Paul is alluding to the appearance of Jesus to him on
the road to Damascus. This becomes clearer in 1:12: *through a revelation of Jesus Christ.* (For further comment on Paul as an apostle, see
TBC below.)

Who are the cosenders of the letter mentioned in verse 2? The
phrase *who are with me* (1:2a) would be a strange way to refer to a
congregation that Paul is visiting at the time of writing. More likely
it points to Paul's missionary associates, those traveling with him.
Philippians 4:21-22, for example, distinguishes between persons
with Paul (as in our text) and all the saints, meaning the church

where Paul is located. The identity of these associates is uncertain since we are not sure of the date of Paul's writing this letter and where then to locate it in Paul's missionary travels as recorded in Acts (see the Introduction).

Addressees 1:2b

The letter is written *to the churches of Galatia.* This is not one congregation but multiple congregations. Just as one can easily miss the multiple senders, so one can easily miss the multiple addressees. The incorrect teaching that Paul combats in the letter is a regional phenomenon. Presumably traveling teachers are visiting the local congregations and promoting the same teaching. Here the word *churches* signifies local groups of believers; the term can also mean the wider body of believers as in 1:13: *the church of God.* Since the churches are not identified more exactly, the question of where they were located has been debated. The uncertainty is made greater by the fact that more than one area could be called Galatia in Paul's day. (See the Introduction for a discussion of the theories of destination.) Paul's practice was to embellish the reference to his addressees with positive descriptions such as "saints" and "beloved of God." The lack of such language here signals a coolness of Paul's attitude. From the fact that several congregations are addressed, we can conclude that Galatians is a circular letter.

Greeting 1:3-5

Verse 3 states the formal greeting. This is the third element in the standard features of a letter opening. The greeting itself conforms to early church practice in combining *grace and peace.* It is an adaptation of the Greek formula that used the verb for rejoice (*chairein*). New Testament writers creatively changed this to the similar *charis,* meaning grace, and added the Jewish greeting of peace (*shalom*). With these words the first generation of believers captured the essence of the gospel, confessing it in the repetition of routine greetings. (Note how *grace* sums up the gospel in 1:6: *grace of Christ.*) *Grace* expresses the ground of gospel reality, and *peace* states its fruit. But the ultimate source is God, seen once again as *God our Father and the Lord Jesus Christ* (1:3; cf. 1:1). What is new is the title *Lord* for Jesus Christ, which was the common confession of the first believers. It points to Jesus exalted to the right hand of God after the resurrection (Rom 1:4; Phil 2:9-11, esp. v. 11) and affirms his authority over the church and potentially over the world. The triple repetition of the designation *Father* in verses 1, 3, and 5 is striking. It discloses the dominance in Paul's thinking of a familial and intimate understanding of God. (See also comments on 4:6 and TLC below.)

Just as the identification of author undergoes a surprising expansion, so the word of greeting is greatly enlarged by verses 4 and 5. The expansion is, in effect, a statement about Christ and has the ring of a confessional affirmation. The Epistles of the New Testament contain numerous formulas of this kind. They usually have Christ as their subject and are marked by a compact and artful style (e.g., Rom 1:3-4; Phil 2:6-11; Col 1:15-20; 1 Tim 3:16). This clearly demonstrates that the faith of the early church was Christ-centered.

Several indicators suggest that Paul incorporates a formula already in existence that was probably known to the readers. First, there is a unique vocabulary for otherwise common Pauline concepts. The verb *to set free*, or *deliver*, and the phrase *the present evil age* are never used elsewhere by Paul. Second, the confessional formula appears to serve as an appeal to traditional material known and accepted by both the writer and the readers. The inclusion of such formulas in the introductions to Pauline letters appears only in Romans and Galatians. In Romans the confessional statement builds a faith tie to believers whom Paul has never met. In Galatians it evokes common beliefs that Paul can use as a basis from which to argue against Galatian error. Thus the greeting looks back to the familiar beliefs of the Galatians and forward to the themes Paul will develop in the letter. This move from the familiar to the new and controversial makes the argument of the letter more persuasive.

Who gave himself for our sins (1:4a) expresses the essence of the gospel from the viewpoint of Christ and his work. The language of self-giving is a reference to Christ's death on the cross, a central theme for Paul. His death deals with the problem of human sin. His life is given on behalf of our sins. The plural (*sins*) highlights the specific ways in which we have violated and fallen short of God's will. In this way the problem is made to focus on the human person, on all persons. By consequence the work of salvation is personal (*our sins*), being directed to the individual's condition. Yet the language can also include the collective sins of the human community.

The thought then moves to a goal beyond that of dealing with sin itself. The ultimate purpose of Christ's self-sacrifice is *to set us free from the present evil age* (1:4b). This purpose clause goes beyond the isolated individual to speak of the context in which the individual and the human community live. It is a social and cosmic (total world reality) context. The sin problem is answered not only by forgiveness of sins, but also through a rescue or deliverance from the *present evil age. Age* does not merely signify a defined period of time but also a social context marked by particular patterns of thinking and behavior.

Although the believer and the believing community are not physically removed from the present world setting, they are changed (converted) to a new understanding of life, a new set of values, and a different way of living. The same idea appears in Romans 12:2, which literally says, "Do not conform yourselves to the pattern (of life) of this age." The concept of rescue implies a movement from an undesirable state of bondage to a favorable condition of freedom. By this traditional formula, then, Paul touches on the later themes of slavery to the *elemental spirits* (4:1-10) and of freedom in Christ (2:4; 5:1, 13).

In his saving work, Christ is not a passive instrument in the hands of God: he gave himself. At the same time, what happened to him is *according to the will of our God and Father* (1:4c). By this phrase the introduction further emphasizes the unity of Father and Son already present in the phrase that pairs the Father and Christ (vv. 1, 3). The emphasis on Christ's self-giving shows him to be an active participant in the love and grace extended by God to a needy world. Moreover, it takes him as a true example of the obedient child of God (Heb 5:8).

To the confessional summary is appended an outburst of praise to God (a doxology): *to whom be the glory forever and ever. Amen* (1:5). Such a response of praise, which turns the flow of address from the reader to God, does not appear in other introductions of Paul's letters; but it is present with the salutation in the book of Revelation (1:6). At the same time, we see similar spontaneous statements of praise elsewhere in Paul's letters (Rom 11:33-36; 16:27; Phil 4:20; and others). They invariably follow a reference to the benefits of God for believers. This explains its presence here in dependence on the preceding confessional formula, which states the benefit of salvation. Thus we view the intense personal faith of Paul, for whom these beliefs are an experiential reality. Glory is the radiant manifestation of God's presence that points to the divine power and majesty. To ascribe glory to God is to acknowledge this highest excellence of God and to own its consequences in one's life and in all creation.

THE TEXT IN BIBLICAL CONTEXT

Galatians as an Apostolic Epistle

Paul's epistles, or letters, of which Galatians is an example, have the form of the normal correspondence of the day. They were written in response to a specific situation (occasional) to achieve a particular goal (task-oriented). They do not aspire to be great literature for a general audience. On the other hand, they have a public character inasmuch as they were intended as (or became) circular letters. None of the New Testament letter writers, including Paul, give evidence of consciously writing literature that would endure or become part of a permanent standard of truth (canon of Scripture).

Nevertheless these writings serve as foundational witnesses to the gospel. As witnesses to God's once-for-all action in Jesus the Christ, they share this good news and its implications for the church and indeed for the whole world. Thus the writings themselves participate in the special and once-for-all character of the gospel. This is the basis for their unique and permanent scriptural authority. In this regard the epistle to the Galatians is of special interest. Here the issue of apostleship and its relation to the truth of the gospel (cf. 2:5) receives specific treatment. Questions of authority come into view. As a result there is a link between the authority of Paul the apostle and the authority of the Galatian letter, and finally the authority of Scripture. Comments on chapters 1 and 2 (below) will explore these matters further.

The Special Function of the Letter Opening

Normally the opening of a letter is little more than a formality. But Galatians is different. Here each expansion of the basic letter form makes a significant point. In these expansions or digressions, we can read the interests of the writer. One might anticipate that those thoughts would parallel the themes of the letter proper—and such is indeed the case for Galatians. The introduction prepares for what follows in tone and in theme. The tone is set by the lack of any praise for the addressees. Paul's reserved and cool tone is further underscored by the absence of a thanksgiving for the virtues and achievements of the readers. This tone prepares for the criticism and rebuke that follow in the body of the letter. The anticipation of later themes focuses on three items: apostleship, the cross of Jesus Christ, and freedom in salvation. Paul speaks to these themes in 1:1 (apostleship) and in 1:4 (cross and freedom).

Apostleship

Paul sees what is happening in Galatia as a challenge to his role as apostle. The attempt by some to introduce new ideas to the Galatians (1:7) has understandably undermined respect for Paul. The message and the messenger are linked and interdependent. On that linkage Paul and his opposition are likely agreed! In the first major section of the letter, Paul defends his qualifications as a messenger and his view of how messenger and message relate. Here in the opening, he makes just one basic but crucial point: his apostleship is fully grounded in divine initiative rather than human authorization.

In the early church the term *apostle* was used in a narrow, specialized sense for that group of Jesus disciples who had witnessed Jesus' life, death, and resurrection and who were commissioned by Jesus Christ himself to preach the gospel. Later *apostle* could refer to any delegated person who represented the church in mission (2 Cor 8:23). Paul clearly lays claim to membership in the first, specialized group. That Paul's status as an apostle was open to dispute is understandable: (1) he was not a participant in the earthly ministry of Jesus (cf. Acts 1:21-22), and (2) he received his appearance at a later time, after the ascension. Paul refers to the latter issue in his acknowledgment of being "one untimely born" (1 Cor 15:8). This vulnerability was clearly being exploited by the opposing teachers in Galatia.

In one sense, then, Paul shares his call as apostle with all apostles in the narrow sense of the term. In another sense, however, Paul excludes the human factor in his case. Although a divine call may involve other persons as the means of divine communication, Paul's language excludes this mediation: Paul's commission is *not from a human source* (1:1, 12). Further comment on this claim and its role in the argument of the letter will appear in the section on 1:11-2:14.

The Saving Benefit of the Cross

The brief statement about the sacrifice of Jesus for human sin is not important for its unique or profound insights. Its significance rests in its witness to belief in Christ's saving work in his death, appearing at the earliest stage of the Christian faith. Because Galatians is one of the earliest writings of the New Testament (if not the earliest) and because this statement shows every sign of being in existence before Galatians, we hear in it the voice of believers within the first fifteen or twenty years after the crucifixion. (A close parallel in language and origin appears in 1 Cor 15:3.) The most plausible explanation for this belief is that the first disciples found in Jesus' own teaching the key to such an astounding claim for a human death (Bruce: 77; Longenecker: 7). That teaching is recorded in passages like Mark 10:45 and 14:24. The Old Testament sacrificial concepts and the suffering servant of Isaiah 53 (see esp. vv. 4-6, 12) provided the framework of thought and language.

Verse 4 begins with stating the benefit of Christ's death for personal sinfulness. Sin has both vertical and horizontal dimensions. In biblical perspective, sin includes wrongful acts against God *and* neighbor. At this point the focus is on the individual's guilty condition. For Paul that point is crucial. However, our text broadens the perspective. Deliverance is not just some private transaction in heaven; it also delivers believers from a world system that is under the apocalyptic power of sin. Here we see redemption in its social and cosmic context. The human problem is one part of a flawed universe. Individuals are in a complex interaction with their social, cultural, and natural environment, molding it and being molded by it. Redemption must address the total web of evil in which person, society, and nature are caught. This view of salvation understands the complex interaction of the human person and the environment. Paul himself describes this larger vision of salvation in Romans 8:18-25.

To explain this situation, Jesus and the first believers used Jewish apocalyptic language to speak of a present wicked age and a future age of righteousness. Early Jewish believers in Jesus agreed that the entire world situation was ruinously influenced by evil. But they differed from some of their fellow Jews by confessing that the power of the coming age was already at work in the coming of the Messiah. This idea saturates the New Testament. It finds most direct expression in a passage like Hebrews 6:5, where believers are said to "have tasted . . . the powers of the age to come." Jesus is the promised agent of God (the Messiah) in whose work the future reign of God is breaking in. The resurrection of Jesus and the coming of the Spirit confirm that events of the coming age are already beginning. Peter is quite specific about this in Acts 2. The resurrection proves that God has begun the re-creating of life from the dead. The baptism of the Spirit makes possible this new life in all believers. In conformity with this perspective, our text asserts that Christ's gift of his own life removes our guilt of sin, which distances us from God, and frees us from entrapment in the system of evil, freeing us for a new life—*a new creation* (6:15). These points are developed in the discussion of 3:13 and especially in 4:1-11.

Centrality of Christ

The Christ-centered faith of the first believers is clearly displayed in these opening verses. In the confessional formula of verse 4, we see an example of how Jesus' actions as Messiah made this liberation possible. Paul embraced this faith, as Galatians shows. In light of Christ as the center, he was rethinking the past and present, in theology and in practice. All of faith must be built up consistently in conformity to Christ. It is precisely this consistency that Paul sees lacking in the Galatians, and it motivates his intense critique of their mixing of so-called gospels (1:6-7).

At two different points Paul places Jesus Christ in full parallel with God the Father. The work of both is done together, as if they are in some sense one. In this context, where Paul is setting human sources for authority over against the divine source, he places Christ with the divine, not the human. Thus our passage unambiguously affirms the divinity of Christ. For the unconverted Paul, ranking anyone with God would have been a blasphemous move. Yet here in one of the earliest Christian documents, he does it without hesitation or apology, and quite unselfconsciously. Although we are still some distance from the later Trinitarian creeds, we are on the way. The monotheism of the older covenant is radically reshaped even as it is being preserved (see 3:20, *God is one*). It is not too much to say that Galatians is a reflection on what it means for Jesus Christ to be equal with God, the Father, in defining the truth.

THE TEXT IN THE LIFE OF THE CHURCH

Practicing a Christ-Centered Faith

Due to the foundational character of the material that Paul incorporates into the introduction, we find ourselves face-to-face with a range of basic faith claims. Here the author uses them in the context of a conventional formality (beginning a letter), but they have the deeper purpose of building a bridge of fellowship and common faith. Paul's faith assertions set the stage for the correctional teaching that follows. Paul argues from the area of agreement to the points of dispute. In this way he maintains a unity of faith amid diversity and debate. Paul also argues from the center to the margin: he looks for direction on the secondary issues of faith by focusing on the elements most basic to the gospel, Christ, and his saving work. This helps the church walk consistently in the truth (2:14) and to maintain a living faith through life in Christ (2:19-20). In these vital matters Paul sets an example both for the Galatians and for us.

Understanding Atonement

Our text states the human problem from the viewpoint of our sin. Jesus' death addresses the problem of sin. One often hears the claim that persons in our time do not experience a keen sense of sin and guilt. Perhaps, however, the loss of a sense of sin is more apparent than real. People today tend to see sin differently. We are often more concerned about social wrongs—unfairness and injustice— than we are about personal or private vices. We feel and assign guilt in regard to world hunger, nuclear threat, violence, and environmental abuses, but seem less concerned about spiritual distance from God. Our sense of a moral universe remains strong, but it may be out of balance. A statement of faith such as that in 1:4 offers a salvation from sin at all these levels. The gospel can speak to the felt need of our age even while it redefines the dimensions of that need.

Believers churches properly emphasize the demand to follow the example of Christ in costly discipleship. However, discipleship goes hand in hand with the gift of forgiveness and new life in the cross—indeed, the former depends on the latter. We cannot hope to follow Christ without first and continuously receiving his grace in our helplessness. If this double emphasis is neglected, we run the risk of a form of Galatian error that relies on the flesh (human work) rather than the Spirit (divine work).

Separation from the World

Churches that stand in the believers church tradition have historically emphasized the sharp distinction of church and world implied in the language of rescue *from the present evil age* (1:4). The language of *evil age* effectively highlights the systemic character of evil that pervades our world. However, this language can also tempt us to overlook the good that is present in the world. Our experience demonstrates how difficult is the task of holding together salt and light—being a truly alternative community, separate from the evil of the world (salt), while also being fully *in* and *for* the world in mission and service (light). It is much easier to drift toward total separation (isolation) or unquestioning participation (conformity).

We gain nothing by renouncing the language of two kingdoms— of evil and of righteousness. Even as believers are freed from the evil of the present age, they continue to live as a special people in that age. What is needed is a missional nonconformity that counters the world in the way it thinks and lives, but encounters the world in the way it critiques, evangelizes, and serves that world. Indeed, Paul illustrates how the gospel can meet culture by the way he uses the standard form of letter greeting, but also modifies it to communicate his message.

Language

In this passage are two examples of language problems for the church today. In some circles the title *apostle* is being reintroduced on the basis of Ephesians 4:11. Since the early church used the term in several ways, misunderstanding can result. There is no reason to reject the title for a person with special delegated tasks in outreach or interchurch ministry. But Galatians (and other NT writings) makes it evident that *apostle* is sometimes used exclusively to refer to persons who were alive in Jesus' day and who witnessed to his resurrection. Perhaps the early church was wise not to use the term after the first generation. Likely the role of bishop (or overseer) was understood to continue the apostles' role in shepherding the general church.

The concern for gender-inclusive language raises a sensitive issue for the church. Our text uses the term *Father* for God three times in five verses. Obviously something at the heart of the faith is surfacing here. This is even more explicit in 4:6. Christ's mediation opens up a new intimacy with God. The loss of this dimension of faith would be costly. At the same time, inclusive-language concerns are valid. Patriarchy and abuse have sometimes robbed women of the very intimacy that this *Father* language can communicate. Under these circumstances, one option is to use feminine parental terms and images along with the masculine ones. In any case, we should not merely replace the Bible's familial language for God with impersonal terms incapable of communicating the profound relational intimacy with God that Jesus introduced and the early church embraced (see esp. the comments on 4:6).

Part 1

A Rebuke: Defending the Truth

Galatians 1:6–4:11

In Galatians, Paul intends to correct what he sees as a problem. The correction takes the form of rebuke and of request. The entire letter falls into two clear parts that correspond to the rebuke-and-request style. (See the Introduction for further comments about this structure.) The rebuke section is signaled by its opening words in 1:6, *I am astonished.* It continues with Paul's defense of a position contrary to the teaching that is being offered to the Galatian believers and is at least partly being accepted by them. The defense of *the truth of the gospel* (2:5, 14) is the unifying focus. The request section begins in 4:12 with the first appearance of an imperative verb in the letter. Thereafter, imperatives are numerous. These exhortations share the aim of assisting the readers in *obeying the truth* (5:7). The structure of the letter reveals a balance of the theoretical and the practical in each of the two parts. The rebuke section is a sustained theological argument that also addresses the ethical implications of right belief. The request section is a focused treatment of ethical dynamics in faithful living, grounded in theological principles.

The rebuke section begins with a statement of the issue. However, this statement reveals more about the depth of Paul's concern than it does about the nature of the problem itself. There follows a defense in two parts. The first (1:11–2:21) is a defense of the divine origin of the gospel that Paul preaches and of his authority as an apostle representing that gospel. The second (3:1–4:11) is a defense of the gospel as the true fulfillment of God's revelation to Israel. In the first part of this defense, Paul claims that the revelation he received from God in Christ makes his commission from God essentially independent of other leaders in the church. But lest the Galatians think that Paul's essential independence represents a break with God's revelation to Israel, the second part of the defense argues that the new revelation continues the truth of the former revelation. It does this by fulfilling the promises in the tradition and by respecting its fundamental principle of faith. As a new revelation and a new act of God in history, both discontinuity and continuity are essential in a right understanding of God's action in the past and present.

The paragraph in 3:1-5 is the key to understanding the problem lying behind the epistle. The Galatian believers are, according to Paul's understanding, leaving a faith-based gospel for a law-based one. The former lives out of the Spirit; the latter lives out of the flesh. The larger emphasis throughout part 1 is that the opening of the gospel to all people (Jew and Gentile) signifies that the law-oriented way of living out the Mosaic Law can be no basis for a universal gospel for all people. Christ's work makes Christ and the Spirit, not the Law, the key to righteousness. The Galatians should reject anything that is inconsistent with this new revelation. Circumcision, which maintains a boundary between Jew and Gentile, is the leading example in the letter.

OUTLINE

The Problem in the Galatian Churches, 1:6-10
Paul's Defense of the Gospel as New Revelation, 1:11–2:21
Paul's Defense of the Gospel as Fulfilled Revelation, 3:1–4:11

Galatians 1:6-10

The Problem in the Galatian Churches

PREVIEW

In place of the usual thanksgiving of Paul's letters, here at the head of the main part of Galatians we find a cry of anguish from Paul about the Galatians' retreat from the gospel! The tone of lament and anguish and Paul's intent to vigorously defend his apostolic authority are implicit already in the opening greeting (1:1-5) as Paul emphasizes his apostolic position and omits positive descriptions of the addressees. Now the intense sentiments of the writer break into full view. In other letters, Paul uses the thanksgiving to allude to his purpose in writing. In Galatians, Paul presents the subject of the letter in a rebuke statement, introduced with an expression of astonishment. This expression of astonishment is typical in Greek letter writing to introduce a reprimand. (See the discussion in the Introduction.)

In our section (1:6-10) Paul wastes no time in getting straight to the point. He indicates his state of mind, clarifies what is at stake in the problem, and says what the Galatians need to do about it. The verses therefore serve to introduce the main body of the letter. The author is deeply disturbed and strongly moved by the situation in Galatia. The problem is that persons from outside the congregation are seeking to persuade the believers to revise their previous understandings of the gospel. Paul is convinced that this is no mere revision: instead, it amounts to an abandonment of the gospel! Paul's approach in responding to the crisis is (1) to set the issue in stark terms as incompatible options; (2) to clarify the true nature of the gospel; and (3) to defend his own person as a servant of Christ.

Paul introduces the letter in such a way as to begin the persuasive process. In other words, he carefully uses rhetorical devices. Verses 6 and 7 undermine the status quo of the readers. Verses 8 and 9 threaten a curse that evokes the action of God in judgment on the situation. Finally, in a surprise move in verse 10, Paul deftly counters an accusation against himself in such a way as to turn the accusation into a supporting argument for his moral integrity! The discourse reflects the repartee and strategy of the courtroom. This lends support to the contention that elements of apologetic or judicial rhetoric are present, at least in this part of the letter.

OUTLINE

Accusation, 1:6-7
Threat, 1:8-9
Counterargument, 1:10

EXPLANATORY NOTES

Accusation 1:6-7

In placing the word *astonished* at the beginning of the sentence, Paul emphasizes it and alerts the reader immediately to the tone of what follows. This word expresses Paul's own surprise and dismay at the turn of events in Galatia. His surprise relates at least in part to the suddenness of the change that is flagged by the words *so quickly*. However, Paul also wants the astonishment to communicate his disapproval of what is happening along with his disappointment in the Galatians themselves. Paul means for his words to have a strong and persuasive emotional impact. *So quickly* strengthens the point. However, no chronological information can be drawn from the phrase. Is the brevity of time from conversion to the present problem, or from the beginning of the deviation to the present stage? Its function here is primarily rhetorical, chosen for emotional effect.

The cause of Paul's astonishment is that the Galatians are defecting! They are *deserting* the true faith! The present tense indicates that Paul understands or assumes the situation as currently happening. Paul intends his intervention, which is this letter, to arrest that defection before it becomes irreversible. The word *deserting* expresses a conversion from one viewpoint to another, seen from the perspective of the position being left. Hence the word has the negative tone of desertion.

When Paul describes what the Galatians are leaving he avoids the abstract language of gospel. Instead, he makes it personal: him *who called you* (1:6c). His readers are breaking a relationship—a relationship with God. This says something about how Paul sees the essence of the gospel. It also heightens the persuasive power of his appeal, since personal relationships generally form a tighter bond than do ideas. Even though the gospel was proclaimed to the Galatians by Paul (v. 11), in that proclamation was a call of God. The parallel statement in 1:15 (and Paul's consistent usage in his letters) makes clear that the one doing the calling is God. Both here and in 1:15, Paul mentions grace in connection with the call.

In 1:15 the meaning is unambiguous—grace is the *means* by which the call came to Paul. But here the wording in the original could express either means or position. The NRSV is probably correct to translate as *in the grace of Christ* with the preposition *in*. Elsewhere Paul can say that God calls *in peace* (1 Cor 7:15 NIV), *in one hope* (Eph 4:4 KJV), and *in holiness* (1 Thess 4:7). These all express a standing condition that the call aims to achieve. Paul may be using this language to suggest that grace is the ground of all faith experience, both its means *and* its end. That would fit the Galatian situation particularly well since these believers were tempted to think that grace marked the beginning of one's life of discipleship, but law was the key to its completion (3:3; 4:21; 5:4). In Paul's view, both the gift of grace and the response of faith (3:2-5) are basic to faith not only in its initiation but also in its continuation and completion. *The grace of Christ* likely has the same meaning as the more precisely worded phrase in 1 Corinthians 1:4: "the grace of God that has been given you in Christ Jesus." In this case God is the giver of grace and that grace is grounded in and mediated by the work of Christ. The expression thus stands as shorthand for the gospel in its entirety.

Paul is at a loss to describe exactly the new position being pressed upon the Galatians. He first calls it as *a different gospel*, but he then qualifies that by denying to it the character of gospel. The distinction is clearer in the Greek text because different words are used for *different* and *another*. The force of the statement is something like this: "You are turning to a different kind of gospel, which is not just another gospel among several similar options." With this clarification, the writer touches one of the main points of the letter. The gospel of Christ is unique. It is without parallel in other religious viewpoints and therefore cannot be blended with them.

The visitors who brought this new teaching to the Galatians probably offered it as an improved or fuller version of their faith, not an alternative to it. Yet Paul characterizes their nongospel in only negative terms. The bearers of the teaching are *confusing* the Galatians (also 5:10), and their handling of the gospel shows that they *want to pervert it*. Both of the verbs, *confuse* and *pervert*, come from the political setting, carrying overtones of agitation and subversion. By saying that the group of teachers (note the plural) want to pervert the gospel, Paul is, of course, portraying them from his point of view. The conscious motivation of the teachers was, no doubt, sincere and well-intentioned. Paul's language is calculated to undermine the credibility of his opponents (cf. 4:17 and 6:13, which are similar).

The phrase that Paul uses to designate the true message is *the gospel of Christ*, the good news whose content and focus is Christ and his work. This reflects an outlook that centers in the person of Jesus Christ, God's Messiah. The rest of this letter, and all of Paul's writings, bear out the centrality of Jesus Christ in his theology as well as in the practice of his ministry. What Paul seeks to emphasize is that Christ is the focal point of the gospel and therefore the standard for what passes as truth.

Threat 1:8-9

In expressing his concern for the Galatians, Paul responds strongly in the form of a curse-threat. He demonstrates his apostolic authority through this threat of sanction. At the same time, Paul's threat also defends the truth of the gospel. The Galatians received the right form of the gospel when they first heard it. This is stated twice: *what was proclaimed to you* and *what you received*. Anything else is a departure from the truth.

Paul constructs his threat with two conditional sentences. Each sentence touches on the same two points: the correctness of the original message and the threat of curse. The intended emphasis is obvious. Yet the two sentences also differ. The double sentences permit the writer to protect the gospel from two kinds of misunderstanding and distortion.

First, rather than beginning with the case at hand, the teachers at Galatia, Paul poses a hypothetical situation in which *we or an angel from heaven* (cf. the role of angels in giving the Law in 3:19) comes forward with a new gospel. The reader in English may miss the nuance that makes this a purely hypothetical event. Paul does not believe that this has happened or will likely happen. He lays out a fictional situation in order to make a point about where truth is found. That point is this: truth is not determined by the character of the messenger but by the origin and character of the message. Even someone's status as apostle does not guarantee the truth of what that apostle says. Peter becomes an example of this at Antioch (2:11-14). The plural pronoun *we* here may be an editorial *we*, referring only to Paul. But a number of verbs in verses 8 and 9 that refer to Paul's earlier ministry among the Galatians are in the first-person plural. This plural language may very well include Paul's mission companions. In fact, Paul may have included his companions as authors of this letter in order to communicate his mind-set in this regard (1:2).

Even the voice of a messenger from the heavenly world does not carry its own authentication. As Colossians 2:18 illustrates, angelic revelations aroused great interest during the first century. The supernatural has always impressed people as evidence of the truth of accompanying claims. Paul is not denying the reality of angelic appearances just as he is not questioning his own apostolic authority. Both experiences of revelation and Paul's authority as an apostle are central features in the next part of the letter. Thus the effect of this statement at this point in the letter is to preclude a misunderstanding. However important the apostolic credentials and divine mode of communication, the ultimate standard of truth resides within the gospel message itself. (See TBC below.)

The second statement of curse-threat (v. 9) relates more directly to the situation of the letter and is where Paul's greater concern rests. *If anyone proclaims to you a gospel contrary to what you received*, that person stands under the divine curse. The form of expression here makes it clear that the condition described is actually taking place. This is different from the previous statement (v. 8)! Paul now has in mind the actual situation in the Galatian congregations as it currently existed. The conditional statement (if . . . , then . . .) allows Paul to speak in the strongest of terms without rudely naming anyone or applying the threat definitively. But there is no doubt about his view of the teaching that is taking root in Galatia! Paul clearly intends that these statements of threat, while not aimed directly at the readers, will cause them to realize the seriousness of their own choice for or against Paul and the teaching they received from him.

The introduction of the second statement (v. 9) is a formula that alerts the reader to a repetition of thought: *As we have said before, so now I repeat.* Whether this refers to the previous verse or to a previous occasion is unclear. Similar expressions in 5:3 and 21 do not help us, since the latter is best taken as reference to an earlier occasion,

while the former is best understood as a general summary of previous points in the letter. Since this is a conventional phrase to introduce emphatic repetition, Paul's main point is to add weight and
seriousness to what follows (cf. 2 Cor 13:2; 1 Thess 4:6).

Let that one be accursed! The same phrase occurs in the same
wording in both conditional sentences. Paul calls on the strongest
expression of condemnation available to him from his Jewish tradition. The word for *accursed* takes its meaning from the Old Testament
word for ban (*ḥerem*)—something given over to God (i.e., given over
for divine destruction; cf. Lev 27:28-29). In Paul it always has the
negative meaning of being subject to God's wrath (Rom 9:3; 1 Cor
12:3; 16:22; cf. Rev 22:3). Here the third-person imperative form of
the verb (*let that one be . . .*), along with the conditional form of the
sentence, leaves open the possibility that the curse can be avoided.
The mode of expression has, therefore, the character of a threat.

It needs to be emphasized that this type of curse turns the person over to the action of God for judgment. This is not Paul's own act
of revenge (cf. Rom 12:19). At the same time the curse-threat is a
form of disciplinary action. Paul is exercising his apostolic authority. Paul's response here anticipates the implied command in 4:30
that the Galatians take action to expel the false teachers from the
congregations.

Counterargument 1:10

Paul's passion for the truth and his willingness to condemn unfaith-
ful messengers (vv. 6-9) gives him the opportunity to defend the
integrity of his motivation as a *servant of Christ*. The sudden intru-
sion of this matter is evidence that Paul assumes his audience will
understand why this point fits the present situation. The rhetorical
character of the questions (the answer is assumed to be clear) indicates the same thing. Paul is countering a charge that someone has
leveled against him. The previous curse-threats allow him to
develop the counterargument at a moment of vulnerability in the
reader/listener. After those strong assertions, the audience is likely
wondering whether Paul is not unduly harsh with his opponents.
They are not predisposed in this moment to think of Paul as a people
pleaser, as his accusers apparently claim!

We cannot be sure what charge lies behind this defensive comment. Many commentators see a link to Paul's practice of allowing a
different practice on circumcision, depending on whether he was in
a Jewish or Gentile setting (cf. Acts 16:3). The same charge may lie
behind Galatians 5:11, which implies that some are saying Paul still

preaches circumcision. By not requiring circumcision of the Gentile Galatians, Paul was vulnerable to the accusation that he adapted the message to the interests of the listeners in order to gain their allegiance to the gospel more readily (cf. 1 Cor 9:22). If so, this might suggest that Paul was "soft," a people pleaser.

Am I now seeking human approval, or God's approval? This question is open to various interpretations. The question is rhetorical since the author assumes that the reader/listener knows the answer. Moreover, the verb can mean either to seek approval or to persuade. If the former is the sense, as in the above translation, then the following sentence, which uses the verb *please*, says essentially the same thing for emphasis, and the general sense is clear: Paul is not seeking to be approved by humans but by God, as the previous curse-threats demonstrate. If it means "persuade," then the answer to the rhetorical question is not obvious. Is Paul affirming or denying that he seeks to persuade? And whom is he trying to persuade: humans, God, both, or neither? Elsewhere Paul never speaks of persuading God, and his comment about persuading humans in 2 Corinthians 5:11 is ambiguous in the Greek, so Paul may be denying that he is trying to persuade anyone—humans *or* God—and that his only intent is to please God, not other humans. The following statement in Galatians 1:10b would then be a denial that Paul uses persuasion to gain human favor (Buscemi: 62–63). In any case, the very concept of persuasion fits awkwardly in the context and is not really relevant to the argument. It is best, then, to see in this first question a parallel to 1 Thessalonians 2:4: "We speak, not to please mortals, but to please God." The assumed answer in the present text is that Paul seeks to please God, not humans.

It follows that the second question (*Or am I trying to please people?*) repeats the first (with different language in the original) in denying any desire to cater to human interests. The reference to the divine side is not repeated. Paul is defending himself against the accusation of ministering with an eye to the dynamics of human approval and of political success, as though Paul uses his ministry to raise his own political or social standing. The point is not that such dynamics are absent from true ministry but that they must be subordinate to a higher value (see below).

If I were still pleasing people, I would not be a servant of Christ. Paul again uses a conditional sentence to make the concluding assertion. The form of this sentence in the Greek makes it clear that Paul is denying that he is trying to please people. At the same time, the basic principle is affirmed that the service of humans and the service of God are in fundamental contrast as ways of governing one's conduct. The point is not that the approval of persons is in itself evil. Paul can desire such approval and acceptance in his own ministry (1 Cor 10:33). In this letter he states this expressly in 4:18: *It is good to be made much of for a good purpose at all times.* But submission to God must be primary. Sooner or later the demands of God and of humans will conflict.

The temporal adverb *still* alludes to Paul's life before his conversion to Christ. That Paul valued human approval in his earlier life is clearly indicated in a text like Philippians 3:3-8. There he uses the phrase "in the flesh" to describe this preconversion perspective, which he had not yet subordinated to Christ. Later in Galatians, Paul describes the authentic life of faith as Spirit led rather than accomplished by the flesh (3:1-5; 5:13–6:10). Of particular significance is Paul's reference to his status as a *servant of Christ.* This is an early signal of how the major theme of freedom, appearing later in the letter, is to be qualified. In fundamental ways the believer is no longer a slave (4:7), yet each believer is a servant (lit. *a slave*) of Christ and of other believers (5:13). In other places in Galatians, Paul gives positive definition to freedom. Here he offers a negative qualification of it. Freedom is not self-centered self-determination.

THE TEXT IN BIBLICAL CONTEXT

Because of its role in introducing the letter's argument, this section touches on key issues and themes for Galatians: grace, authority, discipline, and the uniqueness of the faith. There is an introduction, however brief, to the opposition Paul faces and to Paul's defense of his integrity as an apostle. Since the themes touched upon in these verses receive expanded treatment elsewhere in the letter, comments at this point will be selective and preliminary.

Grace

Paul defines the entire gospel in the phrase *called in the grace of Christ* (1:6). The expression has a typical biblical ring. Grace points to God's favorable disposition and action toward humanity in our neediness. It moves God to take the initiative in relating to the human creature. Throughout the Bible true relationship with God is based on the action of God that precedes the action of persons. This reflects the human inability to place a claim upon God. It also points to the superiority of what God does. Later in Galatians, Paul expresses this divine priority in observing that the believers *have come to know God, or rather to be known by God* (4:9; cf. 1 Cor 8:3; 13:12). God's knowing us is more fundamental than our knowing God.

That God's entrance into our experience takes the form of a call is consistent with the divine initiative. The call is a summons from a greater to the lesser, but it respects the response of the one who is called. Call also conveys an expectation of obedient service. God calls us to complete the purposes that God has set. The concept of call is especially suited to the biblical vision. In every story of God's encounter with a person or persons, at the crucial turning points of the biblical narrative, the elements of call and grace are present. Abraham is called into covenant with God. This includes the specific call for him to leave his native land for the land of God's choice. All Israel is called out of Egypt (Hos 11:1). The prophets of God are marked by a call that authorizes them for tasks beyond their own gifts and status.

The themes of grace and call are key components in the argument of Galatians. But they serve more as assumptions than as items for explanation. The combination of call and grace reappears in Paul's account of his own conversion and call to apostleship (1:15). This way of describing Paul's role as apostle to the Gentiles appears again in 2:9. His call is the outworking of grace. Paul's passion is for a faith grounded in grace. Therefore he is alert to any religious stance that might nullify the grace of God (2:21). He believes the Galatians' use of the Law does just that. See also 5:4 and 8. The concepts of righteousness by faith, promise, adoption, life in the Spirit, which receive the greater amount of attention in the letter, all fit into the framework of grace and call.

In using the concepts of grace and call, Paul links himself with the entire sweep of biblical revelation, claiming that his gospel continues the way God has always worked. However, by adding the qualification that this grace is "of Christ," the new revelation of God in Jesus the Messiah is brought into focus. This new element in the gospel sets it apart from all other religious systems, in some sense including the covenant of Moses, meaning the Law. Just as Paul uses grace as a test for theological coherence, so also he creates a standard of faith and life from the person and work of Christ. In our later exegesis we will demonstrate that in 2:21 the test of grace is paralleled by the test of Christ's work. If the counterteaching in Galatia had been correct, Christ would have *died for nothing*. From this understanding of Christ as the center of the gospel springs the claim to the uniqueness of that gospel. There is no other so-called gospel that takes with absolute seriousness the role of Christ as the agent of God in the fullness of time (1:7; 4:4).

Authority

A central issue of our paragraph is the question of authority. Where is the seat of authority for the church? Who speaks for the gospel and hence for God? The question is crucial for the Galatians, who are caught between two voices claiming to speak for the truth. As one of the claimants of truth, Paul advises the Galatians to look to the gospel itself and its inherent claims. This is more foundational than the messengers and interpreters, even if they were supernatural beings that appeared as likely channels of God's voice. Even though Paul preached the gospel, he is not himself the ground of authority.

We can see a clear tension between the present verses and the rest of chapters 1 and 2 with regard to Paul's apostolic status. Paul appeals to his apostolic status in the salutation of the letter (1:1). He obviously wants to influence his readers by demonstrating his authority as an apostle. The implication of the double emphasis on the gospel itself and the apostolic witness to that gospel must mean that authority begins in the content of the gospel, but the authority of the gospel is necessarily mediated by its messengers and interpreters. The authority of the messenger comes from the message: it is a derived authority. On the other hand, the authority of the message also depends on the messenger and the messenger's integrity.

In the very nature of the case, any witness to saving events and any interpretation of those events as divine revelation depend on a human agent. Therefore the divine message is inseparable from the messenger. The messenger participates in the authority of the message and as a consequence becomes an authority or, more precisely, becomes authorized to represent the gospel. This in turn means that a defense of the gospel may involve a defense of the messenger. That is exactly what is happening in Galatians. Paul identifies so closely with the message of good news with which he was entrusted that the line between defending himself and defending the gospel has blurred. However, while defending himself, Paul does not forget that his authority exists not in himself as an apostle. This is the point of 1:8. It exists in the gospel itself, whose authority is shared with one who witnesses to the central event of Christ's resurrection and who is for that reason qualified to be an apostle, and in his commission as apostle by Jesus Christ himself.

Curse as Discipline

While the present section does not directly defend Paul's status as an apostle, it does show Paul's apostolic authority in operation. Paul speaks for the truth of the gospel and, in his threat of curse on the teachers of error, acts on behalf of God. Paul threatens the use of curse here to bring divine sanction to bear in the act of discipline in the church. The curse evokes the judicial action of God upon the wrongdoer. Similar instances of apostolic discipline are recounted in Acts 5:1-11; 8:18-24; and 13:6-11. The specific use of the curse in relation to truth and error comes out of the Old Testament prophetic tradition. The problem of true and false prophets was a burning issue in Old Testament times (as in the early church and throughout church history). Deuteronomy 13 teaches about how to distinguish true and false prophets and directs that false prophets be removed from the community. Even though curse is not specifically mentioned in that context, Paul is acting in the spirit of this passage from Deuteronomy. (See also Rev 22:18-19 with its explicit use of Deut 12:32.)

The parallel to Deuteronomy 13 suggests that we are to relate Paul's curse-threat to the action of discipline in the early Christian communities. That Paul has in mind the hope for disciplinary action by the Galatians against the adversaries is clear from 4:30: *Cast out the slave and her son.* The disturbers are to be excluded (see discussion there). That Paul applied his authority as an apostle to church discipline is stated expressly in 2 Corinthians 13:10 and is illustrated in 1 Corinthians 5:3-5. The latter passage is similar to Galatians in that a judgment by Paul from a distance is to be followed by concrete action of the church. That passage also is significant since Paul expressly states that his authority is given to him from the Lord and that it is for building up and not for tearing down. The aim of all discipline is to be redeeming, and the one exercising it must act in keeping with that purpose. Whether redemption is the result, however, depends on both the character of the one who disciplines and the one who is disciplined. It is not clear how Paul determined the line between appropriate and inappropriate sanctions. His own struggle on this point is clearly reflected in the case of discipline referred to in 2 Corinthians 2:1-11.

THE TEXT IN THE LIFE OF THE CHURCH

The questions raised by the opening statement of Galatians touch on perennial issues of serious weight for Christians. They are the questions about the uniqueness of the gospel's truth claims, the location of authority that speaks for the true gospel, and the exercise of that authority for the maintenance of faithful community. From this way of formulating the questions, one can readily see their close relationship. Here Paul makes basic assertions on these matters, but he does not develop the case for his beliefs or how believers in Christ are to put such beliefs into practice.

Uniqueness of the Gospel

Paul is emphatic that the gospel of Christ (1:7) is, at its root, a message of good news without parallel or equal. Paul believes that the authority of the gospel is not external to the gospel itself, for instance, in the person who announces the gospel. From the wider statements of Galatians, we can say that, according to Paul, the authority of the gospel rests in the fact of Jesus' life, death, and resurrection, with the particular claims that they carry. At the same time, the gospel invests its human witnesses with authority as they faithfully pass it on (cf. 1 Cor 15:3-7) and rightly apply it to new issues (as in the Antioch episode, Gal 2:11-14).

For the church in the present century, confidence in the gospel's uniqueness is under threat. The relativity of all truth claims is an attractive view for our age. Historical change is so rapid that any sense of permanence is waning. Cultural and religious variety meets us daily in our local communities, through the media and by world travel. Many philosophers offer us a view of truth in process rather than of truth as stable and firm. The scientist finds matter itself to be unstable and subject to change.

Historical change, cultural variety, and the imperfection of all human endeavors is fully consistent with the biblical viewpoint even as biblical faith holds firmly to a God who is above historical change while also involved in the history of constant change. God's character and purposes do not change; the Word of God remains firm and dependable (1 Pet 1:24-25). God adapts to historical change in order to be self-consistent.

The incarnation of God in Christ means that, in the midst of a history in flux, a final action and revelation of God has taken place that will never be surpassed. Christ's followers announce this good news to all people regardless of religious persuasion. They point to the good news of God's action in Jesus the Christ without claiming finality for themselves, their words, or deeds. At the same time they do not shun the task of discerning what is consistent with that center of truth in Jesus Christ and what is not. It will never be easy to stand for a final truth while at the same time displaying the humility that is appropriate for fallible human beings and the tolerance necessary for acknowledging honest differences among sincere people (cf. Galatians to Rom 14:1–15:6).

Authority in Church Life

Taking up responsibility for proclaiming the gospel and for leading the people of God in faithful discipleship calls for exercising authority. In spite of certain tendencies in recent times to question all authority, it will always be present in human communities. The only question is whether or not that authority is exercised in legitimate and productive ways. Will it be expressed in real resources and aptitudes put in service to the community, or will it be expressed to dominate the community? Put concisely, proper authority is earned. Healthy communities confer authority by formally recognizing the genuine giftedness of individuals with the responsibilities of leadership. Mismatches between the formal conferring of authority and individual giftedness weaken communities.

The role of apostle illustrates this principle because the authority of the apostle rests on direct, personal witness to the life, teachings, and death of Christ, and especially to his resurrection. This witness is the ground for the apostle's distinctive role in guiding the church. Apostolic authority is not based in the people, as in a secular democracy, but in the Lord of the church, and in the gospel that announces his salvation. Paul was called by the Lord to be his apostle (1:1, 15-16). In the church, the people are to confirm the calling of God to leadership and recognize the gifts of the Spirit for leadership with a conferred authority that comes from the Lord and the message about him. Authority exercised in the true spirit of the gospel of Christ is legitimate. Authority carried out with respect for the convictions of individual believers and with their consent is productive. (This is the implication of passages like Rom 14:5, 12, 22-23.)

However, as we observed above, the role of apostles as witnesses to Jesus' life, teachings, death, and resurrection could not continue beyond the generation that witnessed those founding events. Therefore, the example of Paul's apostolic authority is relevant for us today only in a modified sense. On the one hand, the authority of the apostles as witnesses to the original revelation cannot be continued by anyone after them. Their witness is contained in the writings that form authoritative Scripture. Galatians is a prime example of apostolic witness becoming authoritative Scripture. On the other hand, the authority of the apostles as interpreters of the gospel and defenders of its practice continues in leaders who bear other titles, such as bishops, overseers, conference ministers, and pastors. These leaders are faithful to their task when they guide the church to live in harmony with the gospel as witnessed to in Scripture.

Discipline, Power, and Peace

It follows from the above that the church needs to be a community of accountability for one another. This requires a process of discipline. (For a fuller discussion of discipline in the history of the church, see TLC on 4:12-31.) The present passage raises a particular issue related to discipline. Paul's use of the curse as an act of discipline makes many present-day readers uncomfortable, especially those in the peace church tradition. When does an act of discipline become inappropriate violence against the person being disciplined? If vengeance belongs to God (Rom 12:19), how can any human activation of that vengeance, as in the case of a curse, be legitimate? Even if Paul's use of the curse is an appeal for God's action of judgment, not his own, Paul is still serving as an *agent* of divine judgment by invoking divine action. Was this just a moment of weakness for Paul, hot as he was about the Galatians' defection? Was Paul just having a bad day?

Early believers, taking their example from Jesus, saw themselves as engaged in spiritual warfare. They did not hesitate to use divine power in confronting evil and countering its effects. At one level, discipline represents the use of power to protect the integrity of the church. What the earliest believers did avoid was the use of coercive power in furthering the interests of the gospel and the church. And they refused to hurt each other in order to protect their own interests. They respected the freedom and integrity of the individual in their response to truth claims. So Paul's curse is an avoidable threat; it is not a definitive, irreparable judgment. This use of divine power to overcome evil, while promoting peace and not perpetuating conflict, is a perennial challenge to the church in its internal life and in its mission to the world. The inevitable tension should not be relieved by nonengagement with the evil of our world, or by pre-emptive use of physical force or political power to achieve good outcomes. Put differently, we must seek justice in our peacemaking and peace in our justicemaking.

Galatians 1:11–2:21

Paul's Defense of the Gospel as New Revelation

OVERVIEW

Who, what, when, where, why, and how? These are the basic build-ing blocks of narrative. After beginning his letter with a passionate and shocking rebuke for the Galatians defecting from the gospel, it would be hard to miss that Paul is quite worked up over something. Already in the first ten verses of this letter, Paul's emotions are raw. He is deeply concerned that the Galatians' change of mind about circumcision is not just a troubling development: it also is a fatal one for the gospel! The situation is desperate!

In light of the obvious passion Paul is expressing, it may seem odd that he immediately moves to retelling his life story, as if the details of that story—the who, what, when, where, why, and how—somehow matter deeply for the theological correction he is eager to communicate. As we will see, getting these details right represents an important reason for his writing this letter!

As a result, the first main part of the rebuke section of Galatians is autobiographical in content and narrative in style. In fact, auto-biographical narrative represents the bulk of chapters 1 and 2. All commentators recognize the unity of this part of the letter. Opinions differ about where the section begins (see comments on 1:11-12) and whether 2:15-21 belongs with this section or not. In any case, 2:15-21 serves as a transition. It completes the Antioch episode immediately preceding and therefore brings to culmination the entire first section. At the same time, it anticipates the next section, which argues not from Paul's life but from theological and scriptural bases.

The various parts of the present section are tied together by the words *when* and *then*. Paul appears eager to recount certain events in their proper chronological order. In fact, a correct understanding of the sequence and timing seems crucial to his argument: what happened when and with whom matters a lot! The tight narrative style also makes obvious the presence of a distinct unit of thought.

The section begins with a thesis-like statement affirming the divine origin of Paul's gospel. A series of experiences and episodes follows. These are selected and recounted for the purpose of proving the thesis. Paul is not interested in recounting his story for its own sake. Paul selects only the events that contribute supporting evidence to his claim that Christ's direct revelation to Paul and Christ's call on Paul to preach the gospel to the Gentiles provide all the authority and truth necessary to support his ministry. No human relationships or structures—not even apostolic ones—can contribute to or challenge that truth or Paul's authority to preach that gospel. While the narrative focuses on Paul's life, the intent of the section is to give evidence that the gospel Paul preaches is based on divine revelation. In this way, Paul's gospel, which moves from the exclusiveness of a Law orientation to a gospel open for all people, including Gentiles, is shown to be according to the will of God. Here Paul is defending his apostolic role as the means of defending the gospel and not as an end in itself.

OUTLINE

Thesis Statement, 1:11-12
Conversion and Call, 1:13-17
Visit with Cephas and James, 1:18-20
Sojourn in Syria and Cilicia, 1:21-24
Visit with the Leading Apostles, 2:1-10
Incident at Antioch, 2:11-21

Thesis Statement
Galatians 1:11-12

PREVIEW

After an introductory statement of the problem to be addressed
(1:6-10), Paul immediately gets to his first main point in opposing
the Galatian error: *The gospel I preached to you did not come to me
through human channels, . . . but by a direct revelation of Jesus Christ!*
(1:11-12 AT). Verses 11 and 12 state this point and serve as the topi-
cal sentence for the section from 1:11 to 2:21. The statement in these
verses makes clear to the reader what is at the heart of the following
material. Since that material is in story form (narrative), the many
details and the various questions they raise can easily distract the
reader/listener. As a result, we do well to allow these two verses to
guide our reading of what follows.

The essential point is clear and straightforward. Paul's gospel
originates in an initiative of God. God disclosed it to Paul apart from
any human channels. The sketches from Paul's life that follow support this claim by showing both the presence of God's working in his
life and the absence of human instrumentality behind his understanding of the gospel about Jesus Christ.

The thesis statement itself is composed of a general statement in
both negative and positive forms: Paul's gospel is *not* of human origin (v. 11). Paul also negates various versions of the argument about
how his gospel is dependent on human agency. Then he positively
affirms the origin of his gospel by divine revelation (v. 12).

EXPLANATORY NOTES

The opening phrase, *For I want you to know* (1:11), is a conventional
expression in letter writing of the time. Paul regularly uses this
form (1 Cor 12:3; 15:1; 2 Cor 8:1) or some variation such as *I do not
want you to be uninformed* (Rom 1:13; 1 Cor 12:1; etc.). The words typically introduce a new argument, as they do here. More important,
they signal what the writer is emphasizing. From these words we
should not conclude that Paul is imparting some information for the
first time. As in the close parallel in 1 Corinthians 15:1, the content
is not new to the audience. Paul is reminding them of something
that is crucial to the issues at hand.

As we stated above, Paul begins this letter with some unusually
stern and harsh words. To soften his tone, Paul chooses the direct

address of *brothers and sisters.* (Although the Greek literally says *brothers,* it is unlikely that Paul intended his letter to be received only by the men. So the NRSV's *brothers and sisters* communicates Paul's intent more accurately for today's audiences.) Paul is concerned to show that the present difference is a family matter. *Brothers and sisters* (or *Friends*) appears often throughout the letter (3:15; 4:12, 28, 31; 5:11, 13; 6:1, 18). It is the primary address used by the New Testament to express the social bond among believers. Both the Jews and some Hellenistic religious groups used this address. The term fits the early Jesus movement particularly well, with its strong emphasis on family metaphors to describe the family of God. Paul draws on this heavily in Galatians 3:26–4:7.

In referring to the gospel as he understands it, Paul uses the rather awkward phrase: *the gospel that was proclaimed by me.* Does Paul use this expression to avoid the ambiguity of the phrase "my gospel," which appears in Romans 2:16 and 16:25? Paul's concern is to show that the gospel he proclaimed is from God, not from himself or others. The gospel is not defined by humans but by Christ (1:7).

So Paul's central point is that the gospel is *not of human origin.* In fact, the meaning is not even as specific as this translation suggests. The gospel is not *according to what is human* (AT). The expression is comprehensive, including both origin and agency, as expressed in the next clause (and in 1:1, of Paul's apostleship). The character of Paul's gospel cannot be defined in human categories. Paul uses this exact phrase to characterize a purely human (natural) way of reasoning (e.g., 3:15) or a way of living (1 Cor 3:3) in contrast to thought and action that is governed by God.

Paul then proceeds to be even more precise about what he is denying: *I did not receive it from a human source, nor was I taught it* (1:12). These statements clarify Paul's previous words. They exclude both origin and intermediate agency. There is a direct link between Christ's encounter with Paul and the origin of the message. The verbs *receive* and *teach* were used by the Jewish rabbis to describe the process of passing on the traditional teaching from past to future generations. Paul may have in mind his own rabbinical training, which he refers to in the next paragraph as *the traditions of my ancestors* (v. 14). If so, Paul is making a contrast between his training in the Law and his encounter with Christ.

How then did Paul receive the gospel? It was given to him *through a revelation of Jesus Christ.* It came by revelation. God set the gospel's character and communicated that gospel directly through Jesus Christ. The contrast to a gospel of human origin or mediation is complete. *Revelation* is a disclosing of something otherwise hidden. The word well expresses the action of God to make known to humans what is otherwise inaccessible. In all likelihood Paul is referring to his encounter with the risen Christ on the road to Damascus, as recorded in Acts 9; 22; and 26. The expanded statement in verses 15-16, which uses the verb form for revelation, supports this.

In verse 12 the prepositional phrase *of Jesus Christ*, which defines the revelation, could mean that the revelation is about Jesus Christ, that Jesus Christ is the giver of the revelation, or both. Both senses characterize the Damascus vision, and Paul may indeed be thinking of both aspects here. In the previous clause the emphasis is on the *means* by which the gospel comes (*not receive . . . not taught*). Revelation represents a means of communication that contrasts with human means of communication. Thus Christ, by revealing himself to Paul, communicated the gospel message that Paul preaches. In verse 16, however, the other side is clearly intended: God is the revealer, and Christ is what is revealed. Because Christ is the central content of Paul's gospel (with God as the author of the revelation), we prefer the second option: Christ is the focus and content of the revelation to Paul.

THE TEXT IN BIBLICAL CONTEXT

Paul's Defense of His Authority

In this first major part of the letter, Paul mounts his argument that his gospel is of divine origin, not human origin (1:11-12). Two kinds of evidence from Paul's experience support the argument. The auto-biographical sketches demonstrate the divine origin of both Paul's gospel and his apostleship. The stories recount the miraculous working of God and demonstrate the gospel's independence from human sources. They also document how other believers have confirmed Paul's claims. Finally, as he recounts the Antioch incident and his second visit to Jerusalem, the stories demonstrate that Paul's apostolic authority was accepted by and effective in the life of the church.

Paul specifically defends (1) his particular role as apostle to the Gentiles and (2) his message of a Law-free gospel for the Gentiles. Paul sees himself as the bearer of a new revelation from God on this precise point of God's full embrace of all nations. He makes this direct claim in verse 1:16. In other writings, Paul calls this inclusion a "mystery" that was made known to him by a revelation for the church (Rom 16:25-26; Eph 3:1-6; Col 1:25-27). The mystery is the direct extension of God's good news to the Gentiles (the nations) and their resulting inclusion into the new universal people of God. In Galatians, Paul is defending the truthfulness of these new claims in his gospel message.

Opposition to Paul

It is clear that new teachers in the Galatian churches were raising questions about both Paul's understanding of the gospel and his relative authority. The letter itself provides evidence that the teachers were countering Paul's policy of not requiring Gentile observance of the Law. Although it is not clear whether they were questioning Paul's right to the status of apostle, it is clear that they were at least subordinating Paul's authority to that of the other apostles.

The false teachers may have been claiming that Paul was inconsistent in his practice regarding circumcision (see 5:11), that he was catering to his Gentile audience's revulsion to Jewish practice of circumcision (see comments on 1:10). If the teachers were successful in leveling this criticism against Paul, it would have undermined the Galatians' respect for Paul (4:12-16). If this were a fair understanding of the teachers' criticism of Paul, we could conclude that Paul's defense of his apostleship serves to restore confidence in him as a spokesperson for the gospel. Nevertheless, Paul's apostolic position was probably being attacked in some way. At the least, Paul was being made subordinate to the Jerusalem apostles whose call preceded his (cf. 1:17; 2:6-7, 11-14). The teachers may even be questioning Paul's right to be called an apostle at all! A similar attack on Paul's person took place at Corinth (2 Cor 12:10-12). Though that situation has many parallels to the Galatians scene, we cannot be sure that the opponents viewed the status of Paul as an apostle in exactly the same way.

Relating the Human and the Divine

In the entire defense Paul's intent is to demonstrate that God has disclosed God's will in the message that Paul preaches. To do this, Paul sets up a contrast between what is merely human and what is divine. The truth of God is not found in the things that reflect merely human dynamics. Paul is not denigrating the human and material. After all, Paul is willing to defend his own human role in the gospel. The human and the divine are not incompatible opposites, as in dualistic worldviews. The presence of the divine becomes the sign of genuine religious experience.

Here we see a unifying theme of the letter. The contrast of flesh and Spirit that predominates in the latter part of the letter makes the same point (3:1-5; 4:21-31; 5:13–6:10). To live according to what is human has the same meaning for Paul as to live according to the flesh. Paul describes the Corinthians as being "of the flesh" and behaving "according to [what is] human," all in the same verse (1 Cor 3:3). The problem is that the human often presumes to live without recognizing the divine, without submitting to it or its empowerment, or (in Paul's words) without walking in the Spirit or keeping in mind the things of the Spirit.

Paul sees evidence for the acts of God in two complementary features. The first is the supernatural form of the event in question. Paul's experience of meeting the risen Christ on the Damascus road was extraordinary. The second is the absence of natural processes that could explain the event. In this example it is the lack of a past tradition or of a learning opportunity. Paul's point in all this is to affirm his direct dependence on God and his total independence from human sources. For Paul, this directness, or nonmediation, provides evidence for the divine stamp of approval on a claim of revealed truth. Later in the letter he uses the same argument to support the superiority of the gospel of Christ over the Law of Moses, which was mediated (3:19b-20).

We need not understand Paul's arguments for the divine origin of his gospel to completely exclude any receiving of information about Jesus from human sources. Paul acknowledges this expressly in 1 Corinthians 15:3 and implicitly in Galatians 1:18 (see comments there). The critical point is that Paul's call and the essential framework of his gospel for all the nations is direct from Christ. The revelation of Christ to Paul on the Damascus road did not communicate everything that Paul came to know about faith. Moreover, Paul's experience is not normative for every believer. Paul can also say that the Galatians received the gospel from him (1:9)—something he denies in his own case with the same vocabulary (1:12). Paul's case is unique because of his unique role as apostle to the Gentiles. What this means is that a faith received by human mediation can be genuine and complete (see more below).

THE TEXT IN THE LIFE OF THE CHURCH

Paul's Experience—Unique or Exemplary?

In the verses under consideration, Paul describes his experience of coming to faith in Christ. Paul came to faith in Christ on the

Damascus road. Every true believer also comes to faith in Christ in some way. But to the extent that Paul's encounter with Christ was a call to be an *apostle*, we must not see his experience as prototypical of all believers. As a result, appeals to this story as an example for other believers must be done with care.

Paul makes clear that the believers in Galatia need not have the kind of direct revelation he had. The spectacular revelation that led to his conversion may not have been required for his own relationship to Christ. But it was necessary for his specialized role as apostle, one who is a witness to the reality of Jesus' resurrection and who therefore has the mandate of God to take the good news to all nations. Later believers do not need to repeat this experience. In fact, we cannot; those breakthrough events of revelation happen only once. Rather, we depend on the faithfulness and truthfulness of those who saw what God did in Jesus and who perceived its meaning. The New Testament Scriptures preserve and share this apostolic witness so that later generations can depend on the original witness for their own faith. In short, when Paul defends his authority as an apostle who speaks for God, he is laying the foundation for what will eventuate in the canon of New Testament Scripture. The call to the Galatians to ground themselves in the testimony of the apostle becomes, for us, a call to accept the authority of Scripture in its unique witness to Christ and to ground our faith in its witness.

That there is revelation which only a select few receive does not mean that other believers cannot sense God's presence and leading. This too can be called a form of revelation. Paul illustrates this here in Galatians. When he made the second trip to Jerusalem (2:1-2), he went up *in response to a revelation*. The language is the same as that in 1:12 and 16. Revelation as a form of divine communication is not limited to the original witnesses of God's deeds whose writings became Scripture. But there is a fundamental and crucial difference between the types of revelation. The difference has to do with the content. The revelation of God's words and deeds that are foundational for the plan of redemption are unique and unrepeatable. This revelation becomes the standard for all believers who follow—it becomes Holy Scripture. Such was Paul's experience of seeing the risen Jesus Christ and receiving the call to evangelize the nations. On the other hand, his experience of receiving God's leading to go to Jerusalem does not tell others what to do. It is an example of what other believers can expect that God may repeat for them in a way particular to their life situation.

Even when later believers receive the truth from a biblical writing or a human teacher, that truth must come alive just as it was for the first witnesses. Otherwise the written word would remain a dead letter (cf. 2 Cor 3:6). The Spirit must enliven the word so that we meet the living Christ just as Paul did. In that sense, every true believer goes beyond the received teaching even while depending on it. Paul understood that the believer knows the deeply personal sense of being a child of God, which the Spirit confirms in the cry of recognition that God is our Father (Gal 4:6; Rom 8:15-16). The living reality of a direct revelation does not necessarily entail a new revelation. The Christian philosopher Søren Kierkegaard captured this concept in his claim that all Christians should know themselves to be contemporary with Christ.

Certainty of Faith

Paul wrestles with what has the appearance of a contradiction. The gospel must be rooted in what truly comes from God. This requires a self-disclosure, or revelation, of God. However, all revelation comes to and through a human person who receives it and passes it on. All who did not directly receive the revelation depend on the human witnesses to that revelation. The following generations have access to divine revelation only through others who first received it and shared it. The experience of every Christian today contains a measure of faith in the *witnesses* to the gospel and their credibility along with ultimate faith in God and God's truthfulness.

Such access to revelation only through human mediation leaves us with the uncertainty inherent in all human existence. This is the inevitable burden we will always bear in this life. Absolute certainty is not available in an imperfect world. Neither those who believe nor those who disbelieve are free from this limitation. All knowledge is partial (1 Cor 13:9). But that is not to say that we are without evidence . . . or ancient witnesses. The experience of God working in one's own life and faith community is evidence that confirms the witness of others. Paul points the Galatians to this in 3:1-5. The Samaritans recognize this when they confess that the basis of their faith has moved from the testimony of the Samaritan woman to the direct word of Jesus himself (John 4:42).

Finally, the problem we have posed points to the profound significance of the character of the witness. The integrity of the witness is crucial for the credibility of the gospel. Paul is understandably concerned to preserve the integrity of his reputation. The people of God in every age must face the same responsibility to reflect the meaning of the gospel in their lives and to do it with integrity. Sensitive believers will realize that they are not equal to such a task (2 Cor 2:16). But this is no reason to be slack in witnessing to the claims of the gospel—both with and without words. We must point to the incomparability of Christ even while acknowledging our own imperfections.

Conversion and Call
Galatians 1:13-17

PREVIEW

Paul has just laid out his thesis statement in 1:11-12, in which he made an impassioned claim for the divine origin of his gospel. Now he needs to support that claim. How will he do it?

In 1:13-17, Paul begins to recite the evidence in support of his claim. He begins with his former life in "Judaism" and his strong resistance to the Jesus movement. Then he recounts his conversion to Christ as the Messiah who fulfills the Jewish faith. Paul specifically mentions the call that accompanied his conversion because this will have particular relevance to the defense of his gospel and apostleship. The paragraph closes with his crucial claim that after the conversion-call experience, he had no significant relationship with others until after a period of seclusion.

The structure of the sentences indicates that the emphasis of the account falls on the words: *I did not confer with any human being* (v. 16). Thus the main point of Paul's argument is that his understanding of the gospel did not come by way of contact with others. Instead, Paul emphasizes that whatever human tradition he knew conditioned him against the faith (vv. 13-14) and that his conversion has all the qualities of a direct intervention by God (vv. 15-16a).

OUTLINE

Life as Persecutor, 1:13-14
Experience of the Divine Call, 1:15-16a
Time of Isolation, 1:16b-17

EXPLANATORY NOTES

Life as Persecutor 1:13-14

You have heard, no doubt, of my earlier life in Judaism (1:13). The text begins with the word *for*, which the NRSV has not translated. The conjunction is the indicator that what follows serves to demonstrate the grounds for the previous assertion in verses 11-12. Paul's reference to the Galatians' previous awareness of these facts means only that Paul acknowledges a degree of familiarity with what follows. No doubt the particular twist on the story is new. Most likely Paul himself had shared his life story during his earlier ministry. In any case, it seems likely that his adversaries had presented their own version of the past to show Paul's inferiority to the Jerusalem apostles. In verse 20 the intensity of Paul's affirmation of his honesty likely reflects Paul's awareness of those counterclaims.

Judaism signifies the way of life that characterized a Jew. The origin of the term is not known, but it appears in the intertestamental books of the Maccabees to indicate a way of life in contrast to the Hellenistic cultural ideals of the time. The term alludes to the relationship between Jewish and Gentile culture. This is a central issue in the early church and in Galatians. And since circumcision was a physical boundary marker between the Jew and the Gentile, the word *Judaism* may also refer to the capacity of a Jewish way of life to serve as a boundary marker between peoples.

I was violently persecuting the church of God and was trying to destroy it. Paul's response to the early Jesus movement was to beat and/or kill its adherents. Through violent persecution he was trying to wipe it out. Paul cites other aspects of his life to explain his actions: *I advanced in Judaism beyond many among my people of the same age, for I was far more zealous for the traditions of my ancestors* (1:14). The presumably laudable intensity of his faith commitment led him to an equal intensity in persecuting the early believers. Crucial here is Paul's use of language to express intensity or excess in both statements. Paul had no inclination to become a follower of Jesus the Messiah before Jesus appeared to him. Far from it!

In calling the community of believers in Jesus *the church of God*, Paul is making an important adjustment to his preconversion viewpoint. The term regularly appears in the Greek translation of the Old Testament to refer to any assembly or congregation of God—that is, the people of God. Now in using the word, Paul clearly includes believers in Jesus Messiah within the assembly, or *church*, that represents the people of God (cf. 6:16). The designation appears elsewhere in Paul, especially in his early letters, of which Galatians is an example. The usage here is highly significant, since it stands for the entire body of believers without specific reference to place or form. Otherwise, the preponderance of occurrences, especially in the early Pauline letters, refers to local gatherings of believers, as in this same chapter (1:2, 22). Although Paul uses the term here primarily for Jewish communities of believers in Jesus, we can see it already beginning to reflect Paul's understanding that in Christ, God has opened the gospel to all people: to Jews *and* Gentiles, to people of all nationalities and ethnic groups.

Behind Paul's fervent opposition to the church was an unbounded ambition to excel in his faith. Paul's advancement to the highest level among his peers does not speak to his social position or political power. The word refers to personal growth in the Jewish religion, with public recognition implied (cf. Luke 2:52 re: Jesus). Paul was a diligent student of Judaism and an uncompromising practitioner of it (Phil 3:4-6). He brought the same basic personality traits to his unconditional commitment to Christ and his unflagging service for the gospel.

The particular expression of Judaism to which Paul is referring is clarified in Paul's reference to his being *more zealous for the traditions of my ancestors*. This involves, at the root, a zeal for the Torah, the Law of Moses. Such commitment to the observance and defense of the Law was an ideal among the Jews (cf. Acts 21:20; 22:3). Zeal was the virtue of defending, at any price, the Jewish way of living from all adversaries. Precisely in this period under Hellenistic and Roman imperial pressures, Jewish zealotry was at a peak. This does not mean that Paul belonged to a particular Zealot party. This zealous attitude, or "philosophy," was widespread in Judaism at that time. Phinehas was the model from Israel's past for zeal, even violent zeal for the Law (Num 25:1-15; Ps 106:30-31). In its historical context, being zealous for the Law or *zealous for the traditions* meant being ready to take radical or even violent action to protect the cultural and religious boundary markers that defined "Judaism" (e.g., 1 Macc 2:44-48). Paul himself later became the target of this same zeal, when certain Jewish believers in Jesus reacted to his perceived weakening of loyalty to the Law (see 2:11-14) *[Judaism in the Time of Paul, p. 311]*.

The phrase *traditions of my ancestors* also includes the authoritative interpretation of the Law by the rabbis. The word *tradition* means "the things handed on." This included passing along knowledge from teacher to student or from parent to child. The rabbinical schools taught the right understanding of the law by passing it on from teacher to student. Paul learned this from his time in Jerusalem in the school of Gamaliel (Acts 22:3). It is precisely this process of religious formation that Paul is at pains to deny in the case of his new faith and vocation (1:1, 11-12).

Experience of the Divine Call 1:15-16a

The remainder of the present paragraph on Paul's conversion and call is one complex sentence. Paul recounts his conversion/call in a dependent clause, while the main assertion is in verses 16b-17. This subordination keeps the focus of the narration on the point that matters in the current argument. Nevertheless the description of that event is elaborate enough to establish its own significance.

Paul does not tell his story like some detached observer. This is clear especially in verse 15, where Paul describes God's perspective on what happened! The entire statement offers spiritual insight into Paul's experience in the Damascus road event (Acts 9:1-19; 22:6-16; 26:12-18; Gal 1:12). Paul's testimony confirms that this event plays for him a foundational, defining role in forming his faith and worldview.

Verse 15 is marked by traditional language for God's call of an agent into service. But it refers specifically to the call of a prophet. The good pleasure of God (*God . . . was pleased*) signifies the gracious disposition of God toward someone. The call narratives of Isaiah and Jesus (Isa 42:1; Mark 1:11 and parallels) assert God's approval and certification of the individual for ministry. The most distinctive parallel to the prophetic call is the awareness of being set apart before birth: *who had set me apart before I was born* (lit. *from my mother's womb*; see Isa 49:1; Jer 1:5). Many of the prophets of Israel reported or reflected on their having been called by God (as did other leaders of Israel). Paul's call has a special tie to that of the Servant of the Lord in Isaiah. In addition to the two references above, the conversion account in Acts 26:12-18 alludes to verses in Isaiah (42:6; 43:10; 44:8; 49:6) that speak of being a light and a witness to the nations.

So Paul's identity emerges here as one who stands in the prophetic tradition. We found an allusion to it already in 1:8-9. With that tradition he celebrates his awareness of God's approval of him, his conviction that God's purposes are being worked out in his ministry, and his experience of God's empowering grace, which has confirmed his call. (On the phrase *through his grace*, compare notes and TBC on 1:6.)

The structure of the sentence leaves some question about the timing of Paul's call in relation to God's setting apart Paul and the appearance of Christ. The grammar of the original language suggests that both the setting apart and the call preceded the actual revelation of Christ on the Damascus road. Does Paul think of the call as happening already in the (eternal) past at the same time as the setting apart? If so, Paul may be recalling the prophetic understanding that the outworking of God's will is seldom spontaneous, but has been determined long ago. The conversion accounts in Acts place the call at the time of the revelation. Whatever the exact timing he has in mind, Paul sees the call as an expression of God's purpose that precedes all historical event and human response. The call of God is expressed both as the revelation of God's intent beyond all time and as human experience within history.

Paul appeals to the prophetic dimension of his experience in defending his apostolic call in order to underscore the divine authority behind his gospel. His encounter with the risen Christ is both a resurrection appearance and a prophetic revelation. In that event Paul saw the risen Jesus (1 Cor 9:1; 15:8). That in itself is the basis for apostleship (see notes on 1:1). But it also reveals two other truths: Jesus is Son of God, and God's will is that all nations be evangelized. Thus the prophetic dimension of his call supports the central claim of Galatians that God, and God alone, stands behind the gospel and ministry of Paul.

The event on the Damascus road is described as God's action *to reveal his Son to me.* As just noted, Paul can view that event either as an appearance or as a revelation. An appearance suggests Christ as the subject and the event as external to Paul the observer. A revelation points to Christ as the object and the event as internal to the experience of Paul. There is no contradiction between these two forms of description. They are two ways of speaking about the kind of event recounted in Acts. Both the objective reality of the resurrection and the subjective reception of its meaning are essential to Paul as well as to other New Testament writers.

Two features in the text suggest what was important in Paul's personal appropriation of the revelation. First, the object or the content of the revelation is the *Son of God.* With this common title for Christ in the early church, Paul confesses that Jesus of Nazareth is no ordinary human being but is uniquely related to God. According to Acts, Paul's first preaching after his conversion was the simple testimony that Jesus is the Son of God (Acts 9:20). Romans 1:4 demonstrates that Paul associated this title with the risen and exalted Christ: the resurrection set forth Jesus Christ publicly as Son of God. When Paul was confronted with the fact that Jesus was alive, he likely concluded, on the basis of his Jewish beliefs, that Jesus was the royal messianic agent of God. This messianic Son of God tradition appears in Psalm 2:7 (and in the Dead Sea Scrolls and the apocryphal writing of 2 Esdras [4 Ezra]) and in the baptism of Jesus, when the voice from heaven announces, "You are my Son" (Mark 1:11). Given the range of meaning of this title, it is difficult to define the precise status for Jesus it intends. In the Old Testament, the king (Ps 2:7) or even all Israel could be called sons or children of God, but divine beings could also be so designated (Ps 82:6). This range permits the title to support the unique divine status of Jesus Christ (when confirmed by his exaltation to God's right hand) while also linking Christ and his followers as children in the family of God. Paul exploits the latter possibility in Galatians 4:4-7.

A second feature in Paul's description of his experience is his comment that God was pleased to reveal God's Son *to me*. This might appear to be nothing more than a simple reference to the one receiving the revelation. However, the prepositional phrase used here normally means *in me*. There is grammatical warrant for *to me* (NRSV), and some commentators prefer this. The similar expressions in Romans 1:19 and 2 Corinthians 4:3 are best translated that way. However, the use of this preposition after the verb *reveal* is rare. This suggests that Paul is reaching for a special meaning. His key concept of being "in Christ" is rooted in this conversion event. Thus we have here a deliberate emphasis on the embodied, personal nature of the revelation. So the better translation is *in me*. The point is not that the event of revelation is purely internal in its form, but that the appearing of Christ was deeply transformative in Paul's embodiment of Christ and of the good news about Christ (cf. Gal 4:19; John 17:23).

The revelation of Christ to Paul is not an end to itself. It has a purpose that points beyond Paul and forms a call for his ministry: *so that I might proclaim him among the Gentiles*. In parallel to the focus on Christ in the appearance itself, the object of the proclamation is Christ. His ministry of evangelism is primarily directed to all those peoples who are not Jewish and therefore have not previously been part of God's covenant people (cf. Eph 2:12; 1 Pet 2:10). The clear implication is that Paul's call to ministry was part of the original event that reoriented Paul's life toward Christ. The Acts accounts of Paul's conversion or call vary on whether the call came in the very appearance of Christ or through the prophetic word of Ananias. But all agree with the close link between conversion and call. Paul's reference to the Gentile mission is essential here, for it authorizes Paul's role as apostle to the Gentiles (2:8) and consequently supports the letter's case for the truth of Paul's Law-free gospel to the Gentiles.

Time of Isolation 1:16b-17

Only here does the sentence beginning at verse 15 come to its main assertion. Crucial for Paul's defense of his divinely given gospel is the absence of human causes and sources. Therefore he traces with some precision his movements and contacts immediately after the encounter with Christ. The adverb *immediately* stands at the head of the entire series. It seems awkward to deny the immediacy of a non-action, that is, do nothing immediately! As a result, some commentators and translators (such as the NRSV) link the adverb to the departure for Arabia: *I went away at once to Arabia.* However, Paul is anticipating here the recounting of his later contacts with other persons beginning in verse 18. The sense is something like, "Immediately I did not confer, . . . but later I did." Paul's point is to show that God—rather than any human person—guided the formative stage of his understanding of the gospel. Therefore the clause should read, *At once, I did not confer, . . . nor did I go up to Jerusalem, . . . but I went away into Arabia.*

That Paul places the negative assertions first, in the position of emphasis, is consistent with the point he is making. They deal with the real issue—the denial of human influence: *I did not confer with any human being.* The words *human being* translate the idiom "flesh and blood." This traditional Jewish expression stands for humanity in its weakness and limitation (cf. 1 Cor 15:50). Using the term *flesh* here is not to stress the human vulnerability to sin, as often in Paul (see on 5:13-17), but the inferiority of the human in comparison with the divine. So the phrase contributes to the main point of Paul's argument.

The sense of the verb *confer* is of considerable significance. This begins a series of verbs (also 1:18; 2:2, 6) that bear the weight of the argument concerning Paul's relationship to human authorities. The first and last in the series negate a certain form of relationship, while the middle two admit a certain kind of relationship. Paul's argument walks a fine line between dependency, which he denies, and the fraternal contact of equals, which he acknowledges. Here in verse 16 the sense of *confer* is "to consult in order to be given a skilled or authoritative interpretation" (Dunn 1993: 110; also Longenecker: 33). Paul needs no one to help him make sense of the strange event on the way to Damascus, or to confirm its validity. (See further on the individual verses cited above.)

This first negation is general and includes all classes of human beings. How does Ananias's story fit this claim? Acts 22 says that Ananias communicated the mission mandate to Paul as it was revealed from the Lord. Acts 9 implies the same (9:6). Ananias leads Paul to be filled with the Holy Spirit (9:16) and baptizes him (9:18). As in Galatians, Paul's account of his conversion or call in Acts 26 makes no mention of Ananias and includes the mission mandate in the revelation from Christ. Thus we are left with enough variety in describing the event that we cannot press the details in attempting to harmonize the total picture.

In Galatians, it appears that Ananias contributed nothing that was essential to Paul's faith perspective. The fact that Ananias also received his instructions for Paul by means of a vision (Acts 9:10) preserves the revelatory character, but it also appears to contradict Paul's claim of having received nothing through any human person (Gal 1:1, 12). Paul may have in mind here the kind of authority figure represented by the apostles mentioned in the next clause. The verb *confer* could suggest this (see the above definition). Also the movement from the present general statement to the next quite specific reference to the apostles makes it likely that the two clauses are more or less synonymous. The first defines the character of an encounter. The second defines a particular instance (place and persons). This would help explain the absence of Ananias in the account here.

Nor did I go up to Jerusalem to those who were apostles before me (1:17). The statement in the same verse that (some years?) later he *returned to Damascus* confirms that Paul is referring to the appearance and revelation of Christ on the road to, and near, Damascus. This rules out the possibility that Paul is speaking about his trance in the Jerusalem temple when the Lord tells him to leave Jerusalem and go to the Gentiles (Acts 22:17-21). The reference to *apostles before me* discloses three important details: (1) Paul considers himself an apostle, but (2) he also recognizes the apostolic status of others, and (3) he acknowledges his own call as the last in chronological order (1 Cor 15:8). Paul is being deferential here, but not *too* deferential. The group of apostles includes, for Paul, the twelve disciples of Jesus (1 Cor 15:5) but also others, including James the brother of Jesus (see on 1:19; also 1 Cor 15:7; 2 Cor 8:23; Rom 16:7).

On the positive side, Paul asserts that he *went away . . . into Arabia, and afterwards . . . returned to Damascus*. The author of Acts gives no hint of such a time in Arabia. Instead, he speaks of an immediate period of preaching in Damascus (Acts 9:20). The appearance of contradiction with Galatians diminishes if we understand *at once* as referring only to the negative clauses (see above). But we cannot pretend any final explanation. Nor can we identify the location with any precision. Arabia was the vast area east of Palestine and extending much farther north and south. Later in the letter, Paul mentions that Mount Sinai is in Arabia (4:25). Might that be a subtle indicator of his destination? Such would be consistent with his keen interest in how the Law given at Sinai relates to the gospel of Jesus Christ (3:19; 4:21-31). However, there is no clear evidence that Paul traveled there. Although Paul does not directly state the purpose of his Arabian sojourn, he was probably assimilating the meaning and implications of his experience of the living Messiah—the resurrected Jesus—and reorienting his beliefs around this new center. He therefore naturally associates that sojourn with the present discussion because of its similar subject matter. On the length of the sojourn, see verse 18.

Paul's reference to his "return" to Damascus implies that the great event that changed Paul's life took place in the area of that city. In the present context, this reference completes the picture of a preliminary period of time when Paul received and developed his understanding of the gospel without depending on the other apostles.

Summary of the Argument. The paragraph under consideration is part of a larger section of the letter providing support for Paul's central claim that his gospel is from God, not from other humans. Within the present verses, four points support the claim:

1. Paul's former life provided him no natural predisposition to become a believer (1:13-14).

2. An eternal purpose of God lies behind Paul's call as one of the prophets (1:15).

3. Paul's conversion or call was a supernatural event in that a heavenly being spoke to him.

4. A period of time elapsed after Paul's conversion or call that precluded human influence on the essential core of his new faith.

THE TEXT IN BIBLICAL CONTEXT

Reconstructing Paul's Life

The passage under consideration is a key one for the reconstruction of Paul's life story and for understanding his belief system or his theology. While it yields significant fruit for these purposes, it also leaves many questions unanswered. Any attempt to reconstruct Paul's life story involves correlating Paul's account with the accounts in Acts of the same events and time period. No full harmonization seems possible based on the evidence we have. Even the Acts accounts have unexplainable variations. Both Luke (in Acts) and Paul have definite purposes in their writing and understandably recount the events in service to these purposes. This largely explains the differences. However, Luke may not have known all the facts. As the participant in the events, Paul should be given first place as witness. This does not mean that we must discredit the historical integrity and value of Luke.

Paul's Conversion

It is common to describe Paul's encounter with Christ as his "conversion" experience. Some object to this since Paul did not change from one religious system to another. At most, he changed parties within Judaism. In Acts 23:6, Luke reports Paul as saying, "I am a Pharisee," not "I *was* a Pharisee." The Christian movement in Paul's day thought of itself as Judaism brought to full realization, since Jesus fulfilled the hopes of Israel.

Although this objection makes a valid and important point, it does not exclude the idea of conversion. In addressing the Jewish people, speakers use the language of repentance and conversion in various biblical settings, including Jesus in his ministry. To accept Jesus of Nazareth as God's agent (Messiah) who introduces the turning of the ages and who includes all nations in the people of God—this act requires a radical reorientation of thinking and life. Such changes can legitimately be called a conversion even while recognizing the deep continuity of the new faith with the previous. Galatians itself defends both the continuity and the discontinuity of the gospel with Israel's faith.

There may be another reason to question whether our account should be called a conversion narrative. As stated in the explanatory notes, the form of our passage is that of a prophetic call narrative, which does not normally involve a religious "conversion." Whatever else was going on in his mind and heart, Paul clearly sees this experience as a call to a prophetic ministry. However, because Paul himself refers to his change from a former life to a new life (vv. 13-14), it is best to describe this event as Paul's conversion *and* call. Here in Galatians, both senses are important to Paul's account of what happened. There is for Paul a close connection between conversion and call.

This close relationship reflects the fundamental characteristic of all biblical religion—to be saved and to be called are bound together. The grace that brings one into relationship with God is also the grace that calls one into service for God (cf. vv. 6 and 15). There is no salvation that does not point beyond itself to a vocation. Not surprisingly, the word *call* can cover both salvation and vocation (cf. again vv. 6 and 15). Since God's purposes extend beyond the salvation of a few to the salvation and blessing of all peoples, every person and people who are the object of salvation become, without exception, the instrument for the salvation of others. The call of Abraham (Gen 12:1-3) and the call of Israel (Exod 19:5-6) illustrate this point. For Paul, the revelation that brings the truth home to him personally contains a *so that*, which communicates the role God has for him. The God of redemption is also the God of recruitment. Biblical salvation is never an end in itself on the individual level.

The Formation of Paul's Theology

There can be no doubt that the Damascus road revelation of Christ formed the nucleus of Paul's faith understanding and the standard for his theological and moral thinking. This is the general impression given by all of Paul's writings. It comes to direct expression in statements like these: "For to me, living is Christ" (Phil 1:21) and "For I decided to know nothing among you except Jesus Christ" (1 Cor 2:2; cf. 3:11). We find the same outlook in the background of a Galatians passage like 2:15-21. The entire paragraph describes the search for an answer to the ethical issue at Antioch by thinking from a Christ-grounded faith (2:16) in a thoroughly consistent manner (2:21).

The foundational role of the Damascus road revelation has led to considerable speculation regarding how Paul's theology developed from it. A surface reading of Paul's words in this chapter might suggest that all of his knowledge of the gospel was revealed to him in that event. But besides being inherently improbable, the accounts of the experiences themselves do not give this impression. Furthermore, we know that Paul received some information about the life of Jesus and the faith of the church before him from other persons. Paul clearly states this in 1 Corinthians 15:3-7 in words that echo the process that Paul denies in Galatians 1:12. Some of this information could have come to him in the visits to Jerusalem reported later in Galatians.

From this we must conclude that for Paul the revelation of Christ consisted of a basic insight or understanding that had the power to shape a whole new faith perspective. The basic skeleton was disclosed to him, but it was fleshed out to some degree from other sources. The Bible (i.e., our OT) continued to provide the basic structure of his faith, but that structure was now built on the new foundation of the lordship of Jesus Christ. Paul was obviously a creative thinker and thought out the implications of the foundational truths of his revelation. In Paul's claim that his gospel is by revelation from God, he means that the foundation, which orients the entire superstructure, was given to him in a direct communication from God. In claiming that he had no interaction with leading Christians in the first years, he implies that he worked out the shape of his entire theology on his own, on the basis of the new foundation.

Can we say more precisely what lay at the heart of the foundational revelation? On two points we can be quite sure. The first and most basic is that the man, Jesus of Nazareth, was raised from the dead and now lives in an exalted (heavenly) state. God has vindicated the messianic claims of Jesus now announced by his followers. Since Jesus had been raised, Paul also concluded that the end-time event of resurrection, which he expected as a Pharisee, had begun (cf. 1 Cor 15:12-28).

The second truth that Paul received through revelation was that God now intended to make good on the promise, made first to Abraham, that all nations would know the blessing of God (cf. Gen 12:3; esp. Gal 3:8). This was the self-evident implication of the command to Paul to preach the good news of Jesus the Messiah to the Gentiles. Paul knew the ancient prophecy that the nations would find the light of God in Israel (cf. Isa 42:6; 60:1-3, 11; Acts 26:17-18). Here one can see that the transforming power of the Damascus road experience issued from the confluence of (1) the content of the revelation, (2) Paul's Pharisaic theology of resurrection, and (3) his awareness of the basic claims of the Jesus movement that he was persecuting. Paul has grounds for claiming that his new belief is given by revelation. However, this does not mean it was given in a vacuum or immediately came to him in full detail. Moreover, we meet here another characteristic typical of Paul's faith: he defends the gospel as new revelation but also as part of a tradition of ancient revelation.

In a study of all Paul's writings, N. T. Wright (1997: 266) summarizes the essential dynamic of Pauline theology in the following way: "Christology is, for Paul, a means of redefining the people of God, and also a means of redefining God himself." Both of these dimensions are at work in our passage. The revelation of Jesus as the Christ leads to confessing Jesus as Son of God and to the conviction that all peoples and persons can equally be children of God (Gal 1:16; 3:26-28). Wright observes that Paul's view of Torah (Law) is then redefined as a consequence. Such redefinition is exactly what will be found in Galatians in Paul's qualification of Law obligation for the Galatians.

THE TEXT IN THE LIFE OF THE CHURCH

Revelation and Tradition

Biblical faith is based on revelation. Such a faith holds that a distance separates the divine world from the human world. God must step across this gap in special acts of disclosure that make known what human beings would not otherwise perceive and could not verify. The validity of biblical faith depends on the reality and the truthfulness of these events of revelation.

The biblical story and church history illustrate the challenge to the people of God for life based on revealed truth. This kind of faith is rooted in great breakthrough revelations of God throughout history, such as the call of Abraham, the exodus of Israel, the life of Jesus, and the coming of the Spirit. Later generations remember these foundational events and their truths. They study the sources that record those things in order to find God's will for their own lives. At the same time, these later generations also desire the sense of God at work in their day and the experience of a living relationship with their God. While living, moreover, they are expecting the new revelation that will come at the next great breakthrough in God's purposes for the world. According to the New Testament, that will be the revealing of Christ at his coming again.

The temptation for the people of God is to lose a proper balance between these two aspects. Some are absorbed with contemporary revelation and Spirit manifestations without a proper grounding in the foundational and authoritative revelation of the past. The opposite temptation is to become a book religion, in which the focus of religious practice is studying the records of past revelation and authoritative interpretations of that revelation by past generations (cf. *traditions of my ancestors* in 1:14; Isa 43:18-19). The first could be called the prophetic extreme; the second, the scribal extreme.

During the Second Temple period, Judaism saw a pronounced shift from prophetic activity to an increasingly scribal approach, which eventually developed into the rabbinical tradition after the destruction of the Second Temple. Distortions of this tradition were the object of criticism by Jesus. He and the early church after him were convinced that the Spirit of God was active in and among them. The prophetic vocation was alive among them (cf. Matt 5:12; Acts 2:16-18; etc.). Paul's comments about his own past reflect these issues. Even his intense reaction to the Galatian situation has a root in these matters. He sees a scribal tendency in the turn to Law observance.

The problem with the scribal extreme is its stagnation in traditionalism and its confidence in moralism or legalism. Paul's opponents among the Galatians show no awareness of being at the cutting edge of the fulfillment of God's purposes under the guidance of a living Spirit. They appear to rely excessively on human formulations, community control, and self-effort at the expense of the divine enabling by grace through the Spirit. This is also the typical problem of second-generation Christianity. On the other hand, the prophetic extreme can be vulnerable to false claims of truth. Often it lacks respect for the authority of past revelation and disdains the established structures of life. Church history is replete with examples of both extremes and of the never-ending search for an elusive balance.

The church must learn to live with a balance of revelation and tradition. Paul's language here seems to oppose revelation and tradition. That is necessary in Galatians because tradition had to step back to allow for the new revelation of Christ. As the bearer of this new revelation, Paul is unique and therefore different from us. In the face of new revelation, the balance of revelation and tradition necessarily shifts. Yet, as we noticed above, even for Paul the meaning of new revelation is partly determined by the tradition of the past revelation that he knows.

Since Paul's new revelation is now a part of our tradition, the role of tradition is greater for us than for him. Still, a sense of the prophetic, present in Paul, is also essential for us. We too have to know the way of revelation, not in the sense of receiving new foundational truth but in the sense of receiving new insight into old truth for our present life. All generations need the guiding work of the Spirit in discerning the will of God for their own day, in the light of the past revelation in Scripture (cf. Rom 12:2).

Revelation through the spectacular appearance of divine

reality, such as Paul experienced, is not common for believers, and it need not be. At the same time, there is no reason to limit such manifestations to Paul. In fact, the reality of encounter with God can and ought to be the experience of every believer. Paul's testimony to the revelation of God's Son *in him* is a truth that penetrated his life. Likewise, our own testimony to the penetration of God's reality in our lives is a sign of authentic faith. Truth given by revelation must be received by revelation in the sense that the same disposition and the same Spirit illumination are required for the truth to be understood and embraced. "No one knows the Father except the Son and anyone to whom the Son chooses to reveal him" (Matt 11:27).

The Relationship of Conversion and Call

The unity of conversion and vocational call present in Paul and generally in Scripture is important to every believer in every age. Within the individual, the movement between gift and task is crucial to spiritual health. The gift of salvation finds its confirmation in the service of God. The calling or task draws its strength from the nourishment of the divine gift. The two build each other up.

The close relationship of salvation and vocation is also crucial for the strength of the church and its mission. The presence of many believers in our churches who are only objects of the church's work and not acting subjects in that work is a major cause of weakness in contemporary Christianity. The church ought to assist every member to discern and practice a vocation that is just as clear as the assurance of salvation. Awareness of what God wants me to do is as important as the awareness of what God has done for me. Whether one's spiritual vocation is directly related to one's employment is a secondary matter. One's spiritual vocation may well be expressed outside of one's occupation and exercised in different specific roles and locations. But God's rule in the world will be greatly advanced when every believer understands one's gift, of whatever kind it may be, as an expression of the calling of God. At the same time, this standard may eliminate certain occupations as inconsistent with a Christian calling.

Practicing the Centrality of Christ

Paul's Christ-centered faith and manner of life is a continuing challenge to the church. Paul had a form of spirituality and a way of discerning God's will from which we can learn. It sets the framework within which the church evaluates the truth claims of other philosophies and religious systems. The finality and preeminence of Christ result from placing him at the center of all thought and life. Menno Simons, the Dutch Anabaptist reformer, was grasped by the same truth and found his anchor point in Paul's words to the Corinthian church: "For no one can lay any foundation other than the one that has been laid; that foundation is Jesus Christ" (1 Cor 3:11).

The centrality of Christ has an important consequence for the interpretation of the Bible. The first Christians read their Scriptures, the Old Testament, in the light of Christ's claims and achievements. Christ is the culmination and fulfillment of God's covenant with Israel. As a result, the meaning of Scripture must always be judged by the standard of the completeness found in the revelation in Christ (cf. Heb 1:1-4). All Christian traditions have continued this emphasis, but not always to the same extent or in the same way. Christians have generally applied the principle to understandings of the means and scope of salvation. The Radical Reformation pressed for a consistent application of the principle to the doctrine of the church and to ethics. As a result, they reaffirmed the New Testament view of a voluntary community of believers distinct from society and based on believers (i.e., adult) baptism, and they emphasized the ethics of a suffering love that rejects violence and war.

Visit with Cephas and James
Galatians 1:18-20

PREVIEW

So was Paul's authority derived from or secondary to that of those *who were already apostles before [him]* in Jerusalem (1:17)? If Paul went up to Jerusalem to learn the basics or even the finer points of the gospel from them, his critics could argue, that would imply that if any different understanding of the gospel should emerge, Paul would certainly need to submit to their understanding and authority.

The second portion of Paul's autobiographical account in defense of his gospel is the story of his first visit to Jerusalem following his conversion. The account stresses the relative shortness of the visit and the limited personal contact. By naming the leading personalities he saw, Paul clarifies the significance of the visit. Paul concludes the section with a passionate declaration that he is being truthful in representing these facts.

The preceding narrative in 1:13-17 presents the activity of God in Paul's experience. The remainder of the autobiographical material (to 2:14) tells of Paul's interaction with other Christian believers. In this second section, Paul's argument becomes subtler and somewhat ambiguous. Paul needs to demonstrate that his contact with the other apostles was quite limited and that it in no way determined his gospel or demonstrated his subordination to them.

The temporal particle *then* marks the structural divisions for this and the following two sections. The specific numbers of the time frame here and in 2:1 (*then after three years, . . . then after fourteen years*) set a contrast to the *immediately* of 1:16 (AT) and create a continuous timeline. This creates the desired impression that all relevant information is present. There is no arbitrary selection of events to favor the argument.

OUTLINE

Stay with Cephas, 1:18
Visit with James, 1:19
Paul's Integrity, 1:20

EXPLANATORY NOTES

Stay with Cephas 1:18

With the word *then*, the reader is informed that the narrative is following a chronological progression. The exact time lapse between the events is expressed: *after three years.* In contrast to the *immediately* of verse 16, *three years* suggests a period of considerable length. That amount of time would allow, or even require, the development of Paul's theology in a definite direction before contact with the older leadership at Jerusalem. It would indicate that Paul was not— nor had he seen himself as—dependent on those leading apostles.

We cannot be sure whether the three years are complete or partial years. The typical reckoning of time would allow for either. Nor can one be sure whether the time period begins from the conversion or from Paul's return from Arabia to Damascus. The likelihood is that Paul means three years after his conversion; otherwise the precision of his chronology, which is his clear intent (cf. 2:1), is lost. The key event in the preceding story is the revelation of Christ to Paul, not his return to Damascus. It is the length of time from that revelation to Paul's first contact with Jerusalem that is crucial for the argument.

If so, Paul's stay in Arabia would have lasted a maximum of three years. All one can say beyond this is that the time in Arabia must have taken a major portion of the time span. Otherwise Paul would have no reason to refer to it in contrast to other activity during the three years. Paul's essential point is that a long period of time elapsed between his commission from Christ and his contact with the apostles.

I did go up to Jerusalem to visit Cephas. Paul uses the traditional manner of speaking of a journey to Jerusalem as going up (cf. v. 17; Mark 10:32; Acts 11:2; 18:22). Given the central role of the city for Jews, this expression sometimes carried connotations of its high religious status. Here the usage is no doubt merely conventional, reflecting geographical relationships. Paul's feeling about the importance of Jerusalem will surface in 2:1-10.

The purpose of his first visit to Jerusalem is *to visit Cephas.* Paul uses the name Cephas for the person better known in the New Testament and the later church as Peter. Cephas appears again in 2:9, 11, 14. This is Paul's normal usage. The only exceptions in Galatians are in 2:7-8, where Paul uses *Peter. Cephas* is the Aramaic form of the Greek name *Peter* (see John 1:42). Both names are related to the word *rock* and were assigned to a man previously known as Simon (Matt 16:17-18). Cephas, or Peter, was the leading figure in the earliest church of Jewish Christians. Paul's visit with him in this first trip to Jerusalem recognizes this fact.

We have already drawn attention to the weight carried by the verb *to visit* (cf. *confer* in 1:16). Paul now says that the human contact he denied in verses 16b-17a did take place, in some form, but after the passage of time. However, *visit* in verse 18 is a different verb from *confer* in verse 16b, and Paul appears to see a difference between conferring with someone and visiting with someone. The word found here can mean "get information from" or "become better acquainted with." The former meaning approaches the idea of *confer* in verse 16b, with its implication of conferring with an authority. The latter meaning, however, differs from *confer.* Given Paul's point in the present context, he certainly wants to avoid implying that he came to Cephas to "sit at his feet" (cf. Acts 22:3) and learn from him! After all, he has just denied being taught by any person (v. 12)! So it is best to translate the word in the sense of "making a friendly visit." This allows the natural exchange of information without suggesting that Peter was teaching Paul or that theirs was a mentor-mentee relationship.

Paul adds that he *stayed with him fifteen days.* Here Paul

acknowledges a period of close interaction. Paul must be aware that the attentive reader will assume an exchange of considerable information, given the amount of time, the persons involved, and the occasion. After all, we have here an extended meeting between a leader of the new movement and a former persecutor of that movement! Many commentators understandably hold that Paul would have been greatly interested in adding to his knowledge about the earthly life of the Jesus who is now his Lord (Dunn 1993: 110–13, 127). And certainly Peter would have wanted to learn about Paul's extraordinary conversion! But from another perspective, the few days were a relatively short time compared to the preceding three years that Paul spent at a distance from Jerusalem.

Visit with James 1:19

Paul now claims that he *did not see any other apostle except James the Lord's brother*. This shows that the Cephas whom Paul has just mentioned is an apostle, thus clarifying that this Cephas is Peter, the apostle. What is not clear is whether Paul means to suggest that James is also among the apostles. The word *except* could be linked to *apostle* or to the verb *see*. The former would make James an apostle: *[no] other apostle except James*. The latter would imply that James is in another group: I saw no other apostle, though I did see James. Commentators are in wide disagreement. The underlying problem is whether James could have been an apostle.

While this James could not have been one of the twelve disciples of Jesus, since he is the Lord's brother, he could have been an apostle. Occasionally the earliest church used the term more widely than for the twelve and those who had seen the resurrected Jesus (see on 1:1). Nevertheless, according to 1 Corinthians 15:7, the resurrected Lord appeared to James. Thus he qualified to be an apostle. Indeed, this fact would help explain his prominence as a leader in Jerusalem. Moreover, 1 Corinthians 15:5, 7 strongly supports his apostolic status. Cephas stands at the head of a grouping with the twelve; James does the same with the grouping of apostles (note *all*). It seems best to understand that Paul is including James among the apostles.

The use of the simple verb *see* differs from the special verb in the previous verse that describes Paul's contact with Cephas. This change of verb and his mention of James as something of an afterthought show that Paul's visit with Cephas was of more substance. However, it is important for Paul to acknowledge this contact with James. The several references to him in chapter 2 likely indicate that as a leader in Jerusalem, James figured prominently in the claims of Paul's opposition in Galatia (see esp. 2:12).

Paul's Integrity 1:20

Before moving to the next stage of his life story, Paul passionately affirms the truthfulness of his account of past events. *In what I am writing to you, before God, I do not lie!* The statement solemnly calls God as witness—as Paul does elsewhere (cf. Rom 1:9; Phil 1:8; 1 Thess 2:5, 10). Here Paul is placing himself under the judgment of God with respect to his sincerity. Whether this reflects the Roman legal terminology for an oath is not clear, but that may be irrelevant.

Presumably the statement covers the entire narrative that begins in verse 11 and that continues after this verse. We noted above the intensity of Paul's concern at the beginning of this letter about the Galatians' desertion of the gospel (1:1-10). The fact that Paul follows up his opening with an extended narrative about his past life indicates that some people are telling that story differently—in a way that suggests a different understanding about Paul's authority in relation to the other apostles. It is even possible that the version of Paul's story offered by his opponents was similar to the one that eventually ended up in Acts (see TBC below). In any case, Paul is at pains to correct the details of his story, especially those that witness to his relationship with the other apostles.

Although we cannot know the precise details of the story the opposition gave, Galatians 1:20 confirms that in Galatians 1–2 Paul is correcting an erroneous account of his story, along with the erroneous implications of that account for understanding the trustworthiness of Paul's version of the gospel. It is also clear that the teachers who were countering Paul's Law-free gospel claimed some kind of support from Jerusalem. This was enough to shake confidence in Paul. Rhetorically speaking, Paul defends his character and integrity in an argument from *ethos* (see the Introduction).

THE TEXT IN BIBLICAL CONTEXT

The First Visit to Jerusalem

In Acts 9:26-30, the account of Paul's first postconversion visit to Jerusalem presents a different impression of its timing and nature. Acts gives no impression of a three-year gap before the visit. With respect to the nature of the visit, the public activity recounted in Acts need not be seen as contradicting the Galatians account. However, Paul's introduction to the apostles by Barnabas in Acts appears to contradict Paul's claim that his contact was limited to just two, Cephas (Peter) and James. F. F. Bruce (101) observes that the author of Acts may be using a generalizing plural. In this case, the plural would not refer to the whole group, but to an unspecified number of the group. The Acts account does reflect Paul's claim that he did not act merely as a learner in Jerusalem. He shares the story of his encounter with the Lord and preaches boldly while there (Acts 9:27-29). Some of the differences between Acts and Galatians 1-2 clearly reflect the different purposes of the two writings. This makes it impossible for us, in the absence of independent information, to pass judgment on the historical reliability of the accounts or to reconstruct a definitive composite picture of the events. Nevertheless, since Paul is writing about his own life and since his account predates the one in Acts by thirty years or more, we must not easily dismiss Paul's version of the story.

Leadership in the Jerusalem Church

Paul's reflections on the early days of the Christian movement grant us a brief glimpse into the leadership of the earliest community in Jerusalem. Paul's interest in meeting Peter (Cephas) and James indicates their prominent role among Jerusalem believers. This is evident again in 2:6, 9, where the two men are named, along with John, as leading personalities (*pillars*). Here the book of Acts supports the general picture.

Interestingly, Peter appears to have the primary status in Galatians 1:18-19, as argued above. This is certainly the impression left by the first chapters of Acts (1:15; 2:14, 37; etc.). However, in Galatians 2:9, Paul lists the names of the leaders with James at the head of the list. This could be a coincidence if it were not that it squares with the picture of Acts in which James replaces Peter as the leader (Acts 15:13; 21:18-19). One explanation for this difference is that Peter's itinerant ministry eventually took him from Jerusalem; such a ministry is implied in Galatians 2:7, 11; 1 Corinthians 1:12; and perhaps 1 Peter 1:1. Acts mentions Peter's departure from Jerusalem in connection with King Herod's persecution of church leaders (12:17). In any case, Peter's exit from the narrative of Acts in 12:17b is quite unceremonious!

The evidence shows that Paul was viewed as the more progressive and even radical leader, and James as the more conservative (see on Gal 2:12). Peter apparently stood between them, as his vacillation at Antioch also shows (2:11-14). Yet no evidence suggests that the three ever broke relationship or no longer recognized one another's ministry. Probably some tension between them continued, as the Antioch episode and perhaps the book of James suggest. Some of James's followers, including Paul's opponents in Galatia, were probably more opposed to Paul's mission and gospel than was James himself (see Gal 2:4, 12). Jewish Christians of the second century continued to honor James, and their writings took strong exception to the Pauline theological viewpoint.

THE TEXT IN THE LIFE OF THE CHURCH

Integrity of Leaders

The autobiographical section of Galatians highlights the close relationship of message and messenger, or more specifically, of truth and truth-teller. This connection may be weaker in the case of more empirical knowledge based on scientific investigation than in the case of personal and religious knowledge. But since no knowledge bypasses human mediation, there is no exception to this relationship of message and medium. The integrity of the truth is inseparable from the virtue of the messenger. Truth and moral values are interdependent. The attempt of the modern world to find a base for truth apart from commitment to a moral frame of reference is an illusion and can lead only to a distorted view of truth. The occasional attempt of some in the Christian church to isolate the communication of spiritual truth from the spiritual character of the ministering person is likewise in error.

When Paul pauses amid his recital of factual information to reflect on his own integrity as a witness, he is acknowledging the link between his person and the truth to which he witnesses. Paul was impressed with the degree to which the issue of integrity or sincerity bears on the role of one who treats the issues of life and death. Can anyone be sufficient for this task? It is possible, but only under the conditions that "in Christ we speak as persons of sincerity, as persons sent from God and standing in his presence" (2 Cor 2:17). Leadership in the church and the ministry of the gospel to the world must give continual attention to the moral and spiritual quality of the person. The incarnation of truth in life is the best evidence for truth.

Sojourn in Syria and Cilicia

Galatians 1:21-24

PREVIEW

After pausing in Galatians 1:20 to solemnly declare the truthfulness
of his version of the story that he is telling, Paul continues his narrative. Although Paul mentions his stay in the territories of Syria
and Cilicia, he is not interested in narrating his activity in that area.
Instead, Paul emphasizes that even at this point, he was known by
the churches in Judea only by reputation. And his reputation was
that he was the one who had changed from being a persecutor to a
proclaimer of the gospel.

Paul continues to tell his story in a way that emphasizes his
essential independence from the new movement's base in Jerusalem
and Judea. But Paul also introduces a new detail in his argument.
He states that the Judean community had already recognized the
true work of God in him. That claim challenges the viewpoint of the
Galatian adversaries, who are trying to discredit Paul. Here Paul is
setting against his opponents in Galatia the testimony of their own
community in Judea! This new argument will continue in the following account of a second trip to Jerusalem (2:1-10).

EXPLANATORY NOTES

The paragraph begins with the second of three occurrences of *then*,
a word that propels the chronological progression of the narrative
(cf. 1:18; 2:1). Following his first trip to Jerusalem, Paul *went into the
regions of Syria and Cilicia* (1:21). This agrees with Acts 9:30 that Paul
went to Tarsus from Jerusalem. Tarsus was Paul's hometown,
located in the territory of Cilicia (Acts 22:3). The two areas of Syria
and Cilicia lay north of Judea and included the cities of Damascus,
(Syrian) Antioch, and Tarsus, all of which figure in biblical history.
Paul's activity in the Gentile mission probably took place in the
areas around Tarsus and Antioch. That Paul was involved in evangelism during the period is stated in 1:23.

Because Paul's earlier stay in Jerusalem was short and rather
private, he was *still unknown by sight to the churches of Judea* (1:22).
The grammatical construction emphasizes the continuing lack of
face-to-face contact. Paul wants to stress to his readers the lack of
direct contact with the Jewish believers in Christ. The reference to
Judea is likely to the entire area included in the Roman province of

Judea: Samaria and Galilee as well as the traditional Judean district. Paul's claim to be unknown presumably includes the Jerusalem congregation(s), in spite of the impression from Acts 9:28 that Paul moved about among the believers there.

Paul normally describes the churches as being *of God*, as God's possession (cf. 1:13). But here and in 1 Thessalonians 2:14, the churches are specified as the churches *in Christ*. The same expression, *in Christ*, is used in the salutation of most of Paul's letters, along with words that refer to members of the church, such as *saints*. The formula is a distinctive phrase in Pauline theology. Galatians itself is marked by it, especially in 3:26-28 (see TBC).

Twice in the New Testament *the churches in Christ* refers to Jewish Christian congregations in Judea. Both appear in Paul's early writings. This suggests that the phrase originally distinguished the Christian congregations, or messianic synagogues, from the traditional Jewish congregations/synagogues. It reflects a time when the word *church* had not yet become a technical term in Christian circles.

Although most believers in the Jewish homeland remained without personal acquaintance of Paul, they did receive news about his activities. This was their sole means of contact: *They only heard it said, "The one who formerly was persecuting us is now proclaiming the faith he once tried to destroy"* (1:23). The tense of the verb *heard* indicates a flow of information over a period of time. In verse 23 the emphasis on the continuing lack of contact and on the persisting flow of information heightens the impact of Paul's point. It also prepares for and explains the statement that the Judean Christians were glorifying God because of Paul. The word of Paul's about-face is in the form of direct address, giving it the authentic ring of a testimonial. At the same time it parallels the language Paul has used in verses 13 and 16.

Of special interest is the use of *faith* as a general term meaning the entire message of the gospel. This usage soon became widespread in the early church and continues to the present day. To find it here in one of the earliest writings indicates its early appearance in Christian vocabulary (cf. 3:23, 25; 6:10). The presence here is rather surprising since in Galatians a central concern is to defend the narrower, precise meaning of faith as trust in God and in the offer or work of God, over against confidence in works of the Law and the flesh (2:16; 3:2-5). For Paul, the central place of faith in the gospel allows him to let that central part stand for the whole of the gospel.

The news that the former persecutor has now become an advocate is a sign of a miraculous deed of God. Therefore, the believers who once had been the object of the persecution now *glorified God because of me* (1:24). The NRSV translation with the simple past tense obscures the continuing nature of this response over a period of time. Their response parallels their not knowing and their hearing of the previous verses. Throughout the biblical record, the praise of God is the spontaneous response to witnessing God's mighty acts of redemption. Paul points away from himself to God, who alone is worthy of praise. At the same time, the words *because of me* are crucial since they strengthen the picture of Paul as an instrument of God. The very faith experience of the Jewish Christians has incorporated the person of Paul into itself. So Paul is telling his Galatian readers that the praise of the believers in Judea stands as a witness against those defaming him in Galatia even as the defamers claim to represent believers in Judea.

THE TEXT IN BIBLICAL CONTEXT

In Christ

Throughout the book of Galatians, Paul uses the language of *in Christ* and related concepts. The terminology is found in Galatians 1:22; 2:4, 17; 3:14, 26, 28; 5:6 (cf. 5:10). The passage in 2:19-20 is a key to understanding the concepts behind the expression. The phrase *in Christ* reflects Paul's Christ-centered perspective in describing the life of believers. It sees Christian experience as participation in the totality of what Jesus Christ represents in his life and work. Not surprisingly, some interpreters of Paul have taken the concept of *in Christ* as the central idea that holds together Pauline theology. Recent interpretation generally is giving increasing weight to it (e.g., Sanders; Gorman; Campbell).

In most of Paul's letters, the phrase describes the relationship of the individual believer to Christ. However, in many instances the corporate sense predominates. The individual and the corporate senses presuppose each other. Our text, with its parallel in 1 Thessalonians 2:14, emphasizes the corporate sense: the congregation is in Christ. The way Paul can move between the individual and corporate senses is illustrated in 3:26-28. The expression *as many of you as were baptized* (3:27) focuses on the individual, but *all of you are one in Christ* (v. 28) speaks to a collective reality. Paul's argument there that old social divisions are removed in Christ is based on the solidarity of all believers in one social entity. The corporate sense of *in Christ* finds its special expression in another distinctive Pauline phrase, the "body of Christ" and its accompanying images. While this language does not appear in Galatians, the idea is already present in the early writing of the apostle.

A fuller definition of *in Christ* must await a study of the later occurrences in the letter. The phrase signifies that the Christian community (and each individual in it) derives spiritual life wholly from the person of Jesus Christ. That life is mediated by a personal relationship of trust in Christ as Savior and Lord and is marked by a way of life that sees Jesus as its model.

THE TEXT IN THE LIFE OF THE CHURCH

Glorifying God

To glorify God is to ascribe glory to God. The glory of God is the manifestation of God's presence in some form that is discernible to humans. Reverently acknowledging God's presence is glorifying God. Such a response is an act of worship. Worship begins with glorifying God and continues with further listening to the divine word and with acts of dedication to the service of God.

The glory of God often takes the form of an unusual event or phenomenon that points beyond the normal and routine. The cloud and pillar of fire that guided Israel and stood over the tabernacle are a case in point. Appearances of God or of angelic beings are typically accompanied by light. The appearance of the risen Jesus to Paul is an example (Acts 9:3). But the glory of God can also be perceived in the more normal processes of life by the eye of faith. The psalmist observes God's glory in the natural world (Ps 19).

The direct and spectacular manifestations are more rare than typical in biblical history and in church history. The kind of experience described in the present text is more common. Here in the life of a human being, something takes place that points to the working of God and the presence of God. Paul's change of character and behavior is a wonderful development that bears witness to God's power. Therefore others can perceive the glory of the Lord in observing this person's life. This form of the glory of God, and the discernment of it, can and should be the experience of every believer and every community of faith. Wherever the saving and transforming power of God is at work, the glory of God is present for those with eyes of faith to see. Where this is not a living reality, faith loses its vitality and worship becomes shallow at best—a mere repetition of the past generations' experiences of glory (cf. Isa 43:18-19).

Visit with the Leading Apostles
Galatians 2:1-10

PREVIEW

What actually happened in Jerusalem? And how does Paul's narrative in Galatians 2:1-10 relate to Luke's narrative in Acts 15:1-21—if at all? Are they talking about the same event, but expressing different understandings of that event? Or are they talking about different events that share some of the same themes? These questions are among the most challenging and perplexing historical issues in the study of Galatians.

As in 1:18, 21, the transitional word *then* marks the beginning of a new event in Paul's life narrative, here a second visit to Jerusalem. The narrative forms a tight logical flow, with no sharp division into parts. Verses 6-10 form one sentence in the original Greek even though the parenthetical statement in verses 3-5 introduces a structural break into the narrative. The opening verses describe the setting and purpose of the visit. In the parenthetical material (vv. 3-5), Paul offers a glimpse into the issues that animated the conversations in Jerusalem. He describes the outcomes of his negotiations with the Jerusalem leaders in verses 6-10. That part of the story is where the emphasis lies.

The report of this visit contributes to Paul's central argument in several ways. In fact, all elements found in the preceding scenes of chapter 1 are present here as well: God reveals God's purpose and guidance; Paul is essentially independent of, while also interdependent with, Jerusalem; and other believers recognize and affirm God's action in Paul's life. All these elements support the central claim that the message and ministry of Paul have God's seal of approval on them.

But there is also a new element in the story. This new event touches on some of the same issues that Paul is addressing in the Galatian churches. This element appears again in the Antioch episode, which completes the autobiographical section. In this way, Paul is linking his own story with the experience of the Galatians. Paul expressly points out this link in verse 5.

In terms of the letter's structure, the introduction of this theme assists in the transition from the focus on Paul and his credentials that have characterized the letter to this point, to a focus on the Galatians and their problems. That theme has to do with whether or how Gentiles should observe the Jewish Law, especially as represented in circumcision (2:3) and table fellowship (2:12). In other words, Paul's experiences not only support the truth of his gospel: they also provide examples that the Galatians can imitate.

OUTLINE

Circumstances of the Visit, 2:1-2
Issues of the Visit, 2:3-5
Outcomes of the Visit, 2:6-10

EXPLANATORY NOTES

Circumstances of the Visit 2:1-2

Paul continues to narrate a crucial period of his life in order to account for all his relationships with the center of the early Christian movement in Jerusalem. The word *then* has practically the meaning of *next* in its three occurrences (1:18, 21; 2:1). The length of elapsed time he mentions is *fourteen years*. Without doubt, this is meant to strike the reader as a long period of time. How unusual that a key figure converts to the faith and launches into a ministry of evangelism and teaching (cf. Acts 9:20, 28; 11:26; 13:1) with so little interaction with the founding leaders! I argued that the three-year period of 1:18 commences with Paul's conversion, since that is the point from which the crucial question of human influence on Paul has to be traced. For this same reason, Paul is again most likely calculating from his conversion in his reference to *fourteen years* in 2:1, with the three years and the fourteen years concurrent.

I went up again to Jerusalem with Barnabas, taking Titus along with me (2:1). According to Galatians, this is now Paul's second post-conversion visit to Jerusalem. Paul's second visit *in Acts* is the famine aid visit in 11:27-30; 12:25. However, the visit in Galatians 2:1-10 sounds more like the visit recounted in Acts 15:1-29. Most interpreters have assumed that Paul's account in Galatians is his version of the so-called Jerusalem Council of Acts 15. After all, how many major meetings in Jerusalem to talk about the critical issue of circumcision for the Gentiles could there have been? And if there are important differences between the accounts in Acts 15 and Galatians 2, should that not be expected, since we already know that Paul is eager to correct some inaccurate accounts of this meeting?

But there are also problems with this view, and some prefer to relate our present account to Acts 11:27-30 or offer other reconstructions (see farther below, and the Introduction). Barnabas is mentioned as Paul's companion in the visits in both Acts 11 and 15.

He was a leader in Jerusalem and Antioch and was an advocate and companion for Paul (Acts 4:36-37; 9:27; 11:22-26; 1 Cor 9:6). The language here and in Galatians 2:9 makes Barnabas an equal partner with Paul, even though the narrative focuses on Paul. In contrast to Barnabas, Titus is clearly introduced as a person under Paul's care. He was a Greek (v. 3), probably Paul's convert (Titus 1:4), and he served as a helper in Paul's mission (2 Cor 2:12-13; 7:6, 13; 8:6, 23).

When Paul reports that the trip to Jerusalem was *in response to a revelation* (2:2), he draws attention to the action of God in his life. Paul is emphasizing once again that *God* is the cause of what Paul does, not human beings. The parallel to 1:12 and 16 is obvious. For Paul's present purposes, the resurrection appearance (1:16) and this revelation (2:2) both support the same claim. But they are most unequal in other respects. The first is a unique form of revelation to an apostle, which is the norm of all Christian truth; the second is a source of divine guidance in a particular case that is not unique to this occasion or to Paul. Paul does not state the *form* of the revelation (dream, vision, prophetic word, or sign). None of the possible parallel accounts in Acts tell of such a revelation to Paul. There is a revelation to Agabus (Acts 11:28) about a famine, but not about the sending of aid to Jerusalem, which was the reason for Paul's trip on that occasion. Acts speaks of the church appointing Paul (and others) to go to the Jerusalem Council (Acts 15:2). But human decision does not exclude the possibility of revelation. The famine visit of Acts 11:27-30 shows how closely the two phenomena can relate.

Paul now states his express purpose of the visit: *I laid before them the gospel.* The verb *laid before* is the third of the four key verbs expressing Paul's special relationship to Jerusalem (see also 1:16, 18; 2:6). The present instance is crucial because the verb admits an exchange with the Jerusalem leaders about Paul's gospel. At first sight, this admission appears to deny what Paul vigorously affirmed elsewhere—that Paul's gospel is independent of Jerusalem. The meaning of the word *laid before* is "to inform for the purpose of consideration or consultation." But the word itself does not indicate the status of the parties involved with one another (Dunn 1993: 114). In this important way it differs from the verb Paul uses in his denial in 1:16 that he was consulting with a greater authority. Paul is therefore saying that his gospel is not dependent on Jerusalem for its authorization, but rather that he is open to mutual discernment and coordination. At the same time, Paul's willingness to discuss matters with the leaders in Jerusalem shows his respect for the position and role of these persons. The wording makes it clear that the subject of the consultation was the innovations Paul had worked out in his mission for the Gentile practice of the gospel.

Paul uses the pronoun *them* without any antecedent. His later reference to *those of repute* (leaders, specifically James, Cephas, and John; 2:6, 9 RSV) indicates whom he has in mind. But this dangling pronoun indicates just how much the issue at Galatia is about Paul's relation to the apostles at Jerusalem. Paul's mind is absorbed with that fact.

The consultation took place *only in a private meeting with the acknowledged leaders*. The NRSV is justified in making this explicit clarification. Some have suggested that the text could refer to two meetings, one with a larger, open group (*them*) and another with select leaders. This suggestion seems to reflect the interest of some scholars in harmonizing Galatians 2 with Acts 15, based on the assumption that they refer to the same historical event. The question of possible harmony with Acts 15 is, in fact, related to the question whether the *acknowledged leaders* in this verse are the three *acknowledged pillars* in verse 9 (James, Cephas, and John), or whether others besides the three were involved. Acts 15 describes an assembly of apostles and elders. A harmonization might suggest that Paul met with a larger group of leaders whose chief representatives were the pillar/leaders. However, if James, Cephas, and John were the only persons in the consultation, that would be a problem for harmonizing Galatians 2 with Acts 15. Paul's statements about the leaders in Galatians 2:2, 6, and 9 make it most likely that his meeting was with only the *pillar* leaders. Such a smaller, more private, meeting fits better with the picture of certain persons who infiltrate and spy on the situation (v. 4). Thus, if Paul is speaking about the same event as that recounted in Acts 15, it is clear that Luke exaggerated the size and official nature of the consultation.

Paul states that he sought out the consultative meeting with Jerusalem leaders *in order to make sure that I was not running, or had not run, in vain*. This statement is astonishing, at least at first blush. For Paul to admit to any uncertainty or apprehension about his work at this point seems to undercut the confident tone necessary to persuade his diffident audience. Such confidence clearly characterizes the rest of the narration! We can be sure that something important to Paul is going on here; otherwise he would surely have avoided this appearance of weakness. Paul is not unsure of his call or of the rightness of his message. He has taken pains to deny just that! He did not need to go to other believers for confirmation of his conversion and gospel understanding (cf. 1:16).

Rather, Paul is aware that the success of his ministry depends on factors beyond himself. One of these factors is the Jerusalem church, meaning the Jewish believers in Jesus there in Jerusalem. Paul clearly wants his Gentile mission to be recognized by Jerusalem. Paul recognizes that if the church leaders in Jerusalem fail to recognize his mission or to bless it, conflicts over his gospel could threaten the success of his work—as indeed was happening now in Galatia. But the matter goes deeper than the question of the immediate success and survival of Paul's own efforts. Paul has a vision of a church of all peoples that fulfills or completes the promise of God to the Jewish people. He therefore sees the unity of the Jewish and Gentile churches as essential to the realization of God's larger purposes (see TBC and TLC below).

Issues of the Visit 2:3-5

One of the points of Paul's message to Gentiles was that circumcision was unnecessary. That this became a central issue in the opposing teaching to Paul is clear throughout Galatians (see 5:2-3, 6, 11; 6:12-13, 15). Now Paul refers directly to this issue by observing that *Titus . . . was not compelled to be circumcised, though he was a Greek* (2:3). Titus's presence became a test case on the question of circumcision. Probably Paul was thinking of this role when he decided to bring Titus along. Paul is more interested in emphasizing the theological significance of this fact than he is in reporting the discussion on circumcision with the leaders. If the leaders had insisted that Titus be circumcised, that would have been a rebuff of Paul's ministry and a signal that his ministry was *in vain*. Hence the strong contrast (*but*) with the preceding verse.

The word *compel* is crucial for understanding Paul's perspective on circumcision and other works of the Law in Galatians. This word appears three times in the letter: (1) here; (2) of Peter, who compels the Gentiles at Antioch to live like Jews (2:14); and (3) of the Galatian agitators, who are trying to compel Paul's readers to be circumcised (6:12). Paul's linking of these passages in this way highlights why he reports this detail of the visit: it speaks directly to the Galatian problem. Paul's emphasis on *compel* indicates that his protest against circumcision for the Galatians is not directed to the act itself, as if it were itself evil, but to the absolute value the teachers were attaching to it. The opponents were teaching that circumcision and other practices of the Law were necessary to be acceptable to God.

This helps explain why Paul at one point can say that neither circumcision nor uncircumcision counts for anything (5:6; 6:15) and at another point he can say that circumcision will cut one off from Christ (5:4). These statements contradict one another unless one understands that circumcision is a threat only when treated as something essential. That is the point where it conflicts with the value of Christ's death and resurrection as the sufficient ground of salvation and right living (see also 2:21; 5:4; 6:14). This clarification of Paul's viewpoint also explains why he did not try to compel Jewish believers to give up Jewish religious practices (works of the Law) and why he could himself circumcise Timothy, who had a Jewish mother and therefore was counted as Jewish (Acts 16:3).

Now Paul focuses on another incident in the visit: *But because of false believers secretly brought in* . . . (2:4). Paul begins a line of thought that he never completes. He never states what actually resulted from the presence of the intruders. Perhaps doing so would only have distracted from his point, to which he shifts in midsentence (v. 5): the intruders were unsuccessful in gaining the upper hand. The linking of verses 3 and 4 suggests that the intruders were exerting pressure to have Titus circumcised.

Who these infiltrators were is not clear. They belonged to the Christian community but were not from among the principal leaders. In the Acts 15 consultation, the opponents of Paul are said to be of the Pharisee party (Acts 15:5). From Paul's point of view, these persons did not represent the leaders, nor did they have their support. Paul describes these persons, their actions, and their motivations in terms of how they would have affected his work. These believers would naturally have thought they were defending the truth. For Paul, they had *slipped in to spy on the freedom we have in Christ Jesus so that they might enslave us.* Paul likely uses the image of infiltrators to discredit these people in the eyes of the Galatians. But Paul may also have used this language to reflect his wish to keep this consultation behind closed doors, with persons he respected. In any case, the language reflects political maneuvering and reinforces the larger theme of freedom and slavery.

With the introduction of freedom/slavery vocabulary, Paul introduces a prominent—some would say preeminent—theme in Galatians (4:3-11, 21-31; 5:1, 13-26). This powerful language serves Paul's polemic well. It has both an immediate emotional impact as well as a profound theological penetration into the issues at hand. Paul is saying that the requirement of circumcision is a matter of freedom and slavery! The obligation of circumcision is an enslavement that encroaches on the freedom Jesus Christ gives. Circumcision is an example of the Jewish way of life under the Law,

from which Christ has redeemed (3:13; 4:5). The intruders are promoting the idea that these practices, commanded in the Scriptures
to Israel, are required of the followers of Jesus the Messiah. Their
attempt to impose their conviction is no less than an attempt to
enslave others.

Ultimately, Paul is alluding to the bondage that results from
mixing Law requirement and Jesus faith. In the present context,
however, Paul is protecting the freedom of the Gentile mission
against the controlling influence of these misguided teachers. The
Galatians, too, are being enslaved to intruding teachers—and by
implication, to the Law. Paul confirms this in his reply: *We did not
submit to them even for a moment* (2:5). Paul has in mind the issue of
political control: who is master and who is servant. He refused to
acknowledge any authority in that group. Thus the impact of the
statement is to support the larger argument of this portion of the
letter, that God directly authorized Paul's gospel, which is therefore not dependent on any human authority.

We come to a high point of the letter, when Paul states the purpose of his resistance to the intruders: *so that the truth of the gospel
might always remain with you*. Again in 2:14 Paul repeats the phrase
truth of the gospel, which appears nowhere else in Paul's letters
except in Colossians 1:5. This phrase is shorthand for the central
concern of the letter to defend correct belief and practice (cf. 1:6-7;
2:14; 5:7). For Paul, it does not mean the reasonableness or rational
coherence of the gospel. It means the gospel that corresponds to
the intention of God. The special emphasis here is on the integrity
of the gospel. The issue is about what is compatible with or alien to
the gospel, both in belief and in action.

The extremists in Jerusalem, whom Paul calls *false believers*, had
attempted to dominate Paul and his companions. However, Paul
understood himself to be fighting a battle leading to consequences
for all believers. It was for the freedom of the Galatians (*you*) that
Paul was struggling. This additional claim to Paul's integrity connects Paul's story with the experience of the Galatians as they were
facing a similar takeover attempt by similar *false believers*. In making
this point, Paul is again inviting the Galatians to identify with him;
he had put himself on the line on their behalf!

Outcomes of the Visit 2:6-10

With verse 6, the account of the consultation at Jerusalem picks up
the story line from verse 2, which treats the relationship of Paul to
the Jerusalem leaders and their response to his understanding of

the gospel. Paul has gone to Jerusalem to consult with the leaders there (2:2); but now he protects that thought from misunderstanding: *those leaders contributed nothing to me* (2:6). Before his second postconversion visit to Jerusalem, Paul had not sought counsel from the earlier leaders. Now that he does submit to accountability (*mutual* accountability, Paul would certainly say), he is recognizing a certain authority at Jerusalem. This does not negate his claim that God's authority is behind his work. The fact that the Jerusalem leaders did not add anything new to him demonstrates the truth of his stance and the equal position he has with them!

The verb in the expression *contributed nothing* is the same one used in the crucial statement of 1:16, *I did not confer with any human being*. That the Jerusalem leaders are the subject of the verb requires a different sense in English, as the translation shows. However, in both cases the thought is of a consultation in which the influence of a greater authority affects a lesser. Thus in the present verse, Paul is saying that the Jerusalem leaders did not use their position to modify Paul's stance. What those leaders did not contribute, or did not add, was the requirement of observing the Law, such as circumcision— which the false believers sought to impose. The real leaders did not press these on Paul. In this way Paul shows that his authority as an apostle was confirmed by Jerusalem, but not conferred by Jerusalem, nor was it somehow inferior to Jerusalem or subject to it.

In order to defend the integrity of his own authority, Paul must be careful about how he describes the Jerusalem leaders. He must refer to them as they were commonly known in the church and as he himself recognizes them—as *acknowledged leaders*. Yet he must combat the conclusion drawn from this term by the teachers in Galatia that their position as leaders makes their word more important than Paul's. This difficulty explains the variation in language that he uses in speaking of them (v. 9). The literal meaning of *acknowledged leaders* is "those who appear to be something." This has a negative connotation to the English ear. However, people of that time used this language for persons *of repute* (2:6 RSV) in society. It could refer positively to a truly outstanding person or negatively to a person whose reputation was without substance. Paul is walking a fine line between these two senses of the language.

The formulation of verse 6, *who were supposed to be acknowledged leaders*, clearly shows that Paul is distancing himself from the commonly accepted language even while adopting it in verses 2, 6, and 9. The same expression is found in 6:3, *those who . . . think they are something*. In this latter case a negative tone is evident. But the two passages are not fully parallel because Paul is not saying that the Jerusalem leaders' reputation is nothing. Rather, the larger context in 2:1-10 suggests that Paul is acknowledging the leadership and authority of James, Cephas, and John, but not in any way that diminishes his own leadership and authority. Their authority and accountability are fully mutual.

Paul doubly reinforces the point with two statements in the form of a parenthesis. The first is a common proverb: *What they actually were makes no difference to me.* This does not mean that Paul places no significance on the position of these leaders. His desire to work with them lest his work be in vain indicates the contrary. The key to understanding the statement is the past tense: *what they were at one time* (lit.). Paul is likely implying that the association of James, Cephas, and John with the historical Jesus is unimportant. It gave them no higher status than Paul, who had not been a disciple of the earthly Jesus. Less likely, it could mean that the relationship of these leaders to Paul in that Jerusalem visit has, in any event, no bearing on the present issue with the Galatians. In either case, Paul is making a point over against those who are trying to pit Jerusalem authority against Paul's authority. Paul concedes neither that Jerusalem disagrees with him nor that its authority can be invoked against him. What matters is the question of truth on its own merits. The Antioch episode, which follows, illustrates this point in practice.

The second statement in the parenthesis makes a theological point: *God shows no partiality.* Paul is clearly not trying to discredit the leaders at Jerusalem. God does not make judgments on the basis of some previously existing status or condition of an individual. Here Paul uses an Old Testament principle (Lev 19:15; Deut 1:17; 2 Chron 19:7; Ps 82:2) to make the point that in God's sight, neither Jerusalem nor Paul has an edge on the truth by reason of social status. This principle places all leaders on an equal level, with shared authority in discerning God's will for the church.

As we have seen before, although Paul is arguing for his personal authority, he is always looking beyond himself to the cause of the gospel among the Gentiles (cf. Gal 2:5). The theme of God's impartiality shows the same linkage. Paul uses the concept of God's impartiality in his letters to defend the principle of a church that includes all peoples in an egalitarian community, regardless of race, gender, or social standing (Rom 2:11; Eph 6:9). Romans 2:11 and 3:22 speak specifically of the equality of Jew and Gentile (cf. Acts 10:34; Gal 3:28; Col 3:11). This is a central issue in Galatians.

Paul does not spell out the equality of Jew and Gentile before God in the present context. Yet here Paul reflects an interest in preserving the equal status of Gentile and Jewish believers in setting direction for the church. The subordination of the Gentiles to Jerusalem would support their submission to Jewish legal requirements, such as circumcision. Both would compromise the equality of all peoples in Christ and their freedom in the gospel (see 2:4-5). Therefore Paul opposes both. He gives the point theological grounding in 2:15-17 and touches on it throughout the letter.

In Paul's view, the Jerusalem leaders did not presume to correct his gospel by adding something that it lacked. Rather, they recognized Paul's gospel for the Gentiles as from God. The words of strong contrast with which he begins verse 7, *on the contrary*, suggest that it was the Jerusalem leaders, rather than Paul, who came to new understandings from the consultation. The new understanding was based on their observation and acknowledgment that God had given Paul an effective ministry among the Gentiles and that God's grace was operative in that ministry (v. 9a). As a result, the *pillar* leaders recognized Paul and Barnabas as partners in a common cause (v. 9b).

The Jerusalem leaders saw that Paul *had been entrusted with the gospel for the uncircumcised, just as Peter had been entrusted with the gospel for the circumcised* (2:7). This gives evidence that during the visit, Paul had reported about his own call and also about his actual ministry with its attending results, as in Acts 15. Titus was a living example of the gospel's effects in Paul's converts. From this reporting, the leaders were able to gain spiritual insight into the divine working in Paul's ministry. The passive form of *had been entrusted*, so typical of biblical statements of this kind (the divine passive), points indirectly to the action of God. That is, *God* had entrusted Paul with this message of salvation to the uncircumcised. The word *entrust* has the double effect of expressing God's approval of the message Paul preaches and God's appointment of Paul to a special work.

The terms *uncircumcised* and *circumcised* are common designations for Gentiles and Jews, respectively. Their use here and elsewhere indicates how much circumcision symbolized Jewish identity versus Gentile identity. The phrases *gospel for the uncircumcised* and *gospel for the circumcised* are, on the other hand, not common. On the surface the reference to two different gospels appears to contradict Paul's emphasis in 1:6-9 that there was only one true gospel. But Paul's distinction of gospels here refers primarily to the division of labor in promulgating the message. Behind the division of labor between Paul and Peter is perhaps also the acknowledgment that

Jewish and Gentile Christians practiced their faith within the different cultural frameworks from which they came (see also 2:3, 11-14.) Paul otherwise assumes that the essential message he preaches is the same as that of the Jerusalem leaders.

That Paul was entrusted with the gospel *just as* Peter is a crucial point. It places Paul on an equal footing with the original leaders of the Christian movement. This supports Paul's claim of interdependence with Jerusalem rather than dependence on Jerusalem. The statement implies that Peter received a divine mandate for a particular people. Indeed, we read about such a mandate for Peter in Acts 15:7, except there, his mandate is for work among the Gentiles, not the Jews. Peter's call was presumably rooted in the appearance of the risen Christ to him (John 21:15-19; Luke 24:34; 1 Cor 15:5). Peter's mission to the Jews likely developed on the basis of circumstances and/or a decision about which we do not read in the New Testament. In any case, the present passage reflects the clear public recognition of Peter as head of the mission to the Jewish people.

That Paul indeed had received a divine commission is stated in verse 8: *for he who worked through Peter . . . also worked through me* (2:8). Here too we see a parallel with Peter. In both cases the evidence for God's approval upon a ministry lies in the practical evidence of God's actual blessing on that ministry. The book of Acts supplies such documentation for both Peter and Paul, whose preaching is accompanied by signs of God's powerful action against evil and in spiritually blessing the believers. According to Acts 10:47; 11:17-18; 15:8, 12, the discernment of God's will to include the Gentiles *as Gentiles* in God's reign was made on the same basis. The evidence of spiritual power at work among the believers is an element in Paul's argument against the Galatian error (3:5; 4:6).

The language in verses 7-8 is not typical of Paul (e.g., the use of Peter for Cephas), leading some to speculate that Paul is deliberately using the official wording of the agreement worked out at the meeting. The suggestion is speculative. The related claim that Paul applies the word *apostle* (lit. apostleship) to Peter but not to himself may reflect that Jerusalem did not use the title for Paul. But one can hardly conceive of Paul allowing such ambiguity to stand at the very place where he is arguing for his equality with Jerusalem and in a letter defending his apostleship (1:1)! Such ambiguity would only play into the hands of the opposition. Probably Paul does not repeat *apostle* for economy of words in parallel phrases, just as he did in the previous verse with the words *had been entrusted with the gospel*. The elliptical grammatical style is normal in the Greek.

Not only did the Jerusalem leaders observe the evidence of Paul's call from God; they also *recognized the grace that had been given to me* (2:9). *Grace* here has the meaning of a divine virtue or power. It is closely related to the gifts of the Spirit, which are called grace-gifts in the New Testament. Paul's ministry reveals God's favorable disposition and action (grace) as a power for ministry. The grace that called Paul into ministry (1:15) is also the grace that empowers the ministry (Rom 15:15-16; 1 Cor 15:10; cf. 1 Pet 4:10).

Only now are the Jerusalem leaders named as James, Cephas (or Peter), and John. That *James* heads the list may indicate that he has become the leading personality at Jerusalem. Before persecution and mission activity took him away from Jerusalem, Peter may have been the leading person (see 1:18). These three persons are *acknowledged pillars*. The language that describes the leaders in verses 2 and 6 is repeated here, but with the additional word *pillar*. The use of *pillar* for a leader is known in Jewish and Greek contexts. In Judaism the word typically referred to the three patriarchs: Abraham, Isaac, and Jacob. Since this is the only use of *pillar* for a church leader in the New Testament, it may have been important only in the area around Jerusalem. There is a close parallel to it in the image of the apostles and prophets as the foundation of the church (Eph 2:20; cf. Matt 16:18). The term places considerable significance on the role of these men in guiding the church's life. But to suggest that the church saw itself as the new Israel founded on new patriarchs, intriguing though this thought may be, is to venture into speculation. On Paul's ambivalent use of the term, and the reason for it, see verse 6.

This brings Paul to the specific outcomes of the consultation. He begins not with a formula of agreement but with a symbol of accord: *They gave to Barnabas and me the right hand of fellowship.* The common cultural practice of clasping right hands to show friendship and to confirm agreement is used here with both senses. The handshake emphasizes the elements of relationship and trust, as does the word *fellowship.*

Now the agreement itself is stated: *that we should go to the Gentiles and they to the circumcised.* This is the recognition of distinct spheres of responsibility within an overarching shared mission. The language is similar to that of verse 8, but no verb is present (*go* is supplied by NRSV) and the language of *apostle* is absent. The latter is understandable, since Paul now includes Barnabas alongside himself, and James and John are grouped with Peter. Peter and Paul as leaders of the respective missions to Jews and to Gentiles are named in verses 7 and 8. Now Paul mentions the wider circle to communicate the broader base for this agreement. Significantly, James and John identify with the Jewish mission rather than with both missions. The fateful move will have some bearing on the subsequent conflicts (cf. 2:11-12) and perhaps the eventual decline of Jewish Christianity in the second century CE.

The specific agreement is more practical than it is theological: it has to do with mission strategy. Believers in Jesus Christ will branch out with two movements of outreach, one to Jews and one to Gentiles. The fact that the agreement deals with operational matters and not theological or ethical ones is significant, since Luke's account of the discussion in Acts 15 is clearly more theological. Did the meeting actually conclude with an informal mutual blessing of ministries? Did the theological justification for that mutual blessing develop later? If so, it would not be the first time this happened in the Christian church.

This does not mean that theological issues are not present. They clearly exist in the background. Paul naturally concludes from the visit that circumcision would not be required, given the experience of Titus. But that is different from a formal agreement. Later events at Antioch make it clear that the mutual blessing of separate Jewish and Gentile ministries left a number of important theological and practical issues unresolved (see comments on 2:12). Paul's immediate point here is that the leaders in Jerusalem recognized Paul's divine commission without trying to correct or control it. And Paul's account admirably achieves this purpose.

At this point Paul mentions that the leaders did make one particular request of Paul: *They asked only one thing, that we remember the poor, which was actually what I was eager to do* (2:10). This is expressed as an exception, the *only* exception, to the preceding agreement. As Paul declares, this additional request does nothing to threaten the equality and mutuality established between the parties, and it is not pertinent to the Galatian problem. Moreover, Paul implies that this is no imposition on him because he is already committed to this work against oppression (see below).

The poor referred to here are certainly a group connected with Jerusalem. In fact, the term may stand for all the saints in Jerusalem. The expression *the poor* was used in some Jewish circles (e.g., the Qumran community) to describe a positive spiritual quality of the group (cf. Matt 5:3). A later group within Jewish Christianity used a name with the same meaning: the Ebionites. At the same time, the term could carry its natural meaning to designate the economically deprived. That connotation is clearly an aspect of the meaning in our passage. The book of Acts documents the material needs in the Jerusalem church (Acts 6:1; 11:29). That the reference is to economic aid to all (or part) of the community in Jerusalem is strongly supported by the evidence of Paul's activity in collecting money among his churches for that purpose (Rom 15:25-28; 1 Cor 16:1-4; 2 Cor 8–9; Acts 24:17).

The point here is not that Paul agreed to round out his theology with social concerns. Indeed, Paul confirms that his theology was already holistic in that way. Rather, the Jerusalem leaders hope to avoid a practical split between the two branches of the church resulting from separate missions. Given the poorer social and economic conditions of the Jewish context in comparison to the Greco-Roman context, such a split would have resulted in greater economic disparity at the expense of the Jerusalem church. Clearly the Jerusalem leaders are concerned about the material needs of their people. But their concern could also be grounded in a larger vision of unity and fellowship. Paul certainly understood the relief aid to Jerusalem as carrying symbolic and theological implications. To the believers in Rome, he described the financial aid as a debt to the Jewish believers owed because the spiritual blessings of the gospel had come from them (Rom 15:27). Here is further evidence (see Gal 2:2) that Paul was committed to a theological and practical continuity between the older (Jewish) people of God and the newer (Jewish *and* Gentile) people of God in Christ.

In light of the shared perspective between Paul and the Jerusalem brothers, we can understand his closing words: *which was actually what I was eager to do.* To assist the needy believers at Jerusalem was no mere obligation for Paul. He was inclined to this of his own will. Indeed, the language may suggest that Paul had already been committed to this before the agreement. This would be in accord with the report of Acts 11:29-30 that Paul and Barnabas carried relief aid from Antioch to Jerusalem. That action was either part of this same visit to Jerusalem (see on 2:1) or previous to it. Part of the agreement, then, is that Paul will continue his interest in the material needs of the Jerusalem saints. This aspect of the agreement should also help impress upon the Galatians how unfounded is any attempt to alienate him from the church in Judea.

THE TEXT IN BIBLICAL CONTEXT

Leadership and Authority

A major issue throughout this part of the letter is that of authority in the church. The source of the authority of the gospel message and its relation to human authority was considered at 1:8 and 12. Beginning at 1:16 and culminating in 2:1-10, the focus is on how the authority vested in persons operates in the life of the church. That is the question of how leadership is structured and practiced.

Throughout the Scriptures, leadership is crucial in the life of the people of God. Times of strong leadership are times of spiritual prosperity (but also, at times, of spiritual dearth). Times of weak leadership are never times of spiritual strength. Leadership is therefore essential to the people of God, though it is no guarantee that the people of God will be faithful to God's purposes.

Biblical leadership shows considerable variation in form in different times and places. There is no basis for linking biblical faith with one ideal type or philosophy of leadership. However, one can discern characteristics that pertain to good biblical leadership. Since "the people of God" is itself a prime biblical theme, good leaders serve the people, not the contrary. Second, leadership is often shared among several types (e.g., king, prophet, priest) or individuals (e.g., Peter and Paul, or the three pillar leaders at Jerusalem). Within this plural pattern, even though an individual can appear as "first among equals" (e.g., James), mutual accountability exempts no one from testing and correction (e.g., King David in 2 Sam 12; Peter in Gal 2:11-14). Finally, all leadership is accountable to God, who alone is a self-sufficient authority and whose will is the standard to which leader and people must answer. Leadership in the church is a stewardship, a gift shared from God for the benefit of the church.

These ideals point to a form of leadership characterized by equality and mutuality. With this understanding of leadership, the people submit to a leader when the leader speaks for God (Heb 13:17), but the leader is always in the service of the people and therefore answerable to them. At the same time, there is an element of inequality in leadership. The very concept of authority involves some form of difference in role and influence. Even the principle of service implies that one has a resource that the group does not have of itself. The interplay of equality and inequality makes leadership a delicate and complex matter. This goes far in explaining why problems of leadership are never finally put to rest and why patterns of leadership necessarily vary in response to cultural difference and change.

Church Unity and Truth

The consultation between Paul and the leaders in Jerusalem shows that both sides want to preserve the unity of Christian community. Despite his strong autonomy in faith and ministry, Paul acknowledges the value of cultivating relationship among believers. This requires opening oneself and one's work to evaluation by others. Therefore, Paul risks rejection or attempted subjection from the Jerusalem circle in the interest of building a unity of faith and mission. He is especially concerned with the relation of unity to mission. Without the tie to the Jewish believers in Judea, polemic and distrust may undermine his efforts in mission. But behind this practical interest lie loftier concerns. Unity is important for demonstrating the universality of the gospel (Jew and Gentile). It is also essential to preserve the continuity of God's people from past to present and future (see on 2:2). Thus unity reaches out laterally to include new peoples. It also reaches back to link with the past so that God's people stand within God's purposes as they unfold in time. Both of these points will be elaborated in Galatians 3–4.

Reaching out to the Gentiles while holding to continuity with the past is essential to the New Testament. In the Old Testament, the continuity of the people of God, the elect, was central. Universality, while anticipated (Gen. 12:2-3 and the prophets), remained largely unrealized. Within the New Testament, there is considerable tension between the two dimensions of unity. The Jewish Christian leaders in Jerusalem and the pro-Law party in general were inclined to greater emphasis on continuity with the Jewish way of life. Paul placed a relatively greater emphasis on the inclusive universality of the gospel, which rejected the second-class-citizen status of the Gentiles. The result was the tension present in our passage and in the Antioch episode that follows (2:11-14). All Christian groups believed in both continuity and universality. On that there was unity. But they differed on the relative weight of the two and on the practical implications of those different weightings.

The problem we have just described can be expressed as the tension between unity and truth, between maintaining Christian fellowship and being faithful to God's purpose. Paul claims to be committed both to the truth of the gospel and to mutuality. The consultation at Jerusalem well illustrates how compromises may be necessary to preserve the two chief values of unity and truth as all sides seek to speak the truth in love (Eph 4:15). Diversity is a given in how the gospel is given expression in life. Convictions about ethical practices naturally differ (cf. Rom 14). The New Testament writings reflect considerable diversity in language, emphases, and practices among the earliest communities. But they also reveal common basic beliefs about the identity of Jesus as God's Messiah, source of salvation, and Lord of life. According to Paul, genuinely held personal convictions are more important than superficial groupthink (Rom 14:22-23). Yet he also calls the church to the continual search for a common mind on the will of God based on the mind of Christ (Phil 2:1-5).

THE TEXT IN THE LIFE OF THE CHURCH

Leadership and the Faithful Church

Even a superficial glance at church history shows how the church swings between expressions of leadership that are more egalitarian and less egalitarian, more hierarchical and less hierarchical. In parallel fashion, we see a constant vacillation between reaction against authority and desire for greater authority. One side experiences authority as oppressive and restrictive; the other side experiences it as reassuring and protecting. Some groups of Christians have a single leader with absolute power, while others have no formal leadership structure at all. Both extremes conflict with biblical ideals. Good leadership provides for the participation of all members in the maintenance of group life. Each member must own the vision of the whole people and must contribute their gifts to the common good. On the other hand, certain leadership functions help the group live as a group and create the conditions in which individual members can make their contributions. This, in turn, is based on the conviction that God gives special gifts for leadership to certain ones and uses particular individuals, such as prophets, as instruments for communicating God's will to the community.

Authority for Christian leadership must be lodged with persons who actually possess the gifts of leadership. Such persons are "authoritative" because of who they are intrinsically. Moreover, authority is effective only when those exercising it are duly "authorized" for that role by the community. In the Christian community, such authorization resides primarily in the call of God and then secondarily in the confirming call of the group. The group commits itself to submit to the authority of the leader while also holding the leader accountable for the faithful and unselfish exercise of authority. Leadership based on this view of authority is flexible in form and structure. It keeps communication open between leader and those who are led; and it shares authority with other group members. It is servant leadership (Mark 10:42-45).

Leadership is closely related to questions of unity and truth. The desire to preserve unity and truth drives churches toward more centralized and formalized leadership patterns. Churches with shared authority among congregations and among members tend to exhibit more heresy and schism. Nevertheless, the capacity of a centralized authority to control these problems is largely an illusion. Sometimes facades of unity and truth ("orthodoxy") are created at a great price. The members lose a sense of close identity with the church. Wrong ideas and diverse practices develop behind the scenes, undermining the integrity of the church internally and in its relation with the world. Finally, there is no guarantee that the Lord of the church values our perspective on the truth as much as we do. As church history shows, error and evil can be even more difficult to oppose and eradicate when authority is centralized.

So how can we honor the truth while preserving unity in the church? First, we must recognize that no guarantees are available this side of the fullness of God's kingdom. But this does not leave the church without security or direction. God has revealed God's will and purpose in many ways, yet supremely in Jesus Christ (Heb 1:1-4). The church has access to this revelation in the written Scriptures. That word is true. It is reliable. Here is the most secure foundation that is immediately available to us.

But we know how much interpretations of Scripture can differ. Even if God's Word serves as a sure foundation, that does not mean that our understanding of Scripture serves as a sure foundation. We do better to trust not in our private interpretation but in the corporate discernment of the people of God, whose many gifts and experiences are available to us. Those gifts come from the church of the past (available in history and tradition), the church of which we are a part, and the global church—the church of other groups, ethnicities, races, nations, and cultures. Even with those gifts, we must confess our lack of access to the truth in some final, definitive form (cf. 1 Cor 13:9). We are finally thrown back on the promise of our Lord when he said that the Spirit would guide us into all the truth (John 16:13) and on the indispensability of love, without which all of our understandings amount to so many clanging cymbals (1 Cor 13:1-2). Our certainty rests ultimately in God.

Incident at Antioch
Galatians 2:11-21

PREVIEW

When is compromise legitimate, necessary, and wise? And when is compromise an expression of unfaithfulness, lack of courage, or duplicity? When is it a courageous expression of love, and when is it a betrayal of the truth? When does "religious adaptation" reflect loving cultural adaptation (as perhaps in 1 Cor 9:20-23), and when does it reflect betrayal of the gospel or even hypocrisy (as perhaps in Gal 2:11-13)? Oh, if the church knew how to answer that question!

This part of the letter takes us to the very center of those knotty questions. It marks a major transition in the letter. Paul seems to be continuing the narrative of events in his own life when he recounts his confrontation with Cephas at Antioch. But in the midst of the paragraph, Paul's writing takes on the characteristics of a theological treatise. That style then dominates the remainder of the letter, except for his autobiographical comments in 4:12-20. The precise point of transition is unclear. For that reason we are treating 2:11-21 as a unit.

In verse 14 Paul is clearly reporting the conversation at Antioch. At some point, however, Paul's direct reply to Cephas at Antioch ends as Paul begins to address the Galatian readers. By verse 17 the transition is complete. Thus the material in the paragraph serves both to conclude Paul's own narrative about his relationship with the leaders in Jerusalem and to introduce his theological argument against the error in Galatia.

The confrontation in Antioch speaks directly to the question of Paul's apostolic authority and the consequent authority of his gospel. After all, Paul can even correct one of the pillars of the Jerusalem church! This paragraph sets out the heart of the Pauline gospel that tests all aspects of Christian beliefs and behavior. Interestingly, the theological claims of these verses (2:15-16, 20) are apparently not themselves in dispute in Galatia. They do not even directly describe the problem in the Galatian churches. The first paragraph of chapter 3 comes closer to doing that. But just as these claims were able to test the action of the Jewish Christians at Antioch, so they also hold the key to demonstrating the incompatibility of the Galatian heresy with the true gospel, when rightly understood. Paul states certain common Christian convictions (note the *we* in verses

15-16) in such a way that exposes inconsistencies with those essential convictions. That common ground is reflected especially in verses 15-16. The issues in Galatia begin to surface in verses 17-21.

OUTLINE

The Nature of the Confrontation, 2:11-13
Paul's Theological Argument, 2:14-21

EXPLANATORY NOTES

The Nature of the Confrontation 2:11-13

Paul recounts an event in Antioch of Syria when he was again with Cephas (Peter), as in the previous account of the Jerusalem visit. (See on 1:18 re: the dual names for Peter.) This time the encounter was not friendly. In this strong confrontation, Paul directly accuses Peter—*opposed him to his face* (2:11). Paul felt justified in confronting Peter because he considered Peter to be engaging in activity that put him at fault: *he stood self-condemned*. The implication is that Peter was being inconsistent, making the condemnation self-evident. Paul makes this explicit by using words like *hypocrisy* and *inconsistency* in verses 13-14. However, the verb *condemned* could also be a divine passive, which could suggest that God was doing the condemning, even though God is not directly mentioned. This would only heighten the seriousness of Peter's action. In either case, Paul's judgment merely exposes what is already true.

Verse 12 states the cause of the controversy: Until certain people came from James, Cephas had the practice of eating with the Gentiles. But after they came, he drew back and kept himself separate *for fear of the circumcision faction* (because he didn't want to offend the people from James?). The key issue has to do with table fellowship between Jewish and Gentile Christians. This may have involved both regular meals and the Lord's Supper, which the early church typically celebrated in a meal context. Jews were careful not to associate closely with Gentiles because it violated the regulations of ritual purity and dietary laws. Eating at the same table compromises these standards. James and Peter are not technically inconsistent with the stance they had taken in Jerusalem in the previous account. There the issue was circumcision and mission responsibility. Here the question is table fellowship. The former agreement recognized and blessed two separate spheres for Jewish and Christian believers. Table fellowship, however, raises a new kind of question because here the two groups must be together—as equals. Clearly for Paul the two matters are inseparable, as the following verses show (see also above on 2:4-5).

Neither James nor Peter has moved as far as Paul has on the implications of the Gentile mission. James has sent the delegation to review the situation at Antioch. This is interesting for what it reveals about the oversight role of the mother church in Jerusalem. All parties appear to accept it. Presumably word had gotten back to Jerusalem that the dividing wall between Jew and Gentile was not being respected at Antioch. This delegation represents James and his viewpoint and is apparently not to be equated with the "false believers" in 2:4.

The term *circumcision faction* likely refers to the delegation from James. However, the NRSV use of *faction* is unduly negative; *party* or *group* would be preferable. The expression is descriptive, not pejorative. Some commentators understand it to refer to non-Christian Jews. If so, Paul's reference to fear of the circumcision group would indicate that Jewish Christians are afraid of persecution from non-messianic Jews if they are too open toward Gentiles. There may be an element of truth in the latter point. Like Paul (1:14), some Jews could militantly defend the boundary markers (such as not eating with Gentiles and circumcision) that separated them from the nations. The early Jewish Christians probably wanted to avoid further conflict with their fellow Jews whenever possible.

However, it seems more likely that *circumcision party* refers to Jewish Christians who practice the marks of Jewish distinctiveness, of which circumcision is the leading example (hence the name), and who observe the regulations of separation from Gentiles. Only Gentiles who accept circumcision and who observe Jewish practices could be in full fellowship with them. James belongs to this group and, in fact, is their leader. However, Paul depicts James as moving toward the position of not requiring the Jewish way of life (cf. 1:13 and the distinctives for Gentile believers in 2:3). But against Paul, James maintains that ritual separation from Gentiles overrides the unity of fellowship, even though they are believers.

Peter's situation is more ambiguous. As a Christian Jew, he appears to have been part of the *circumcision party*. But he was moving more quickly to accept the Gentiles because of his experience with Cornelius (Acts 10). Interestingly, that acceptance brought him criticism from the "circumcision party" (Acts 11:2, using the same term as here). He has now drawn the conclusion that God's acceptance of the unclean Gentiles means that he can engage in table fellowship with the Gentile believers at Antioch. Peter's problem is that he feels political pressure from the circumcision faction—or perhaps he wants to be appropriately deferential or adaptive. So he decides that maintaining good relations with others in Jerusalem is more important than continuing the close fellowship with Gentile believers. Peter no doubt continues to recognize these Gentiles as true believers, but he also wants to respect the "weak" conscience of the circumcision party (perhaps temporarily in this situation), as Paul seems to recommend under certain circumstances (cf. 1 Cor 8:12-13; Rom 14).

The other Jews join him in this hypocrisy (2:13). The influence of Peter causes others to follow his example. These other Jews are apparently Jewish believers residing in Antioch who previously have practiced table fellowship with the Gentiles. Paul uses the term *hypocrisy* to describe their action. It comes from a word meaning "actor" and could be translated "playacting." Here it has the negative sense of putting on an outward act intended to disguise the true inward reality. Paul believes that Peter and the other Jews who follow him are acting in a way that is contrary to what they know and believe, as shown in their previous fellowship with Gentile believers. In light of the following verse's emphasis on the truth of the gospel, Paul is not interested in analyzing Peter's *intention* so much as the logic of his position.

Even Barnabas was led astray by their hypocrisy. Barnabas was Paul's companion in ministry during this period of Paul's ministry. He was present in the Jerusalem meeting (2:1, 9). Acts recounts this partnership in Paul's early ministry and mentions their extended stay in Antioch (11:25-26, 30; 12:25; 13:1). Barnabas, too, plays the hypocrite. However, the passive form of the verb *led astray* and the result clause (*so that*) indicate that Barnabas was the victim of the arguments and pressure of others. Paul's disagreement with his own partner was particularly painful for him, but in the argument to the Galatians, this detail of the story enhances the image of Paul as a defender of the truth.

Paul's Theological Argument 2:14-21

But when I saw that they were not acting consistently with the truth of the gospel . . . (2:14). With these words Paul makes his clearest evaluation of the situation. This is the second occurrence of the phrase *truth of the gospel* (see 2:5), marking it as a key indicator of the letter's intent (see also 4:16). For Paul, the coherence of the gospel, rooted in God's will and action, claims our allegiance. God's action in Christ has revealed the good news that there is no distinction between Jew and

Gentile in needing God's grace or receiving that grace, based on faith with respect to Jesus (cf. esp. Rom 3:21-26). In fact, this good news is not peripheral to the gospel. Part of Paul's role as apostle is to preserve the truth of that good news, centered in the action of God in Christ. According to Paul, truth involves both right belief and right behavior. Here Paul emphasizes moral integrity. The word translated *acting consistently* means (lit.) *to walk straight.* It is related in form to the English word *orthodoxy,* but it refers to one's manner of life rather than to one's doctrinal beliefs. So it would be equivalent to our word *orthopraxis,* or right action. In keeping with his Jewish background, Paul takes truth to involve both behavior and belief (ethics and theology).

I said to Cephas before them all. The focus remains on Peter because Paul sees him as the key personality in the conflict. In contrast to the Jerusalem meeting, which was held in private (2:2), this confrontation is a public event. Is Paul deliberately trying to shame Peter into change? Or is Paul addressing the problem at the level where people are affected—the entire community, in this case? We cannot be sure of Paul's strategy or even if he thought much about it. In any event, Paul risks losing face himself by bringing everything to a head at once before all the parties he opposes.

If you, though a Jew, live like a Gentile and not like a Jew, how can you compel the Gentiles to live like Jews? Paul's question to Peter reflects his concern for both theological truth and ethical consistency. At Antioch, Peter has adapted his behavior in relating to Gentiles. Now that he has reverted to some form of separation between Jew and Gentile, he has effectively obligated the Gentiles to take on all the cultural markers of Judaism based on the Law (Torah). The use of *compel* does not mean that Peter is actively pressing Gentiles to become Jewish. But by accepting separation of Jewish and Gentile believers, he is giving the Gentiles no choice if they are to enjoy full fellowship with Jewish believers. Peter is thus introducing a hidden obligation. Here Paul's underlying concern surfaces: in Christ there must be full equality of all persons without regard to ethnicity or other human differences. This concern is visible in Galatians 2:6 and will reappear in the verses to follow. It is stated explicitly in 3:28. *Compel* links back to 2:3 and has the effect of underscoring Peter's inconsistency between his action at Jerusalem and at Antioch (see comments on 2:3).

The reader is left to wonder about the outcome of the confrontation. It is hard to conceive that Paul would not have stated the outcome if he had prevailed. Most likely he did not persuade either

Peter or the Jerusalem delegation. At the same time, a powerful rhetorical effect is created by this lack of resolution. The reader is invited to enter the debate and to take a position on the issues. What this incident meant for Paul's subsequent relationship with Antioch (and by extension, to Jerusalem) is debated. Some assume a marked break of Paul with Antioch because of this incident; others do not. The evidence of Acts can be read either way.

Verse 15 begins as a theological defense for Paul's position at Antioch. As already noted, the section in verses 15-21 is transitional. It concludes the Antioch incident and begins the case against the Galatian error. This is signaled by the change from *we* to *I* in verse 18. The *we* of verses 15-17 is the voice of Jewish believers, specifically Paul and Peter. However, verse 17 reflects a common accusation against Paul's teaching (see below) and one likely used also by the Galatian opposition. This statement of Paul may therefore be aimed more at the Galatian opposition than at Peter in Antioch. In any case, the transition from Antioch to Galatia is subtle.

We ourselves are Jews by birth and not Gentile sinners (2:15). In good debate style, Paul begins with a point on which his opponents will agree. This affirmation expresses the typical perspective of a good Jew. All non-Jews were commonly referred to as sinners. Jews are *by birth* (lit. *by nature*) in a class of their own, meaning that they are natural-born Jews and beneficiaries of covenant status with God. This is where Paul's argument begins. But it ends in verse 17 with another perspective entirely: both Gentiles and Jews are sinners (cf. Rom 1:18–3:20).

Yet we know that a person is justified not by the works of the law but through faith in Jesus Christ [or, *the faith* of *Jesus Christ*, as in NRSV footnote; see below] (2:16). Paul again states a principle that he assumes to be a conviction he shares with Peter. Justification by faith in or of Jesus Christ is the true ground of Christian identity. It is of paramount importance to recognize that this belief is not in dispute, either at Antioch or in Galatia. Paul never implies that this doctrine is being expressly denied in the controversies. What is in dispute is the implication of justification by faith for the Christian life and whether it is necessary to supplement this bedrock belief with submission to the Law of Moses. Paul believes that some are unwittingly denying this doctrine by not seeing that it changes the status of the Law in significant ways. Later parts of the letter spell out these changes. Christ needs no supplement. Paul will not countenance the idea that the Law is a master along with Christ. The issue is *not* whether believers fulfill in Christ and by the Spirit the central spirit and intent of

the Law. They do. The Law thus has a continuing role, but a subordinate one, a role that is subordinate to Christ [*Paul's View of the Law in
Galatians, p. 316*].

With this verse we strike one of the rich veins of Paul's theology. The three concepts of (1) justification, (2) works of the law,
and (3) faith of or in Jesus Christ are each crucial in Paul's thought.
A central problem for the interpreter is the unusually terse and
tight nature of this paragraph, which makes multiple interpretations possible. So the passage is as controversial as it is important.
(We will include some comments here but expand them in TBC and
TLC below.)

Justify means to make or find someone just, right, or righteous,
and therefore innocent (in biblical languages the same word group
is translated into English as either "just" or "right/righteous"). It
can mean "to vindicate" or "to acquit." The language comes from
the judicial (legal) realm. In the Bible, the term refers to establishing
or affirming right relationship between God and humans. Here the
setting is more covenantal than judicial. Moreover, the word
expresses God's initiative in restoring right relationship. This saving
action of God is particularly important for understanding Paul's
justification language. The point of our text is that our relationship
with God is now based on God's provision in Christ, not on observance of the Law (or *works of the law*; see TBC).

We can anticipate where Paul's argument will go by noticing the
ethical implication of righteousness/justification language. Since
good relationship can exist only when behavior is consistent with
that relationship, righteousness has moral implications. That is, it
involves right living. This is true in both testaments. In one sense, the
moral implications are dependent on the relationship. Relationship
precedes moral action. But in another sense, the relationship is
dependent on moral action. Moral action sustains relationship.

Paul states both the negative and the positive means of justification. It is not by *works of the law* (2:16). By this expression Paul means
all acts of obedience to the commandments of the Mosaic Law. In
some sense, he is setting the covenant of the Law over against the
new covenant of Christ. Some have argued that Paul is referring
only to those Torah regulations that set boundaries between Jew
and Gentile, such as circumcision or food laws, and not to the entire
Law (Dunn 1993: 136). This argument is theologically attractive. It
is true that the boundary-marker aspect is prominent in this context.
Paul is concerned about true equality between Jew and Gentile—an
equality that is damaged or destroyed by those boundary-setting

regulations. Unfortunately, this argument is incapable of accounting adequately for Paul's argument in the rest of Galatians, where Paul is in some sense contrasting the Law as such with Christ's work. Moreover, Paul's contrast of life in the Spirit with life under the Law (3:2-5; 5:18, 23) contains a logic that sees the Law as a matter of legal requirement. This supports understanding the phrase *works of the law* as something more comprehensive than or deeper than the Law as boundary marker.

Paul's use of works in a negative sense has led to the common and persistent misunderstanding that he views Judaism as a legalistic religion, in which salvation is a human achievement based on the merit of observing the Law. This is a harmful caricature. On the contrary, most Jews understood that God's grace called Israel into covenant. Human effort did not earn that status. Most Jews in this era held that Law observance was necessary to maintain covenant status. Common practice today is to respect this distinction by describing the Jewish view as "nomism" (from *nomos*, law) rather than "legalism." A more difficult question is whether some or many Jews were veering into legalism and whether Paul is reflecting that actual situation. There is some basis for arguing that Paul is afraid that the Galatians, most or all of whom are Gentiles, will fall into such a legalistic mind-set if they embrace the Law (see 3:1-5).

Stated positively, justification is *through faith in Jesus Christ* or *through the faith of Jesus Christ*. Either of these translations of the Greek is possible (see the NRSV footnote and similar wording in 2:20 and 3:22). An additional issue is whether to translate the Greek word *pistis* as *faithfulness* or *faith* (or whether to use such equivalents as *belief* or *trust*). Scholars are divided on how *pistis* should be translated and interpreted. Since the publication of the Revised Standard Version in the late 1940s, the translation *faith in Jesus Christ* has been so dominant that most readers are not aware of any option, despite the fact that the King James Version translated many of these expressions *faith of Jesus Christ*. Both translations clearly reflect Pauline and New Testament truth expressed elsewhere. Christians express faith (i.e., they believe) in Christ to receive right standing with God, as Paul says in the next part of this same verse. On the other hand, our right standing is based on the faithful, obedient action of Jesus Christ (Rom 5:19; Phil 2:6-8). In Paul's theology this two-sided truth is the basis for right standing (justification) with God. That is the essential point here.

But can we say more about the meaning Paul intends by the particular phrase *faith of/in Jesus Christ*? The option is typically stated this way: Is he contrasting human obedience to the law with human believing in the work of Christ? Or is he contrasting human action with God's action in Christ for us? Unfortunately, setting up such a contrast is unhelpful and even misleading. The two expressions in this context, *works of the law* and *faith of Jesus Christ*, are technical phrases that serve as shorthand for two religious perspectives: one that is Law-oriented and one that is faith-oriented. The focus, in this case, is not on *anyone's* action, whether that of the believer or of Jesus Christ.

Whenever the context in Galatians makes the meaning clear, the concept of faith or believing consistently refers to the human response to God's action in Christ. (A probable exception is *faithfulness in* 5:22, where it has an ethical meaning.) However, in 1:23 and 6:10, likely also in 3:23, 25, Paul clearly uses the word *faith* to stand for the gospel itself, not a human act. So when Paul uses the word *faith* to speak of the human response to God, he can also use it of one part of the gospel to stand for the whole of the gospel. The technical term for this is metonymy. That Paul would use this word, so key to his current polemic, as shorthand for the whole is understandable. Even today we continue to use the word *faith* to refer to our beliefs as a whole (e.g., the "Christian faith").

In light of these considerations, the phrase *faith of Jesus Christ* is best taken to mean something like this: "the belief system that has its central, defining reality in Jesus Christ and his work, and is made effective for those who have faith." Even though the word *faith* preserves its original reference to the human response, the focus here is on the gospel itself, which is centered in God's action for our salvation in Jesus Christ, not on the particular human action of believing. This means that no one English translation is fully satisfactory. *Faith in Jesus Christ* puts the focus on the human act of believing. At the same time, English readers tend to limit *faith of Jesus Christ* to the faith that Jesus himself exercises. Both alternatives miss the mark when seen as alternatives. As a result, in the comments that follow we will mostly use the phrase *faith of/in Jesus Christ* to signal both senses. At the same time, we should be open to recognizing that in different contexts, one or the other of these senses may come to the fore.

Those familiar with this debate will notice that the position taken here answers two arguments in support of the view that the phrase refers to the faith/fulness of Jesus Christ. There is now no question of redundancy in those contexts (Gal 2:16, first of two occurrences; 3:22; and Rom 3:22) where the phrase is immediately followed by the verb expressing the human action of believing. Our phrase states the truth claim followed by a statement of the response to that claim. Moreover, the explanation above puts to rest the argument that only a reference to the faith/fulness of Jesus keeps Paul's gospel grounded in God's action instead of human action. The phrase focuses on the message that is totally defined by Jesus Christ rather than on any action implied by the word *faith* (see TBC on "Faith in Paul and James") [*The Faith of Jesus Christ, p. 305*].

We have come to believe in Christ Jesus, so that we might be justified by faith in Christ, and not by doing the works of the law. Or in a more literal rendering of 2:16, *Since we know that a person is justified . . . through the faith of/in Jesus Christ, we* [Jews] *also have come to believe in Christ Jesus.* Paul begins with a principle that both Peter and he himself agree on, and then affirms that a particular group (we Jews) must *also* (a word in the Greek but not in NRSV) follow that principle. Knowing that one's standing with God is dependent on accepting Christ's work puts Jew and Gentile on equal footing. This gives the Jew who has observed the Law no prior advantage. Consistent with the explanation above for the phrase *faith of/in Jesus Christ*, the faith of that expression closely parallels the verb *believe* in the present clause. Since the second refers clearly to the human act of faith, the first likely also refers ultimately to human faith (but with a different focus, as explained above).

The English words *faith* and *believe* have essentially the same meaning in the New Testament. *Believe* simply means "to have or to exercise faith." Faith in the biblical sense combines three ideas: (1) accepting something as real or true; (2) where a person is the object, trusting someone in a relationship to be true to promises and commitments; and (3) making concrete responses in life that reflect that acceptance and trust. The last aspect bridges faith/fulness with obedience. Paul's usage throughout his letters traverses this entire range, though he emphasizes the believer's trust in God and in God's provision (see TBC).

Given the argument of Galatians, *faith/believing* refers to the human's trust in and acceptance of God's offer or promise of reconciliation in such a way as to stake their life on it. This is amply demonstrated by the example of Abraham's faith when he embraces the offer (promise) of God (cf. 3:6-9) and is confident that God will make good on it (4:21-31). This pairing of promise and faith is prominent in chapters 3–4. Faith as dependency on God's action is what Paul contrasts with Law observance, which is dependency on human effort (i.e., the flesh) in the key 3:1-5 passage. Although Paul would never have contrasted faith with faithfulness, the latter aspect of faith does not predominate in Galatians. In the present verse, *believe in Christ Jesus* means to trust Christ, totally depending on him and his work for one's standing with God (see TBC on "Faith in Paul and James").

The clause *so that we might be justified* expresses the intended outcome of believing in Christ Jesus. Paul is repeating the thought of the clause at the beginning of the verse for emphasis: people are put into right relationship with God by faith of/in Christ and not by Law observance. Paul thus means, "We have acknowledged the theological truth of justification by faith of/in Christ. As Jews, we acted on that truth by exercising faith so that we might experience the reality of justification by faith of/in Christ."

Paul is not finished. He offers additional support for rejecting righteousness by works of the Law: *because no one will be justified by the works of the law* (cf. Rom 3:20). This allusion to Psalm 143:2 provides Paul with scriptural support for his argument. The form of the Old Testament text Paul has in mind reads, "because every living being shall not be justified before you." Paul adds the crucial phrase *by the works of the law* to apply the text to the present topic. The psalmist says that the sinfulness of all humans leaves them without right standing before God. For Paul, works of the Law do not overcome that condition.

Verse 17 marks a shift in the flow of the argument. Paul is no longer (or, not only) in conversation with Peter at Antioch, but also with other adversaries, likely those in Galatia. *But if, in our effort to be justified in Christ, we ourselves have been found to be sinners, is Christ then a servant of sin? Certainly not!* For Paul to speak of an *effort* to be justified may seem strange in light of his insistence that justification is *in Christ*; that is, God does the setting right in and through Christ. But this merely demonstrates that Paul holds together divine and human action in salvation. We can acknowledge the cooperation of persons with God in redemption as long as we see it as a receptive cooperation, responding to God, who brings the initiating and formative operation. The encounter with Christ by Paul and other early believers in Christ caused them to see Jesus as God's messianic agent of salvation. To participate in this salvation and enjoy right standing with God, people—Jews and Gentiles alike—must believe and trust in God's agent. Everyone, Jew and Gentile alike, stands in equal need of what Christ offers. Encountering Christ and his message makes us aware of our distance from God as sinners.

With this affirmation, Paul explicitly corrects the Jewish practice of calling only Gentiles sinners (v. 15). But to acknowledge that

Christ makes sinners even of those who faithfully practice the Law sounds irresponsible to the Jewish ear. Where is any appreciation of moral achievement? All ground for moral exhortation and guidance appears to be taken away, especially when Paul goes on to say that the Law is no longer our authority. Paul will hear this accusation more than once (Rom 3:7-8; 6:1, 15). No doubt the Galatian opposition is making just this claim against Paul's gospel. It is a major issue in Galatians: if the law is not in force, where will moral motivation and concrete guidance come from? In the following verses, Paul begins to answer that question. He gives a fuller response in chapter 5. Here he simply makes an emphatic denial: Christ does not promote sin!

Before moving to the response in verse 19, Paul responds to the accusation that his gospel promotes sin by making a counter-accusation. In an ironic turning of the tables, Paul claims that the person who reverts to the way things were before Christ is in the wrong. *But if I build up again the very things that I once tore down, then I demonstrate that I am a transgressor* (2:18). Paul writes in the first person to state a universal principle applicable to him as well as to others. Undoubtedly Paul is politely referring indirectly to those in Antioch who changed their practice of fellowship with Gentiles. These Law-loyal Christians are transgressors. The word *transgressor* is different from the word for sinner in verse 17. A transgressor is one who violates a specific standard of right, such as the Law. Peter's inconsistent behavior at Antioch is a transgression. In using this word, Paul strikes an ironic note: the very ones claiming loyalty to the Law are the lawbreakers! But Paul's theme of destroying and rebuilding does not only look back to the Antioch incident; it also looks forward to the verses that follow. In dying to the Law, the believer has torn down the authoritative status of the Law, and it should not be rebuilt to its former status.

For through the law I died to the law, so that I might live to God (2:19). The first-person language continues to the end of the section. Here the theological claims carry the poignancy of personal testimony, giving vividness and pathos to the points being made. The conjunction *for* signals that an explanation is being offered to the surprising claim just made in verse 18. But here Paul also begins to explain how Christ, apart from the law, answers the problem of sin posed in verse 17.

Galatians 2:19 is one of the more difficult verses of the letter. No further explanation of its meaning is offered here or elsewhere. The statement has the feel of a riddle—how and why would the Law bring about the demise of its own relationship with Paul? The general claim is clear enough. To have a living relationship with God, the believer must end a relationship to the Law. Such a claim is nonsense to the average Jew, who sees the Law precisely as the means of cultivating covenant life with God. Indeed, Deuteronomy emphasizes the point again and again.

So what is the basis for Paul's claim? Perhaps we find some hint later in the letter. The Law cannot make alive (3:21). Only the Spirit can overcome the flesh and create the true fruit of righteousness (5:18, 23). The Law cannot do so. It simply does not have the capability to bring about spiritual and moral renewal. In the coming of Christ, God has now given the Spirit (4:6), who provides the power that the Law lacks. The implication is that the Law by its own limitation has brought death to the authority it had over Paul. In one sense the Law is the agent of its own death. But in another sense the new gift of life in Christ and in the Spirit is the cause of that death. As a result, it is important to notice the link that Paul is making between death to the Law and being crucified (and made alive) with Christ in the next sentence. They are two aspects of the same event. To die with Christ is to die to the Law. This thought is expressly stated in Romans 7:4.

Romans 7 lays out a fuller explanation of death to the Law and how the Law itself is the means of death to the Law. Although the Law *tells* me what is right, it does not *empower* me to do the right. Knowing the Law makes me more responsible for my conduct (it "is holy and just and good"), but without the power to overcome sin, this knowledge only gives sin more leverage over me, causing spiritual death. In this way, the Law becomes the agent that ends my relationship with it. By implication, the Law itself tells me to seek life elsewhere. To do that is to die to the Law as the governing authority in my life.

The expression *live to God* is key to Paul's larger argument. (Note how *life* and *live* mark the next verse as well.) It might also be translated *live for God*. Paul is picking up on the Jewish Christian concern for upright living. He grounds his response in the assertion that coming alive to God and living for God is precisely what his view of the gospel and of justification entails. Here and throughout Scripture, *life* (v. 20) has rich connotations of human existence in its many dimensions and in its ideal and fulfilled form. To *live to* someone speaks of a vital, nourishing relationship with that one. For Paul, *life* encompasses the right-making action of God in justification in the totality of its effects. Justification *in Christ* (2:16) begins in the court-like declaration from God that we are children of God, but it results in a new relationship with God that is life-changing because our whole life is given godlike shape by an encounter with Christ, the Son of God (2:20).

Paul now explains what justification in Christ and coming alive to God actually involves. *I have been crucified with Christ* (2:19c). Here Paul thinks of the work of Jesus Christ as more than a historical transaction that resulted in some saving benefit for him and other believers. Paul himself *identifies* with the experience of Jesus Christ, allowing the death of Jesus Christ and its way of existing in the world to be replicated in his own life. This death with Christ is a transformation of life. On the formative impact of Christ on the life of the believer, see especially 4:19.

The perfect tense of the verb is significant, indicating an action in the past in a way that stresses its continuing impact in the present. Likely Paul is referring to his conversion as the past action, although some see here a reference to the believer's participation in the original event of Jesus' crucifixion. However, Paul's emphasis in the current context seems to be on his spiritual experience, not the historical event of Christ's death. Especially crucial is Paul's point that he continues to have his life shaped by the death of Christ. The death of Christ is the paradigm or model after which Paul's life is patterned. His life is formed by the crucifixion; it is a cruciform life that unfolds day by day (for detailed studies, see Gorman 2001; 2009).

And it is no longer I who live, but it is Christ who lives in me (2:20a). The terminology of life continues to dominate, linking back to the former phrase *live to/for God* in the previous verse. Christ living in the believer is the means for living to God. Thus in some sense Paul himself is not alive, which must in turn depend on Paul's previous assertion of his crucifixion with Christ. Paul's death refers not only to the end of his relationship to the Law and to sin (see above), but also in some sense to the death of his self-life. Obviously Paul cannot mean he is physically dead. The very next sentence speaks of *the life I now live*. What he means is that the defining agent for his existence is no longer his own ego but Christ. Paul's ego is not canceled (see below), but it is displaced as the guide in his life. To use another Pauline expression, the mind of Christ now controls his life (Phil 2:5). This is not a controlling set of ideas, principles, or rules, but a living person who acts in and through the believer in response to each particular circumstance of life, in obedience to divine purpose.

And the life I now live in the flesh I live by faith in [or *the faith of*] *the Son of God, who loved me and gave himself for me* (2:20b). Paul does not pretend to suppress his own ego or despise his own personality. The *I* still lives, but is no longer in control. Nor does Paul set his new spiritual life over against his material existence (flesh). His passion is to express the will of God in Christ in his body, in the down-to-earth dimensions of life. This positive use of the word *flesh* is noteworthy because Paul later uses the term in a negative sense to describe life without the power of the Spirit. We are thus reminded that the flesh is not necessarily opposed to God.

The important point Paul is making is how this Christ-in-me life is realized. His answer is *by faith*. Again, the translation could either be *by faith in the Son of God* or *by the faith of the Son of God*. In light of the dominant concern of Galatians to emphasize faith as the way in which God saves, Paul probably has in mind his own response to the loving, self-giving work of Christ, not the faith/faithfulness of the Son himself. However, as argued elsewhere (see the explanations at 2:16 [*The Faith of Jesus Christ, p. 305*]), this unusual phrase places the emphasis not so much on the *act* of believing as on the *object* of believing: on Christ and his loving, self-giving death. That is the event on which Paul's own spiritual crucifixion is based. That is what completely defines his present way of life (on *Son of God*, see 1:16).

This Christ-oriented faith is for Paul a way of life: *I live by faith in/ of the Son of God*. Faith is about more than the initial act of becoming a Christian. Authentic Christian faith involves constant trust in and reliance on Christ in every aspect and at every stage of living. This is a major point in Galatians, beginning in 3:1-5, where Paul castigates the Galatians for moving from a faith-based mode of relating with God to a Law-based mode. It also explains why Paul refuses to allow the Law equal status with the gospel. Such parity would detract from the believer's unvarying trust in the living Christ (note the contrast of Law and faith in 3:2, 5.)

With this emphasis on faith, Paul's argument has come full circle. He began by defending justification as God's act based on the believer's faith. He ends by testifying that participation in the life of Christ is also by faith. By linking justification with participation in Christ, Paul has given a powerful answer to the question of whether his gospel of justification can overcome sin. Faith, according to Paul, is the unconditional opening of one's life to the presence and lordship of Jesus Christ. Expressed in this way, faith assures that the likeness of Christ, and hence the will of God, comes to clear expression in that person's life, totally apart from observance of the Law.

I do not nullify the grace of God; for if justification comes through the law, then Christ died for nothing (2:21). This is the clinching assertion that baldly states the contrast between Law and the gospel. The verb *nullify* comes from the legal field that deals with wills and covenants. Paul has in mind the concept of covenant, a concept he will develop in 3:15-18, where the same verb is used. The grace of God as mediated through the death of Christ is here thought of as a covenant with an integrity that must not be violated. Mixing the covenant of Law with the covenant of Christ without regard to their differences renders the new covenant in Christ null and void. For Paul, God's grace, the sacrifice of Jesus Christ, faith, and justification form a complete recipe for salvation and discipleship; any other ingredient ruins the final product.

There is yet another way to state the contrast. If the previous covenant of Law had been able to achieve righteousness, then there was no need for the death of Christ (cf. 3:21). Paul, of course, is denying that the Law can make righteous. He is convinced that the death of Christ has achieved something new and wonderful. Behind this line of thought lies Paul's conviction that the work of Christ is so complete and final that nothing can stand alongside it. Paul's argument here provides a key insight into his view of the Law. The reason he is against the Law is that something better has come. To hold on to the Law implies that nothing fundamental has changed. Now that Christ has taken up what is good in the Law into himself, the Law has a different meaning and plays a different role. Paul realizes that his opponents have not made this radical shift in perspective. What they are teaching the Galatians is therefore dangerous to their faith. For that reason he puts the issue in stark terms: either Christ or the Law.

Paul's mention of justification in 2:21 brings us back to the starting point of the argument in 2:16. The entire paragraph is an exposition of Paul's view of justification. Paul is not explaining or defending the concept itself as much as he is setting out its consequences and implications. Now the implications of his view are evident. First, there are social implications. God's way of rectifying the world places all persons on equal footing as sinners. And those now made righteous are likewise equals in Christ. There is unity and oneness in Christ. This truth affects the full range of social interaction, such as eating meals together at Antioch! Second, God's rectifying work has ethical implications. Justification (making right) involves a formative process that results from personal interaction with Christ, who is the ground of righteousness. We have called this process identification or participation with Christ. It is out of this bedrock conviction that Paul will make his case regarding the particular issues in Galatia.

THE TEXT IN BIBLICAL CONTEXT

Justification and Righteousness in Scripture

The verb *justify* (along with *just, justification*, and *justice*) is part of the family of biblical words also translated by *right, righteous*, and *righteousness*. The terms have their home in the law court, where the judge pronounces a verdict of acquittal or condemnation on the accused, and of vindication or rebuff of the plaintiff. If the judge is just, justice is rendered to the person who is in the right. All of these levels of meaning help one understand the biblical image of God as a judge, with people facing accusation or seeking vindication.

In the context of Old Testament covenant, the family of words takes on even richer meaning. God enters into covenant relationship with Israel out of love and grace. Righteousness exists where God recognizes this relationship and the people obey the terms of the covenant. God's act of recognizing right relationship in covenant is justification. The idea of justification is forensic (juridical) at its root, but it includes other dimensions of relationship and uprightness of life. Not only does God declare a righteous status for covenant partners; God also brings about a living relationship based on loyalty and justice among covenant partners. Moreover, God expects from covenant partners a behavior that respects and builds that relationship. Paul affirms all of this Old Testament perspective while also making the claim that all of this covenant making centers in Christ and is based on his work.

There are other crucial aspects to our words (*justification*, etc.). Already in the Old Testament, especially in Isaiah, God is depicted as actively creating right or just conditions by engaging in deeds of salvation for the people. God is involved in a mission of making right or rectifying. God does not just make pronouncements, like a judge, about innocence and guilt, right and wrong. God is also an activist and reformer who works to right what is wrong. In light of Paul's conviction that God has acted in Jesus Christ to save, it is best to understand justification as God's act of rectifying (making right) the sinner. In doing this, God recognizes the forgiven status of the sinner (acquittal) *and* sets the sinner on the path of righteous living (spiritual relationship and moral renewal).

In Galatians, as in Isaiah, the idea of right making includes, by implication, the liberating action of God that overcomes the various forms of human bondage (see Gal 3–4). God corrects, or rectifies, the context in which we live by overcoming the enemies of right (see 1:4; 4:1-10). All of this demonstrates the important breadth of meaning in the idea of righteousness/justification. God's mission of righting the world has the total creation in view, a process that God will complete only at the end of this age. This last aspect appears in Paul's expression *the hope of righteousness* (5:5; cf. Rom 8:19-23).

Faith in Paul and James

For Paul, the word *faith* usually refers to the believer's response to God. Moreover, Paul usually emphasizes that faith reflects a posture of receptivity to an offer of God. Paul often uses *promise* to describe the initiating offer of God (see the many occurrences of *promise* in Gal 3; 4:21-31). So faith is the embracing of God's promise. This is typically expressed in English as trust in God or as reliance on God. Paul even makes the point that in Abraham's case, his faith preceded any action of obedience, specifically the act of circumcision (Rom 4:10-11). Thus we must be careful not to read the idea of faithfulness into Paul's use of the word in a way that denies, ignores, or minimizes the believer's embrace of God's gift. *Faith* also expresses dependency on God rather than on human or material means. Abraham illustrates this faith when he relies on promise instead of his own action *according to the flesh* (4:23, 29). This is why faith is not just another form of human work. Faith is the admission that human action and effort are insufficient.

Paul knows that *faith* has broader meanings in the biblical languages. This range includes the English words *faith, believe, trust, fidelity,* and *faithfulness.* As is typical of biblical language (cf. *righteousness* and *holiness*), the same word naturally and necessarily spans the spiritual dimension of relationship with God and the moral dimension of behavior consistent with that relationship. So Paul can refer to God as faithful (Rom 3:3). Faithfulness is likewise a Christian virtue gifted by the Spirit (Gal 5:22). Indeed, the whole argument of Galatians is geared to demonstrate that the one who has faith will live faithfully in a posture of faith (3:1-5) and will faithfully work out the implications in life (5:13–6:10).

But the point here is that in Galatians (and Romans) Paul uses, almost exclusively, *faith*-related words in the narrower sense of trust and reliance on God's promise and provision. That is due to Paul's concern that faithfulness in the age of Christ and the Spirit not be misunderstood as continuing submission to the Law as the opposition teachers in Galatians understood it.

Paul's usage of *faith* bears on the debate about the meaning of the phrase *faith of/in Jesus Christ*. In the context of Paul's argument in Galatians (and Romans), it is unlikely that Paul is using *faith* to mean the faithfulness of Jesus himself. Apart from this ambiguous phrase, Paul elsewhere never speaks about Christ's own faith. Because of the weight and importance *faith* carries in Paul's thought, he no doubt developed and explained the concept with some care and precision. When discussing Jesus' own submission to God's purpose and will, Paul typically uses the language of obedience (Rom 5:19; Phil 2:6-8). It would be fair and accurate to translate this as *faithfulness*. However, in the present context, Paul chose not to use that vocabulary.

The letter of James represents a more traditional Jewish perspective on faith. Here faith and faithfulness, or faith and works, are held tightly together. "Faith without works is dead" (James 2:17, 20, 26 KJV). In all likelihood the polemical tone of James reflects the debate between Paul and the Jewish Christian party. One has to wonder about the extent to which the differences between Paul and James here are substantive or semantic. Paul has his own way of calling for a consistent way of life in harmony with one's commitment to the gospel. Paul would certainly agree that faith without the fruit of new life (works) is not true faith. While James is concerned about faith disconnected from works, Paul is more concerned about works that are disconnected from faith, the faith of/in Christ. For Paul, faith entails a living relationship with God through Christ and through reliance on the Spirit's enabling. Because he sees these values as threatened in the traditional understanding and practice of the Law, he tends to employ the word *works* in a negative sense to describe actions divorced from those gospel values.

Identification with Christ

The motif of identification or union with Christ is pervasive in Paul. Paul often expresses this theme in the phrase *in Christ* (2:6–17; for a comprehensive study, see Campbell). Both the crucifixion and the resurrection of Christ are played out again in the believer (cf. Rom 6; Phil 3:10). In Galatians, Paul emphasizes crucifixion (as in 2:19) in order to accentuate death to the Law. However, 2:20 makes clear that Paul also has in mind participating in Christ's resurrection (cf. Rom 6:4-5).

Identification with Christ involves encounter with the person of Christ. Paul expresses his powerful experience of Christ as the Living One in the expression *Christ . . . lives in me* (2:20). Some refer to this as Paul's mysticism. This captures one dimension of the experience but is misleading insofar as it limits the meaning to inner spirituality. In fact, all aspects of Paul's life are touched by the presence of Christ. Paul also explicitly links the ethical and the vocational realms to this theme. As for the ethical implication, he will say in Galatians 5:24: *Those who belong to Christ Jesus have crucified the flesh with its passion and desires.* To be crucified with Christ is to die to the control of sin in one's life.

Paul alludes to the vocational connection in Galatians 5:11 and 6:12, 17, where ministry for Christ involves persecution because of the cross. More direct is the statement in 2 Corinthians 4:10. In his ministry, Paul is "carrying in the body the death of Jesus, so that the life of Jesus may also be made visible in our bodies." Paul understands that the implications of Jesus' life and message are so vast that no part of life is left unchanged. The comprehensive dimensions of the Pauline concept are expressed well by the language of formation, as in Galatians 4:19, where Paul hopes to see Christ formed in the Galatian believers (see the discussion there). Paul's understanding of the complete and comprehensive work of Jesus Christ lies at the root of his passion to exclude all other claimants, including the Law, from a share in the central vision of the gospel (see comments on 2:21). (On this theme of formation, see 4:19 and TBC/TLC there.)

THE TEXT IN THE LIFE OF THE CHURCH

Equality in Church and Society

Throughout Galatians 2, Paul has been stressing God's purpose in creating a people inclusive of all peoples. For this people of God to be truly inclusive, all members must enjoy equality of status. Paul wants the Galatians to know that he has been defending their freedom and equality against the idea that believing in Christ also requires one to observe the Jewish way of life based on the Law. The Antioch incident focuses on this issue. Recognizing someone else as a fellow believer while refusing to sit down at the same table in fellowship is, according to Paul, violating God's intent of including all people under the lordship of Christ.

In defending his conviction, Paul appeals to the theme of justification by faith. This is remarkable because it demonstrates that this great doctrine about a person's relationship with God has clear social implications. From this doctrine, Paul argues that all have sinned and need to be made right by God's action, based on faith. Thus all are equal in their need. The Jew does not necessarily have a head start in spiritual matters. And even though the religious practices of the Jewish way of life are based on the Law, those practices have no final authority or privileged position. Being equal before God means being equal with all in God's family.

The church has often failed to see or take seriously the social implications of Paul's teaching. Social status and ethnic privilege have marked the church almost as much as the surrounding culture. In the days of slavery, the practice of segregating the slaves into a separate section during church services closely parallels the situation in Antioch. Even some churches that rejected slavery sometimes promoted an equal-but-separate practice, separating churches for blacks and whites. Paul would have rejected this practice. The racism that continues to plague the church is simply inconsistent with the foundational belief of justification by faith.

But other areas of life also need to be examined. It is all too common to argue that spiritual status and social status are different things. For example, some attempt to narrow the implications of Galatians 3:28 on the question of women's role. They claim that Paul is thinking only of spiritual status, not social roles. But Paul's argument in Galatians 2 makes such a move indefensible, whatever our understanding of Paul's views on gender (see discussion at 3:28). Paul will not allow a separation of the social and the spiritual. The point is crucial to the vision and lived expression of Christian faith in every time and place.

Justification, Sanctification, and Discipleship

This part of Galatians offers helpful insight into the relationship of three key terms in Christian experience. The Protestant tradition sees justification as the center of Pauline thought and right Christian theology. Holiness groups emphasize sanctification or holiness of life. The Anabaptist tradition focuses on discipleship (following Christ in all of life). Some students of Paul have concluded that identification with Christ (*in Christ* language) is the central idea in Paul. Galatians 2:11-21 offers insight on the meaning and relationship of these concepts. Paul uses the term *justification* and the concept of identification with Christ here, but not the language *sanctification* or *discipleship*, even though the latter concepts are implicitly present.

First, Paul does not allow a separation between justification and sanctification (holiness) or discipleship. Paul draws out implications for living from the concept of justification. Traditional Protestant thinking draws too sharp a distinction between justification and sanctification, in the interest of guarding against any tendency to see saving merit in human effort. Martin Luther classically expressed this concept in the slogan "justification by faith *alone*." While this preserves the important truth that salvation is God's pure gift, it can result in devaluing or obscuring the place of right living in the gospel. In our passage, Paul places equal emphasis on what we might call "justification by faith *consistently*." This is to say, justification has clear ethical implications. Paul is concerned that Peter and the Galatians live in a way that is consistent with this truth.

Likewise, Paul ties together justification and identification with Christ. Justification makes us alive to God for a life in Christ. Paul thus closely relates justification, sanctification, and discipleship. It is best not to see justification and sanctification/discipleship as stages that follow one another in Christian experience, with justification as the beginning and sanctification as the development. Rather, these are different ways of viewing the same encounter with God, with each having multiple stages of development from the initiating act of God, through lifelong transformation, to fulfillment at the end. Justification (making righteous) looks at God's act in Christ and the believing life of response from the perspective of what is right or just according to some standard or ideal. Sanctification (making holy) looks at lived response from the viewpoint of what is godlike, what conforms to God's character.

Second, if we take Paul seriously, we will find a close relationship between identification with Christ and discipleship. As noted in the discussion in TBC, identification language covers the spiritual, ethical, and vocational dimensions of life. This language is comprehensive in its underlying imagery. It connotes both a depth of formation in the person and a breadth of impact in life. Some have unjustly contrasted discipleship in the Gospels with identification in Paul. Identifying with Christ means having a personal relationship with him *and* walking "in his steps" (1 Pet 2:21). Identification language keeps discipleship and spirituality connected—an important point for the Anabaptist discipleship tradition. It also reminds us that following Jesus is not a matter of merely imitating the actions of a personality in the past; it is also based on a relationship with the living Lord, who guides us to faithful action in every changing time and place.

Practicing the Centrality of Christ

Even at this early point in Galatians, we are beginning to see how Paul works out his convictions and governs his behavior in constant reference to the person of Jesus Christ—his life, teaching, and ministry. When he speaks of *acting consistently with the truth of the gospel* (2:14), he has in mind the gospel centered in Christ as revealed to him (1:16). His most basic reason for rejecting the authority of the Law is that Christ simply fills all the space in his view of God and the world. Christ relativizes all other truth claims in the sense that nothing else is absolute. Everything must be understood in relation to the revelation of truth in Christ. For Paul, this is not just high-sounding theory. Paul assesses the everyday issues of life in the church and in mission on the basis of how they conform to God's action in Jesus Christ. This is not simply a matter of repeating words and actions from the historical Jesus. It involves understanding Christ well enough that believers can discern the will of the present, living Lord Jesus Christ for each new situation of life (Rom 12:2; Phil 1:9-10).

Galatians 3:1–4:11

Paul's Defense of the Gospel as Fulfilled Revelation

OVERVIEW

Paul's defense of the new revelation of God in Christ is beginning to raise some serious questions about the status of the Law—the Old Testament, in Christian terms. Was the Law a mistake? If not, why is it not still fully valid? Does God change? We can easily imagine that the opponents of Paul were making the simple and convincing claim that the only Scriptures the Galatians could have known, the Jewish Scriptures or the Christian Old Testament, remain the true revelation of God. Belief in Jesus as Messiah does not change the authority of God's earlier revelation! Therefore, its commands, such as circumcision, continue to apply to those who believe in Christ as God's Messiah!

On one level, the next major part of the letter is a discussion of how Christians are to interpret the acts and commands of God in the past. The essence of Paul's response is that the concept of faith itself actually represents the fundamental continuity of divine purpose between the old and the new. Christ has fulfilled the promises, explicit or latent, of all previous revelation. Moreover, he has fulfilled or completed the Law in the sense that Christ does all that the Law did while also doing what it could not do. The gospel has, in effect, moved beyond the Law, not rejecting it but taking it up into the gospel itself and going beyond it by conforming it to Christ.

Paul carries out his discussion by way of contrasts. This is not surprising in a letter of rebuke and debate. Paul sees a fundamental clash of theological perspectives being played out in Galatia, and he describes this clash with contrasting pairs of words. Listing the contrasts here may help the reader perceive the larger picture behind the details.

Paul's Gospel	The Other "Gospel"
Promise	Law
Spirit	Flesh
Faith	Works
Freedom	Bondage
Blessing	Curse
Children of God	Slaves
Unity of all peoples	Disunity (implied)

OUTLINE

The Issue Identified, 3:1-5
The Theological Argument, 3:6–4:7
The Application to the Galatians, 4:8-11

The Issue Identified

Galatians 3:1-5

PREVIEW

You foolish Galatians! Who has bewitched you? If the fire with which Paul began this letter in 1:6-10 receded somewhat in the paragraphs that followed, here it bursts to the fore again with this new outbreak!

This paragraph is crucial to understanding exactly what is going on in Galatia. Here is the place in the letter where Paul is most explicit about the situation that occasioned this letter. Interestingly, the topic of justification does not appear here, though the questions of faith and works of the law from the previous discussion do. New to this section is Paul's introduction of Spirit and flesh as a contrasting pair. These latter terms rise to prominence in the rest of the letter, overshadowing the theme of righteousness/justification. This signals that although justification is a supporting theme in Galatians, it is not the principal theme, as many have supposed.

So what *is* the issue as Paul sees it? It appears that the Galatians were being taught that how they began their life in Christ has little to do with continuing in their faithfulness to the Law of Moses, and that it is this continued faithfulness that determines their inclusion in the people of God. But Paul sees this theology as inconsistent and problematic, a deviation from the truth. Here again we see Paul's passion for the consistency and coherence of the gospel. The Holy Spirit not only began the Galatians' new life in Christ; the Spirit also sustains that life. The teachers were happy enough to acknowledge the role of the Spirit in the Gentiles' initial incorporation into the people of God, but here Paul's theological critique is that the teachers' insistence that the Gentiles observe the regulations of the Law means that they are abandoning the Spirit in order to live on the basis of human energy (flesh). Doing so is not only inconsistent; it also amounts to an abandonment of the gospel!

EXPLANATORY NOTES

You foolish Galatians! Who has bewitched you? (3:1). After the long narrative of Paul's experiences and the theological statement growing out of the Antioch incident, Paul turns to confront the Galatians directly. Throughout the letter, Paul moves back and forth between language of affection and respect, and language of rebuke and shame. The Galatians are *foolish*! They are unthinking and unwise in their judgment of the issues they face! They are *bewitched*! They have come under a spell, cast by Paul's adversaries. This last description comes from the world of magic and sorcery and refers to what is known as the "evil eye." Paul may be deliberately arousing in his readers/hearers fear of an evil magical spell and revulsion against the teachers who would do such harm. Magic was a powerful cultural feature of Paul's day. But the parallel reference to Paul's preaching that follows suggests that the primary reference is metaphorical, pointing to the persuasive power of words that have the false appearance of sophistication. The adversaries who were teaching observance of the Law were, according to Paul, spellbinders.

The Galatians should not have fallen for the tantalizing rhetoric! Why? Because they had experienced an equally powerful presentation of the cross in Paul's preaching. *It was before your eyes that Jesus Christ was publicly exhibited as crucified!* Paul had graphically portrayed the death of Jesus Christ on the cross. He must have narrated Jesus' crucifixion vividly to impress on the listener the reality and significance of the cross. This reference to the cross links back to 2:19-20, where the cross of Christ marks Paul's spiritual experience. In both cases the perfect tense of *crucify* is used, emphasizing the continuing effect of a past event. Paul sees the cross of Christ as an event with relevance for every moment and for all persons. These two references in places where Paul is summarizing his argument show that the cross is a foundation stone in the edifice of the gospel.

The only thing I want to learn from you is this: Did you receive the Spirit by doing the works of the law or by believing what you heard? (3:2). The word *only* is of more than passing interest. There are at least two possible nuances in this word. It signals that Paul is about to indicate what in his mind is the central issue in Galatia. That issue is not a doctrinal dispute, such as about justification. Paul does not accuse the Galatians of knowingly rejecting any of his teaching. Rather, they are being duped into changing the source out of which they live the Christian life! The letter Paul writes them, then, is about how one pursues the life of a disciple, not primarily about how one becomes a believer or even stays a believer, though these matters are touched on.

The word *only* also signals that Paul will identify what can best help the Galatians perceive the nature of the issue before them. The key is the Holy Spirit and the Spirit's work. So in a rhetorical question, Paul asks what the secret was to the work of Spirit among them. And he suggests two options: either Law observance or trustful believing. The right answer is clear to the readers. They had received the Spirit on the basis of faith apart from practice of the Law (and, perhaps for some Gentile believers, even apart from *knowledge* of the Law). From Paul's perspective, the Galatians are foolishly being led to reject the centrality of the Spirit for the centrality of the Law! The choice is between a religious experience from above (God) or one from below (cf. the concept of flesh in v. 3).

The phrase *believing what you heard* (lit. *hearing of faith*) is open to various interpretations. The word for *hearing* can mean either the act of hearing or the thing which is heard (i.e., report or message). In the latter case, the phrase would refer to the message of the gospel, which has faith as its focus. Paul would be contrasting works of the Law (see on 2:16) with the divine offer in the gospel message. That meaning is less likely here. In 3:5 the phrase appears again. There God's action of supplying the Spirit and working miracles is said to depend on the *hearing of faith* (implied in the rhetorical question). It would be more relevant to Paul's point to say that this action of God depends on a human response (act of hearing) rather than on a message (what is heard). The allusion then is to human action that opens the door to the divine action. This is supported by a similar statement in Romans 10:14, where the two human actions of hearing and believing are related, with hearing as the prerequisite for believing.

Contrary to some interpreters, the faith referred to here can hardly be a faith or faithfulness of Christ himself (see on 2:16; 3:22). The opening words, *just as*, in verse 6 indicate that Abraham is an example of the faith being spoken of in verses 1-5. Verse 7 makes clear that those who believe like Abraham are his children. Such are the Galatians when they, like Abraham, act in faith. This same parallel to Abraham (and the likely parallel of Rom 10:14, as noted above) supports the idea that faith in the expression *hearing of faith* means the act of believing—that is, a hearing accompanied by faith. Above I argued (on 2:16) that in the phrase *faith of/in Jesus Christ*, faith comes closer to meaning "message." But in the present phrase, the action of faith is prominent. This understanding of the phrase fits well with Paul's view of faith in the letter as response to divine promise. One learns of promise by hearing the divine offer; one responds to promise by the embracing action of faith.

Are you so foolish? Having started with the Spirit, are you now ending with the flesh? (3:3). The rebuke for being foolish is repeated (from 3:1) for emphasis. But here the question form softens it. The rhetorical questions to the Galatians continue, thus effectively drawing them into the discernment process. The second question shows where Paul's mind is going in analyzing the Galatian situation. The Galatians are moving from Spirit to flesh. Paul sees this disturbing shift not as one of degree, but of kind (cf. 1:6-7). The new teaching on Law observance is threatening to undo the work of the Holy Spirit, just as Paul argued earlier in relation to Christ (2:18-21). The language of starting and ending reflects on one level that change is happening in Galatia. On another level, it shows yet again Paul's fundamental viewpoint that life in Christ is of one cloth: its essential character remains the same through all times and circumstances.

The concept of *flesh* in Paul's thinking is as crucial as it is difficult. In short, it means humanity in its material dimension. When used negatively, as here, it is material existence operating on its own without God. So in Galatians, *flesh* has the connotation of human life and activity apart from the power of God (the Spirit) and therefore based on human and material resource (see the clear example in 4:23). Here the term *flesh* probably also alludes to circumcision, an act done to human flesh, and thus connects with a central theme in the letter. However, we should not limit it to that allusion. The term carries deep and broad implications for Paul's thought, describing life that is an alternative to life in the Spirit. The theme of Spirit versus flesh, introduced here, is expanded in chapter 5 (see also TBC).

The clear implication of verses 2-3 is that the reception of the Spirit is part of conversion, the beginning point of life in Christ. In fact, the Spirit's presence defines basic Christian experience (cf. Gal 4:6; Acts 2:38; 10:47; Rom 8:15). A person without the evidence of the Spirit's presence is not a New Testament believer (Rom 8:9). The promise of the Spirit is a defining reality of the new covenant in Christ (Gal 3:14). Without the Spirit we would still be under the covenant of Law. With the Spirit we need not and ought not remain at the level of that covenant. Paul argues this point more thoroughly in 5:16-26.

Paul's particular point in verse 3 is that the beginning relationship with the Spirit must characterize the believer's life from beginning to end. The same basic quality should always be present. Life must be lived on the basis of the Spirit's enabling, not on the basis of human ability (flesh). What is truly striking is that Paul creates a parallel between doing works of the Law in verse 2 and living by the flesh in verse 3. In the false teaching in Galatia, he sees a view of the Law that is closer to flesh than to Spirit! As we will see, Paul has a more positive view of the Law than this might imply. The Law is not purely and simply defined by flesh. Rather, Paul fears that the Galatians will use the Law in a (wrong) way that substitutes reliance on the flesh for reliance on the Spirit, that substitutes reliance on human resources for reliance on God [*Paul's View of the Law in Galatians, p. 316*].

Did you experience so much for nothing?—if it really was for nothing (3:4). With this question, Paul asks the Galatians to consider how much they value the beginning of their new life in Christ. The language of the question contains the same stark contrast that Paul has been hammering home. The new so-called gospel in Galatia would render the earlier experiences meaningless and worthless. The word translated *experience* is elsewhere in the New Testament always used with the meaning "to suffer." But the positive sense, "to experience," is found in Greek usage, and that is the only meaning that fits the context here. There are references elsewhere in the letter to persecution in the form of Jewish pressure for Gentile believers to fully embrace Jewish practices (4:29; 6:11). However the expression *so much* found here refers most naturally to the Galatians' early spiritual experiences, mentioned in the immediate context.

Well then, does God supply you with the Spirit and work miracles among you by your doing the works of the law, or by your believing what you heard? (3:5). Paul comes back to the comparison of *works of the law* and *hearing of faith* made in verse 2 (see definitions there). The question there focuses on the initiating experience with the Spirit. Here the present-tense verbs draw attention to the continuing ministry of the Spirit in life. The same basic issue is present in both verses. What is the key that opens one's life to the work of the Spirit? The reader has no doubt about Paul's answer to his own rhetorical question. It is trustful reception of the good news about God's offer that activates God's action for us, *not* human actions in conformity to the stipulations of the Law, even granted that they are given by God (3:19-21).

This verse goes beyond verse 2 in defining more specifically the Spirit's work. The verb *supply*, perhaps implying even *liberally supply*, speaks of God's giving the Spirit to believers as an ongoing nourishment and provision. Paul strongly emphasizes the Spirit's provision in chapter 5, where the Spirit is the key resource for the day-to-day life of obedience. Moreover, God's work through the Spirit is manifested in *works of power* (lit. *miracles*). This indicates that Paul's proclamation of the gospel in Galatia was accompanied by powerful manifestations of divine working.

That they are here called *works of power* indicates the important role of demonstrating the power of God as overcoming the power of evil in the spiritual, physical, and social realms. Moreover, the miraculous work of God illustrates well Paul's point that what counts in genuine Christian faith is God's work rather than human works. The reader should not miss the subtle play on the word *work*, which highlights the contrast between God's work and human works (of the Law). God's work in the Spirit is a true source of power for life and ministry rather than human flesh (see v. 3). This is a strong theme in Galatians (e.g., 2:8; 5:6).

THE TEXT IN BIBLICAL CONTEXT

Signs and Wonders in Paul and the New Testament

Miracles were part of Paul's role as an apostle, as he states explicitly (in Rom 15:18-19; 1 Cor 2:4; 2 Cor 12:12; 1 Thess 1:5). In calling them "signs of an apostle," he gives them a key place in his ministry and in the apostolic role generally. As signs, they are not an end in themselves. Rather, they point to the presence of divine power as authenticating evidence for the gospel—God's kingdom now at work for salvation. Like Paul, Acts also links miracles with the Spirit. The reception of the Spirit was not an invisible dimension of early Christian experience merely confessed in belief or symbolized in baptism. If the Spirit was present, it showed itself. Paul makes clear that deeds of power must be balanced with other elements of Christian practice. The New Testament is aware that the spectacular character of signs and wonders can distract from the larger concerns of the gospel. Yet the New Testament writings give witness to the importance of miracles in the early church while also illustrating the variety of specific forms they took.

Dualism

Like Paul, other New Testament writers contrast Spirit and flesh. The classical statement is found in John 3. But we must not misunderstand this contrast. The early followers of Jesus held to an ethical duality, in which the two forces of good and evil struggle against each other on the stage of history. They did not believe in an absolute dualism, in which reality is divided into two fixed realms of good and evil. Their belief in one God, who is good, rules this out. And since God created the material world, that part of reality is essentially good even though evil has gained temporary control over much of it. Human life belongs to this material realm, which biblical writers describe with the word *flesh*. This is how the term *flesh* comes to have the double connotation of good and evil. Even though the flesh is vulnerable to the influence of evil and easily becomes its servant (Rom 7:13-20), under God, through Christ, and with the aid of the Spirit, the flesh is able to serve the good (Gal 2:20!). Paul expands on this theme in Galatians 5:16-21. He is not espousing a spiritualist stance that finds the highest good in the inner, mystical realm of spirit, as detached as possible from the material world. The values of God's reign can be and must be expressed in the material world and lived out in the affairs of everyday life. What Paul is resisting in Galatia is the external, material form of religion without the Spirit to give it authenticity (cf. 2 Tim 3:5). He stands in the tradition of the prophetic emphasis on the heart (Jer 31:33) and the Spirit (Ezek 36:26-27; Joel 2:28-29).

THE TEXT IN THE LIFE OF THE CHURCH

Miracles

Signs and wonders have been part of the biblical world from the beginning. Though sometimes deliberately rejected and often absent, they have been part of church history as well. Miracle is at the foundation of the Christian faith. The founding figures of Jesus, Peter, and Paul were all miracle workers. Some have held that miracles belong only to the time of the New Testament, citing a passage like 1 Corinthians 13:8. But besides misunderstanding that passage, such a view overlooks how Paul sees the presence and powerful action of the Spirit as an indispensable part of the gospel. This point of view is expressed even more strongly in the book of Acts, which presents the effectiveness of the early church's mission as dependent, to a significant degree, on signs and wonders. The point is confirmed again and again in the history of missions and young churches, and in times of renewal up to the present. At the same time, both Scripture and church experience treat signs and wonders with some caution, since they can be counterfeit and need to be tested (see Deut 13:1-5; 18:21-22).

The presence of the Spirit will always be accompanied by evidences (signs), but the presence of signs is no guarantee that the Holy Spirit is behind them. Signs can be the evidence that other spirits or powers are at work. Moreover, there is no reason to limit the signs of the Spirit's presence to the spectacular, what is popularly thought of as miracle. Moral transformation, expressed as fruit of the Spirit (Gal 5:22-23), and deeds of loving service are signs that can elicit the wonder of a watching world (cf. Matt 5:16; 1 Pet 2:12). If we respect the freedom and spontaneity of the Spirit (Heb 2:4), these signs can and will vary and change with time and place. We should, no doubt, expect that the Spirit's acts of power will differ, to counter the type of evil being confronted in a given setting. But the Spirit's work, when present, will be visible! For a church in the age of science, which is easily skeptical about divine intervention in life, openness to signs and wonders may be difficult. But for all that, it is no less important. Otherwise we risk treating God as an absent Creator (deism) who makes no real difference in daily life.

Spiritual Maturity

The New Testament speaks of two opposite ways that believers mistakenly relate to the basics, the foundational realities of the faith. One is not to progress beyond them to the mature and ever-growing expressions of faithfulness (cf. Heb 6:1). The other is to leave the first things behind and to disconnect from them, as here in Galatians. Both of these are constant temptations to believers. The latter temptation is particularly insidious for churches that emphasize discipleship and obedience in all of life. It is easy for such persons and groups to focus on applying the gospel to moral and justice issues in the personal and social arenas in a way that ignores the presence and power of the Holy Spirit. We begin to assume that the basic questions of knowing God and living in the Spirit are taking care of themselves. We can become so practiced in the habits of Christian living, supported by community expectations and accountability, that we are unaware of a spiritual vacuum in ourselves or in the new generations of believers who may have heard precious little about the basics. The appearance of godliness is there, but the source of nourishment is flesh, not Spirit.

The Theological Argument
Galatians 3:6–4:7

OVERVIEW

Paul has now identified the core problem in the Galatian churches, and he has stated what they should do about it: They are being seduced into thinking that faithfulness means keeping the Law of Moses, including the rite of circumcision, but they should instead recognize that the apocalyptic power of the cross has ended the Law's reign and made it possible for the Galatians to live by the Spirit. That much is clear. But what is the basis for Paul's critique and alternative? Is this wishful thinking on his part, a manifestation of his unfortunate tendency to say what people want to hear (cf. Gal 1:10), as his opponents are claiming, or is Paul right? Does Paul have any good theological or scriptural basis for his teaching?

After describing the core problem in Galatia, Paul now turns to defend his understanding of the gospel. His defense is an argument from Scripture, although in 4:1-7 the theological argument draws on a Greek philosophical concept. In every instance the arguments consist of dialogue between the scriptural evidence and the event of Jesus Christ. In making his defense, Paul's intent is to show that the work of Christ is the faithful and full response to earlier revelation.

A key concept that ties the individual arguments together is promise. Abraham and the promise that God made to him provide the main example. Paul's decision to use Abraham is a strategic move. The teachers countering Paul likely made much of Abraham, the "father of the faith." Wasn't Abraham righteous because he obeyed the command of God to be circumcised? And wasn't

Abraham the original Gentile, the original proselyte, whose circumcision sealed his role as father of the people of God? Abraham served their case well.

But Paul argues that Abraham better fits the gospel of righteousness by faith. Throughout the section, Paul sets the faith of Abraham over against the Law of Moses. Abraham stands for blessing; the Law stands for curse. God's promise to Abraham has priority over the Law both temporally and theologically, making the Law temporary but the promise permanent. More specifically, God's promise to Abraham, based on faith, is more fundamental to God's relationship to humanity than is the Law of Moses. For those who can see it, the principle of faith in Christ was revealed (long before the giving of the Law to Moses) in God's justification of Abraham on the basis of his faith. Moreover, faith is the key to God's blessing for the Gentiles who, along with believing Jews, are united into one people in Christ.

OUTLINE

Example of Abraham, 3:6-9
Curse of the Law, 3:10-14
Primacy of Promise, 3:15-18
Place of the Law, 3:19-24
Fulfillment in Christ, 3:25-29
Freedom of God's Children, 4:1-7

Example of Abraham

Galatians 3:6-9

PREVIEW

So whose champion is Abraham? Is he the champion of those advocating full observance of the Law, or is he the champion of Gentiles freed from the Law through their faith in Christ? In this part of Galatians, Paul is trying to wrest Abraham from the grasp of his opponents, who are using Abraham as Exhibit 1 in their argument that they are right and Paul is wrong.

Remarkably, Paul does not merely seek to neutralize his opponents' use of Abraham as their prime example. Instead, he boldly and creatively turns the tables on his opponents and shows how, understood correctly, Abraham is actually *Paul's* Exhibit 1 in his defense of the gospel! In Abraham, Paul finds proof of the fact that right standing with God is fundamentally a matter of faith responding to promise, not of obedience responding to Law. Furthermore, God's promise to Abraham foreshadowed the inclusion of the Gentiles in the people of God when that promise spoke of Abraham being a blessing to all nations. The whole gospel message is prefigured in Abraham!

EXPLANATORY NOTES

The paragraph begins with the conjunction *just as*, which signals an important link to the preceding paragraph. Paul's citation of Abraham illustrates his earlier point that faith is the key to genuine spirituality, not works of the Law. Paul's use of Abraham as the example of faith in this context makes it clear that *faith* (NRSV, *believing*) in the preceding verses (3:2, 5) refers to the believer's faith in response to the gospel proclamation. Some argue that faith in 3:1-5 refers to the faith/faithfulness of Jesus Christ. But that does not fit well with the account of Abraham, who is used in chapter 3 as an example for the believer, not as an model (type) to which Jesus corresponds (see on 3:2 [*The Faith of Jesus Christ, p. 305*]).

Abraham *"believed God, and it was reckoned to him as righteousness"* (3:6). Paul's reference to Abraham consists of a quotation from Genesis 15:6. He quotes this same verse in Romans 4:3. It fits his theology well because it uses the key concepts of faith, believing, and righteousness. In the Genesis account, Abraham is counted as right in God's sight on no other basis than his faith. Abraham's obedience to specific commands of God is not a precondition for his right relationship with God, even though Abraham does obey God later. This interpretation contradicts the teaching that Abraham's observance of circumcision and his readiness to sacrifice Isaac were the primary evidence of his righteousness. Thus Abraham's example actually supports Paul's contention that faith is the fundamental category of all biblical covenants. The Mosaic Law is a secondary, conditional, and temporary component in God's covenant relationship (3:23-25).

From this scriptural evidence, the Galatians should be able to draw the same conclusion that Paul does: *So, you see, those who believe are the descendants of Abraham* (3:7). The *true* children of Abraham are those who stand in this spiritual heritage. Neither biological descent nor circumcision (cf. Rom 2:28-29; 4:11) nor keeping of the Law of Moses (cf. the rest of Gal 3) define this heritage. With this claim, Paul makes faith a central, ruling feature of biblical religion. Paul has already claimed for Christ (and the cross in particular) the same essential status (2:21). Promise and Spirit share the same position in his argument. These features, with Christ at the center, form a cluster that functions as the pillars of Paul's theology.

This stance on faith opens the possibility for anyone from any nation to be a child of God. And Paul finds an anticipation of this in God's promise to Abraham. *And the scripture, foreseeing that God would justify the Gentiles by faith, declared the gospel beforehand to Abraham, saying, "All the Gentiles shall be blessed in you"* (3:8). Paul reveals his respect for Holy Scripture by attributing to it what was actually the person and voice of God as reported in Genesis (cf. 3:22 for another personification of Scripture). Moreover, he treats the Genesis story as prophecy. The Scripture has prophetic vision because it foresaw that God would justify the Gentiles. In fact, the proclamation of universal blessing to the nations through Abraham is *described* (lit.) as a preproclamation of the gospel. Thus the Scripture can look forward or backward, closing the gap in time between past and present.

The key to Paul's use of Scripture here is that he sees God's work in Christ as the fruition or fulfillment of all divine promises in previous times. So Paul can say in another letter that all the promises of God find their yes in Christ (2 Cor 1:20). This type of interpretation is known as *pesher* and was used in the Qumran community as well as by the early Christians. The basic idea is that since the present time is the end time (e.g., see 1 Cor 10:11), all scriptural vision and expectation speak to the present as their culmination.

For this reason, those who believe are blessed with Abraham who believed (3:9). Paul draws his conclusion by putting together the elements of faith and blessing from the Abraham story. God grants God's blessing to all, Jew and Gentile, who have faith like the faithful Abraham. The use of the adjective *faithful* (lit.) to describe Abraham is striking since the adjective usually describes a person who stays by their word and commitment. The context here, however, requires the sense of one who is *full of faith*. NRSV expresses this with the clause *who believed*. But the use of *faithful* here does give evidence that Paul sees a close tie between *faith* and *faithfulness*. Paul's point is that the people of God are defined not by ethnic origin but by the sole criterion of faith. This is *the* true *Israel of God* (cf. 6:16).

THE TEXT IN BIBLICAL CONTEXT

Faith and Promise

For Paul, faith is trust in the God who makes promises. This is clear from Paul's repeated use of promise as a corollary to faith in his argument in Galatians (3:14, 18, 19, 21, 22, 29; 4:23, 28). Faith involves accepting the promise and making oneself available for its fulfillment and outworking in one's life by divine, not human, action. This understanding accords with the account in Genesis 15, in which Abraham receives God's promise of posterity and land, and believes God as the one who can make good on the promise. The allegory of Hagar and Sarah in 4:21-31 makes the same point. The exercise of this faith is the condition for effecting the covenant relationship offered by God. In God's sight, this makes Abraham righteous—a covenant partner in good standing.

The Blessing of Abraham

The reference in Genesis (12:3; 18:18; 22:18) to a universal blessing in the context of God's particular choice of Abraham's family is remarkable. There is no way of knowing exactly how the blessing was originally understood. Subsequent narratives in Genesis illustrate how Abraham and his descendants are a blessing to certain outsiders. But the meaning of blessing to all the families of the earth is not explained. That Genesis connects Israel to the nations with whom Israel shares the blessing of their God is clear enough. The election of Israel is not a limiting of God's blessing; it is a means by which all peoples receive God's blessing. A vision for mission is latent here.

In the Second Temple period, God's people came to think that this promise would be fulfilled at some future time when all the nations would accept Israel's God and would stream into Jerusalem in worship of this God (see esp. Isa 56, 60). When Paul cites this blessing in 3:8 he sees the fulfillment of this promise of blessing in God's justification of both Jew and Gentile as equals, brought out of their former religious practices into life in Christ, in pilgrimage to *the Jerusalem above* (4:26). Gentile and Jewish believers meet, as it were, in the middle, in a new place defined by Christ, not in the Law of Moses or Gentile paganism. In 3:14 he will identify the blessing with the gift of the Spirit to believers.

THE TEXT IN THE LIFE OF THE CHURCH

Faith

Faith sometimes refers to the whole belief system of Christianity as in the expression "Christian faith." Already in the New Testament, *faith* can serve as a shorthand expression for the beliefs and way of life characterized by the Jesus movement, as in Galatians 1:23. Some parts of the church think of faith as mental assent to a system of ideas or doctrines. While this is an appropriate extension of the word, it is neither its beginning nor its center. In the story of Abraham, *faith* refers to one's reception of God's offer and one's trust in God to make good on the offer. To believe, or to have faith, involves making oneself available to God for the working out of God's purpose. God's offer is known in Scripture as God's *promise*. So *faith* is a companion word to *promise*. As the hymn expresses it, "Faith . . . grasps the promise God has given" (P. Herbert, 1566).

Paul has good grounds for understanding promise received by faith at the root of biblical religion. God in gracious love takes the initiative with humankind, offering a promise of blessing. This promise is made good as humans trust (have faith in) this God of promise. As the Genesis narrative shows, Abraham's commitment to availability is not just an instantaneous act, but a stance that marks his daily existence. Faith involves walking with God toward the fulfillment of God's promise into the future. This can be called obedience or faithfulness. In biblical thought, obedience is faith acted out consistently in daily living.

Seen this way, both Paul, with his claim of faith-*not*-works, and James, with his stance of faith-*with*-works (James 2:18-26), are right, so long as neither excludes the other! When Paul says in Romans 14:23 that "whatever does not proceed from faith is sin," he is expressing a commitment to the centrality of faith in every aspect of biblical spirituality and ethics. What this says is that the flow of virtue and power for our salvation and blessing is from God to humans. God initiates, we do not. God does not respond to our initiative; we respond to God's. Nevertheless, that response is important because God's response is conditioned on it. This is the attitude and stance that mark the Christian life from beginning to end. It is the distinctive feature of biblical faith, old covenant and new.

Curse of the Law

Galatians 3:10-14

PREVIEW

Clearly the key word in this paragraph is *curse*. As the antithesis of blessing, *curse* signals that Paul is presenting the negative side of the positive statement in the preceding paragraph. The teachers undoubtedly saw the Law of Moses as a place of refuge or protection. And although Paul "upholds" the Law (Rom 3:31) and considers it "holy and just and good" (7:12), here he insists that any commitment to "the works of the Law" puts one under a curse rather that under the Law's protection. The two paragraphs function as point/counterpoint in the argument. The contrast is between faith that leads to blessing, and works of the Law that lead to curse. The first way of being righteous results in the inclusion of all peoples. Although the contrasting result is not stated as such, dependence on the works of the Law results only in the exclusion of everyone who does not fully obey the Law, which is, unfortunately, everyone (3:11a)!

Paul continues to interweave the two themes of true biblical faith and God's universal gospel for all peoples. The concept of curse permits Paul to explain why works of Law lead to a dead end, yet it also provides the occasion to explain the benefit of Christ's death on a cross: Christ took the curse of the Law upon himself, releasing those under the curse. God's act of redemption in Christ has the effect of opening the blessing of Abraham to the Gentiles and of realizing the promise of the Spirit in all believers. Paul's reference to the Abrahamic blessing and to the Spirit (v. 14) ties together the entire section of 3:1-14.

EXPLANATORY NOTES

This is one of the more difficult paragraphs of the letter. Nearly every phrase is disputed. The larger context of the letter will have to arbitrate among the options.

For all who rely on the works of the law are under a curse (3:10a). The opening clause reads (lit.), *For as many as are from* [i.e., *who take their identity from*] *works of the law are under a curse*. The inclusive expression *all* (lit. "as many as") indicates that Paul is thinking not only of the traditional Jew but also of anyone who embraces this perspective. Paul is thus inviting the Galatians to see themselves in this group if they accept the new teaching of his opponents. Paul is not simply characterizing the spiritual attitude of this group, as the English translation *rely* might imply. He is simply identifying anyone who is loyal to the Jewish Law. The same mode of expression is used in 2:12 (lit.), *those from* [*the*] *circumcision*, meaning the circumcision party. On the phrase *works of the law*, see on 2:16 and 3:2.

Paul now pronounces a severe judgment on the law-observing group: they *are under a curse*. *Curse* is the antonym of blessing and signifies that one is disapproved by God and subject to divine retribution. As the following quotation from Deuteronomy shows, Paul has in mind the concept of blessing and curse that is so basic to the covenant and is spelled out in detail in Deuteronomy 27–28. In the immediately preceding statement, Paul has spoken of the blessing that comes to those who have faith. Now he speaks of a contrasting parallel: the *curse* that comes on those who define themselves as observers of the Law. In fact, he has in mind more than a contrast. The conjunction *for* suggests that what follows supports Paul's preceding argument of blessing to all nations. How? By showing that curse results from a view of the Law that does not give faith priority. But setting up the contrast in this way would have struck the average Jew as most odd, for it appears to set one aspect of the covenant against another. What might Paul mean?

For it is written, "Cursed is everyone that does not observe and obey all the things written in the book of the law" (3:10b). Paul cites Deuteronomy 27:26 as scriptural support for his claim that Law observers are under a curse. We can well imagine that this verse was in the arsenal of the Galatian opponents. For Paul to use it against them was good strategy. He makes a slight modification with the words *book of the law*, which has the effect of broadening the sense to the entire Torah, not just the law code of Deuteronomy. The quoted statement itself is clear enough: failure to put the Law into practice brings divine disapproval. The teachers would have used a verse like this to show why failure to accept circumcision puts one under the curse. But Paul takes this same verse to support his claim that all Law observers are, in fact, under a curse. It is not the ones who disregard the law who are under a curse. How can that be? Something in Paul's thought is not apparent. There seems to be an unexpressed assumption in the argument.

The usual explanation is that Paul holds that no one is capable of obeying all the law perfectly because of human sinfulness. Therefore, because all disobey, they come under a curse. That Paul believed in universal sinfulness is clear in Romans 3:9-18. No Jew *or* Gentile keeps all the Law (cf. Rom 2:17-24; 7:7-11). Furthermore, Galatians 3:11a and 6:13 may suggest that Paul's opponents themselves do not keep the *entire* Law. Paul's reference to the obligation to obey the entire Law in 5:3 suggests that the opposition party was requiring circumcision, but not what Paul considered the whole Law. (As a former Pharisee, Paul would have held the strictest of views on Law observance.)

In point of fact, however, the argument may not require such a presupposition at all. Paul may simply be drawing a self-evident contrast between the Abrahamic and Mosaic covenants in that blessing alone appears in the former covenant, but the second involves both blessing and curse. Note that the beginning statement of 3:10 speaks of being *under a curse*. In keeping with the apocalyptic nature of Paul's thought, this could mean under the *threat* of curse, rather than under an *actual* curse (cf. Paul's use of the preposition *under* in Rom 3:9; 6:14-15). All that Paul is trying to say here is that those who choose a Law identity have chosen to place themselves where curse is possible. That contrasts with the blessing of God's covenant of promise to Abraham. But Christ has now redeemed us from this threat of curse under the Law (v. 13; for this approach, see Young: esp. 79–92). For a similar contrast, compare the debit-versus-credit language of 5:2-3. Another possibility, which could supplement rather than contradict the above explanation, is that Paul has in mind the historical reality that Israel is under the curse of exile for disobedience to the Law as Deuteronomy warned. That exile began with the Babylonian captivity but continues in the subjection of the Jews to foreign powers in the first century CE. Paul's point then would be not just a theoretical truth but a historical fact. (For a defense of this position, see Wright 2013: 863–68.)

Paul sees a fundamental contrast between the Law and faith. On the one side, *it is evident that no one is justified before God by the law; for "The one who is righteous will live by faith"* (3:11). Now we hear what the bottom line is for Paul with respect to the Law: it cannot be the basis for covenant relationship with God. Law observance is not the key to the divine-human relationship. Faith is that key—as it always has been! Evidence for this is present in Scripture itself. Paul quotes Habakkuk 2:4, a passage that he cites at another crucial point, in Romans 1:17. Second Temple Judaism could take this verse to refer to the Messiah as the righteous one. Similarly, some modern interpreters take it to support the concept of *Christ's* faith/faithfulness (see on 2:16; 3:22). However, the context here seems to indicate that Paul is referring to the *believer* as the righteous one (on this point, see Bird and Sprinkle: 155–63).

Whether this passage emphasizes *righteous by faith* or *live by faith* (either translation is possible) is not decisive for Paul's present argument. Throughout his letters, Paul holds that life before God is based on faith from beginning to end (cf. Rom 1:16-17). Justification by God (*the one who is righteous by faith will have life*) and faithful living before God (*the one who is righteous will live by faith*) are both important to Paul. However, given Paul's quotation from Leviticus in what follows (see next paragraph below), Paul seems to be emphasizing righteousness that comes by faith. Life is the result of a prior condition—either doing the Law (as in Leviticus) or being righteous by faith (as in Habakkuk). Moreover, in Galatians and Romans, the formulation *by faith* is typically tied to righteousness, not to life. Paul's argument from Scripture here is likely persuasive for the Galatians since they had come into new life with God by the Spirit's work, through faith, apart from law (3:1-5). It is on this basis that they are righteous.

The other side of the argument now follows: *But the law does not rest on faith; on the contrary, "Whoever does the works of the law will live by them"* (3:12). Literally, the Law is not from (or by) faith. Paul uses the same form of expression throughout the letter in the phrases *by faith* and *by works of the law.* Faith is not an intrinsic operative principle for law, Mosaic or otherwise (see TBC below for important qualification). The Law's operative principle is action, *doing* it. Paul documents this in the quotation of Leviticus 18:5, a passage used again in Romans 10:5. According to this text, the actual *doing* of the Law is what secures meaningful existence (life). The language of this verse supports Paul's interest in the concept of life as an ideal, fulfilled existence (see 2:19-20; 3:21). Of course, Paul does not believe that the Law achieves the life it envisions, as he expressly denies in 3:21. This less-than-life condition is precisely the curse he has described in verse 10.

Christ redeemed us from the curse of the law by becoming a curse—for it is written, "Cursed is everyone who hangs on a tree" (3:13). After demonstrating that the way of Law threatens curse rather than blessing, and after identifying the intrinsic tension between faith and the Law, Paul announces the resolving action of God in Christ. The work of Christ answers the condition of curse by an act of redemption. The word for redemption comes from the world of commerce in slave trading. It has the meaning of buying from or buying back in an act of purchase. Here the word means freeing from an undesirable situation without any necessary reference to a purchase exchange. Paul uses the same word again in 4:5, where the redemption is from the Law, rather than from the *curse* of the Law, as here. The meaning is substantially the same, although in 4:5 the image of enslavement is more explicit in the context.

The redeeming benefit of Christ could be understood as removal of the curse (or guilt), resulting from specific acts of personal and corporate disobedience to the will of God. But the context suggests that Paul has in mind primarily the effect that Christ's work has on the external, historical situation within which we live. (Of course, that situation in turn affects our personal lives.) The stage of time in

God's salvation plan has changed. The time of the Law's control is terminated, and the time of salvation in Christ has begun. This perspective would cohere with the explanation of verse 10 above.

In the following paragraphs Paul develops this point from various angles, especially in the assertion that Christ brings the time of our confinement (bondage) under the Law to an end (3:23; 4:1-7). The key to this change of situation is the crucifixion of Jesus, when he carried the curse of being a lawbreaker and became himself an outsider to the covenant people. This is the meaning of the quotation from Deuteronomy 21:23, *Cursed is everyone who hangs on a tree*, a passage from the same general context as the quotation in verse 10. Understood in this way, the curse of which Paul speaks is not relevant just for the Jews who were under the Law. *All* nations, who are outsiders to the blessing, are also affected by this change of historical situation in the death of Christ. The pronoun *we* (vv. 13-14) includes Jew and Gentile, but each in their own particular way, given their unique histories.

Christ's bearing the curse of the Law on our behalf is one aspect of the shift to the new order of salvation. The Mosaic Law is neither the final definition of the will of God nor the final authority for the follower of Christ. Thus the curse of the Law is not something the Galatians need to fear. They are free to explore the meaning of faithfulness in the light of Christ and his law (6:2), as guided and empowered by the Spirit (5:16-25). In particular, they can know that the curse of being a lawless Gentile outsider is now overcome because the curse of the Law has been nullified. It was God's intent *that in Christ Jesus the blessing of Abraham might come upon the Gentiles, that we might receive the promise of the Spirit through faith* (3:14).

Paul uses two statements of purpose to express the intended outcomes of Christ's curse-bearing death. The first is the realization of the pre-Law vision of a universal blessing to all nations given to Abraham. This is possible because those aspects of the Mosaic Law that effectively excluded non-Jews are without force in Christ. With this comment the present discussion links back to verses 6-9, showing that the primary issue in Paul's mind is the effect of the Law's curse on the Gentiles.

The second purpose or result of Christ's curse-bearing death is that believers receive the Holy Spirit. Once again (see 3:2-3), Paul shows that redemption in Christ and receiving the Spirit are inseparable for the believer. The second purpose statement further explains the first. By the word *promise*, Paul apparently means that the gift of the Holy Spirit is the blessing (or at least an expression of it) for the nations that God promised Abraham. While the first purpose has to do with the Gentiles alone, the second is inclusive of Jewish and Gentile believers. The use of the simple pronoun *we* sends this signal of inclusion. Christ has indeed made all people one and equal. With the reference to the Spirit and the reminder that the promise comes through faith, a link is made all the way back to 3:1-5. Paul is now giving a theological rationale for the Galatians' experience of the Spirit—apart from Law. Thus the entire section of 3:1-14 is tied together.

THE TEXT IN BIBLICAL CONTEXT

Law and Faith

This paragraph contains one of Paul's sharpest contrasts of faith and the Law. Its generalizing form sounds categorical and unconditional: *The law does not rest on faith* (3:12). Does this radical contrast set one part of Scripture against the other? Are the covenants of Abraham and Moses opposed to each other? Are faith and law totally incompatible? From Paul's writing, it is not immediately clear to what extent he sees the contrast inherent in Scripture itself, and to what extent he is referring to the understanding of the Galatian adversaries and how the believers are hearing their message.

We can be quite sure Paul thinks that in the actual experience of the Galatians, faith and Law represent alternatives. But is Paul going further? Does he mean to criticize his own Jewish faith? Scholars do not agree about how to describe the prevailing views of faith, grace, and Law in Second Temple Judaism. We can say with confidence that Christian interpreters have often wrongly interpreted late Second Temple Judaism as basing salvation purely on obeying the Law (legalism). But the Scriptures of Second Temple Judaism make it clear that God's gracious initiative was the basis of the Jews' relationship with God.

Some evidence indicates that in late Second Temple Judaism, some Jews were preoccupied with ever-increasing detail in the observance of the Law. Some saw the gradual accumulation of additional regulations as a safeguard or a hedge (Mishnah, *Abot* 1:1) *around* the Law that can protect one from accidentally violating one of the 613 written laws. But other Jews, such as Jesus himself, saw this development as a kind of dehumanizing servitude to the Law rather than service to God or to one's brothers and sisters. Jesus, Peter (Acts 15:10), and Paul all criticize the way some of their brothers and sisters approached the Law. We cannot avoid the conclusion that on the road to Damascus, Paul came to see his own experience with the Law as a distortion of God's will. In Galatians, the exclusive attitude of the Jews puts them on a different level than the Gentiles. Thus some Jews in Paul's day saw God's promise to Abraham as subordinate to the covenant at Sinai (Abraham's obedience to the command of circumcision is the central point). However, Paul sees the covenant at Sinai as subordinate to God's promise to Abraham (Abraham's faith is the main point).

Does Paul see the contrast of faith and Law within Scripture itself? Here one needs to speak with caution. In the paragraphs that follow in Galatians 3, Paul affirms the basic compatibility of faith and Law as represented in the two covenants with Abraham and Moses. He is careful to deny that the coming of the Law set aside the covenant with Abraham. The Law is *added* (3:19) to the earlier covenant, implying that the Sinai covenant is a combination of faith and Law when understood in God's intention. In 3:21 Paul affirms that the Law is not opposed to promise (the corollary of faith). Moreover, Paul explicitly relates faith and Law in a fruitful way in Galatians 5–6. Thus faith and Law are not inherently contradictory.

So what then is the point of the contrast in 3:10-14? Paul does not describe the historical situation of the covenant at Sinai as if it had nothing to do with faith. Rather, he acknowledges that faith and Law are different things and that, taken on their own terms and in the abstract, they represent contrasting religious perspectives. He can find scriptural references to illustrate this. Law naturally points to doing. Faith points to trust in the promise and action of God. While the logic here is hypothetical, Paul clearly thinks that some persons fall into the temptation of building religious practice around one of these to the detriment of the other. For the Galatians, their error is emphasizing Law at the expense of faith. Paul's mode of argument parallels his contrast of flesh and Spirit. These are different realities that can become adversaries when split apart. In God's purpose they are meant to be together and are indeed compatible when rightly related—that is, when the Spirit controls the flesh. In a similar way, faith and Law are compatible when faith has the priority.

From the perspective of the all-sufficiency of Christ, Paul sees the Law of Moses as incomplete, even though it all reflects the intention of God at the time. The Old Testament prophets themselves saw that an inner spiritual power was necessary that was not provided by the Law. (See the continuation of this discussion in the next four subdivisions of the letter [*Paul's View of the Law in Galatians, p. 316*].)

Christ and the Curse

This passage in Galatians is the only place where Paul or any other New Testament writer uses the concept of curse to explain Christ's redemptive work (though cf. 2 Cor 5:21). Paul apparently found this perspective on the death of Christ appropriate to the Galatian situation, though the fact that it appears only here suggests that it is not his preferred or primary perspective. In this case Paul's argument would seem particularly effective to the Gentile believers in Galatia. From a Jewish point of view, the Gentiles are under the curse of God. The adversaries in Galatia were likely pressing the believers to become full Jews to avoid the curse. In making his point, Paul is likely using the very same verses the adversaries were citing. Paul claims that Christ has nullified the curse of the Law by becoming a curse in his crucifixion.

Paul's understanding of the cross as the removal of curse is in harmony with his wider explanations of the cross. In 4:4-5 he speaks of redemption for those under the Law, but there he uses the image of bondage under the Law rather than curse. The thought, however, is similar. Typically Paul speaks of the cross as the place where humanity's sin is removed. For example, in 2 Corinthians 5:21, Christ is said to have become sin in order to carry out his redeeming work. To become sin is parallel to the idea in our present context of becoming a curse. The two statements look at the same reality from different points of view. "Sin" describes our condition in itself, while "curse" describes our condition in the sight of God. In any case, the idea is that Christ has played a representative role for us by taking upon himself a condition that is really ours. Christ takes our place and frees us from our unsaved condition.

THE TEXT IN THE LIFE OF THE CHURCH

Faith and Law in Judeo-Christian Tradition

One of the enduring issues in the Judeo-Christian tradition is the relationship of faith and law, the issue that Paul is treating in the letter to the Galatians. (In this discussion, as elsewhere in the commentary, *Law* stands for the Mosaic Law, and *law* for any definition of the divine will that places a demand on the child of God.) This history reveals a tendency to turn religious experience into formulation. Doing so makes the experience easier to teach and transmit, and easier to regulate proper behavior on the part of adherents. Such a reliance on law, as we can call it, is probably unavoidable, given our human condition (cf. Gal 3:19-22). Historically, Christianity, like Judaism, has affirmed and benefited from some form of law. At its best, law is a protecting fence or wall around some object or place of value. It is not itself the thing of value; it serves what is more essential.

What easily happens is that law moves to center stage and becomes itself the object of religious attention. This problem is "legalism," or an improper and one-sided emphasis on law as external regulation. Every tradition with biblical roots sooner or later faces this temptation. Throughout the centuries, the history of revival and renewal is the story of recovering an essential faith reality after a period of routine and regulation. Leaders in both the early church and the Reformation leveled the accusation that, in some sense, law had encroached on faith.

The Radical Reformation, as embodied in the Anabaptist movement, sought a middle way between the perceived legalism of Catholicism and the tendency toward fideism (the view that faith can and must be protected by downplaying the demand of obedience) in the mainline Reformation. The Anabaptist leader Michael Sattler captured this third perspective in the phrase "filial obedience," which refers to the obedience of a true child of God, motivated from a living relationship with God. The opposite of filial obedience is servile obedience, in which one obeys out of obligation (fuller discussion at TLC for 5:1-12).

There is no real safe haven from legalism. This is amply illustrated by the subsequent history of the Radical Reformation tradition. Its strong interest in discipleship emphasizes that all of life must be conformed to the will of God. Commitments to faithfulness lead to identifying particular practices and standards to guide those practices. With the passing of time and the turn of generations, these forms tend to disconnect from the spiritual energy and commitment that originated them. Under these circumstances, the religious life of the church changes focus. The agenda shifts to the protection and promotion of the standards. The new temptation that accompanies this shift is to employ human power and strategy (what Paul in Galatians calls *flesh*) in preserving the faith. This then short-circuits the true biblical mode of building obedience on faith, and law trumps faith.

From a biblical perspective, faith has priority over law for at least two reasons. First, the biblical tradition places relationship between God and people as the basis of everything. This relationship is expressed in covenant and takes the form of personal fellowship. The human contribution to this covenantal relationship is

trust, or what Paul calls faith. The relationship has a source of nourishment in the Spirit of God. The word *spirituality* is often now used
to name this aspect of life before God.

Second, only faith can adequately respond to the ever-changing
form that faithfulness must take in a diverse and changing world.
Law by nature is rigid and resistant to change. The more time
passes, the harder it can be to change law. This is a key concern of
Paul. For example, he finds that the Law does not fully accommodate the change that Christ has brought, with its full inclusion of the
Gentiles. Only a living faith can meet the challenge of fresh and
relevant interpretation of God's will in the changing human
experience.

Primacy of Promise

Galatians 3:15-18

PREVIEW

There is one small problem in what Paul has been saying. He has
been arguing that the Galatians, *as Gentiles,* have their place within
the purposes of God on the basis of their continuity with Abraham,
the one whose standing with God was based in faith. But doesn't
God's giving of the Law *after* God's covenant with Abraham logically
imply that God intended for the Sinai covenant to *supersede* or
replace the Abrahamic one? How are we to understand the relative
authority of these covenants?

Paul's answer to this question is that the first covenant has priority over the later one. The character of promise in the first is not
modified by the legal character of the second.

EXPLANATORY NOTES

Paul uses various types of argument to persuade his readers. He has
appealed to experience (3:1-5) and to Scripture (3:6-14). Now he uses
yet another type of argument. *Brothers and sisters, I give an example
from daily life* (3:15a). Paul's direct address of his readers as *brothers
and sisters* obviously softens his earlier description of them as *foolish*
in 3:1 and reassures the Galatians of his spiritual bond with them
even when he rebukes them (as in 1:11; then increasingly in 4:12, 28,
31; 5:11, 13; 6:1, 18). The argument itself is based on an example that
is referred to (lit.) as *according to man.* Paul's point is not that the
example is from typical human experience (NRSV, *from daily life*),

but that it is of human origin rather than from divine revelation (as in the case of the argument from Scripture just preceding; cf. also 1:11). Paul is preparing the reader for the fact that he is about to use a human analogy for a divine action and that the argument, therefore, has its limits.

The example is stated thus: *Once a person's will has been ratified, no one adds to it or annuls it* (3:15b). The Greek word for *will* is the same as the word for *covenant* used in verse 17. This is what makes the comparison work for the reader even though a will (or testament) made by a human being is fundamentally different from a covenant made by God, as Paul has forewarned us. The point is that no one other than the will-maker can terminate or modify a will. (The terms are legal; the Greek word behind *add* here is different from the one rendered as *add* in v. 19.)

However, this does not seem to support the particular case of the Jewish covenants since the one who made the first covenant, God, is also the one who made the second and therefore could presumably change or add to the first (cf. v. 19!). But Paul's intent here is simply to draw attention to the permanency of a will or covenant. His point is that in making the covenant with Moses, God did not and could not invalidate the covenant with Abraham, given God's constancy. In fact, the emphasis in the statement is on the fact that the will of which he is speaking is the *human* will. Paul is saying that if the terms of a human will persist, how much more does an agreement established by God!

Before directly stating the conclusion of his line of thinking, Paul introduces another point that is crucial to the case he is making. *Now the promises were made to Abraham and to his offspring; it does not say, "And to offsprings," as of many; but it says, "And to your offspring," that is, to one person, who is Christ* (3:16). Already in verse 14 Paul associates the person of Christ with the promise to Abraham. It is *in Christ* that the blessing of Abraham is brought to realization for the Gentiles. Now Paul pushes that linking of Christ to Abraham one step further by finding reference to Christ in the Old Testament text itself. He observes that the word for *offspring* is in the singular and concludes that it refers to Christ rather than to the whole biological progeny in Abraham's family line (also in 3:19).

The modern reader finds this perplexing since the word *offspring* in Genesis naturally refers to all Abraham's children. As a collective noun, it is singular in form but plural in meaning. Here Paul is using a technique of interpretation typical of the Jewish rabbis. Finding meaning in subtle technicalities of the language not related to the plain sense was a normal, acceptable form of exegesis. That Paul knows *offspring* is collective is shown by his use of it in 3:29 in that sense. In this mode of interpretation, the flow of proof is not from the cited text to current belief, but the other way around. In other words, Paul has a belief about Christ as the fulfillment of all Old Testament promises (cf. 2 Cor 1:20) based on other evidence, and he projects that belief onto the text. Today's experience illuminates the text.

The value of this move is to demonstrate a unity in the purposes of God through time, and this is precisely Paul's concern in this chapter. The deeper idea is that Christ is the representative head of the renewed people of God in the last days. Christ is the one who represents the many. (Note *in Christ* in 3:14, 26, 27 and *of Christ* [lit.] in v. 29, which reflect this solidarity.) Therefore, Christ is the primary *offspring* in and through whom God fulfills God's promise to Abraham. The concept of one person being the representative head of a group is typical of Hebrew thought and of Paul himself (cf. Rom 5:12-21).

Some see the parallel being drawn between Abraham and Christ as support for translating *pistis* as faithfulness (Hays 2002, who thus supports his view of Christ's faith/faithfulness in 2:16 and 3:22). But this is not Paul's concern here. Paul's identification of Christ as the *offspring* demonstrates the continuing validity of the Abrahamic covenant of promise/faith up to the present. Indeed, this is the main point of the paragraph. We see here no development of the idea that Christ, like Abraham, exercises faith in the promises of God.

My point is this: the law, which came four hundred thirty years later, does not annul a covenant previously ratified by God, so as to nullify the promise (3:17). Paul now returns to the question of how God's covenant with Abraham relates to that with Moses, the covenant of Law. Verse 15 emphasized the permanency of a will, or covenant. Now Paul appeals to the chronological order of the covenants. A long period of time, 430 years, separates the two covenants. This figure apparently comes from Exodus 12:40 (Gen 15:13 and Acts 7:6 say four hundred years). All of these numbers are for the sojourn in Egypt, not the full span of time from Abraham to Moses. The number in a general way refers to the time period and emphasizes its length (see below).

Paul's main point, as he states, is that the later covenant does not cancel out the former. As noted in verse 15, this claim is based on the assumption that God's consistent character would not allow God to turn against a covenant once made. Therefore, the promise aspect of the first covenant is still valid and will always remain so.

Furthermore, the lengthy time suggests that right relationship with God is possible without the Law. (Note that Paul is *not* denying that obedience was part of the covenant with Abraham.)

Paul's opponents might well have responded that circumcision, their primary concern, was already part of the Abrahamic covenant (Gen 17:9-14). Paul may have pressed the point that the covenant-making accounts in Genesis 12 and 15, where the righteousness-by-faith motif is found, preceded and did not include the circumcision command. Consequently, the faith/promise form of spirituality is primary and sufficient in itself to establish the divine-human relationship. In Paul there is a kind of primitivism that sees the purer form of a thing in its first or early appearance. In this Paul stands on good authority. The same viewpoint is present in Jesus when he gives priority to the creation account over Moses on the question of divorce (Matt 19:3-9).

For if the inheritance is by the law, it is no longer by promise (3:18a-b RSV). The word *inheritance* introduces new vocabulary, but not a new concept. *The blessing of Abraham* and *the promise of the Spirit* (3:14) refer to something passed down through the generations. Inheritance now becomes an important concept in what follows, as in 3:29; 4:1, 7, 30. The concept reflects the forward-looking (eschatological) perspective of the early church, when looking backward on the history of salvation, when looking forward to the present time, and when looking at the fulfillment of God's purposes in the future. Here Paul's point is that the inheritance depends on promise, not on the Law. God's blessing of the Gentiles and God's gift of the Spirit (3:8-9, 14) are inseparable from the mode by which they were given, that is, by promise. In any case, the Law would not be able to deliver the kind of spiritual benefit the Galatians have experienced: their new status in the people of God and the empowerment of the Spirit.

The inheritance came by means of promise: *God gave it to Abraham by a promise* (3:18c RSV). Significantly, the word here for *gave* has the special meaning of a giving out of graciousness, as gift. Paul's use of this verb touches on another key concept for him: grace. Grace, promise, and faith are perfectly matching ideas. Out of grace God is moved to offer a promise that is received and made effective on the basis of human faith. The tense (perfect) of the verb emphasizes the ongoing validity and relevance of God's ancient promises to Abraham, which are precisely what make it an inheritance.

THE TEXT IN BIBLICAL CONTEXT

The New Testament View of the Old Testament

All the writers of the New Testament had to come to terms with the relationship of the old and the new. The confession of Jesus as Messiah and as exalted Lord was so novel and weighty a matter that radical shifts in perspective were bound to follow. In some manner all writings in the New Testament reflect the need to define the consequence of God's new deed in Jesus the Christ for the older biblical tradition. All the authors acknowledge that Christ has brought a significant change. Furthermore, Christ is granted a position of authority over the Law of Moses. This perspective is grounded in Jesus' own teaching, in which he criticized certain contemporary interpretations of the Law, redefined some priorities within the Scriptures, pointed to a level of spirituality beyond the Law, and placed himself over the Law. Yet he accepted the Old Testament's fundamental truthfulness and validity (see esp. Matt 5:17-48). At the same time New Testament writers themselves show considerable variety in the way they describe God's action in Christ and its continuity and discontinuity with God's action of old, and in the degree of unity and diversity they find between them.

In Galatians 3 Paul offers an interpretation of Scripture that is one of most explicit and compelling in the New Testament. Paul attempts a nuanced balance of unity and difference both within Scripture (for Paul, the OT) and between God's past and present acts in history. Because the Abrahamic covenant, which is based on faith, is irrevocable, Paul places it at the foundation of all biblical covenants. This creates a unity across the entire Bible. By implication, Paul thus acknowledges that God intended faith to be the ground of the Mosaic covenant as well. He does not say this directly, but in 3:21 he explicitly observes that the Law is not against the promises (of the Abrahamic covenant). Compatibility is possible. (Modern biblical study also recognizes that the Law regulates a relationship that earlier was established on the basis of God's gracious act of redemption, as observable in the prologue to the Decalogue [Exod 20:2]).

Thus Paul affirms, by implication, the essential unity of all God's covenantal relationships with humanity. Within this picture of unity, however, Paul's view differs from others in two important ways. First, the Law is secondary because life with God existed before the Law, and it is temporary because its rationale existed only until Christ came. Second, the coming of Christ represents a significant fulfillment of the divine purpose. The fulfillment surpasses what preceded it, even though the fundamental principle of faith is present in old and new. It is the *promise* character of the Abrahamic covenant that is important in this regard. A promissory covenant signals future developments with greater fulfillment. Therefore the promise correlates with the new and better covenant in Christ. Since the Law, taken by itself as legal demand, does not contain promise (cf. 3:12), it cannot anticipate Christ and consequently does not serve as the ground of unity in God's purposes.

THE TEXT IN THE LIFE OF THE CHURCH

A Christian View of the Old Testament Scriptures

Just as the continuity and discontinuity of God's action in Christ with God's saving action in the past exercised the New Testament writers, so the continuity and discontinuity of the Old and New Testaments have never entirely been put to rest in the history of the church. Some have rejected the Old Testament completely, claiming that it reflects a different god than the God of the New Testament. Others accept the two testaments as fully equal. The seasoned view of the greater part of the Christian church is that the Old Testament remains authoritative Scripture for the church as long as it is interpreted in the light of the fuller revelation in Christ. The Protestant Reformation interpreted the Old Testament so as to show its anticipation of Christ. The Radical Reformers (Anabaptists) made Christ the norm for interpretation not only in matters of salvation but also in questions of ecclesiology and ethics. One implication of this is that the union of church and state reflected in the Old Testament can no longer serve as norm for the Christian church. Another is that warfare cannot be normative for the church because Jesus' demand is to love one's neighbor and enemy unconditionally.

Largely because of the habit of some reformers to qualify or limit the lordship of Christ by appealing to Old Testament Scriptures, the Anabaptists stood near the discontinuity end of the spectrum in their views on how the testaments relate. However much we can appreciate the historical reasons for this, Anabaptists today would do better to retain the Anabaptists' emphasis on the centrality of Christ as an interpretive criterion while letting go of the Anabaptists' relative denigration of the Old Testament.

Paul's teaching has a particular relevance in our time in relation to a popular teaching called dispensationalism. According to this school of thought, the time of the church is a parenthesis between the dispensation (or time period) of the Law and a millennial (thousand-year) age (based on Rev 20) at the end of time. During the millennium, the Old Testament economy of salvation will be re-established, it is alleged. From this comes the idea of the church age, also known as the age of grace, as a parenthesis between two similar ages of Law. Clearly, Paul would turn this scheme of dispensations or covenants on its head. For him, the time of the *Law* is a time of parenthesis, since it has the character of a temporary arrangement within the larger and more fundamental covenant of faith. The gospel of Jesus Christ, based as it is in the gracious work of God in Christ and the Spirit, is the climactic development in the story of salvation. The future will bring this salvation to full realization but will never replace it with another form of covenant between God and humanity.

Place of the Law
Galatians 3:19-24

PREVIEW

Now that Paul has satisfactorily shown how the Law does not replace or supersede God's promise to Abraham, he has a new problem. If the Abrahamic covenant of promise/faith remains in force and has clear priority over the Law of Moses, what good was the Law in the first place? If Paul wishes to preserve the authority of the Scriptures and the unity of God's purposes, he will need to show how the Law had a positive role to play, even if its role was limited. In response, Paul describes the role of the Law as preparing the way for Christ. The specific role is that of bringing some measure of control over transgressions until Christ would come. But now Christ offers more. He offers new life before God by faith that overcomes our enslavement to sin. Since the Law could not achieve this, the Law must give way to what is better.

EXPLANATORY NOTES

To this point the argument has set the Law over against promise and in an inferior position. The reader will naturally wonder why the Law was necessary at all, perhaps even whether it could be from the same god! Two rhetorical questions articulate these thoughts. In 3:19 Paul answers the first question, *Why then the law?* The second question will be addressed in verse 21 with the assertion that promise and Law are not incompatible when each is understood rightly.

We therefore immediately observe that in Paul's view the Law is not entirely negative. In short, the Law is good (cf. Rom 7:12) as long as it does not claim too much or usurp the place of honor that belongs only to faith-based-on-promise.

It was added because of transgressions, until the offspring would come to whom the promise had been made (3:19b). The Law then was given *because of transgressions*. This key statement is open to various interpretations. The preposition can mean either "on account of" or "for the sake of." There is a range of views on what exactly Paul means here, with a corresponding range of negative to positive implications for the Law's role. At the negative extreme is the idea that the Law was intended to provoke (i.e., cause or increase) transgressions: God gave the Law to increase awareness of the need for salvation by grace. One translation of Romans 5:20 communicates this sense: "Law came in, to increase the trespass" (RSV). Another sees it otherwise: "Law came in, with the result that the trespass multiplied (NRSV). At the positive end of the spectrum is the idea that the Law was given to provide a *remedy* for sin in the sacrificial system prescribed by the Law.

However, Paul's own subsequent comments in Galatians 3:22-25 offer the most reliable window on his thinking. The role of the Law is that of the disciplinarian or the moral guardian of a minor. In this sense, the Law raised moral awareness (and thus also rendered a person morally accountable) and corrected moral lapses. In this sense, the purpose of the Law in "increasing sin" is to be understood as increasing awareness and responsibility. What is increased is actually *transgression*, a breaking of the law. Paul is thinking about sin committed after the giving of the Law, for, as he says in Romans 4:15, "Where there is no law, neither is there violation" (lit. transgression). This is why Paul speaks of an increase—an increase not of moral decadence but of moral accountability. Paul probably means that ultimately the Law was given to deter sin. Such an idea does not contradict Romans 7, which speaks of a stimulus to sin when there is knowledge of law. That is what happens when sin *exploits* the Law, but such exploitation was not God's intent for the Law, which is the point Paul is making here.

In describing the function of the Law, Paul makes several additional points. The Law was *added*. This does not contradict 3:15, since here the same one who made the original covenant modifies it. Clearly this does not mean that the Law completed the defective covenant of promise. Rather, it indicates the subsequent arrival of the Law and its secondary status as an addendum to the principal covenant with Abraham. At the same time, the expression shows that the two covenants are not fundamentally incompatible. In fact, the implication is that God intended the Sinai covenant to be grounded in the Abrahamic covenant, that is, in faith (cf. v. 21).

Second, the phrase *until the offspring would come* (3:19c) makes the point that the role of the Law is limited in time. It functions until the arrival of Abraham's offspring, who is Jesus Christ, the one to whom the promise was made (cf. 3:16). The clear implication is that the Law has both a beginning and an end. That this claim could have come from the mouth of a Jew would have been stunning to the average Jew, for whom the Law shared in the eternal character of God, who gave it.

We encounter another major issue with Paul's observation that the Law *was ordained through angels by a mediator* (3:19d) and with his commentary on that fact: *Now a mediator involves more than one party; but God is one* (3:20). The perceptive reader may notice that Paul is profuse in naming God as the author of the covenant with Abraham but avoids doing the same with the Law. In verse 19 he uses the passive voice of "add," which implies God as the acting subject without naming God directly (called the divine passive). Paul believes that God gave the Law, but he consciously or unconsciously wants to associate God more with the covenant of promise than with the Law. This is confirmed by Paul's comments about the role of angels and a mediator. The Law was ordained *through* angels and *by the hand of* a mediator (lit.). We should understand the mediator to be Moses (cf. Lev 26:46 LXX). The assistance of angels is based on Jewish interpretation of Deuteronomy 33:2, an interpretation also reflected in Acts 7:38, 53; and Hebrews 2:2.

Paul's cryptic comment on this implies that the mediated character of the Law is an imperfection. The Law has a mixed origin, with multiple actors. In contrast, God is one. Paul's appeal to Israel's monotheism suggests some kind of compromise in the giving of the Law. What exactly that might be, Paul does not say. Is he suggesting that the directness of communication and fellowship with Abraham represents a higher spiritual value than the distancing of mediation? We should perhaps not read too much into this. Paul may be using an ad hominem form of argument meant to put the opposition on the defensive by posing a logical quandary, rather than setting forth an important and firm truth (see TBC, "Rhetoric and Truth").

In any case, Paul's argument turns the most basic theological conviction of Judaism—monotheism—against its most important source of identity, the Law. Clearly Paul believes that God has authored the Law. After all, Paul clearly identifies the angels and the mediator as agents, not the source. That leaves only God as the originator. In some sense, therefore, the Law serves the purposes of God and, as defined above, has a positive role to fill. But Paul also appears to question whether the Law in its giving represents monotheism in its purest form.

If Paul's critique of the Law raised the issue of its purpose, it also raises the burning question of whether the Law and the promises are fundamentally antithetical. Paul states the question rhetorically: *Is the law then opposed to the promises of God?* (3:21a). He responds with a typical Pauline rejoinder to his hypothetical interlocutor: *Certainly not!* It is crucial to hear Paul on this. However much the way of promise and the way of law differ in their character, they play complementary roles in a compatible relationship, in a way comparable to how spouses with different personalities can make a happy marriage. So Paul's problem is not with the Law itself but with a view of the Law that loses touch with its foundation in promise. When the Law is not subordinate to promise, it becomes an absolute that distorts the larger will of God (e.g., blessing to the nations), and it fails to give way to Christ, who is greater.

A further explanation of the emphatic denial follows. *For if a law had been given that could make alive, then righteousness would indeed come through the law* (3:21b). Paul states this thought in the form of a conditional sentence indicating that the condition is not true. Righteousness cannot come by the Law since the Law cannot make alive. What light this contributes to the claim that the Law is not against the promises is not immediately evident. The thought may be that since life cannot come by the Law, then there is no competition with the promises, which are, in fact, the key to life. This would confirm the observation (above) that Law and promise are compatible when each is granted its rightful place and role.

We have already encountered the concept of life at several places in the letter—2:19; 3:11-12. There we noted that Paul uses the concept in Galatians to indicate quality of life—the vitality that makes possible a full existence—in relationships and in behavior. Thus righteousness, both in the sense of right standing with God and of right living before God, must be grounded in a life-giving source. The Law does not qualify for this. Only God, active in Christ and in the work of the Spirit, enables the promise/faith mode of relating to God. The present verse is the clearest expression of this perspective.

The assertion that the Law does not *make alive* appears to contradict Leviticus 18:5, *Whoever does the works of the law will live by them,* which Paul himself cites in Galatians 3:12. But Paul's point may be that although the Law intended life, it could not, in fact, achieve it. This is the clear sense of Romans 7:10, which attributes to the Law (as commandment) a promise of life, but then states that, in practice, the Law brought death because sin exploited it for evil ends (cf. Rom 8:3-4). Paul acknowledges that the Law aspires to give life, but he holds that it fails to achieve this apart from faith in Christ. With this insight we are at the heart of Paul's thinking on the Law.

But the scripture has imprisoned all things under the power of sin (3:22a). The emphatic *but* announces a sharp contrast. While the Law does not give life, the Scriptures (which contain the Law) disclose all creation's bondage to sin. Thus the Law functions as an agent of imprisonment rather than a giver of life. Paul chooses to attribute the imprisonment to the Scriptures themselves, which contain the Law. Specific texts of the kind Paul may have had in mind can be seen in Romans 3:10-18. As those texts show, Paul sees the explicit claim of universal culpability before God throughout Scripture, not only in the Law itself (the Torah). That explains why he here makes *Scripture* the agent of imprisonment, even though in the following verses the *Law* is the actual cause of the bondage. Paul personifies the Scripture as he did in 3:8. Here Paul portrays Scripture as the expression of the will and action of God (cf. Rom 11:32, where God is the acting subject in a parallel statement).

The verb translated as *imprisoned* rightly evokes confinement in prison. But does Paul have in mind the more negative sense of punitive confinement, or the more positive sense of protective or disciplinary custody? No doubt the emphasis is on the negative, even though an element of the positive appears even here. To be under sin and its power is undesirable. Still, the ultimate aim is constructive (cf. v. 24). In the nearest parallel to this statement in Romans 11:32, Paul says, "For God has imprisoned [same verb] all in disobedience so that he may be merciful to all." Here the positive intent of the imprisonment is explicit. Moreover, in our present passage Paul is still answering the question of whether the Law is contrary to God's promises. One would therefore expect his response to have a positive implication. The section from 3:22 to 4:11 plays on this two-sided condition of existence under the Law; it is a kind of benevolent bondage.

The Scripture thus openly and clearly reveals that all things are under the dominion of sin. Like a drumbeat, the recurring use of the preposition *under* throughout this larger section of the letter announces the universal condition of enslavement. Two other details are significant. The words *all things* imply the imprisonment of not only the human world but also the entire created order (cf. Rom 8:20-21!). By using the word *sin* in this context rather than *transgression*, Paul indicates the moral disorder of the entire world, including Jews who have disobeyed the Law, which is transgression (see on v. 19).

The positive purpose of Scripture's negative judgment on sin is *so that what was promised through faith in Jesus Christ might be given to those who believe* (3:22b). Here it is the ultimate positive result that is Paul's focus. Paul states this result in the now-familiar terms of *promise* and *faith*—the primary themes of the whole section beginning at 2:15. Although Paul does not use the word *grace* here, the concept is present in the idea of a promise that is given by God. This is God's promise to Abraham that is fulfilled in the coming of Jesus Christ. In the present context, that promise focuses on receiving the Spirit (3:14) and becoming a child of God (3:26). It is a promise made effective in human experience to those who believe, those who have faith.

Here again we have the question of how to translate the phrase *faith in Jesus Christ*. Either *faith in Jesus Christ* or *faith of Jesus Christ* is grammatically possible. In the second case, a question still remains whether the faith is Christ's or whether Paul thinks of faith as referring to the whole event of Jesus Christ—faith defined by Jesus Christ. Up to this point we have argued for the second option (see on 2:16 [*The Faith of Jesus Christ, p. 305*]). The expression is thus Paul's short-hand for the gospel message, which has to do with Jesus Christ and his work, the benefit of which is received by faith. Although the believer's faith remains in the background, *faith* has come to stand for the whole of the gospel. This fits well with Paul's use of *faith* in the following verses (3:23, 25, in the expression *faith came*) to encompass the entire life and ministry of Jesus Christ. We have taken our cue from Galatians' clear uses of faith to stand for the entire Christian message, as in 1:23 and 6:10. In this case, Paul's emphasis is on the work of Jesus Christ and not on the believer's act of faith, which is stated in the next clause: *to those who believe*.

In sum, the expression *the promise by faith of Christ* (AT) describes God's plan of redemption in the work of Jesus Christ, which fulfills the promise rooted in the covenant with Abraham. The expression *to those who believe* describes the human reception of the divine provision. Thus the first expression is something of a technical label for the gospel. The second expression emphasizes the need for human acceptance of that gospel in order for the divine-human relationship to be realized.

Now before faith came, we were imprisoned and guarded under the law until faith would be revealed (3:23). The statement begins with a description of faith as an event: *faith came*. The prepositions *before* and *until* indicate a specific moment in time. The context shows unmistakably that this event is the appearance of Jesus Christ (note *until Christ* in the next verse). But Paul describes it here as the coming of faith. This coming of faith appears to be equivalent to the coming of the gospel. Once again (see on 3:22) we see *faith* standing for the whole of the gospel. Here Paul emphasizes that the gospel of faith is grounded in the story of Jesus the Christ. This is the meaning we have suggested for the expression *faith of Jesus Christ* (lit. as in 2:16; 3:22). Significant also is the characterization of this coming of faith as revelation: it is a divine disclosure. The good news based in the work of Jesus Christ is the revelation of God's purpose, not the revelation of mere human imagining (Gal 1:12; Rom 1:17).

But why does Paul speak of faith "coming" and being revealed when he has earlier argued that faith came to Abraham, before the Law? Is Paul suggesting that faith reenters the picture after the parenthesis of the Law? This is unlikely, since, as we have argued (3:19), Paul does not exclude faith from the time of the Law. More likely it indicates that Paul thinks of the time of Christ as significantly, though not totally, new (cf. "But now, apart from the law . . . [though] attested by the law," Rom 3:21). This is a fulfillment, a fulfillment of the promises contained in that preliminary appearance of faith in Abraham, not a mere repetition of it.

The NRSV reverses the original order of the verbs with its *imprisoned and guarded*. The literal translation would be: *we were guarded, being imprisoned*. The second verb, *imprisoned*, links this verse with the same verb in the previous verse. The two verbs are in the passive form, with no expressed doers of the action. The unstated actor of *guarded* could well be the Law, as suggested by the phrase, *under the law*. Moreover, the following two verses express the same idea with clear reference to the Law as disciplinarian. Thus Paul is saying that Scripture and the Law overlap in this function of custody. As already stated, Paul deliberately alludes to both negative and positive aspects of this custody role. The unspoken actors of these verbs allow for such a double play in the mind of the reader. As it is, the passive verbs draw attention to the ones receiving the action, expressed here with the pronoun *we*.

In this and the following two verses, the pronoun *we* surely refers to the Jewish people, with Paul identifying himself with his people. *We* were the ones under the Law. The pronoun *you* in verses

26-29 refers to the Gentile Galatians. But this distinction should not be understood as a sharp separation. It reflects different past experiences. The shift here and in 4:5-6 has the intended effect of linking the two experiences, even while recognizing the different histories of Jew and Gentile. All are under the bondage of sin. The Galatian believers should sense their detachment from the Law just as the Jewish believers should. At the same time, they should embrace their inclusion as children of God, equal participants with their fellow Jewish believers in the grand story of redemption.

Therefore the law was our disciplinarian until Christ came, so that we might be justified by faith (3:24). In the original this sentence is a subordinate clause, expressing the result of the guarding action in the previous verse. The Law has the role of a *disciplinarian*. We have already noticed that Paul uses this word in a positive sense with respect to the Law (3:19, 22). The reason lies in the relative precision of the image of the disciplinarian. The word transliterates as *pedagogue*. However, it does not have the modern meaning of one who instructs or teaches.

In this image some have seen a view of the Law as a teacher pointing to Christ. This is certainly incorrect. In the Greco-Roman world the *pedagogue* was the person, usually a slave, who was a constant guardian of a young boy. The role of the *pedagogue* was primarily positive, meant for the good of the young person. The *pedagogue* guarded the youth from bad influences and thus assisted in the youth's moral development. This might well involve correction and discipline. The NRSV translation as *disciplinarian* is appropriate so long as the word is not understood only in a punitive sense. As important for Paul, the authority of the *pedagogue* lasted for a limited time, until the youth reached maturity. This fits with Paul's point about the temporary role of the Law. Paul makes the connection explicitly in 4:1-2.

Earlier English translations reflected an educative role (schoolmaster, tutor) for the *pedagogue* and understood the prepositional phrase about Christ to mean *to Christ*. The Law was to be a teacher that would bring us to Christ. But this is surely wrong. The preposition is the same as that in the preceding verse, which speaks of imprisonment *until* faith is revealed. The preposition has an undeniable temporal meaning, as in the NRSV reading, *until Christ came*. Indeed, the preposition gives the nuance that the guarding action (of vv. 23-24) has the purpose of preparing for Christ.

A purpose clause completes verse 24: *so that we might be justified by faith*. It is couched in language that goes all the way back to

2:16—*justified by faith*. Paul, of course, does not mean that the Law's role as disciplinarian makes one right with God. Rather, he means that the Law held God's people in a protected state so that, when Christ came, they were ready for the gospel, which offers right relationship with God based on faith. Exactly how Paul conceives of this protected state he does not say (but see the discussion on 3:19-23). The primary point is that God's people have been kept (or guarded) within the realm of God's will and purpose so that they are ready for the Messiah's coming. The idea is thus closely related to the concept of *fullness of time* in 4:4.

THE TEXT IN BIBLICAL CONTEXT

Monotheism in Paul and the Old Testament

Paul's theology is rooted in his Jewish heritage, as clearly shown in the way he draws applications from Deuteronomy's teaching that God is one: there is one God (Gal 3:20). The Jewish rejection of all idolatry, so central to their theology, appears in Paul's criticism of paganism (4:8) and in his denial of spiritual significance to food offered to idols, since those gods have no reality (1 Cor 8:4-6). Consequently, Paul finds fresh insights and applications of monotheism in support of the gospel. Belief in one God implies a basic oneness and unity in the world created by God. God excludes other gods and other systems of truth.

One temptation for Israel was to use monotheism to set itself apart from other peoples as the exclusive people of God. Deuteronomy itself repeatedly warns against this (e.g., 7:7-11). Here Paul exploits Judaism's insistence on monotheism to strengthen his argument for the oneness of Jew and Gentile in the gospel, both of whom are made right with God by one means, by faith (Rom 3:29-30; cf. the book of Jonah). Here in Galatians, Paul claims that monotheism privileges immediacy and singularity in God's relationship with humans over any form of relationship that is mediated (3:20). This insight supports Paul's argument for the secondary position of the Law within the economy of God. Finally, Paul's commitment to monotheism protected the early church from conceiving of Christ or the Spirit as divine beings separate from God.

Life and Law

In our passage Paul is emphatic that the Law cannot give life. At key points throughout the letter, Paul uses *life* to describe the ideal human condition before God. On this last point Paul is simply following a biblical tradition that shows up particularly in Deuteronomy and in John's gospel. John agrees with Paul that life in its true and full form, "abundant life," is found in Jesus Christ (John 1:3; 10:10; 14:6). However, in Deuteronomy, life is related to the observance of the Law that God gave to Moses (Deut 5:33 and throughout). And in Psalms 1 and 119, the psalmist is thankful for the Law as an aid to fellowship with God and to happy living.

The positive claims for the Law in Deuteronomy and the Psalms appear to contradict Paul's claims in our Galatians passage. How are we to think about this? To begin with, Paul's view is more complex than a simple denial that the Law cannot make alive. In Romans 7:10 Paul acknowledges that the Law promised life. In that same context, Paul clarifies that while the Law aspired to life, sin used it to produce death. The Law did not arrive at its intended goal. Paul does not deny that good may come from the Law or that it may accomplish some control of evil. However, Paul does see the Law as powerless in itself. As a result, it can come under the power of either good or evil. In this sense, the Law is ambiguous.

A careful reading of the Deuteronomy and Psalms passages cited above shows that life does not come from the Law itself. The Law is a protector of the relationship with God, teaching and reminding people of what will threaten or enhance life before God. Law observance does not constitute the relationship itself. Loving God with heart, soul, and might is the ground of that relationship (Deut 6:5). Like the Old Testament prophets and Jesus himself, Paul is aware that the Law can become, and has become, an end in itself rather than the means to spiritual ends and human good. When this happens, Law is out of its proper place. Paul often sees the Law as a guide in defining what is right and good, if it is clearly subordinated to the faith relationship in Christ and reinterpreted in light of what is new in the gospel. There is, then, broad agreement throughout the Scriptures on the essential relationship of Law and life, although the particular angle of vision varies according to an author's context and interest.

Rhetoric and Truth

In interpreting Paul's letter to the Galatians, it is important to recognize the considerable significance of the rhetorical style Paul uses. Rhetoric has to do with how one says something to achieve a desired outcome. Truth relates more particularly to what is said and its veracity. Yet the two are interrelated. For example, I may choose to use hyperbole (exaggeration) to make a point more forceful. If so, the truthfulness of what I say must be judged in the light of my mode of communication; otherwise an understanding of that truth may be distorted. It is clear beyond doubt that Paul uses a highly charged form of rhetoric in Galatians. Paul is passionate about persuading the readers of the truth (as he sees it). In Galatians we should not expect a finely tuned, carefully qualified, and comprehensive treatment of the themes he addresses.

Paul uses arguments he thinks will persuade his particular audience, even when he does not actually consider them the strongest arguments. These are called ad hominem arguments. That this is the case is indicated by the fact that Paul does not repeat some of these arguments in his later letter to the Romans, which treats similar themes under less polemical circumstances. And this is true even where the same fundamental perspective in the two writings is clearly discernible. Possible examples unique to Galatians are the offspring (3:16) and intermediary (3:19-20) arguments, and the allegory of Hagar and Sarah (4:21–5:1). The practical implication of all this is that Galatians needs to be interpreted in the light of Paul's complete writings [Literary and Rhetorical Features of Galatians, p. 314].

THE TEXT IN THE LIFE OF THE CHURCH

The Law and Christians

With the apostle Paul, we can and should confess that the Law was a legitimate part of God's unfolding purpose for the people of God. It was not a mistake, nor was it incompatible with the rest of God's plan of redemption. However, it was an incomplete and imperfect solution to human need. Now, in light of God's decisive act in Christ, it would be retrograde to base one's spirituality in the Law. That would be moving in a backward direction, while God's purposes in history always move forward.

The basic reason we do not give primary authority to the Law is that One who is greater than Moses is here (Heb 3:1-6). This in turn has both negative and positive implications. From the new perspective of Christ's coming, the Law had shortcomings (as even Peter acknowledges in Acts 15:10). They can be summed up in the idea that the Law does not mediate life. Although the Law describes and defines what is right and wrong, it does not bring to life what is right as a reality in human lives. Law is a thing, something without life in itself. It has no inherent energy to accomplish its ideals. So the Law makes us aware of sin, but it does not provide help for our weakness as sinners (cf. Rom 8:3-4).

That brings us to the positive implication of the news that Christ brings. The source of life has always been in God. Now, apart from the Law, life is available at a new and greater level. In the living person of Christ, we can have a living relationship with God, the source of life. And in the Spirit of God, who is the living God present with us, we have a source of living energy, empowering us to do good and to resist evil. In Galatians, Paul focuses on these very points: how we live to God through Christ and how the Spirit assists us in such a life.

In our personal lives and in the life of the church, it is crucial that we give priority to the true sources of life. Our ministries of nurture should focus on the spirituality of our relationships with Christ and on being open to the Spirit. In the pursuit of righteousness, it is good to urge people to do what is right. But in making this appeal, it is too easy to fall back on group standards or social expectations to gain our leverage. However, this is the way of law and flesh, to use Paul's terms in Galatians. It is a shortcut, creating an artificial righteousness that will last only as long as the external pressure to conform remains present.

Does all this mean the Law is now worthless to the Christian? Not at all! Paul holds that it has continuing worth. Although he does not develop a full rationale for his continuing embrace of the Law, Paul's practice of appealing to the Law in numerous contexts in his writings, as in Galatians 5–6, supports this. He can even speak of *the law of Christ* (6:2). When Paul urges believers to identify the will of God, he does not hesitate to cite the Law. Nor is Paul contrary to formulating new laws in the sense of specific rules or guidelines of conduct for his churches. According to Paul, even though the danger of legalism is real, the way forward is not antinomianism—the rejection of any form of law as ethical definition. With Paul, we need a keen sense that the Mosaic Law, and indeed any law, (1) is subordinate to the high principle of life and fellowship with God; (2) answers to the values and ideals that Jesus Christ lived and taught; (3) makes room for the decisive revelation of God in Christ; and (4) is subject to the living discernment of the Spirit in changing times and places.

Fulfillment in Christ

Galatians 3:25-29

PREVIEW

Few messages in this world are as powerful or as revolutionary as the message we have in this paragraph. The good news of Christ Jesus has created a wonderful seismic shift—an earthquake of grace that has suddenly leveled the previously jagged terrain of unequal social status. *There is no longer Jew or Greek, there is no longer slave or free, there is no longer male and female; for all of you are one in Christ Jesus* (3:28). Hallelujah! But not only are those *in Christ* on a level playing field; God's reintroduction of faith through Christ also has the effect of including all, Jew and Gentile, in the family of God, making all, Jew and Gentile, children of Abraham!

The status of the Christian believers as children of God is central to this paragraph. This image serves Paul in several ways. As family imagery, it connects with the theme of standing in the heritage of Abraham (3:29). In applying the phrase *children of God* (3:26) to followers of Christ, Paul is radically expanding what was an important Jewish self-designation. *All* believers in Christ, Jew and Gentile alike, can now claim the heritage of the people of God (cf. 6:16, *the Israel of God*). Moreover, Paul uses the intimate family imagery here to support his contention that the good news restores intimate relationship with God (see the *in Christ* language here and contrast 3:19-20). Finally, the image of children of God strongly reinforces the theme of unity of Jew and Gentile while extending that theme to all areas of life (3:28).

EXPLANATORY NOTES

The transition point from the previous paragraph to the next is not sharply defined. Verse 25 closes the discussion of the Law as disciplinarian, but it also begins the description of what existence in the time of fulfillment is like. A conjunction (*but*) links verses 25 and 26 closely. By verse 26, the topic is clearly no longer the place of the Law. The transition is clear, but the exact point to mark it is not.

But now that faith has come, we are no longer subject to a disciplinarian (3:25). With this statement, Paul concludes his illustration based on the figure of the *pedagogue*. Again Paul depicts faith as historical event, referring to the entire saving event of Christ (see also 3:23). That the role of the disciplinarian is temporary was alluded to in verse 24: *until Christ came*. Now Paul states that fact in bald terms: *no longer subject.* Paul is referring, of course, to the termination of the Law's authority and control. The pronoun *we* reflects the perspective of believing Jews. They are the ones who have experienced the transition from the Mosaic covenant to Christ. But the real point Paul wants to make is that there is now no reason for the Gentile Galatians to think that the Law has authority over them. This explains the sudden shift of pronouns, *we* to *you*, from this verse to the next.

Paul appears to accept the continuation of Jewish practices for Jewish Christians on the condition that such practices not conflict with the covenant ideals of Christ-centered faith or the unity of all persons in Christ. However, neither Jew nor Gentile is obligated to the Law as Law. Paul's insistence on freedom for the Gentiles put him in conflict with the more conservative party, which was requiring all believers to take on a Jewish way of life. That Paul extended this freedom also to the Jewish believers apparently put him in conflict with the *pillars* (2:9) in Jerusalem. For Paul, neither being circumcised nor being uncircumcised had any moral weight in themselves, as he states explicitly in 5:6 and 6:15.

For in Christ Jesus you are all children of God through faith (3:26). Paul emphasizes the word *all* and the phrase *in Christ Jesus* by means of their positions in the sentence. NRSV is certainly correct to connect *in Christ Jesus* to the status of children of God, rather than to *faith* (not *faith in Christ Jesus*), as a wooden adherence to the Greek word order might suggest. The next verses clearly connect being *in Christ* with being a child of God. Paul is accenting the points, by now familiar to the reader/hearer, that all people are now invited into the family of God and that Jesus Christ is the norm that determines everything for the true people of God. To these points Paul adds the other dominant theme of *faith* as the means by which persons enter into the new reality in Christ. Paul restates these points here to explain why the time of the Law is necessarily ending (note the conjunction *for*).

What is novel is the concept of *children of God*, introduced here for the first time in the letter. (But notice the parallel concept *children of Abraham*, in 3:7, 29 NLT.) The phrase figures significantly in 4:5-7 and in 4:21-31 (cf. Rom 8:14-19). The terminology is common in many religions to express relatedness to and ownership by the deity. Paul, however, is reflecting the tendency in Scripture to refer to Israel as the elect people of God, as a son (e.g., Exod 4:22-23; Hos 11:1) or sons/children (e.g., Deut 14:1). For the multiple resonances of this family language with Paul's interests in Galatians, and its persuasive power, see the Preview above. In the light of 4:7, Paul is keen to contrast being a son or daughter and being a slave. Indeed, these two metaphors illuminate the difference between being under the Law and being in Christ.

The phrase *in Christ Jesus* both continues a previous theme (1:22; 2:4, 17; 3:14) and opens up a discussion in the next three verses, expanding on it. Here, where Paul is noting key features of the gospel that surpass the Law, he shows just how central it is to his thought (see also TBC on 2:20-21 and TBC/TLC on 4:19).

For as many of you as were baptized into Christ have clothed yourselves with Christ (3:27). The verse begins with the same conjunction (in Greek) as the previous verse, indicating that Paul is making an additional comment on the phrase *in Christ Jesus*. Not surprisingly, therefore, Paul describes baptism here as *into Christ*. The same idiom was used at the time in commerce to indicate a change of ownership. That nuance is likely present here, as the expression *you belong to Christ* in verse 29 confirms. But like *in Christ*, the phrase *into Christ* also connotes a depth of personal identity with the one in whose name believers are baptized (see additional comments on baptism at 3:28 and TBC).

The main assertion of the verse is that believers have put on Christ. The imagery is that of putting on clothing. Paul elucidates the more abstract image of being *in Christ* with a graphic variation. The image of clothing oneself was used widely at the time in the metaphorical sense of taking upon oneself a certain characteristic or even personality. For example, it was used of an actor who played a part or assumed the role of someone. This is particularly pertinent here where the believer puts on Christ. The clothing image appears throughout the Old and New Testaments for virtues or characteristics that someone assumes (e.g., Isa 61:10; Zech 3:3-5; Col 3:12, and of the power of the Spirit, e.g., Luke 24:49).

Paul speaks of putting on Christ in Romans 13:14 and uses the expression "clothe yourselves with the new self [lit. new man]" in Ephesians 4:24 and Colossians 3:10. All three passages have strong ethical concerns, and the latter two speak of the transformation in conversion from the old self to the new. Colossians 3:10-12 is particularly relevant because of its parallel to the next verse in Galatians. Here in Galatians 3:27, Paul confirms the close tie between conversion and ethics that we also found in 2:17-20. This is the basis for Paul's confidence that life in Christ is complete. It has no need of the Law for ethical direction or motivation. But the real point is that the genuine child of God has so deeply encountered the person of Jesus

Christ that the personality of that One, in all of his humanity, has been taken on by the believer. In using the image of clothing, Paul is clearly not suggesting that conversion is an external thing, put on, as it were, to cover up the real person underneath. Paul uses the metaphor to speak about actual change in the person.

The verb, *have clothed yourselves,* is in the aorist tense, which expresses a completed event. Paul is referring here to one's initial encounter with Christ, symbolized by baptism. (On the question of what Paul means by baptism, see comments on v. 28 and TBC). Paul says that everyone who has been baptized into Christ has put on Christ. The parallel passages of Romans 13:14 and Ephesians 4:24 assume that such action is an ongoing imperative for the believer. This is an example of the typical Pauline practice of using the language of a past divine action as the basis for an imperative in the present, the latter gaining its rationale and resource from the former. The reflexive form of this verb normally refers to the action of clothing oneself. However, when Paul uses this expression in the context of Christian experience, it connotes a human action of submission to the action of another—in this case, the action of God.

There is no longer Jew or Greek, there is no longer slave or free, there is no longer male and female; for all of you are one in Christ Jesus (3:28). The view has become popular that in verses 27-28 Paul is citing traditional material used in the practice of baptism. That is less likely for verse 27 because of its smooth connection with the preceding verse. We have noted that the shift of pronoun from *we* in verse 25 to *you* in verse 26 is Paul's editorial choice. The use of *you* in verses 27-28 continues that usage and is therefore not evidence of a quoted source. Nor is it even certain that the mention of baptism here is directly tied to the ritual practice of baptism (Dunn 1993: 203; Witherington: 276; see TBC on "Baptism in Paul"). It may reflect the spiritual reality of incorporation into Christ, which is the theme of verses 26-29.

There is a stronger basis for supposing that the first part of verse 28 represents a conventional formula used in baptism, since it recurs in similar, though not exact, forms elsewhere in Paul (1 Cor 12:13; Col 3:11) along with a reference to baptism. The statement is grammatically independent from the context and is quite formal in style. A primary reason that some take this as a baptismal formula is that only the Jew/Greek pair seems to relate to the argument of Galatians. But Paul may have included the slave/free and male/female pairs for other reasons (see below). In any event, Paul likely originated this expression because it fits his thought better than any other sources of early Christian convictions that we know about. Paul thought and spoke in novel and radical ways. In what setting he may have first used the formulation is uncertain. Judging by his marginal participation in the ritual of baptism (1 Cor 1:16-17), he most likely formulated this language in his teaching or writing ministry. Whether it was used in baptismal ritual is unknown.

The transition is abrupt from the idea of clothing oneself with Christ (v. 27) to the negation of social distinctions in the contrasting pairs, with which verse 28 begins. Only at the end of the verse does the connection with the preceding discussion become clear. There it is affirmed that being *in Christ* involves a condition of oneness that explains (note the conjunction *for*) the negation of social distinctions. None of those distinctions defines identity or social role as fundamentally as does being in Christ. None represents the ground of true oneness. Such oneness exists only in Christ Jesus. The sense is that our social unity and cohesiveness is not to be based on one of these social markings in our natural experience of life—ethnic/national identity, social class, or gender. Unity resides in the spiritual connection that believers share in Christ.

With this argument we find another confirmation that humanity's unity in Christ was central to Paul's gospel and a major concern in his ministry. Indeed, unity is one aspect of the realization of God's reign. For Paul, this unity requires a commitment to equality in all areas of social interaction, as illustrated in the Antioch incident (2:11-14).

Not surprisingly, the first pair in the list is *Jew or Greek* (as in 1 Cor 12:13; Col 3:11; cf. Rom 10:12). This was the big issue in Paul's ministry and the most divisive issue in the earliest church. It is one of the main themes in Galatians. Rather than the usual *Gentile*, we find *Greek*, a variation with basically the same implication. The succinct phrase is a direct denial of the Jewish self-identity based on exclusion of the Greek or any other people (cf. 2:15).

The *slave or free* pair evokes significant vocabulary in Galatians. However, Paul uses it here in reference to socioeconomic status—the institution of slavery in Greco-Roman culture over against the status of free citizen. Elsewhere in the letter, Paul speaks of bondage to sin and to the elements of the world, and of the Law over against freedom in Christ. This does not mean that Paul sees no connection between the two kinds of usage. Paul rejects any division between the spiritual and the material realms, as illustrated by the Antioch episode regarding how Jew and Gentile should relate (2:11-14). (On the question of how Paul applied the slave/free principle, see TBC.)

Conspicuous in the case of the male-female pair is the fact that the words are joined with *and* rather than *or*, as in the other two pairs. This is usually taken to reflect a conscious allusion to Genesis 1:27. Another possibility is that Paul's world did not know the same level of polarization in this area as it did in the areas of ethnic difference and social class. That is, Paul may be acknowledging that the patriarchy of his day had not risen to the level of public discourse in the way the others had. In any case, this formulation shows that Paul believed the gospel vision called for change in the way women and men relate in the church. Gender must not impede the unity and equality we have in Christ.

Parallel passages in 1 Corinthians 12:13 and Colossians 3:11 do not include Paul's leveling of gender. So why is it here? Perhaps Paul sees some readings of the Law as having negative effects on the position and role of women. After all, circumcision, which is central to the letter, is itself gender-specific since it excludes women. Paul thus celebrates the new level of freedom made possible in God's fulfilling action in Christ. The pair's absence in the other places *may* indicate that misunderstanding and abuse arose around this issue, as perhaps demonstrated at Corinth (1 Cor 11:1-16; 14:34-35).

A recent study has helpfully pointed out that the three pairs in this verse are found, either explicitly or implicitly, in the Genesis 17:9-14 passage, which sets the terms of the covenant of circumcision. Circumcision theoretically separates Israelites from other peoples. Although the practice was common in Egypt and its practice in Canaan was mixed, it was not practiced among the Philistines. Foreign slaves in Israel had to be circumcised, but free sojourners in Israel did not. Because only males carried the mark of circumcision, Paul may be deliberately referring to the three areas where the Old Testament observed social distinctions to underscore his point in Galatians that Christ has transcended the stipulations of the Law (cf. Martin: 111–25).

The last clause of the verse, *for all of you are one in Christ Jesus*, closely parallels verse 26. The word *all* is in the emphatic position in both statements. The phrase *in Christ Jesus* closes both sentences. What changes is the theme: the status of God's children in the earlier verse, and the reality of oneness or unity in the latter one. Our unity within the body of Christ expresses our common participation in the family of God, based on the shared communion in Christ.

And if you belong to Christ, then you are Abraham's offspring, heirs according to the promise (3:29). The statement has the character of a summary. It is cast in the form of a condition, but the grammar assumes the reality of the case in point. *Since you belong to Christ* catches the sense better. The expression *belong to Christ* is a variation on the previous *in Christ* and *put on Christ*. The reference to Abraham and to promise ties together the entire section that begins with 3:6. *Heirs* continues the theme of 3:18 and prepares for the opening of chapter 4. New, however, is the application of the word *seed* (*offspring*) to the followers of Christ. Earlier Paul argued that the promised seed of Abraham refers to Christ (3:16). Now Paul understands it as also referring to *believers* in Christ. This move is understandable in the light of Paul's insistence in verses 26-28 that believers are in full solidarity with Christ. One expression of this solidarity is the share they have in the heritage of Abraham.

THE TEXT IN BIBLICAL CONTEXT

Baptism in Paul

In our text the mention of baptism draws attention to the time of initiation into the Christian life. Paul obviously assumes that every believer receives baptism. What is not clear from this context is how much Paul thinks of the ritual itself as the occasion and means of the putting on of Christ, or whether he is referring to the action of the Spirit in conversion, using the symbol of baptism. First Corinthians 12:13, which parallels Galatians 3:27-28, associates baptism with the action of the Spirit. This is likely Paul's emphasis here as well. Paul's experience at Corinth indicates that he understood the rite of baptism as distinguishable from the spiritual event of conversion itself (see 1 Cor 1:14). This is consistent with Paul's argument in Galatians that the work of the Spirit counts above all else. Paul does not contrast the rite of baptism to the rite of circumcision, but does contrast the Spirit to circumcision.

At the same time, Paul's thought assumes a close connection of Spirit and water baptism. In ideal terms, the rite of baptism is a material action that symbolizes a spiritual action. The external action supports the spiritual reality by deepening its public and personal effects. The importance of the internal and the external in salvation is shown in Romans 10:9-10, where Paul similarly links verbal confession with believing in the heart. First Peter 3:21 reflects the same point of view.

Equality Issues in Paul

Paul's radical call to end racial and social distinctions in 3:28 must be guarded from distortion from several angles. On the one hand,

Paul does not presume to obliterate all such distinctions in human experience. The physical distinctions of gender are essential to God's purpose, and ethnic characteristics are morally neutral. Paul is not simply denying or rejecting any and all distinctions.

On the other hand, the Antioch incident in Galatians 2 shows beyond any doubt that Paul scrutinized situations around him with an eye for applying the spiritual principles of unity and equality to the mundane affairs of life, such as eating meals together. In explaining Paul, it does not work to harmonize New Testament passages by making this verse on equality apply only to some purely spiritual level while making other verses (e.g., 1 Tim 2:12, restricting women) apply to the practical level. If we are equal in the vertical relationship with Christ, we are also equal in the horizontal relationships with other persons.

Paul's ideal is to put into practice as much freedom and equality as possible without violating another ideal specific to Christ and the new people of God. It appears that sometimes Paul had to live with what was less than the ideal because of limitations within the wider culture (cf. slavery) and within the churches (cf. role of women). The book of Philemon shows Paul finding his way between the ideal of equality and the socioeconomic realities of his time on the question of slavery. Paul addresses the role of women in the church at several points (1 Cor 11:1-16; 14:34-35; and 1 Tim 2:8-15, where Paul's authorship is debated). There the picture is more complex because these texts use theological norms, such as headship, to address local and transient problems by calling for temporary restrictions. Paul sees the gospel as pressing toward maximal freedom without compromising an orderly church life (see TLC). In this stance, Paul appears to be ahead of other biblical writers but in step with the practice of Jesus, who included women in his ministry in an unprecedented manner for his time.

THE TEXT IN THE LIFE OF THE CHURCH

Gender Issues in the Church

Galatians 3:28 has become the rallying cry for the voices of freedom and liberation in the church. And with good reason! No other affirmation in Galatians offers such a striking and concrete articulation of the vision for freedom that pervades the letter. Paul's vision for the church, living in the freedom of Christ, is that it should demonstrate equality of status before God. Particularly significant here is that Paul uses this spiritual ideal to defend concrete questions of equality in social relationships (see the Antioch incident in Gal 2). How shall the church maintain a vision that drives toward full realization of the *glorious freedom of the children of God* (Rom 8:21 NIV 1984)? And how does this work out in the relationships and roles of women and men?

According to Paul's letters, three dimensions of experience bear on issues of gender. They are (1) creation differences in gender, (2) cultural conventions regarding gender, and (3) new creation effects on gender. First, God created male and female with differing physical features, some of which have a bearing on roles (e.g., childbearing). Less obvious are differences of personality traits typical of each gender—differences that true freedom and equality will respect.

Second, cultures develop customary ways in which women and men interact, sometimes turning social conventions into role prescriptions that exert powerful control over individuals. These conventions may reflect creation realities, but they also go beyond them. So, for example, typical gender differences may become rigid caricatures that do not respect individual differences and exceptions (e.g., not all men are less feeling than all women). Social expectations and structures can exert enormous force on people to submit to prescribed roles. Even if this differentiation makes the social mechanisms work smoothly, it does so at the price of violating individual freedom, which is also part of God's creative handiwork. In theological terms, because culture is a human creation, it may do much good even though it also inevitably reflects the sinful condition of the human race. Only the presence of sin limits full freedom and equality for gender (and other) relationships, and the church is justified in naming such limitations wrong and calling for change.

This brings us to the third dimension: new creation effects on gender. The good news of the gospel proclaims freedom and equality. The Spirit makes both men and women capable of tasks that go beyond natural endowments and cultural expectations. God calls the church to live by the ideals of the kingdom rather than the ideals of the unconverted world. This presents the church with one of its greatest challenges. As God's agent of change, the church respects human culture as a gift of God for the ordering of human life. But it also proclaims and lives out an alternative vision with a more just reality. This leaves the church with constant questions of how, where, and when to challenge society's norms. But amid these challenges, which require the best of the church's discernment, the will of God for justice and equality is clear enough and can serve as the grounds for confident action.

Freedom of God's Children
Galatians 4:1-7

PREVIEW

At this point Paul challenges the Galatians with an analogy. What do you want to be? Heirs or slaves? Being subject to the Law is like being minors in a household managed by guardians and trustees. For such minors, freedom is minimal indeed. But the redeeming action of the Holy Spirit has adopted the Galatians as children of God, which in turn has made them full heirs of God's promises! So Paul is asking, "How do you want it? Do you want to return to being slaves managed by others, or do you want to be free adults who will inherit the best of God's promises?" Paul tries to make the choice easy.

With the mention of *heirs* (3:29), Paul introduces another aspect of his theological argument for a gospel that does not depend on the Law. Being an heir is the overarching idea for this section. The word *heir* appears in the opening and closing clauses in a structural device known as inclusio. The metaphor *heir* lends itself well to Paul's interest. He wants to picture a movement in divine purpose from the promise given to the promise fulfilled, from Abraham to Jesus the Christ. Within that picture, he wants to show a period of time in which a special, if temporary, arrangement is made until the fulfillment. That temporary arrangement is the Law. The passing down of a family heritage has the same features. The child is the prospective owner from birth but must be under special custody and protection until reaching the age of maturity. That special custody is important, but only temporary. So it is in God's dealing with the family of God.

Within this analogy, Paul develops other ideas as well. He likens the status of the heir, while still a minor, to that of a slave. This permits further reflection on the condition of servitude under the Law, using a Greek philosophical concept of *elements* (4:3 KJV). The high point of the section comes when Paul describes the redemption in Christ that brings believers into the full status of children of God, ending the period of subjection under the Law.

EXPLANATORY NOTES

My point is this: heirs, as long as they are minors, are no better than slaves, though they are the owners of all the property (4:1). The thought picks up on the immediately preceding verse with the word *heir*. That metaphor has served the argument thus far to make both Christ and

Christian believers the rightful inheritors, or heirs, of the promises given to Abraham. Now Paul presses the family analogy further to illustrate the delay in time (during the time of the Law) between the beginning of God's family with Abraham and the entrance of the children into full possession of their rights and privileges.

During infancy and youth, a child is incapable of carrying responsibility for the family affairs. This is the status of the minor, who must wait for the time of maturity to enter fully into the benefits of family membership. The context (4:3 specifically) lets the reader know that the time of delay stands for the time of the Law. The analogy therefore lends itself to explaining the role of the Law as a necessary but temporary preparatory period, which anticipates its displacement by something better.

Paul is clearly reflecting cultural practices of inheritance in his social setting. What precise legal arrangement (Jewish, Greek, or Roman) he has in mind is a matter of debate. However, the basic concept of a period of minority status is understandable enough. As with most analogies, it is important not to press this analogy beyond the essential point Paul is making. For example, the fact that the older generation passes away before the new generation enters into the inheritance is irrelevant in the present case, where God is depicted as the father.

There is some tension between the analogy in verse 1 and the analogy of adoption in verse 5. This is due to the fact that the adoption as a child in verse 5 comes when entering into the maturity of the new covenant in Christ, but the analogy of the heir assumes the status of a child already before the time of maturity. This difference is, however, the result of the multilevel argument Paul is pursuing. The analogy of the heir deals with the movement of salvation history from Abraham through the Law and up to Jesus Christ. Here the Jew is already a child of God but not yet mature. On the other hand, the analogy of adoption focuses on the decisive event of redemption in Christ, when one moves from the status of slave to that of child. (Paul is consistent, however, in his belief that for both Israel and the church one becomes a child of God by adoption; cf. Rom 9:4.) More important for the unity of Paul's thought is his use of the image of slavery here in verse 1, even though (as described above) it creates a mixed metaphor and in verse 5 forces the change to the status of *sonship* (the literal form of a word Paul clearly intends to be gender-inclusive, as *childship*).

A child who is a minor differs in no way from the slave. This is not true in every sense, but is true in the area of inheritance, which is Paul's point here. The child is the prospective master of the household but does not have that full privilege during the years as a minor. This lack of control is no different from the situation of the slave in the same household.

But they remain under guardians and trustees until the date set by the father (4:2). The reference to oversight of the young child clearly connects with the *disciplinarian* of 3:24-25. Both instances speak of protective custody. The terms here are different, however. The terms *guardians* and *trustees* had a technical usage in cultural practices of the time, referring to roles in the household. The distinction between the two terms is not completely clear, but *guardian* was often used as a near synonym of *disciplinarian*, while *trustee* refers specifically to the administration of property. The fact that the trustee typically had a slave background fits well with Paul's point that the minor is no better off than a slave.

The word translated with the phrase *the date set* was used for legal deadlines and here refers to the time when the child gains majority status. The exact conditions under which a father had the power to set this date are unclear. The various terms used in the analogy could indicate that Paul is thinking of the case of an orphan. The father has already committed the family inheritance to the son and has set the date when the son receives full responsibility to manage the inheritance. However, Paul is obviously not making any application of the father's deceased status in the analogy.

So with us; while we were minors, we were enslaved to the elemental spirits of the world (4:3). Paul now clarifies the application of the analogy. The first-person plural pronouns (*we, us*) have the Jewish people as their logical referent. The analogy of the minor, as noted above, assumes the historical stages of Israel's faith experience. Verses 4-5 continue this frame of reference with the concepts of *fullness of time* and *under the law*. At the same time, the larger context makes clear that recent Gentile believers are incorporated into this story of God's people as *seed* of *Abraham* (3:29 KJV).

Paul now picks up the slave figure from the previous verse. He asserts more directly what was there only an allusion: people who are under the Law are in bondage! The precise expression is *enslaved under*, thus making a link to the repeated usage of the preposition *under* in relation to the Law (3:23), the disciplinarian (3:25), and the guardians and trustees in the preceding analogy. Paul's thought here is apocalyptic in the sense that all of these entities "under" which one might be are powers that can serve or oppose God's purposes. The inevitable and startling conclusion is that life under the

Law is, in some sense, enslavement. This would certainly have gotten the attention of Paul's audience!

Modern readers may be perplexed by Paul's description of the agents of enslavement as *elemental spirits of the world*. The term has no apparent connection to the story of Israel and the Law, about which Paul has been speaking (to say nothing of our own experience). This term comes not from the biblical tradition but from Greek philosophical thought. Paul is bridging two linguistic and symbolic worlds, the biblical and the secular. To translate this word as *elemental spirits* already offers a debatable interpretation. The NIV 1984, for example, translates it as *basic principles*. In these differences one can observe the basic choice between a more personified reference (*spirits*) and a more impersonal one (*principles*). As a neutral way to refer to the word, we might simply say *elements* (the word *spirit* itself is not present but is an interpretation).

The broader scope of Paul's writing (Gal 4:3, 8-10; Col 2:8, 20) suggests that he understood the term to refer primarily to ideas or practices by which a person, but especially a society, gives meaning and order to life. The term also connects realities on the historical plane with realities or beings in the spiritual realm. (For a defense of this interpretation, see TBC.) That Paul shares with his contemporaries this understanding of a connection between historical realities and spiritual beings is shown, for example, in his comments about angels being involved in the giving of the Law (3:19). This may be a particularly appropriate example because it may approach what Paul means in our verse when he links the Law to the *elements*. His real concern is with the way the Law is a regulating, ordering power in Israel that is inferior to Christ. At the same time he acknowledges a role for spiritual powers in mediating the Law to humans.

The main point in the present context is this: the Law is for the Jew an expression of the *elements* that hold sway over people by the power they wield to determine what is thought and done. Although Paul does not explain how this is true, we are probably to understand him in the following way. Because Paul views the Law as powerless to achieve its otherwise good ends, it has fallen prey to powers that use the Law for their own ends. Certain powers have evil intent and exploit the Law for evil purposes. In Romans 7 Paul develops a parallel argument, naming sin and death as evil powers that abuse the Law. And in 1 Corinthians 15:56 Paul plainly states, "The power of sin is the law." Thus, being under the Law is not freedom. It is a form of bondage in comparison to life in Christ, empowered by the Spirit of Christ (4:4-6).

But when the fullness of time had come, God sent his Son, born of a woman, born under the law (4:4). The contrast is temporal; Paul differentiates between the time of bondage under the Law and the time of fulfillment in Christ. The expression *fullness of time* sums up his references to the stages of history in 3:23-25 and 4:2, and to the concepts of promise and inheritance. *Fullness of time* speaks not of the maturation of the children but of the timing in the father's (God's) will (4:2). What follows continues that focus by describing the action of God in redemption. The style of verses 4-6 is unusually polished and symmetrical, suggesting that Paul may be drawing on a traditional formulation. Yet the fact that the main concepts of *childship* and *the Spirit* are so integral to Paul's larger argument in Galatians supports the probability that Paul himself is formulating it while using traditional ideas or forms.

The main verb, repeated in verse 6 for the Spirit, forms the backbone of the larger formulation. It has the nuance of "send out." The noun form of this word is *apostle*, which appears earlier (1:1; 2:8) to express the sending of an agent under divine commission for a particular task. That connotation is certainly present here and applies to the Son. Most interpreters see also an allusion to some kind of preexistence of the Son (existence before his earthly appearance), as is the case with the Spirit in the parallel sentence. (For comment on the title *Son*, see 1:16.) Paul has been building his argument around the theme of *childship* of believers in Christ (3:26). Paul's present link of sonship between Christ and God completes the chain of relationship. This intimate fellowship, linked from God to the believer through Christ, is an important part of Paul's argument for the superiority of the gospel.

Two modifying clauses refer to the birth of Christ. They emphasize the humanity of Christ, *born of a woman*, and his status among the people of God, *born under the law*. The former description could be used of any human birth, but if the sending language alludes to Christ's preexistence, this reference to being born of a woman takes on more theological weight (Phil 2:6-8 is a probable parallel). That Christ is born as a Jew and therefore subject to the way of life determined by the Law is of obvious significance to the context. Paul has already alluded to this in 3:13: Christ came under the curse of the Law in order to redeem those under the Law. The next clause in 4:5a makes the same link between Christ's status and his redeeming work. For Christ to fulfill the redemption story from Abraham through the time of the Law, he needed to be part of that story.

Paul now states the purpose or intended goal of the sending of the Son: *in order to redeem those who were under the law, so that we might receive adoption as children* (4:5). The double statement of purpose touches both the negative and the positive side of redemption. It says what we are delivered *from* and what we are freed *for*. Both statements treat themes being developed in the letter's argument: bondage under the Law; and status as children of Abraham and, more importantly, of God. Paul made both of these points explicitly in 3:13 and 26. Even the same verb for *redeem* appears in 3:13. *Redeem* connotes purchasing a slave in the slave market. It does not necessarily mean purchase for the purpose of setting free as a free citizen. Rather, it is an exchange of owners. This meaning could fit Paul's theology in our letter when he calls himself a *servant* (same as *slave*) of Christ in 1:10. But in the present context, Paul wants to clarify the advantage of maturity in Christ. Thus he speaks of the exchange of ownership as a movement from the status of slave to that of a child. This exchange is an adoption, as Paul now says.

The purpose of redemption, then, is reception into the family of God as adopted sons and daughters. *Adoption* appears in the New Testament only in the Pauline letters (Rom 8:15, 23; 9:4; Eph 1:5). For the apparent conflict between the images of adoptee and heir in 4:1, see the comments there. In Romans 9:4, Paul speaks of Israel as an adopted child. This shows that one's status as a child of God has the same basis in the old and new covenants: it is based on God's choice, not on human virtue or initiative. In Galatians, Paul uses *childship* as a status granted to those who move beyond the Law into relationship with Christ. The pronoun *we* most naturally reflects the historical experience of Jewish believers in Christ, as one would expect, given the theme of redemption from the Law (yet see 4:6). In this context, the adoption theme points to a new quality of spiritual relationship with God that includes rights and privileges not known before.

And because you are children, God has sent the Spirit of his Son into our hearts, crying, "Abba! Father!" (4:6). Here we meet another of the pronoun shifts from *we* to *you* that mark this entire section of the letter. The *you* is directed to the Galatians and is intended to include them in the story of redemption. As noted at 3:25-26, this shift of pronoun is Paul's way of recognizing the shift to a period in saving history that includes both Jews and Gentiles. But it also helps the Galatians identify with Paul's negative description of life under the Law and thus to lose their fascination with Law observance. The shift to the first-person plural (*our hearts*) in the second part of the verse continues this linking, except that now *we* refers to the whole family of believers, not just the Jewish Christians.

The causal conjunction *because* might appear to make *childship* a precondition for sending the Spirit, suggesting a sequence of distinct experiences for the believer (as if salvation is separate from receiving the Spirit). But Paul does not intend such a conclusion. He simply identifies different sides of the same experience, as shown by the description in 3:1-5 and the fact that in the closely parallel passage in Romans 8:14, the order is from Spirit to childship. Paul is emphasizing the link, not the sequence. In Galatians, Paul wants to show the logical connection between sharing *childship* status with Christ and sharing also the same Spirit with Christ, *the Spirit of his Son*. If we are the children of God through the redemption of God's Son, it follows that we should share in the Spirit of that Son as well. Thus, becoming a child of God and receiving the Spirit are two inseparable dimensions of becoming a believer. For Paul, the Spirit is so closely tied to Christ that one cannot have one without the other (cf. 1 Cor 12:3).

The verb *sent* is the same as in verse 4 (see comments there) and creates a balanced structure for this summarizing statement of the gospel around the twin ideas of Son and Spirit. The first *sent* refers to the once-for-all event of Jesus' life on earth, while the second refers to the repeated sending of the Spirit at the moment of individual conversions. The resulting picture is that of a God who is continually sending out gifts into the world, gifts of God's own self, based on the work of the Son and put in effect by the Spirit. This God tears open the heavens and comes down (Mark 1:10; cf. and contrast Isa 64:1).

The sending of the Spirit has a corresponding action in the believer. The grammar of the original makes clear that the Spirit is the one who cries out the words *Abba! Father!* At the same time, this is a human voice, for the point is not the *Spirit's* relationship to God as Father, but the *believer's* relationship to God as Father. It is a typically biblical view of divine initiative and human responsive action. The center of this spiritual encounter is the heart, which in biblical usage means the seat both of rational powers and of the emotions and affections. In other words, the cognitive and the affective are held together, not set over against each other. That this is described as a cry indicates its intense, deeply felt character. This is truly heartfelt religion, true spiritual ecstasy. Whether it implies the presence of ecstatic manifestations, such as speaking in tongues, is not clear. But the language of *Abba* is not evidence of such, as we will now see.

The presence of the term *Abba* is remarkable and therefore significant. This word is Aramaic, a language spoken in Palestine in
Jesus' time, which explains the presence of its translation, *Father*, for
a Greek-speaking audience. This word also appears with its translation in Mark 14:36 and Romans 8:15. It is generally recognized that
the word lies behind all places in the Gospels where Jesus calls God
"Father." Apparently it is the distinctive way that Jesus addressed
God, especially in prayer, and the manner in which he taught his
disciples to address God. Jesus took this term from the everyday
family life of his time where children addressed their father as *Abba*.
That Jesus adopted such intimate language to address God, while
not entirely novel in the Jewish setting, pointed to a new level of
spiritual intimacy with God. Indirectly it indicates that Jesus saw
himself as the basis for such a new, more profound relationship with
God. In Jesus the kingdom of God drew near (Mark 1:14-15); in Jesus
also God drew near. That the early church saw this language as distinctive and fundamental to Christian faith is demonstrated by its
persistence in the church as a loanword, even in other languages.

Paul embraced this language as of primal and indispensable significance for believers. This is all the more remarkable in light of
Paul's sensitivity to anything that had the appearance of Jewish
cultural imperialism in the mission to the Gentiles. That he includes
it in this context is fully understandable. As a word that expresses
intimate family ties, it suits Paul's purpose here of highlighting the
superiority of the child-of-God status in the gospel. Furthermore, it
strengthens his case for the bond between being a child of God and
having the Spirit, since the cry of *Abba* is a gift of the Spirit. Paul's
use of this word puts him in close continuity with Jesus. For Jesus
and for Paul, intimate relationship in the family of God is central to
the new creation inaugurated by Jesus.

*So you are no longer a slave but a child, and if a child then also an heir,
through God* (4:7). The first part of the sentence summarizes the argument, the movement from bondage to the position of child in the
family of God. In using *you* in direct address of the Galatians, Paul
shows that he also wants his Gentile readers to identify with his previous references to being under the Law (even though there he used
we), even though he proceeds in what follows to describe the particular form of bondage in which the Galatians had formerly lived.

There is another switch of pronouns here. The *you* of verse 6 is
plural, but the *you* in verse 7 is singular. This marks Paul's move
from the collective to the individual. For Paul, redemption has both
a community and a personal dimension, and both are significant.

Perhaps the switch to the singular *you* was prompted by the reference to the preceding experience of heartfelt communication with God as *Abba! Father!*, which is inherently personal.

Somewhat surprising, however, is Paul's use of the word *heir* in his culmination of the paragraph. It has the sense of something still unfulfilled (see 4:1). But the apparent meaning here is the same as in 3:29, where the word refers to the heritage of Abraham and signifies that the (Gentile) believer is now heir of that heritage in receiving adoption as a child of God in Christ. In other words, Paul uses the word here at the climax of his long argument from 3:6 to clinch his claim that the gospel is the true fulfillment of the promises to Abraham.

At the same time, we ought not exclude a possible allusion to the hope of the Christian, who continues to anticipate the full reality of God's promises (cf. 5:5 and the parallel passage in Romans 8, esp. v. 17). For Paul, adoption and Spirit have strong future (eschatological) connotations. Elsewhere Paul describes the Spirit as the down payment or pledge of what is yet to come for believers (2 Cor 1:22; 5:5). And in Romans 8:23 he says that the believer is still waiting for adoption (as a child of God), referring in that context to the future redemption of the body. Our life in the gospel has both already-realized and still-unrealized dimensions.

The final phrase, *through God*, does not seem to attach smoothly to any single element in the sentence. So it must apply to the entire preceding statement, to the whole process of liberation from slavery and incorporation into God's family. It underscores that this is a divine rather than human work, a theme that is dominant in the letter from 1:1 onward and is focused in the Spirit-flesh contrast, beginning in 3:1-5.

THE TEXT IN BIBLICAL CONTEXT

The Elements of the World

The meaning of this phrase is one of the more difficult problems in Paul's writings. Yet one can sense that this phrase could give vast insight into Paul's worldview and into his understanding of the profounder dynamics of human existence. A broad range of understandings of *elements* in the Greco-Roman world has been documented. The leading, and more viable, ones are these: (1) the basic materials of which the world is composed (fire, water, earth, air); (2) the elementary or rudimentary principles or teachings that explain the world; (3) the heavenly bodies (e.g., stars); (4) spirit beings and powers. The latter two could be merged into the belief that the heavenly bodies are actually divine powers that control the fate of the world. The third and fourth meanings are not documented in extrabiblical sources until at least a century after Paul's writings. Nevertheless, the association of divine powers with the basic elements of the material world was widespread in the ancient world. (Note how Rom 8:38-39 puts both in the same list and personifies them as actors in human experience.)

Paul uses the expression *elements of the world* four times: Galatians 4:3, 9; Colossians 2:8, 20. Elsewhere in the New Testament, the word *elements* alone is found in Hebrews 5:12 and 2 Peter 3:10, 12. The usages in Hebrews and 2 Peter are clear examples of definitions 1 and 2 above. In Galatians and Colossians, the discussion concerns the concrete beliefs and practices of human society, thus illustrating at least part of the meaning of the phrase. In Galatians 4, the association is with the Law (4:3) and with the observance of days, months, and years (4:10). In Colossians, the connection is with human philosophy (2:8), eating regulations (2:16, 21), special days of the calendar (2:16), or human regulations in general (2:20-22). At the same time, both contexts have references to the realm of spirit beings: see Galatians 4:8 and Colossians 2:15 ("principalities and powers," KJV); 2:18 (angels).

Paul does not directly explain whether or how these all relate to each other. But that there is some connection is quite apparent. Likely Paul chose a term that connotes to his audience the ideas and practices people use to give meaning and purpose to existence. And he shares the dominant assumption of his time that a close relationship exists between the material world of human culture and the spiritual realm of invisible powers, which can influence persons through those material forms.

In any case, Paul gives greater attention to the material expressions of the *elements*, especially if one takes into account that he subsumes all of his analysis of the Law under this concept. On the other side, there is some evidence that Paul diminishes the significance of spirit powers in light of his belief in one God (cf. 1 Cor 8:4-6; see the comments below on Gal 4:8-9). This latter statement could, in various degrees, be made of the biblical writings generally and of Jesus specifically. The spirit realm is acknowledged and confronted, when necessary, but is kept strictly at the margins of God's domain and under God's control.

What is particularly important is what this all suggests about Paul's keen insight into life. He observes the dynamics by which the forms of human culture come into being and the way in which those forms, meant though they are to serve humankind, come to enslave people through their own imperfections or through exploitation by other forces. As a consequence, the *elements* are the means by which evil is able to gain control in human lives. In fact, all humanity outside of Christ is in bondage to *elements*, and the whole world is subject to invisible powers that exercise influence over the human race by means of these *elements*. Those powers can even use something good in itself, like the Law, to increase the grip of evil on humanity. Only Christ offers a way of escape from this otherwise unavoidable bondage. An implication, which Paul does not expressly develop, is that the *elements* can be brought under the control of Christ and the Spirit and therefore serve good ends (something like this is implied in Col 2:15 and Eph 1:21-23). Paul's positive use of the Law in Galatians 5 and 6 illustrates just this viewpoint.

Early Christian Experience of the Gospel

What Paul gives us in Galatians 4:5-6 is a rare glimpse of the subjective side of life early in the Christian movement. That early Christians had profound and moving experiences is everywhere evident. They were joyfully exuberant because of the new blessings from God through the Spirit. Some even had highly ecstatic experiences. The emotion and affect of faith expressed itself in the creativity of song in worship and sentiments of love for fellow believers and neighbors. What those experiences were actually like is harder to detect. No New Testament writer shows interest in detailed description or analysis. The biblical writers emphasize the action of God rather than the experience of the human person and give more attention to the new behaviors of the believers than to their inner states of mind and feeling.

All the more remarkable, then, is the insight this passage offers into the experiential evidence for authentic Christian faith. In Romans 8:16, Paul says that the *Abba!* cry is the "Spirit bearing witness with our spirit that we are children of God." For Paul, the most basic sign of authentic experience of the Spirit is this heart cry of parental bond with God. This is more fundamental than any particular fruit of the Spirit (ethical evidence) or gift of the Spirit (worship, including speaking in tongues, and fruitful ministry), important though they may be.

Both the Galatians and Romans passages show that this *Abba!* reality emerges spontaneously from a source beyond oneself, though it is not independent from one's own spirit. As elsewhere in our letter, Paul thoughtfully recognizes both divine initiative and human response. This then is another insight into Paul's chief concern for the Galatians: only the spirituality that is grounded in divine action is authentic. The Spirit-created bond with God is the root from which flow the energies that inspire and nourish genuine Christian living. Finally, this sign of authentic faith shows that early Christian experience was profoundly affective and emotional even as it was intensely communal. The *Abba!* experience, along with the believers' adoption as children of God, reinforces the family metaphor that Paul uses to describe these believers' intimate relationship with God and with fellow believers.

THE TEXT IN THE LIFE OF THE CHURCH

The Elements of the World: Contemporary Relevance

As we have seen, Paul's concept of *elements* appears to encompass the breadth of human culture—the things we create to support meaningful life. But it refers especially to the things that are foundational to the meaning of that life. Some suggest, with good reason, that our modern term *worldview* expresses much of what Paul means by the *elements*. Worldview is the basic framework of convictions about the world that all cultures and ideologies develop in order to make sense of life, giving it meaning and purpose. Specific rituals and practices give expression to worldview and allow it to be lived out. It is religion-like. In fact, religions are prime examples of it.

Contemporary thinkers emphasize that human communities create the stories and myths that provide a rationale for how they live. Some of these same thinkers like to unmask these "big stories" (metanarratives) by showing how little basis they have in any ultimate, absolute truth and how much they inevitably reflect mere personal or corporate interests. As a result, we become slaves in the very house of meaning that we build. What we thought was the way to freedom ends in bondage. The situation is similar to that of the spider that spins its web. The spider's existence depends on the web, but the web also limits the spider. The spider's prey is the victim of the web, but in some sense the spider is a victim as well.

In contrast to the presumed dead end of this human bondage, Paul invites us to see Jesus Christ as God's offer of a way to true freedom, beginning with Jesus Christ as God's Son who was sent into our world. He therefore breaks out of the limitations of earthbound *elements*. In Jesus, God has authored a big story about life that is anchored in God's love, not in human interests. The life this story offers is not a system of ideas or a set of ethical guidelines. It is a family-like relationship with God through the person of Jesus Christ and the enabling work of the Spirit. It does not resort to human knowing as its ground of certainty, but rests in the assurance that God knows us and that is what counts (see comment on Gal 4:9a). God's story encompasses us, rather than our story encompassing God. This does not make sense to those who, while seeing the bondage of human knowing, demand to be in control of their own fate. It does make sense to those who, embracing faith as a way of knowing, have met Jesus the Christ face-to-face and have experienced him as true Liberator.

The Application to the Galatians
Galatians 4:8-11

PREVIEW

In the previous paragraph, Paul pressed home the choice facing the Galatians: do they want to continue to live by the Spirit as God's children and inherit the promises of God, or do they want to return to their previous status as slaves? Here Paul continues to press the choice while clarifying (esp. in v. 10) in practical terms how they are showing their slavery. Paul's expression of exasperation in 4:11 clarifies what is at stake in this choice for Paul's relationship with the Galatians.

With this paragraph, the major section beginning at 3:1 comes to a conclusion. Thus the paragraph is at the transition point between the two major parts of the letter. Its content is in keeping with this crucial position for it speaks directly and concretely to the situation in Galatia, as Paul perceives it. As its frame of reference, the theological argument begun in 3:6 has the story of God's dealings with Israel. Paul brings the Galatians into the picture subtly (but significantly) by his use of the pronoun *you*. Now Paul describes the spiritual journey of the Galatians as a journey from the valley of ignorant paganism to the hilltop of knowing the true God, yet heading back down to the valley of enslavement again through their submission to the empty forms of religious observance. How can this be? Why would the Galatians want to head back downhill to the valley of enslavement?

It is here that Paul's letter to the Galatians reveals most clearly the Gentile background of his readers. The themes in the paragraph are not new, but their application to the Galatian experience is new. In observing the Law, the Galatians were not returning to something they were doing before they experienced new life in the Spirit. They no doubt thought their observance of the Law was simply the next logical step in their growing faithfulness to God. But Paul makes it clear here that their "progress" in observing the Law is actually a regression to their former enslavement!

EXPLANATORY NOTES

Formerly when you did not know God, you were enslaved to beings that by nature are not gods (4:8). The reference to enslavement recalls 4:3, where Paul is referring to the condition of the Jew under the Law. Now the parallel situation for the non-Jew will be described. The phrase *know God* or *known by God* marks the section, appearing three times in this and the next verse. Paul is revealing his roots in the Jewish Scriptures, where the knowledge of God is a key concept. In that context knowing God means both understanding the things of God and actually serving this God. Knowledge of Yahweh God marked Israel off from the nations whose gods were mere idols.

Paul's monotheistic perspective lies behind his observation that the gods of the Galatians were by nature not gods. Paul is reluctant to concede the term *god* to anything but the God of his Jewish tradition (Isa 37:19; Jer 2:11). He is not necessarily denying any and all reality to those deities. He probably means to deny their status as gods while allowing that they function in some way as part of the *elements* (see the next verse and the discussion on 4:3). The term *by nature* has a Greek philosophical background and reflects discussions about what constitutes the true nature of things. So Paul is weaving together Hebrew and Greek concepts for his Gentile audience.

We do not know the identity of the religion to which Paul is referring in this paragraph. Some think of astrological practices, since Paul mentions spirit beings and calendrical practices (4:8-10), which may derive from observation of heavenly bodies. Others notice that the emperor cult organized worship around a human being within an elaborate calendar of celebrations. Given the broad sense of *elements* in Paul's usage and the probable variety of religious backgrounds of the Galatians, we need not assume a narrow reference for Paul's description.

Now, however, that you have come to know God, or rather to be known by God, how can you turn back again to the weak and beggarly elemental spirits. How can you want to be enslaved to them again? (4:9). The tense of both verbs *know* indicates that they refer to the time of conversion, when the Gentile Galatians came to know the true God. God now intends for the gospel to go to Jew and Gentile. As a Jewish believer in Christ, Paul thinks of spiritual matters in relational terms. We should thus not be surprised that he sees knowledge in the divine-human encounter as personal and mutual. Here Paul places the human knowing of God and the divine knowing of the human person side by side. But Paul says more. He gives priority to *God's* knowledge of *us*.

Paul's giving priority to God's knowledge is found elsewhere in Paul (see 1 Cor 8:3; 13:12). While distinctive among biblical writers, it does not contradict them. It is an important clue to his theology and to the message of Galatians in particular. True faith, from beginning to end, flows from God's initiative and action to humans' response. We met this same perspective in *through God* in verse 7. Paul linked this action of God to the work of the Spirit in the Christian community (cf. 3:1-5 and the *Abba!* cry of 4:6). The work of the Spirit shows God acknowledging, and hence knowing, the believers as God's own (cf. Rom 8:16). In Paul's eyes, therefore, the Galatians had experienced the best and the highest in their initial turning to God through Christ. Any alleged supplement to it is by definition a regression.

But shockingly, the Galatians are now "turning" in a different direction! The word used for *turn* is the characteristic biblical term for turning from sin to God, or for the reverse. It connotes a radical change of direction (cf. 1:6, but with a different word). In this case, the tragedy is that the Galatians are "returning" to their previous position of enslavement! Paul emphasizes this through his repeated use of *again*. He uses the term *elements* to describe that to which the Galatians are turning (cf. 4:3 and the full explanation there). Paul thus implies that the false gods the Galatians had served in their paganism are closely aligned with (less likely, synonymous with) the *elements*. Second, it confirms (see 4:3) that Paul understands the Law as an expression of the *elements*, since the letter clearly shows that the Galatians are moving in the direction of Law observance.

We gain further insight into Paul's view of the *elements* from the adjectives *weak* and *beggarly* (impoverished). These words focus on the lack of resource and strength. The thought fits well the theme we hear throughout the letter. The Law is not able to give life (3:21; cf. Rom 8:3-4). The Spirit can do mighty deeds, which the (human, material) flesh cannot do (Gal 3:3-5). Paul makes the same contrast of Spirit and flesh in 5:16-24 with respect to victorious Christian living (cf. Col 2:20-23).

The *elements* are thus those things that assume religious-like influence over people, but have no real power. The idols of paganism and the Jewish Law share in this impotence, even though, for Paul, the Law is God-given and not the invention of human imagination, as with pagan religion and philosophy. The Law itself is a powerless system of religious beliefs and practices. The key to Paul's experience in Christ is that the Spirit of Christ provided the power to fulfill the just and right standard of the Law (cf. 5:14-16; Rom 8:3-4). When the Galatians submit to the Law observance being urged by the Galatian opponents, they are embracing a *weak and beggarly* condition instead of building on the strength of the Spirit and the riches of grace in Christ—both of which are constant themes in Pauline writings. Such a condition is tantamount to slavery. (See also the discussion on "The Elements of the World" in TBC for 4:1-7.)

You are observing special days, and months, and seasons, and years (4:10). The verbs in verses 9 and 10 are in the present tense: *turn back, want to be enslaved*, and *are observing*. Does this imply that the Galatians are actually accepting this new teaching? Have some actually submitted to circumcision? Probably so, though Paul would not be writing if he had considered the situation unredeemable. The present verse likely indicates that the Galatians have begun to participate in these rituals. The list of things being observed can easily make one think of the Jewish calendar, with its rituals and festivals. However, these terms are more general. They lack the greater precision of the list in Colossians 2:16—festival, new moon, and Sabbath. Perhaps Paul uses more general terms here to make them applicable to both Greek and Jewish observances, thus underlining the parallel he sees between the Galatians' former paganism and their new turn to Law observance.

It would not be surprising if Paul's opponents were promoting the observance of holy days and their related rituals. In particular, the Sabbath symbolized Jewish identity and faithfulness within the Hellenistic culture. In the first century, when Paul was writing, different Jewish groups had different opinions about the calendar and when various festivals should be observed. The priesthood in Jerusalem observed a lunar calendar, while the Essenes held to a solar calendar. This resulted, for instance, in the Day of Atonement being celebrated at different times by different groups (cf. also *1 Enoch; Jubilees*). These calendrical debates may thus provide the link Paul is making between the Galatians' former pagan practices and the Jewish way of life being promoted by the teachers. They are both examples of the *elements* that govern people's lives.

I am afraid that my work for you may have been wasted (4:11). With this confession Paul ends the reasoned argument of the previous section to make a more personal appeal. With this reference to his intense labor on behalf of the Galatians, Paul intends to evoke feelings of shame and remorse in the readers. The same idea of the entire past being for naught is found in 3:4. Paul consistently presents the options faced by the Galatians as an either/or.

THE TEXT IN BIBLICAL CONTEXT

Knowing and Being Known

Paul's statement regarding the mutual knowing between the believer and God is profoundly revealing. This knowing goes both ways. In affirming the importance of knowing in religious experience, Paul stands in a strong biblical tradition. Knowledge in the Bible is both informational and relational in character. God is informed about all things; nothing escapes God's awareness. Humans are limited in knowledge but have a level of awareness of who God is and what God does.

Biblical writings portray knowing in personal relationships as going beyond cognitive awareness to include deeper understanding and bonding. Such knowledge is necessarily mutual. This personal kind of knowing marks God's relationship with God's people. In one sense, God knows only Israel among the nations (Amos 3:2; yet cf. 9:7). In turn, God expects Israel to know their God (Hos 5:3-4). Not surprisingly, true knowledge is practically synonymous with a committed relationship that is loving and faithful. This same perspective is particularly strong in John's gospel, where knowing characterizes the close personal fellowship of spiritual relationship that exists between the believer, Jesus, and God the Father (John 10:14-15).

Paul's contribution to this theme lies in his insistence that God's knowledge of the believer has priority over the knowledge that the believer has of God. With the language of Galatians 4:9, this is clear in the comparative word *rather*. It is also implied in 1 Corinthians 8:3 and 13:12. From these latter passages we learn that the priority of God's knowledge is grounded in the facts that (1) human knowledge is limited until we are face-to-face with God and (2) knowledge constitutes a particular temptation to human pride. Paul concludes that love is more important for the believer than knowledge (1 Cor 8:3). The implication is that love, based on partial knowledge from the believer's side, is the adequate precondition for relationship with

God. Once in relationship, the believer becomes the beneficiary of the perfect knowledge that God possesses without needing to possess that full knowledge (see TLC).

TEXT IN THE LIFE OF THE CHURCH

Freedom and Bondage

Galatians is the principal treatise in the Scriptures on the theme of freedom. Paul touches on the subject in 1:4; 2:4; 4:21-31; and 5:1, 13; but Paul's most detailed treatment of freedom comes in the present passage in chapter 4, even though he does not use the language of freedom here. What becomes immediately clear in Galatians is that freedom is not an absolute and independent value. Freedom needs something to define its content; it needs a larger frame of reference to have any meaning. The complete autonomy of the individual is an illusion. Humans may aspire to full liberation from outside control, but they can never achieve it. Absolute freedom requires complete control of one's situation, something humans do not possess. According to Galatians, external powers exercise control over the human race.

God created humans to serve something greater than ourselves. It is in our nature to be in the service of something or someone. When we throw off one authority, we may indeed experience a sense of self-determination. But that sense is fleeting, for in choosing another way of life or way of seeing reality, we become subject to something that limits and manipulates our future options. This illustrates what Paul means by *elements*. As the real tragedy of the human situation, the forces that control us are not friendly to our best interests. Our striving for freedom always lands us in bondage.

Here is where the story of liberation in Christ is revealed to be good news indeed! It is not the case that in Christ we gain access to absolute freedom and self-autonomy. Rather, in Christ we gain a master who brings us back to our true condition as children of God. According to Paul, true freedom lies in being able to choose a master in whose care our full human potential can be realized. To hear the gospel and to receive it is just such a freedom. This is freedom under God within a community of mutual love and care (5:13). It is not an illusory dream of godlike autonomy as an isolated self (see also TBC for 5:1-12).

Knowledge and Faith

Christian faith appreciates the intellect as an essential part of our humanity and of our relationship with God. Reasoning is not more important than other aspects. Moreover, knowing is more than reasoning, since knowing can include intuition and experience. Even faith is a way of knowing. So knowledge, or understanding, is important to our faith. Knowledge is one dimension of who we are as human beings. There are no grounds for a bias against knowledge and reason in Christian experience. Jesus himself affirms using the intellect in loving God as (part of) the most important commandment in the Bible (cf. Deut 6:4-5; Mark 12:28-34).

However, we are always tempted to overestimate our ability to know. We assume that we know more than we actually know and with more certainty than is warranted. The philosophical outlook called postmodernism has taught us to be skeptical about the limits of human knowing. But this is no novelty for those steeped in biblical thinking (cf. Eccl 5:2; 1 Cor 8:1b-2). The human mind is limited and susceptible to error and deception.

However, belief in God offers a way out of the morass of meaninglessness. There is a God who knows fully and truly, and faith is a way of connecting to that knowledge. Faith does not provide knowledge, but it does provide the link of relationship with One who is all-knowing. That is why Paul prioritizes God's knowing of the believer instead of the believer's knowing of God. The practical implications are profound. Confidence in God who knows all and who knows us better than we know ourselves gives us confidence for living. First, we can be confident that the world in which we live is a world of sense and meaning even if we cannot see it or prove it. Second, God's knowing involves a personal knowledge of each believer. We can thus be confident that God holds every circumstance and every future eventuality. Indeed, to know God is a great privilege; to be known by God is the greatest privilege!

Part 2

A Request: Obeying the Truth

Galatians 4:12–6:10

OVERVIEW

We finally come to the end of the first major part of the letter to the Galatians, which is in the rhetorical form of a rebuke. So far in Galatians, Paul has given a reasoned defense of his position, which counters that of the opponents. Paul does not shrink from direct rebuke, as 1:6 and 3:1-5 make clear. But with 4:12, Paul assumes a new rhetorical form, the form of request. Imperative verbs mark this form. The command *Become as I am* (4:12) is the first real imperative of the letter. (The imperatives in 1:8-9 are not directed to the Galatians, and the possible imperative in 3:7, which NRSV translates as an indicative, *you see*, is in any case a stylistic feature of narrative.) The key motif for this entire section is *obeying the truth* (5:7). Here Paul beings to focus questions of conduct (ethics) without losing sight of the theological underpinnings in the first part of the letter.

Paul begins this section by appealing to his personal relationship with the Galatians. He follows this up with another extended argument from Scripture that culminates in a call to action against the false teachers. After appealing directly to his readers to maintain their position in freedom, Paul explains how right living is based on the resources of the gospel rather than on the Law. The leading themes are freedom, flesh, Spirit, and Law. Paul has introduced them earlier in the letter but now applies them to the underlying question about how a faith-centered gospel leads to holy and righteous living if it does not appeal to the demands of the Law. Paul's response is that the Spirit is the key. The Spirit makes upright living achievable in a way that is impossible for the Law. The Spirit goes beyond the Law even as it fulfills the basic spirit of the Law, which is love.

OUTLINE

Example of the Apostle, 4:12-20
Scriptural Case for Corrective Action, 4:21-31
Standing Fast in Freedom, 5:1-12
Overcoming the Flesh by the Spirit, 5:13-24
Acting in Conformity to the Spirit, 5:25–6:10

Galatians 4:12-20

Example of the Apostle

PREVIEW

In this section Paul returns to the autobiographical style of chapters 1 and 2. However, in contrast to the more rational argument of that previous section, Paul here appeals more directly to the feelings and emotions. He recalls his initial favorable reception by the Galatians and contrasts it with their present loss of respect and trust. Paul remembers his sacrifices for them (and theirs for him) in a way that exposes the behavior of the teachers, who are motivated by other, baser interests. In a final burst of pathos, Paul wishes he could birth the Galatians into full conformity to Jesus Christ! What an image! Paul enduring labor pains! This must be one of the most powerful expressions of what Paul means when he writes of becoming a believer and living in the Spirit!

EXPLANATORY NOTES

Friends, I beg you, become as I am, for I also have become as you are. You have done me no wrong (4:12). The NRSV uses the inclusive word *friends* to translate the literal *brethren*. However, this mutes the religious bond the term had for early Christians. In Galatians, where Paul uses the term at regular intervals, this nuance is crucial. Paul is seeking to maintain fraternal ties during a time of stress in relationships with his readers. A better translation would be *brothers and sisters*, as the NRSV does in 3:15 and 5:13.

The intensity of Paul's feeling comes through in *I beg you*. Paul's appeal to his converts to imitate his way of following Christ is typical of him (cf., e.g., 1 Cor 4:16; 11:1; Phil 3:17). Here the emphasis is not on Paul's way of life in the spirit and character of Christ in a general sense, appropriate though that be. Here he is defending his way of dealing with the issue of Law observance, as he has else-where in the letter. The force of Paul's appeal resides in the emo-tional impact it could have when the Galatians recall Paul's full identification with them as Gentiles even at the cost of renouncing aspects of his Jewish way of life, when Paul sacrificially contextual-ized the gospel in his life with them (cf. 1 Cor 9:21).

Verse 17 portrays the false teachers as doing the opposite—withholding fellowship unless the Galatians become as they are. Paul is trying to help his readers see the Antioch incident (2:11-14) being played out again with them. Also in that case Jewish believers pressured the Gentile believers to observe their Law-based prac-tices. Paul's assurance that the Galatians have done him no wrong is meant to head off speculation that there may be hidden agenda from the past behind Paul's passion. It may also subtly allude to a future harm that the Galatians would do to him if they were to side with the false teachers.

You know that it was because of a physical infirmity that I first announced the gospel to you (4:13). This is a clear reference to a health problem that Paul experienced. What that problem was is largely a matter of speculation. From 2 Corinthians 12:5 and 7, we know that Paul had physical ailments of some sort. Whatever the exact ail-ment, it caused Paul to go into the Galatian region. This geographi-cal reference has led to the suggestion that Paul had a disease like malaria. Galatia, which is not in a coastal area, would have offered some relief from such a disease. (But see more on the next verses.) The temporal reference *first* might imply multiple visits to these churches, but most likely Paul is contrasting a former time of posi-tive relationships with the present crisis.

Though my condition put you to the test, you did not scorn or despise me, but welcomed me as an angel of God, as Christ Jesus (4:14). In all events, the ailment just mentioned was not something Paul could hide. It created a trial for the Galatians, something that caused a burden and could have ruined the relationship with this itinerant preacher. Despite Paul's burdensome and possibly revolting condi-tion, the Galatians did not allow it to cause feelings of disgust and revulsion. The word translated *despise* is particularly interesting. Its literal meaning is *to spit (out).* The word alludes to the ancient prac-tice of spitting as a ritual to protect against illness or demonic influ-ence (cf. the possible allusion to the evil-eye magic in 3:1). That could fit Paul's decision to allude to his ailment and suggest why it might have been easy for the Galatians to turn from him.

Whether the usage here is figurative or literal is unclear. The figurative meaning would simply be *to disdain* or *despise*. Some have conjectured that Paul's illness was epilepsy, since that was widely associated with demonic possession. But an ordinary illness fits the evidence better. Paul emphasizes the physical nature of his problem. Moreover, in the next verse (15) Paul's reference to the Galatians' willingness to give their eyes to him could suggest that Paul had an eye disease. Such a disease best fits the various clues in the passage. Paul's comment at the end of Galatians about writing in large letters (6:11) could be explained by a problem with his eyesight.

If the previous language alludes to the Galatians' possible rejection of Paul because they feared evil influence, the following comment about receiving someone as an angel would make a fitting, contrasting parallel. The Galatians were not put off by Paul's weakness. Rather, they chose to show him the hospitality one would extend to a messenger from God. The belief that angels appeared on earth in human guise was common at the time (see Acts 12:15; Heb 13:2). The incident in Acts 14:11-12, which happened in one of the cities to which Paul may now be writing, reflects the popular mindset. The crowd took Paul as Hermes, a messenger god. There is also behind our text the idea that the messenger carries the full authority of the one represented (cf. Matt 10:40). Paul clearly thought of himself as the commissioned representative—the apostle—of Jesus Christ, as Galatians 1 shows. Now Paul is saying that the Galatians first accepted his apostleship, though they are now questioning it.

What has become of the good will you felt? (4:15a). The apostle wants his readers to recall their state of mind and spirit when he was with them, when relationships were good. He describes that condition as blessedness. Paul's question can be expressed literally: *Where is then your blessedness?* This leaves the exact meaning open. It may refer to the blessing the Galatians themselves experienced or to the way they expressed blessing toward Paul in his physical need. The first meaning fits Paul's use of the word elsewhere (Rom 4:6-9) and the idea (but not the same original word) of Gentiles receiving the blessing of Abraham (Gal 3:9, 14).

But the immediate context here suggests the second meaning (supported by the translation *good will*). The statement about the Galatians being willing to give their eyes supports this assertion. Paul may even intend the double connotation. Given the nature of blessing in the Bible (and in all human experience), blessing experienced by one may quickly be enjoyed by others as well. The Galatians' goodwill toward Paul was the result of and the evidence of the blessing they had received from God.

For I testify that, had it been possible, you would have torn out your eyes and given them to me (4:15b). As just noted, Paul offers this hypothetical, and certainly hyperbolic, statement as support for his previous claim about the Galatians' goodwill toward him. This is clear from the conjunction *for*. The force of the illustration is that eyesight is of such great value that giving it up would be an extreme sacrifice. That Paul chose the particular image of offering one's eyes to someone else most naturally suggests that his physical ailment had to do with his eyes (see on 4:13-14 above), but this is not certain. In any event, Paul clearly regards the previous loyalty and support of the Galatians as unconditional and unequivocal.

Have I now become your enemy by telling you the truth? (4:16). This sudden and drastic shift catches the reader off guard. Paul no doubt intends the dramatic effect. The conjunction (*now* in the translation) normally introduces the result of a preceding clause. Its use here must be ironic. If so, the punctuation could well be an exclamation point. Paul's thought may be expressed this way: "So what is the result? I have become your enemy for telling the truth!" Paul means to elicit feelings of guilt and shame! His shocking use of *enemy* may seem extreme, but he uses it in part for rhetorical effect. Later Jewish Christian writings show that some, in fact, saw Paul as an enemy of the truth. Paul's writings and Acts show that angst over issues like circumcision was high. The truth that Paul speaks about here is presumably the truth of the gospel that he has preached in Galatia and to which he refers in 2:5 and 14.

They make much of you, but for no good purpose; they want to exclude you, so that you may make much of them (4:17). The third party (*they*) in this confrontation means the teachers, who have set the Galatians against Paul. Paul has mentioned these opponents in places like 1:7 and 3:1, but he has not really characterized them. Their teaching has been the focus, but Paul's references to them have been rather indirect. Now Paul directly attacks the teachers themselves. Even then Paul's description is brief and cryptic. Obviously the original readers know their situation! The statement has a catchy, chiastic style, with Paul using the same key verb at the beginning and the end of the verse. (The verb appears a third time in the next verse.)

This key verb, translated by the NRSV as *make much of*, is difficult to render in English. It carries various possible nuances with its root concept of zeal and is freighted with meaning in a Jewish context. It evokes the religious zeal of the Jews to maintain the standards of faithfulness to the Law (see Acts 21:20 and esp. Gal 1:14). When the word has a person as the object of the action, as it does here, the translation could be either *be deeply concerned about someone* or *court someone's favor*, or even *be envious of someone*. The second of these options is preferable here. The teachers are courting the favor of the Galatians in the hope that the Galatians will court their favor.

For Paul, this mutual desire between the teachers and the Galatians is based on false grounds. The teachers do not have the good of the Galatians in mind. In fact, they want to exclude or shut out the Galatians! Perhaps they want to prohibit the Galatians from contact with Paul. More likely, the teachers want to enforce the Law-based boundary lines between Jews and (uncircumcised) Gentiles in a zealot-like fashion (hence Paul's choice of a verb that connotes zeal). This would parallel the action of the Jewish Christians at Antioch (2:12-13).

In this strategy, the teachers want to marginalize the Gentile converts in the hope that this will arouse in them an even greater desire to court the favor of the teachers—a classical control technique. The teachers' ultimate goal is to get the Galatians to embrace a Jewish way of life based on the Law. This is actually a missionary strategy with a positive intent on the part of the teachers. It is not that they are disinterested in or dislike the Gentile believers. However, for Paul, this does not change the fact that it is ill-conceived and of no benefit to the Galatians. In fact, their strategy illustrates the enslaving dynamics against which Paul is so exercised throughout the letter.

It is good to be made much of for a good purpose at all times, and not only when I am present with you (4:18). The verse begins with the same verb that appears twice in the preceding verse with the same translation: *make much of*. There the term has a negative sense, but here Paul affirms the positive side. To *court the favor* (see comment above) of someone is appropriate, if the goal is worthy. The first part of the verse is a general principle, so perhaps Paul is using or adapting a well-known saying or proverb.

Only in the second part of the verse does the reader discover that Paul is now thinking not of his opponents but of himself. Paul *too* is zealously courting the Galatians and hoping that they will reciprocate, but for worthy purposes. Still another twist comes with Paul's indirect accusation that, while Paul and the Galatians shared this mutual interest when he was with them, it has now weakened or ceased.

My little children, for whom I am again in the pain of childbirth until Christ is formed in you . . . (4:19). Now the mood changes once again. Paul reflects the wide range of emotions he feels, based on the love he has for the Galatians and the concern he has for the truth, even as he admits some element of self-interest. Now he discloses his parent-like love and bond. It is typical of Paul to call his converts children (1 Cor 4:14; 2 Cor 12:14; 1 Thess 2:11) and himself a father or parent. In the present text, Paul pictures himself specifically as their mother (cf. also 1 Thess 2:7). Paul communicates his sentiment through a powerful image of human bonding—one that also reflects the profound personal formation that can take place in the relationship of two human beings. The picture of a mother straining to give birth to her child serves the purpose. The pain and labor of childbirth illustrate the anguish Paul is experiencing over the Galatians' possible defection. Great anticipation accompanies labor and childbirth. What will be the outcome? Will the Galatians come out healthy, or will they be stillborn?

Here Paul's appeal to the Galatians elicits one of the more basic and powerful sentiments of human experience. But at midbirth, the analogy suddenly changes! Now the strain and anguish refer not to Paul's labor pains, but to the Galatians' own nurturing formation of Christ within them! Paul suddenly becomes the midwife! This odd mixture of images makes sense, however, if we recall that Paul sees himself as one who bears the image of Christ and thus whom others can imitate (cf. the comments on 4:14; see Rom 8:29; 2 Cor 3:18; Col 3:9-10). Because Paul bears the image of Christ, what he births will bear that same image (cf. 2:20; 6:15).

The word for *formed* is a close variant of the verb used in 2 Corinthians 3:18 ("being transformed into the same image [of the Lord]") and Romans 12:2 ("be transformed by the renewing of your minds"). Being formed into Christ's likeness or image is the same as Christ being formed in the believer. These related passages show that formation involves all levels of human experience: the world of thought and beliefs, the world of relationships and community, the world of character and personality, and the world of action and behavior.

Labor pains had additional overtones for Paul. The literature of late Second Temple Judaism used the image of labor in childbirth to depict the birthing of God's new order at the end of time. The new order arrives with suffering and travail. This perspective is visible in Matthew 24:8; Mark 13:8; and Revelation 12:1-5 (see comments on Gal 4:27). It links directly to the concept of *new creation* in Paul (see 6:15; 2 Cor 5:17).

Paul portrays life in the Spirit and ministry as the bringing forth of new life in Christ through acts of death (sacrifice and suffering) in emulation of Jesus himself (2 Cor 1:5-7; 4:10-11). That is precisely how Paul sees himself in relation to the Galatians. Here at the end of the times (1 Cor 10:11), God's new world is taking shape, and Paul's ministry is helping to bring it to birth. As Paul's experience with the Galatians shows, evangelism is more than a quick and simple decision for Christ. It is an extended and formative process that involves change in one's values, character, and behavior, to which the whole self of the evangelist contributes as model (see TBC and TLC).

I wish I were present with you now and could change my tone, for I am perplexed about you (4:20). At the close of this section, based in personal experience, Paul displays yet another sentiment in his attempt to woo the Galatians. He admits to uncertainty and doubt about what is really going on. More than just the inconsistency of the Galatians baffles him. Perhaps the separation of time and space is making it difficult for him to understand the situation completely. Or perhaps the situation has changed and his letter may have unintended effects. So he expresses his desire to be with the Galatians to alleviate these problems of communication. That Paul talks specifically of changing his tone of voice indicates that he hopes things really are better than he has heard or supposed. In any case, this verse shows some openness and flexibility. Paul thus gives some space to the debate in order not to polarize feelings.

THE TEXT IN BIBLICAL CONTEXT

Formation in Christ

The image of conception, labor, and childbirth in verse 19 is unusually powerful in its theological importance and in its rhetorical impact. Paul's allusion to labor pains conveys the intensity of his pain-with-affection with regard to the Galatian problem. At the same time it connects with a central and distinctive feature in Paul: the theme of identification with Christ or formation in Christ, and being *in Christ*.

At the heart of the reality to which this language points is the conviction that Christ is the full expression of God's redeeming purposes. He is both the one who illustrates the God-directed life and the one through whom such a life is possible for others. Christ shows us what full salvation looks like and is also the one who, through the Spirit, works that salvation in the believer. The preposition *in*, typical of Paul's language on this theme, conveys well this inclusive view of salvation. Paul does not have in mind the literal sense of material place; he is speaking figuratively of spiritual formation: total investment in a larger reality that encompasses something else and that, in some sense, defines or controls it. Moreover, in Greek the word *in* can have the sense of *by means of* or *in association with*. These nuances also seem to be present in Paul's thought. They pick up the point made at the beginning of the paragraph that Christ is both the one by means of whom we are saved and the one with whom we walk in a common life like his.

In Paul's ideas some see an expression of what is termed a Hebraic corporate personality concept, that is, the idea of one personality representing a whole tribe or people. Paul's view of Adam as the representative of the human race (and Christ as the representative of the new humanity) supposedly illustrates the concept (Rom 5:12-21). The existence of the concept itself in the biblical tradition is disputed. Yet the strong sense of social solidarity in biblical cultures is certainly an important presupposition for Paul's ideas. Paul is aware of the formative influence that accompanies interpersonal interaction, and he applies that to the divine-human encounter. To be in relation with Christ is to experience the formative impact of his person. This happens not only to individuals, but also to a people, the church, which must bear the likeness of Christ.

Paul's language of identification with Christ has both relational and behavioral (ethical) aspects. The relational aspect speaks to the communion or fellowship that exists between the believer and Christ. This is the Christian mode of communion with God. The work of Christ in his death reconciles us to God, making possible the communal relationship. Some describe this aspect of identification with Christ as "mystical." That is helpful insofar as it points to the unique spiritual modes of communion across the great divide between the divine and the human. But it is misleading for Paul (and for biblical thought in general) if it carries overtones of dualism, in which spirituality is an escape from the material world and an absorption into God. Moreover, mysticism is typically too individualistic to support Paul's social vision. Indeed, an important subset of the relational dimension in Paul is the fellowship between believers, that is, the experience of being *in* the body of Christ, the church.

The other aspect is the behavioral. This refers to the moral or ethical dimension, which includes both character and action. To be *in Christ* is to be transformed into the likeness of Christ (1 Cor 3:18-23), to be conformed to his image (Rom 8:29). Galatians 2:19-20 describes this as a process of dying and rising (the latter being

implied). Questions about virtue and right behavior are often linked
to the identification theme. Christ's servant life is grounding for the
believer's life. The classic passage is Philippians 2:1-11 (with *in Christ*
language in Phil 2:1, 5). In the Pauline writings, the range of application to life suggests that this conformity to Christ is as large as life.
Paul does not presume to spell out all the implications. He wants
believers to explore the will of God amid their own circumstances
under the Spirit's guidance and the standard of Christ (Rom 12:2;
Eph 5:1-2, 17; Phil 1:9-11).

The other New Testament writer to make major use of *in Christ*
language (or its equivalent) is John (e.g., John 15:4-7; 17:21; 1 John
5:20). For the gospel of John, spiritual communion is prominent. The
relationship between the believer and Christ (*in* one another), as
well as between Christ and God, is mutual. This mutuality image is
perhaps not as common in Paul. The theme of discipleship in the
synoptic gospels is closely related to this identification language in
Paul and John, who recast discipleship for a time when a literal following of Jesus is no longer possible.

Although 1 Peter (2:21) uses the language of discipleship, Paul
does not (but see Eph 4:20-21, where the believer is a "learner" or
disciple of Jesus Christ). Following Jesus was, for his disciples, both
profoundly relational and behavioral, much as Paul's *in Christ* language. All of one's life is potentially touched and changed by the
close sharing of life with another. The *in Christ* language of Paul and
John is an extension of the Gospels' discipleship language in a modified form. This new form accords with the change from material
ways of relating to the earthly Jesus, to spiritual ways of relating to
the exalted Christ (see TLC below and TBC on 2:20-21).

Imitation in Paul

The text we are considering sheds interesting light on a common
theme in Paul's letters—his exhortation that the readers imitate
him in the faith. At the beginning of this paragraph in the letter,
Paul begs the Galatians, *Become as I am*. This appears to have the
same meaning as other passages, which use the word *imitator* to
define the readers' relation to Paul (1 Cor 4:16; 11:1; Phil 3:17;
1 Thess 1:6; 2 Thess 3:7, 9; and with different language, Phil 4:9).
Later in the paragraph he recalls, favorably, that the Galatians
received him as Christ Jesus. This point is relevant here in light of
Paul's perspective, sometimes explicit but always implicit, that
because he imitates Christ, to imitate him is to imitate Christ. Paul
sees himself so closely identified with Christ that he can represent

Christ to others. Clearly, then, the theme of imitation is related to the themes of formation and identification (see preceding section in this TBC).

This theme in Paul offers both theoretical and practical insights. The practical one is that Paul is dealing with first-generation converts who have no resources for knowing what a Christlike way of life looks like. They had neither written resources (the NT Gospels did not yet exist) nor eyewitnesses or older believers to instruct them. This is why Paul regularly moves from abstract concepts, such as "becoming like Christ," to concrete illustrations of what this means. Also, the invitation to imitate a person resists the rigid codification of rules, since personal existence is dynamic. It involves growth in maturity and adaptation to change.

The idea of imitation further shows that morality for Paul is narrative in character. The moral life is based in a model of virtue and action that is not discernible in the abstract, but is handed down as one sees and emulates the wisdom that is lived out by others. The model for the Christian surely is Jesus Christ, whose life represents the one time and place in history where perfect godliness has been realized. Imitation is the manner by which a moral vision is handed on from generation to generation. So Paul's imitation concept is an extension of the discipleship theme in the life of Jesus. This is why the Gospels were written and became part of Scripture. Narrating the life of Jesus assisted believers to learn Christ—"as truth is in Jesus" (Eph 4:20-21).

A close study of this theme in Paul discredits the accusation that Paul's appeal to imitation masks an arrogant spirit and a readiness to use power in a manipulative way. Paul's appeal to become like him in the present text is based on his already having become like the Galatians. In other words, Paul claims to practice a mutual exchange in which he disciplines himself to identify with his converts. Imitation is a two-way experience in which one submits as well as controls. Certainly, to be a model for imitation is to exercise power. The issue is whether, in so doing, one points away from oneself to the greater model of Christ and participates in a mutual process of learning from and submitting to others in love (cf. 5:13, *Become slaves to one another*).

THE TEXT IN THE LIFE OF THE CHURCH

Discipleship and Life in Christ

Pauline spirituality, with its focus on identification with Christ, has often been obscured in the church. Some groups favor Paul by taking justification by faith as his chief idea, rather than identification with Christ. In its emphasis on discipleship, the Radical Reformation tradition has tended to favor the Gospels and 1 Peter over Paul. Neither justification nor identification was thought to connect as well with its central ethos. In particular, the mystical or spiritualizing understanding of Paul's identification language made it more alien to a tradition interested in the practical following of Jesus. Even the liberalism of a century ago favored the supposedly simple ethical religion of Jesus over against the supposedly otherworldly Christ worship of Paul.

However, Paul's emphasis on identification with Christ suggests that such dismissals be rethought. Paul's language actually *integrates* discipleship, personal spirituality, life in community, and Christlike living (cf. TBC above with regard to the relational and the behavioral aspects of living *in Christ*). The language of discipleship can keep us focused on what faith means in day-to-day life. However, it is also vulnerable to the misunderstanding that Christian faith is all ethics and that faithfulness is literal imitation of the historical Jesus.

Judging from Paul's wider viewpoint, he was concerned about these very misunderstandings. With this identification language, he directs our attention to both spiritual and moral dimensions, plus their intrinsic connections. Moreover, following Christ does not mean focusing on his past earthly life, but on his present lordship. Believers are to apply the mind of Christ to their present circumstances. Paul is concerned with how the church can be faithful in ever-new and changing situations under the guidance of a Lord who is our contemporary.

The church need not choose between discipleship and identification, nor should it choose between the Gospels and Paul as its leading light. One of the puzzles of the New Testament is its paucity of evidence for how the Gospels and their Jesus stories relate to the proclamation of the gospel. Why is the example of Jesus cited so rarely outside of the Gospels? Perhaps the preceding paragraph helps explain why. In any event, the early church decided that it needed both the Gospels and the Epistles to support its discipleship and its experience *in Christ*.

Paul and other writers give hints of how they understood the relationship. To illustrate in brief—Paul exhorts his readers to behold the glory of the Lord, as if reflected in a mirror, in order that they might be transformed into that image (2 Cor 3:18). He does not describe exactly how one is to do this beholding. He assumes his readers/hearers will understand. In light of the whole New Testament, the narratives of Jesus' life, first preserved in oral retelling and now in our present Gospels, function as the mirror for contemplating the glory of Christ. Where else is there access to the face of Jesus Christ (see 2 Cor 4:6!)?

These concrete narratives in the Gospels keep us from falling into nebulous and subjective contemplation. On the other hand, Paul's language indicates that this new life in the Spirit must not be primarily a trip into history, but a living encounter with this same Jesus as Lord. Christ, as living Spirit, makes contemporary and relevant the meaning of Jesus for the church. This perspective keeps us from falling into legalism and formalism (see 2 Cor 3:4-17). This point of view should inform the faithful church of any tradition, and certainly the discipleship tradition of the Radical Reformation.

Galatians 4:21-31

A Scriptural Case for Corrective Action

PREVIEW

The so-called allegory of Hagar and Sarah is especially difficult for today's reader. The primary reason for this difficulty is the unusual type of interpretation Paul adopts (cf. 3:16 and discussion there). This use of Scripture is not unique to Paul. What is unique to the passage is the unconventional result! The conclusions he draws from the Old Testament texts are, at certain points, counterintuitive both for the original and the modern audience. That he is engaging in a distinctive approach to Scripture is signaled by Paul's use of a term that appears only here in the earliest Christian writings: *allegory* (4:24).

Another challenge with this passage is that Hagar and her child, representing as they do, slavery and the *lack* of God's favor, come off looking bad. Many modern interpreters of Galatians criticize Paul for not taking Hagar seriously as a person in her own right—for not respecting her courage, her strength, and her own faith in the face of a difficult situation. But Paul is not trying to take her or her story seriously, nor is he trying to interpret the Genesis passage on its own terms. He is using her story *allegorically* to make a certain point. In fact, few authors attempt completely fair, comprehensive, or balanced interpretations when using a story or person to illustrate a point.

Yet another challenge with the passage is why it is placed here. Paul has already made his argument from Scripture and has moved

219

on to more experiential matters. Is this now an afterthought, or is there a deeper explanation for its placement? There are, in fact, at least two deeper reasons. First, the reference at the end of the text to casting out *the slave and her child* is an indirect call for the Galatians to expel the offending teachers. This exhortation fits this part of the letter, which is characterized by imperative verbs requesting specific responses from the readers/hearers (see explanation at 4:12). Second, the ideas in the text form a bridge between the earlier theme of promise and Law, and the theme of Spirit and flesh, which dominates the material that follows. For these reasons it fits the present location well, even though it may appear an afterthought, perhaps belonging better in chapter 3, with the discussion of (OT) scriptural evidence.

Despite these challenges, Paul's main point and how it connects with the wider message of the letter are clear enough. Paul uses Hagar and Sarah, and their respective sons, to illustrate two covenants, or ways of living before God. These two ways correspond to the by-now familiar contrast in Galatians between the way of slavery and the way of freedom. Hagar, the slave woman, stands for slavery. Sarah, Abraham's wife and the one through whom God's promise was to be fulfilled, stands for freedom. The shocking irony is that in holding on to Law observance, the teachers are actually identifying with Hagar, the Gentile, rather than with Sarah, the Jew! Just as shocking is the implication that the present Jerusalem, center of the Jewish people and seat of the pillars in the church (2:9), is the symbol of slavery!

Paul describes Abraham's decision to force the fulfillment of God's promise by using Hagar to bear Ishmael as a birth *according to the flesh* (4:23, 29). It was based in human intent and effort. On the other hand, the miraculous birth of Isaac to Sarah is God's act, consistent with the promise. Therefore, Paul calls Isaac the son *through promise* and *according to the Spirit*. It was based on God's purpose and action. To this point, Paul has not engaged in allegory, but in a conventional interpretation of the text. In this letter Paul's observations illustrate his conviction about the fundamental difference between promise or faith, leading to freedom, and Law or flesh, leading to slavery. The allegorical features then follow.

The basic elements of the account and its logic can be set out this way:

Story: Abraham's Two Sons

One son by a slave woman	One son by a free woman
Born according to the flesh	Born through promise

Allegory: Two Women as Two Covenants

Hagar	[Sarah]
Sinai/present Jerusalem	Jerusalem above
Children for slavery	Children of promise
According to the flesh	According to the Spirit

EXPLANATORY NOTES

Tell me, you who desire to be subject to the law, will you not listen to the law? (4:21). After the preceding emotional appeal, Paul suddenly turns to a more rational argument. The opening statement makes the clearest assertion yet that the Galatians are submitting to the requirements of the Jewish Law. This verse also illustrates the multiple meanings of the Law in Paul. The first occurrence refers to the specific demands in the Torah, but the second refers to the narrative material in the Torah to which Paul is about to appeal.

Paul wants to show that the very Law being pressed on the Galatians can support his understanding of the gospel. The suggestion is plausible that Paul is here giving his interpretation of a passage that his opponents had used to show that true sons (!) of Abraham are descendants of Isaac, who was circumcised, and not Ishmael, who represents uncircumcised Gentiles. Paul's use of the verb *listen* reflects the cultural setting in which the average person heard Scripture being read, rather than reading a written text. In typical biblical fashion, the word also connotes giving heed and submitting to what is heard.

For it is written that Abraham had two sons, one by a slave woman and the other by a free woman. One, the child of the slave, was born according to the flesh; the other, the child of the free woman, was born through the promise (4:22). Here Paul rehearses the facts of the story that interest him. The interpretation he gives the story is based on its literal features. He does supply language absent from the original text in Genesis in the phrases *free woman* and *according to the flesh*. The former describes Sarah's status in contrast to Hagar's. The latter is

Paul's way of describing Abraham's human act of taking a woman who is not his wife to help God fulfill God's promise of offspring. Paul's choice of vocabulary obviously supports his linking of the story with the themes of the present letter, but to this point, Paul's thought is grounded in the meaning of the Genesis text. Here Paul focuses on the first two sons of Abraham, Ishmael and Isaac, although neither is named (Isaac is eventually named in 4:28). Given the use he is making of the story, Paul has more interest in the allegorical value of the persons than in their character or identity.

It is clear enough that the key to 4:22–23 lies in the two contrasting pairs: slave versus free, and flesh versus promise. The pairing of flesh and promise as opposites is significant because it demonstrates a correlation between the more usual contrastive pairings of promise versus Law, and flesh versus Spirit. Thus Law and flesh share common ground, and promise and Spirit share a different ground. The linking of Law with flesh and promise with Spirit is a key move in Galatians and essential to Paul's argument (see 3:2-3; 3:14; 5:16-18). It would have been anachronistic for Paul to have used Law, which had not yet been given, as the contrast to promise in the story of Abraham's sons. However, one cannot miss Paul's intended connection to the Law in the allegory itself at 4:24-25.

Now this is an allegory: these women are two covenants (4:24a). The introduction of the word *allegory* at this point signals the existence of two stages in Paul's rendering of the account: story and allegory (see the structural layout in Preview; on the concept of allegory, see TBC). The present passage is a mixed allegory. Paul first finds spiritual insight based on the plain meaning of the story of Abraham's sons, and then Paul offers an allegorical extension based on those insights.

The narrative focus now shifts from the sons of Abraham to their mothers. Apparently the mother figure serves better to symbolize a covenant tradition. So Paul returns to the image of bearing children (cf. 4:19) and plays again on the mother image (4:26): *Jerusalem above . . . is our mother.* Paul's allegorical move is to make these two women, Hagar and Sarah, stand for two covenants. This step places the origin of the contrast between covenant types in the story of Abraham himself. As we will see, Paul has in mind the contrast he has been making all along between promise and Law, between freedom and slavery.

One should notice that this contrast *precedes* the giving of the Law at Sinai. The contrast is not between Abraham and Moses, or between the old and new covenants, though Paul will later refer to such contrasts in salvation history. Here Paul is using *covenant* not of specific covenants in history, but of *types* of covenants and their respective modes of living before God. Paul is not contrasting the Old and New Testaments (as if he were even *aware* of the NT)! Rather, Paul is contrasting two *types* of covenant that interact down through the history of God's interaction with God's people, beginning in Genesis. Paul's concern in Galatians is to show that his gospel of freedom connects more authentically with how God has related to humanity over the long haul than does the Law of Moses.

The one woman, Hagar, is from Mount Sinai and bears children for slavery (4:24b AT). Hagar "is" Mount Sinai in Arabia and corresponds to the present Jerusalem, for she is in slavery with her children. Hagar, the servant woman in Abraham's household, is the representative mother of slavery. In that role she stands at the head of a family line. It is interesting that in this allegory Paul traces *matriarchal* lineages (from Hagar and from Sarah) in a patriarchal context in which male-centered family lines were the norm. Whether Paul is consciously seeking to elevate women in doing this is unclear, but this move is consistent with his more gender-inclusive perspective on the gospel (Gal 3:28) and his complete comfort in associating himself with feminine imagery (Gal 4:19; 1 Thess 2:7). Paul is, perhaps, thinking of Isaiah 51:2, which mentions Sarah, along with Abraham, as the one who bore Israel (see 4:27 for another possible link to this Isaiah passage).

A key to the allegory is Mount Sinai, because that geographical location can be connected both to Hagar and to the Law of Moses. Mount Sinai is where the Law was given, as anyone familiar with Judaism would immediately have recognized. The link to Hagar is more tenuous since no Old Testament text puts the two names together. Nevertheless, the narratives in Genesis 16 and 21 do place her in the Sinai Peninsula (the Negeb) where Mount Sinai is located. Other suggestions about specific associations of Hagar with Sinai are speculative and unlikely to reflect Paul's thinking (for details see Longenecker; or Dunn 1993).

Paul's expanded statement, *Now Hagar is Mount Sinai in Arabia* (4:25a), is grammatically unclear in the Greek. This has led to variations in the early Greek manuscripts, with Hagar sometimes present and sometimes absent. The Greek could also be translated *Now Mount Sinai, which is Hagar, is in Arabia.* Is Paul more intent on identifying the location of the mountain or in identifying Hagar with Mount Sinai? She is *from* Sinai in verse 24, but in verse 25 she *is* Sinai. Paul's reference to the *present Jerusalem* in verse 25 could suggest that in verse 24 Paul is geographically situating the elements in the allegory.

Paul then makes a further link to the present Jerusalem. The word for *corresponds* means "to be in the same list or column." Hagar (and Sinai, i.e., the Law) are in a category with Jerusalem. The *present Jerusalem* (4:25) refers to the center of Law observance, with particular allusion to Paul's adversaries, who claim to represent Jerusalem and defend the Law. This category stands over against the category of Sarah and the *Jerusalem above* (4:26). The first category is characterized as slavery, the second as freedom.

The double reference to the slavery of Hagar and her offspring indicates what Paul is emphasizing. In the allegory, the concept of slavery comes from Hagar's status as slave. But Paul has already given other grounds for associating the Law with bondage (3:23; 4:1-10). This illustrates how an allegory is an illustration for a truth originating on other grounds. If the earlier allusion to Law observance as bondage would scandalize the Jewish Christian, this association of the Law and Judaism with the Gentile Hagar and her descendants would appear even more startling to them. Paul seems to want to shock his hearers!

But the other woman corresponds to the Jerusalem above; she is free, and she is our mother (4:26). This other woman is Sarah, who, like Ishmael and Isaac, goes unnamed (see 4:22; Isaac is named in 4:28). Sarah belongs in the category with Jerusalem above. The characterization of this category as free comes as no surprise at this point of the letter. Although unstated, Paul's gospel is also in this category. The same effect is achieved in the assertion that the Jerusalem above is our mother. The pronoun *our* is shorthand for those believers, Jew and Gentile, who live in Christ and beyond the Law. This is the gospel that Paul preaches. The reference to Jerusalem as mother is not new (see Isa 50:1; 51:17-18; Jer 50:12; Hos 4:5).

The concept of a Jerusalem above is introduced in pure allegorical style without being linked to any of the passages that figure in this allegory. The idea of a new Jerusalem is firmly rooted in the prophetic tradition (cf. Isa 2:1-5; Mic 4:1-4; Jer 31:38-40; Isa 65:17-25). In Jewish apocalyptic circles, prophecies about the restoration or renewal of Jerusalem developed into hope for a new Jerusalem from heaven that would anchor the restored kingdom of God (cf. Isa 65:17-25; 2 Esd 10:25-28; Rev 21:2). A similar evolution of prophetic hope developed with regard to the temple (cf. Ezek 40–48; Heb 8:5, citing Exod 25:40; for expressions of antitemple sentiment within Judaism, see Acts 7:47-51; John 4:21-24; Heb 9:1-14; *Epistle of Barnabas* 16.1-2). This provided a means by which some faithful Jews could critique the present establishment in Jerusalem (note *present*

Jerusalem in 4:25!), contrasting it with the (heavenly) ideal and laying out prospects for a better future. Paul is here directing this critique against the false teachers in Galatia, who claim to represent the Law-observing mother church in Jerusalem, the earthly Jerusalem.

For it is written, "Rejoice, you childless one, you who bear no children, burst into song and shout, you who endure no birth pangs; for the children of the desolate woman are more numerous than the children of the one who is married" (4:27). The mixed character of our account is again highlighted by this quotation of a prophetic text from Isaiah 54:1 (Greek). In a manner typical of late Second Temple Judaism, Paul applies a prophecy concerning God's intention to reestablish Israel after the exile to fulfill God's final purposes through the Messiah (here, Jesus Christ) in the messianic people (here, the church). The Isaiah passage may well allude to Sarah, as the explicit mention of her in Isaiah 51:2 suggests. In any event, Paul uses the reference to barrenness (*childless one* and *the desolate woman*) as the contact with his allegory of Sarah, who was the barren one, but stands for the gospel of freedom in the age of fulfillment. The joy and exuberance are signs of an eschatological ecstasy, the joy of realized expectations!

For Paul, the high point of the quotation is probably in the final clause. The paradox is that the barren woman has more offspring than the married (fertile) one! The women are Hagar and Sarah. The greater number of the barren woman's children refer to the Abrahamic blessing of the nations, a blessing that is now being fulfilled through the influx of the Gentiles into the messianic people of God (see 3:8-9, 14). The covenant of freedom is a place of fertility and procreation, where God continues the miracle of creating adopted sons and daughters in the power of the Spirit. Did the Galatians catch the force of this quotation and share the enthusiasm Paul wanted to convey?

Now you, my friends, are children of the promise, like Isaac (4:28). Lest the Galatians miss how this allegory relates to them, Paul states the matter plainly. The pronoun *you* lies in the place of emphasis at the beginning of the sentence. The *Galatians* are children of the promise. They are the offspring of Sarah, like Isaac. Paul returns to the language of promise to describe this lineage (see 4:23). On the expression *my friends*, see on 4:12.

But just as at that time the child who was born according to the flesh [Ishmael] *persecuted the child who was born according to the Spirit* [Isaac], *so it is now also. But what does the scripture say? "Drive out the*

slave and her child; for the child of the slave will not share the inheritance
with the child of the free woman" (4:29-30). Here the allegory takes a
novel turn! And it may well be the turn that Paul had in mind to
begin with when he decided where to place the allegory in his letter.
The story of Hagar and Sarah provides Paul the resource to prescribe the exact course of action he wishes to urge upon the
Galatians in relation to the false teachers. From Genesis 21:9 Paul
picks up the motif of persecution of Isaac by Ishmael. Its reference
to persecution depends on a later Jewish understanding of the word
playing in the text to mean "to make fun of, to make sport of." But
here it may refer to the difficulties being caused by the circumcision
party (cf. 5:11). The opponents of Paul in Galatia represent that
group, and they are to be expelled, as the next verse will say. But
this persecution is of a piece with the larger persecution of the
Christian sect, in which persecution Paul himself participated
before his conversion (1:13; cf. 2 Cor 11:24; 1 Thess 2:14-15).

The language Paul uses to describe the two sons of Abraham is
significant. He has already used the phrase *according to the flesh* in
4:23, where he contrasts it with *through the promise.* Here, however,
Paul uses the more common pairing with *according to the Spirit.* This
is the first time in the allegory that the Spirit is mentioned. As elsewhere in Galatians, *according to the Spirit* refers to what is in harmony with the divine promise and has the direct empowerment of
God in its realization. Specifically, here it refers to the miraculous
birth of Isaac.

Now Paul quotes the statement of Sarah in Genesis 21:10 (in the
Septuagint, the Greek translation) where she demands that
Abraham send away Hagar and Ishmael. Although Paul does not
spell out how this command applies to the Galatian situation, his
intent is unmistakable. Without being unduly brash, he wants the
Galatians to send the other teachers packing! The Law-promoting
teachers do not share in the true inheritance of biblical faith. The
distinction between the viewpoint of those teachers and the true
gospel must be preserved! The concept of inheritance provides yet
another link between this allegory and the preceding discussion
(see 3:18, 29; 4:1, 7). Paul's use of the concept reflects his view of a
divine purpose that gives unity and continuity to history as true
faith passes from generation to generation. A practical application,
as seen in the present context, is that believers have a responsibility to preserve the integrity and purity of this stream through time.
Such a task calls for some form of defending the truth and preserving the integrity of the faithful community.

So then, friends, we are children, not of the slave but of the free woman
(4:31). Paul has now used a respectful designation *friends* (better,
brothers and sisters; see on 4:12) twice in this passage alone—in verse
28 and here. The usage intensifies as the letter progresses. This
verse serves to summarize the whole passage. Paul uses the vocabulary of slavery and freedom once again, returning to the point of
beginning in 4:22. At the same time, it prepares for what follows as
Paul further expounds these themes.

THE TEXT IN BIBLICAL CONTEXT

Allegorical Use of Scripture

Paul calls his treatment of the Hagar/Sarah story an allegory. How
does allegory work in this passage? In the story, Paul associates the
Abraham/Sarah/Isaac line with the gospel. Paul made this point
already in chapter 3. What is new here is the way Paul uses Hagar to
make the connection between slavery and the Law. Both Hagar and
the Law have a common link to Mount Sinai, but no essential link to
each other. On the basis of this accidental link, Paul associates slavery with Law. He then extends the association of slavery/Law to
include the present Jerusalem, and lets the freedom/gospel association include the Jerusalem above. These links are not in his biblical
source. The connection of Law with Jerusalem makes logical sense
to the reader/hearer because Jerusalem is the center of the religion
that observes the Law. The connection of the true gospel to the
Jerusalem above has no basis other than Paul's spiritual insight and
conviction that Israel's eschatological hope in God's restoration of
Israel (symbolized in the Jerusalem from above) is being realized in
God's action in Christ—that is, in Paul's gospel.

As a method, allegory does not seek insight from the texts being
treated. For this reason, it is somewhat misleading to speak of the
allegorical "interpretation" of Scripture. Rather, insights (and their
warrants) come from *outside* the text, either from other texts or
from the theology of the interpreter. This does not mean that allegorical uses of Scripture are necessarily wrong. Their truth is not
based on the cited text itself but on something outside that text that
is brought to the text. Strictly speaking, it is not an interpretation of
the text, but a *use* of a text to illustrate a truth derived elsewhere.

Allegory was developed by the Greeks as a way of using old writings to speak in an age that no longer accepted the texts' old myths
and superstitions. This was not the last time in history when a
change of worldview created the need for a drastically new way to

give meaning to old, respected texts! Something parallel happened for the Jewish people who lived amid Greek cultures. Philo of Alexandria used allegory to build a bridge between the Jewish Scriptures and Greek philosophy as he tried to show that the new insights of philosophy were already present in Scripture. Paul's use of the word *allegory* indicates his intentionality in using this approach. Paul's conviction that God's action in Christ is the key to understanding God's action throughout history is what compels his allegorical reading of the Hagar story. Thus, in our passage, he brings his understanding of the gospel *to* the text rather than taking his understanding *from* the text.

The present passage is really a mixed allegory (Witherington: 323). The elements of allegory coexist with other types of interpretation as well. Paul engages in a more literal interpretation when he states that Abraham acts outside the spirit of promise by acting on his own initiative to have a son. Here we also see a form of interpretation called typology. *Typology* comes from the New Testament word *type* to describe the linking of an Old Testament precedent (the *type*) to a New Testament parallel (the *antitype*; e.g., Rom 5:14; Heb 8:5). New Testament writers who employ typology usually see the type as an anticipation of what is now a more perfect example (cf. Heb 10:1). In other words, typology links the type and antitype as promise and fulfillment. The assumption behind this method of interpretation is that God is guiding history purposefully and that one can observe a certain coherence or unity in God's action.

Typology gives allegory a historical context. As a result, the parallels an interpreter draws are not arbitrary, but actual links in the larger story of God's saving action. Our present passage features a typological framework within which Paul makes his allegorical moves. This framework is Paul's view of salvation history based in a divine promise to Abraham that is fulfilled in Christ after the interlude of the Law. Paul worked out this framework carefully in chapter 3. Thus Paul is not using pure allegory. By placing his allegorical moves within a typological and literal framework, he grounds his interpretation of Scripture in something other than his own presuppositions or arbitrary reconstructions of the text.

Discipline among the People of God

One of the purposes of this section of the letter, as we have noted, is to motivate the Galatians to dismiss the false teachers. Paul wants the Galatians to discipline these teachers. The theme of discipline was first touched on in relation to the pronouncement of a curse on heretical teachers in 1:8-9. Paul exercised discipline in his churches based either on his action as an apostle or the action of the congregation. Galatians illustrates both: apostolic discipline in 1:8-9 and congregational discipline here in 4:30 and 6:1. A parallel case appears in 1 Corinthians 5, where Paul refers to both types of discipline.

Paul appeals to Scripture in support of his idea of a disciplined community that with integrity reflects Israel's covenant with Yahweh. In the present passage, he quotes Genesis 21:10. In 1 Corinthians 5:13 he cites Deuteronomy 17:7. The latter passage is particularly pertinent because it concludes a set of instructions, in this case for the discipline of idolaters.

In both testaments the concept of discipline is rooted in the vision of a special people who reflect the uniqueness (holiness) of God in the world. The integrity of the covenant relation with God and of the mission of God's people in the world demands the protection of this unique vision. Doing so requires actions that preserve the distinctiveness of God's people by dissociating them from what is inconsistent with it. The same perspective is obvious in Paul's use of the leaven imagery in 1 Corinthians 5:6-7—a little leaven (adversely) affects the entire loaf. Both God (e.g., Heb 12:5-11) and the people of God (Matt 18:15-20) have a role in discipline. The New Testament teaches about church discipline in such places as Matthew 18; Acts 5; and Revelation 2.

In general, the New Testament emphasizes the restorative intent in disciplinary action, though the account of Ananias and Sapphira in Acts 5 seems an exception. Galatians 6:1 reflects this intent to restore and adds the important corollary that those who exercise the discipline bear in mind their own vulnerabilities (cf. 1 Cor 5:5; 2 Cor 2:5-11). Moreover, Paul is concerned that the commitment to preserve a community with an identity separate from the world not lead to an isolated community without missional engagement with the world (1 Cor 5:9-11). Matthew 5:13-16 shows that Jesus viewed the integrity of the disciple community as essential to its missional effectiveness in the world.

THE TEXT IN THE LIFE OF THE CHURCH

Biblical Interpretation in the Life of the Church

The question about how any religious group is to interpret the texts it considers religiously authoritative is a critical issue. How can one faithfully apply a text written in one time and place to other times and places? Answers to that question are in constant flux and change. The Christian church faces an even greater challenge because it treats both testaments as authoritative, with the newer testament reading the older one in a distinctive fashion. That is, the writers of the newer testament read the older one in the light of God's action in Christ. Thus already in the New Testament itself, we see the challenge of reinterpreting an older text for a new time.

In the secular realm this issue is illustrated in debates about how to interpret and apply a society's constitutional documents. Some advocate a strict or literal interpretation as the only way to ensure faithfulness. Others insist that faithfulness to the original intent requires a broader, more dynamic mode of interpretation.

We should recognize validity in both of these approaches. The broad approach rightly recognizes that changing circumstances require new applications, given the change in meaning that culture can attach to things. And since all human knowledge, including the revealed truth of Scripture, is enmeshed in ever-changing cultures, these changes require shifts in our reading and application of Scripture. This means that in applying an authoritative text, one may need to depart from a literal application of the text in order to be true to its deepest intent. On the other hand, a literal approach guards against the temptation to accommodate the text to new cultural contexts so thoroughly that the text cannot critique that culture.

The Anabaptists of the sixteenth century illustrate the above points. By employing a simple, direct, and literal reading of the Bible, they discovered the basis for criticizing and rejecting certain accommodations of the day, such as infant baptism and the state's control of the church. On the other hand, in their attempt to recapture the New Testament teaching on discipline, their literal reading of those texts often led to harsh applications that missed the spirit of reconciling love (see below).

The Anabaptists demonstrated some wisdom on how Christians should use the Old Testament. Because they took literally the command of Jesus to love enemies, they needed an interpretative approach that did not have to take Old Testament texts on warfare and violence as the literal standard for the church. The approach they adopted is today called a Christocentric hermeneutic, in which Christ and his teachings are the standard by which to interpret and apply other Scriptures. In Galatians, Paul uses the same approach in arguing that the coming of Christ has modified the role and relevance of the Mosaic Law in significant ways.

The dilemma of broad versus strict interpretation can be resolved only by attention to the Spirit and to the spirit of the text.

Hence readers must penetrate the surface of the text in order to understand how a larger spiritual vision expresses itself in concrete human forms and actions. This awareness *can* point to an appropriate application for a new time and place. Postmodern sensitivities make us aware that our personal social location and interests inevitably color this work of interpretation, easily distorting and limiting our understanding. The church has a resource for answering to this challenge in the doctrine of the Holy Spirit. The Reformation emphasized the twofold work of Word and Spirit in discerning the mind of God. When the church faces difficult discernment about some matter, it must depend on the dialectic of Word and Spirit to negotiate its challenge (cf. 1 Cor 14:26-33a). This means listening to the Holy Spirit as we read the Word. The process is messy and unmanageable, but crucial. Specifically, the church must heighten its reliance on the Spirit, who "guides into all the truth" (John 16:13), doing so through the variety of Spirit gifts present in the whole body of believers (the hermeneutical community).

Discipline in the Believers Church

The believers church has typically taken the biblical teaching on discipline seriously. In this tradition the true church is made up only of those who have a personal faith commitment, which requires an ongoing maintenance of that integrity. Therefore, a mark of the true church is discipline. This discipline aims at preserving the integrity, or purity, of the church. Churches with less emphasis on these points (e.g., state or establishment churches) tend to see the church as a service institution that ministers to the religious needs of the entire society. The distinction between church and society receives less, or no, emphasis.

The believers church tradition, including the sixteenth-century Radical Reformation, from which it derives, is a study in the success and the failure of discipline. At one extreme, the use of the ban and the shunning of the disciplined person have contributed to perfectionism, legalism, factionalism, and disunity. Partly in reaction to the harsh forms of discipline in the past, and partly because of the influence of modern individualism, relativism, and tolerance, some churches today have largely abandoned their historical commitment to being communities of mutual care and accountability.

Some sense of ongoing tension here cannot be avoided since the church is both an open community engaged in evangelism and mission, and a closed community with its own unique identity within a world of many identities, religious and nonreligious. Even within the church, tension remains between the high vision and ideals of righteousness and the reality of believers who encounter failure along their journeys of faith. At the heart of this tension is the dynamic relationship between truth and love, a relationship beautifully stated in the phrase "speaking the truth in love" (Eph 4:15). This same double emphasis on truth and love lies at the center of the Galatian letter, which holds onto both the truth of the gospel (2:5) and love for one another (5:13).

At its best, discipline makes community effective in evangelism because it has the appeal of an alternate community where righteousness and love are genuinely displayed. Its discipline encourages and supports the faith development process of each believer. The primary emphasis of discipline must always be on positive encouragement to spiritual growth. We can call this *formative discipline*, illustrated in Galatians when Paul calls for the formation of Christ in the believer (4:19) through a life-giving process of identification with Christ (2:19-20).

At the same time, the church must not abandon its practice of corrective discipline in dealing with moral failure and doctrinal error. Such discipline aims at restoration, rather than punishment. Later in Galatians, Paul himself says that the community should *restore . . . in a spirit of gentleness* (6:1; see comments there), which is itself a fruit of the Spirit (5:22-23).

Galatians 5:1-12

Standing Fast in Freedom

PREVIEW

Having completed the allegory on slavery and freedom, Paul is now ready to make a strong, direct appeal to the Galatians. Paul wants them to remain firm in their first commitment to the gospel as he had preached it. Happily, the "cost" of this commitment is freedom from the yoke of slavery!

The letter is moving to its climax. Paul's strong affirmations carry a note of finality. Now we come to the heart of the matter. As we would expect in this section, marked as it is by request, imperatives are numerous, and the language of personal appeal dominates. At this crucial point Paul's use of *freedom* confirms that it is a unifying theme of the letter. After announcing this theme in his appeal to *stand firm*, Paul explores several specific weaknesses in the visitors' false teaching and several strengths of his gospel. Paul's summary formulation in 5:5-6 is one of the most striking and memorable statements of Pauline theology.

OUTLINE

Yoke of Law Righteousness, 5:1-4
Freedom of Christ Righteousness, 5:5-6
Call to Action, 5:7-12

EXPLANATORY NOTES

Yoke of Law Righteousness 5:1-4

For freedom Christ has set us free; stand fast, therefore, and do not submit again to a yoke of slavery (5:1). There is some question whether this verse belongs to what precedes or to what follows. It continues the freedom and slavery theme of the preceding allegory, but the lack of a connecting word suggests a break. Furthermore, Paul's description of Christ's liberating work does not grow out of the allegory. On the other hand, a more obvious break separates verses 1 and 2. It is probably best to take 5:1 as transitional, a bridge that gives continuity to the material.

Paul's double use of *freedom* in the verb (*set free*) and in the noun (*freedom*) contributes to the strong impact of his opening assertion. Which English preposition best expresses the sense with which Paul is modifying the noun is debated: is it *for, in,* or *by* freedom? This may be one place where the distinction between purpose and result is minimal. Christ set us free *so that we might continue* in freedom. Christ's liberating action was not just a temporary stage until further "growth" requires submitting to the Law of Moses! This affirmation serves well at the head of a section that explores the implications of redemption (see 4:4-5) for the way we live. Christ frees believers *for a life of freedom*. This is the first place in the letter that Paul uses the word *freedom* to describe the work of Christ. He did, however, introduce the *theme* of freedom in 1:4; 3:25; and 4:5 (see the discussion there about what this freedom entails).

To the affirmation of God's liberating action in Christ, Paul now joins the command to continue steadfastly and firmly in the resulting condition. This is a classic illustration of how Paul typically links the indicative of divine action to the imperative of human response (see TBC). Such use of language provides another window into the heart of Paul's religious conviction, which he is struggling to express in Galatians: spiritual authenticity exists only where human religious deeds are consistent with and continuously nourished by the deeds of God.

Paired with Paul's positive command to stand firm is his corresponding negative command not to submit again to the *yoke of slavery.* The word *again* indicates that Paul has in mind the Galatians' bondage under paganism, described in 4:8. Although the form of bondage into which the Galatians are now falling is different, it is bondage all the same. The word *submit* is not the same one that New Testament writers use in calling for the submission of believers to one another. It has the nuances of "being entangled in" or "loaded down with." Its negative connotations well fit the image of slavery.

Paul's reference to the *yoke of slavery* has a double allusion. The Jewish community used the expression "yoke of the law" to describe commitment to observing the Law (cf. Jer 5:5; Acts 15:10). But *yoke* also evokes the image of war captives who are bound by yokes and led away into slavery (cf. *yoke of slavery* in 1 Tim 6:1). In a context where Paul contrasts the freedom of Christ and the bondage of Law, the aptness of the image is obvious (cf. Jesus' positive use of *yoke* in Matt 11:29, and its possible parallel in Paul's expression, *the law of Christ* [Gal 6:2]).

Listen! I, Paul, am telling you that if you let yourselves be circumcised, Christ will be of no benefit to you (5:2). Paul begins verse 2 with a call to attention, two personal pronouns, and a citation of his personal name. It is a solemn, forceful, and authoritative appeal to pay attention. Paul sustains the intensity of his tone through verse 4. By now the perceptive reader of the letter knows that the teachers in Galatia are trying to impose circumcision on the Gentiles and hardly notices that this is the first time in the letter that Paul has made this fact explicit. The grammar of the conditional sentence leaves open the question about whether the Galatians are just contemplating circumcision, or whether some of the Galatians have already consented to being circumcised.

In either case, the principle underlying the hypothetical statement is crucial for Paul: for the Galatians, circumcision and Christ are incompatible. Submission to the Law, which is what circumcision involves, amounts to a repudiation of any benefit from Christ. The word *benefit* connotes economic profit and loss (see also the next verse). The idea is parallel to 2:21—Christ's death is meaningless if the Law can put us right with God. There is no reason to take the future tense of *benefit* as a reference only to the future, final rewards for the believer (for that aspect, see 5:5). Paul obviously means no benefit of any kind at any time. (The English future tense is required by the type of Greek conditional sentence here.)

How are circumcision and Christ incompatible? First, this is not a statement about God withholding something as a consequence of law observance. Moreover, circumcision is not intrinsically evil. After all, Paul accepted circumcision for Jewish Christians. But, in Paul's mind, for *Gentile Galatians* to accept circumcision meant accepting the full validity of the Law's demand and devaluing the work of Christ. In effect, this means denying the full sufficiency of identification with Christ (in the strength of the Spirit)!

Moreover, Paul clearly believed that if Gentiles had to become full Jews through circumcision, their new life in Christ would no longer be a fulfillment of the Abrahamic promise of blessing to all nations. Gentiles *as Gentiles* would not be redeemable. Since God's promise to Abraham had been fulfilled in Christ, the free entry of the Gentiles into the people of God is a benefit of Christ. Christ removes the wall that separates Jew and Gentile. He does not make the one side *become* the other; he makes the two become a new *one* (3:28; cf. Eph 2:13-16). To embrace the Law in the form of obligation to receive circumcision means rejecting this benefit of freedom and equality (see 2:4 and the elaboration in 2:11-14 and 3:6-14).

Once again I testify to every man who lets himself be circumcised that he is obliged to obey the entire law (5:3). Now the solemnity of the courtroom is evoked with the language of witness. Paul's *once again* could point back to 3:10, or the expression might merely mean that this is the second of two definitive assertions (vv. 2 and 3) to which Paul is bearing witness. In any case, the thought itself may be linked with 3:10 (see notes there). English translations do not catch the wordplay between the *benefit* of verse 2 and the *obliged* here. The first has the connotation of credit and the second indicates debt. Paul is saying that in Christ the believer is the creditor of the riches of grace, but in the Law a person is always a debtor. Christ offers a relationship through which flows divine provision. The Law offers obligation without any provision for fulfilling it. This economic image parallels the image of life: the Law cannot give life (2:19; 3:21), but God in Christ (2:19-20) and through the Spirit (3:1-5; 5:25) can and does give life.

The central point of the assertion is that if one accepts obligation to part of the Law, however small that part, one becomes a debtor to the entire Law. This is the logic found in James 2:10 and often in Jewish literature. Paul wants the Galatians to feel the weight of the all-encompassing Law. Perhaps the Galatians have not been made aware of this. There is no evident reason why the opposing teachers themselves would have had a selective view of the Law's requirements. Yet Romans 2:17-29 suggests that some in the Jewish community did operate, in practice, with a selective view. In this letter, Paul assumes that the proponents of circumcision in Galatia themselves fall short of full observance of the Law (cf. 6:13). Beyond that, we have little basis for making deductions from this text about Paul's understanding of the Law—or even about Jewish views in general.

You who want to be justified by the law have cut yourselves off from Christ; you have fallen away from grace (4:4). Here Paul moves from being the witness to being the judge. He renders judgment on their submission to circumcision. The present-tense verb, *be justified*, correctly communicates the Galatians' desire to be justified, but from Paul's point of view, that justification is unachievable, given their approach. Even if some of the Galatians have already submitted to circumcision, their justification depends on their returning to the real grounds for justification: faith in Christ. Paul does not believe that justification is ever possible by the Law. The verbs *cut off* and *fallen* are in the past tense, indicating completed action. This might well be evidence that some of the Galatians have indeed submitted to the teachers' exhortation to "advance" in their faith by submitting to circumcision. Yet in that case, as Paul will make clear in 5:6, all is not lost; what is crucial is that they return to *faith working through love.* However, these same past-tense verbs could, according to Greek usage, also be used for dramatic effect, to bring home the full reality of what would result from the action of circumcision. In this case the action would not necessarily have yet taken place. This would be consistent with the hypothetical tone of the context set by the conditional sentence in verse 2.

It has been some time since Paul has used the language of justification in his argument (see 3:24). Here Paul states the negative side: justification by means of the Law depends on keeping the Law of Moses. Paul rejects this in favor of justification by faith, as in 3:24. The phrase *by the law* is found also in 3:11 (cf. *through the Law* in 2:21) and is practically synonymous with *works of the Law*, the other key formulation in the letter. The close parallel of this verse to the previous shows clearly that circumcision is a concrete example of seeking justification by the Law. Paul's fullest discussion of these matters came at 2:16 and 3:10-12 (see comments there).

The consequence of embracing a Law-based righteousness is being cut off from Christ and falling from grace. The word translated as *be cut off* means to be separated from or loosed from. Here Paul is not alluding to the physical act of circumcision. He is talking about the serious matter of breaking off a personal relationship. That deeply personal bond to Christ, which came to expression in places like 2:20 and 4:19, is threatened by loyalty to the Law. Another way to express the consequence is that they have fallen from grace. Although present, *grace* is not a dominant theme in Galatians. Already in 1:6 Paul has characterized the gospel experience as a calling into the grace of Christ (also 1:15; 2:9). In a close parallel to our present passage, Paul claims that justification or righteousness through the Law is tantamount to nullifying the grace of God (2:21).

Again we hear the sharp either/or of Paul's logic. The Law is not inherently alien to Christ or grace, but trusting it as a basis of securing one's relationship with God amounts to rejecting God's decisive action in the cross of Christ. *Christ* defines the will of God, and doing the will of God depends on the Spirit's empowerment. Anything else is slavery, something less than freedom from sin and freedom for righteousness. Moreover, believers who have entered into grace might later abandon that same grace. In emphasizing the freedom of God in choosing a people and the initiative of God in salvation, Paul does not displace or diminish human responsibility in the covenant relationship with God. The loss of salvation is a real possibility that demands vigilance on the part of the believer (see TBC).

Freedom of Christ Righteousness 5:5-6

For through the Spirit, by faith, we eagerly wait for the hope of righteousness(5:5). Now Paul turns from describing the negative option of righteousness based on Law to describing the positive option of righteousness based on Christ. The pronoun *we* stands for all those who identify with the gospel of freedom as Paul has presented it. This verse illustrates Paul's delight in formulating short, memorable statements of Christian belief. In the Greek there are only eight words, compared to fourteen in our translation. Even in translation, the economy of words and the vast scope of thought are evident. Paul is attempting a summary formulation of his gospel, setting before his readers its essential difference from what the opposing teachers are offering. Verse 6 may be part of the summary statement, especially the last phrase, *faith working through love*, which adds a new and crucial dimension.

It is therefore no surprise to find here several of the key terms in the argument so far. *Spirit, faith,* and *righteousness* have carried much of the conceptual weight in Paul's exposition. The Greek makes no distinction between *Spirit* and *spirit*, making various meanings possible. Here it probably refers to the Holy Spirit and not generally to the realm of spirit and certainly not to the human spirit. For Paul, the power of God for justification comes through the action of the Spirit of God.

The grammatical construction allows the meaning of either *in the Spirit* or *by* [or, *through*] *the Spirit*. The discussion of the Spirit's work in the letter attributes to the Spirit the role of effective agent.

This supports *by the Spirit*. On the other hand, *in the Spirit* connotes something of a personal relationship with the Spirit (see 4:6), with the instrumental idea (*by*) implicit. While we are forced to choose one option or the other in translation, it seems best to allow this entire range of nuances to stand in our understanding of the text.

The order in the sentence is important. With what we know of Paul's thinking thus far, we should not be surprised that *Spirit* stands at the head. This reflects Paul's theology that God is the ground and source of Christian existence and the Spirit is the effecting agent. Next in order is the human response—secondary but essential. That response is *by faith*. Faith alone is the human response that recognizes full dependence on divine source and power. It is also the necessary condition for God's work to be realized in our individual and corporate lives. However much the Spirit's initiative draws out the responding faith, faith is a real human act that makes the person a genuine partner in the covenant relationship we call salvation. *Righteousness* is also familiar to the letter's reader. We have defined it in the letter to this point as right relationship between God and persons within God's covenant terms. Here the term is linked closely with the new terminology of the verse, as discussed below.

If we were not surprised by some of the vocabulary in Paul's gospel summary, *eagerly wait for the hope of righteousness* may indeed surprise us. So far this letter has not said much about the future. We noted a possible future theme in 4:7 (and see 6:8-9). The issue in Galatians has been the relationship of the previous covenants of Israel to the present covenant in Christ. Paul emphasizes the greater benefits in Christ in the present. But now Paul introduces the future as a dominant feature of the gospel.

The main verb expresses a longing for the future to arrive, *eagerly wait for*. The object of that verb is *hope*. Hope, in turn, conditions (and is conditioned by) righteousness. It is not obvious why Paul introduces this future orientation here. It certainly appears important to his thinking. For Paul, moreover, the present and the future are so interrelated that the movement from one to the other is easy and natural. Here the verb *eagerly wait for* demonstrates the bridge between future and present. It reflects Paul's understanding of the real presence of the power of the Spirit in justification, yet recognizing that the fullness of redemption remains incomplete.

In this bird's-eye view of the gospel, Paul portrays its attractiveness in order to draw the Galatians to it. Part of that attractiveness is the great future hope that the gospel offers. Paul formulates that hope in relation to righteousness, a central theme in the letter, with the phrase *the hope of righteousness*. This phrase could be taken in several ways. In light of the argument of the letter, it probably points to the future dimension contained in the concept of righteousness.

Already in the Old Testament, *righteousness* expresses the divine intention to bring all creation into conformity with God's will. Paul stands in this tradition. For him, the gospel offers us more than we presently possess and powerfully draws us toward its realization, motivating us to action on its behalf. Even our status of right standing with God has a future dimension. A final verdict on our standing by the divine Judge is still to come at the end of history (Rev 20:12-13). That gives Paul not anxiety, but optimism and motivation for present living. So this verse adds a new dimension to righteousness, giving it a fuller meaning, even as it builds on Paul's earlier uses of *righteousness*.

In Paul, *righteousness* always has a future dimension. Paul's very gospel is future-oriented (eschatological) in character. Thus life in the Spirit is a mix of the present foretaste of God's future *and* the hope of complete fulfillment of that future. Paul has been highlighting the present virtues of life in Christ, which make it superior to all else. Here Paul reminds the reader that not all is perfect. Present righteousness in Christ is not an end point, but a genuine beginning on the way to a glorious culmination. Moreover, in keeping with biblical thought generally, the hope of righteousness includes all of God's creation, when all will be made right (Rom 8:19-25; cf. 2 Pet 3:13). The culmination of God's purpose embraces creation in all its dimensions.

For in Christ neither circumcision nor uncircumcision counts for anything; the only thing that counts is faith working through love (5:6). Here is the bottom line. In some ways, this verse summarizes the whole of what Paul wants the Galatians to understand. It continues to expand the positive picture of the gospel of freedom. The phrase *in Christ*, the beloved expression of the apostle, stands for the whole of Christian faith and illustrates the Christ-centeredness of Paul's theology. The tight style of the previous verse reappears in the expression *faith working through love*. That this last phrase belongs in the summary statement with verse 5 is suggested by the presence of the conventional triad of virtues—faith, hope, and love (1 Cor 13:13; 1 Thess 1:3; 5:8).

Now Paul turns to the issue at hand: circumcision. That Paul believes circumcision has no value for the Galatian believers is not new to the reader. But Paul's statement that *neither circumcision nor uncircumcision counts for anything* is new and startling. (The phrase *neither circumcision nor uncircumcision* also appears in 6:15 and 1 Cor 7:19, with a parallel idea in 1 Cor 8:8 related to food.) Paul does not see right or wrong in circumcision itself. Neither its presence nor its absence has any relevance to life in Christ. It is morally indifferent. However, it does become important if someone is trying to attach moral freight to it, as the opposition in Galatia is doing. That is a threat to the integrity of the gospel.

This also explains why Paul tolerates circumcision if it serves some real advantage to the gospel (see Acts 16:3). The word translated *counts* has the root idea of strength and ability, which is relevant here. The latter part of the verse speaks of the *working* of faith (see below). What has the power and strength to produce good outcomes? Faith has such power, but circumcision and uncircumcision do not. This point is made even more explicitly in Colossians 2:23: "Self-imposed piety, humility, and severe treatment of the body . . . are of no value in checking self-indulgence."

One of Paul's happiest turns of phrase now follows: *faith working through love*. This captures the heart of Pauline ethics (moral teaching). Together with the summary statement of the preceding verse, it covers the breadth of Paul's theology, without the detail. By linking faith and love, Paul binds ethics to the rest of his theology in a way that answers his critics' charge that without Law observance, there are no moral guidelines (cf. 2:17). Faith certainly has been a central theme in the letter. Paul mentioned love as a quality of Jesus Christ in his self-giving (2:20). In the present formulation, love serves to define the shape of the moral life for believers. Love, for Paul, is defined by Christ. Even the Law of Moses contributes to this definition, as we will see in 5:13-14. Love is more action than sentiment.

Of special importance is the verbal idea in the expression *faith working*. The word *working* means more than being occupied in labor. It speaks of expending energy to effect a result. The distinction is reflected in the two phrases in 1 Thessalonians 1:3: "the work of faith" and "the labor of love." Faith comes to expression through actions of love. Faith works itself out in the form of love deeds.

As we have seen before and will see even more, here Paul is consumed by the question of where to find the source of vitality and power for achieving God's will under the present condition of human weakness. *Faith working through love* is part of his answer. The same faith that is the sole means of right standing with God is also the power that energizes the believer to loving action. That power has its source in the Spirit (5:16-25). Faith appropriates that source. Faith is absolutely crucial for ethics in Paul's thought, as he states powerfully in Romans 14:23: "For whatever does not proceed from faith is sin."

Call to Action 5:7-12

In this unit, Paul again (as in 4:12-20) moves from a theological argument to specific contextual and personal appeals. *You were running well; who prevented you from obeying the truth?* (5:7). Paul praises the Galatians for the time when they showed a way of life consistent with the gospel. He commonly portrays life as a race. In 2:2 he pictured his own ministry as the running of a race. The metaphor well expresses Paul's conviction that life in the Spirit is a journey, with interdependent stages. What is well begun must be completed. Without the good ending, the beginning is worthless. The word translated *prevented* should be taken in its literal sense, *cutting in on*, with the idea of blocking or impeding someone in a race. The reference surely is to the opposition in Galatia. The teachers are *cutting in on* the believers, forcing them off the right track! In doing this, they are not obeying the truth of the gospel as first presented to them (cf. 2:5, 14).

With *obeying the truth*, Paul maintains his emphasis in the letter on truth linked closely with practical conduct. He does not allow a separation of knowledge and action. Head and feet are closely connected. Paul said this explicitly in 2:14, when he accused Peter and others of not walking the talk. Galatians is one of the biblical sources that most clearly reflect this holistic perspective of truth. Paul argues abstract ideas (theology), but they are based in God's concrete actions in history (the gospel proclamation) and must lead to consistent action in the believer (lived-out ethics).

Such persuasion does not come from the one who calls you. A little yeast leavens the whole batch of dough (5:8-9). The word *obey* in the preceding sentence has, in the Greek, the underlying idea of being persuaded of something. Now the language of persuasion is explicit. Paul clearly has in mind the teaching of the opposition in Galatia. Also interesting is the present tense in the clause *the one who calls you*. In 1:6 and 15, Paul used the past tense of *call* to speak of the initial stage of faith. The present tense here gives the divine calling a present relevance when the Galatians are hearing a different call from the opponents of Paul.

The saying about the leaven is probably a well-known proverb of the day. The same saying appears in 1 Corinthians 5:6. The basic meaning is clear enough, but how Paul is applying it to the present situation is not. Because the saying stands alone, without any grammatical link to its context, the reader must discern how it applies to the present situation. Clearly the tone of it is negative (cf. Mark 8:15). It could mean that false teaching on one point (about circumcision) could lead to error on other points. Or it might allude to the fear Paul has that the small number of those who have already submitted to circumcision could easily influence the whole body of believers in the province of Galatia. Paul likely wants his readers to think of all the possible applications!

I am confident about you in the Lord that you will not think otherwise. But whoever it is that is confusing you will pay the penalty (5:10). To the previous play on the idea of persuasion (see above), Paul, by way of contrast, adds his own persuasion: *I am persuaded in the Lord* (lit.). In such a way Paul likes to express his confidence in God and persons, and in matters of faith. The same form of the statement, with "in the Lord (Jesus)," or "in Christ," appears in Romans 14:14; Philippians 2:24; and 2 Thessalonians 3:4. Paul is engaging in persuasion via anticipated praise. The specific object of this confidence is that the Galatians will think in the same way as Paul. The language here, as in verses 7-8, respects the place of reason in matters of faith. For Paul, the mind matters. Galatians demonstrates that, for Paul, truth involves correct intellectual understanding, trust in God, and integrity in the practice of life. One should both think the truth and walk the truth.

With this note of confidence in his readers, Paul once again sensitively balances his sharp criticism with respect and positive regard. He does not simply blame, criticize, and call down judgment on the Galatians. Paul is careful not to create an unnecessary barrier between himself and his readers. The statement is closely parallel to 1:7-9, where the verb *confuse* (or trouble) describes the effect of the false teachers, and Paul pronounces a judgment or curse on them. Although Paul uses the plural elsewhere in describing the opposition, here he uses the singular (*who . . . is confusing*). Paul is probably is not thinking of the leader. The statement may imply that Paul is not entirely sure of the composition or profile of the opposing group. The indefinite pronoun and singular verb, *whoever it is*, makes the judgment strike home to each individual in the opposition party.

But my friends, why am I still being persecuted if I am still preaching circumcision? In that case the offense of the cross has been removed (5:11; on the translation *my friends*, see on 4:12). This statement comes as a total surprise. The subject changes abruptly, and the content of the statement seems to contradict everything else in the letter. The question implies that someone says Paul is preaching circumcision. The form of the conditional sentence in the Greek indicates that this is not merely a hypothetical situation used to make a theoretical point. Someone, obviously not Paul, is saying that Paul continues to preach circumcision. The information Paul had received about the Galatian trouble, which elicited this letter, apparently referred to this accusation.

The question has led to numerous proposed solutions, none of which is entirely satisfying. Two options have the strongest possibility. *Preaching circumcision* might refer to Paul's preconversion defense of Law observance. The problem with this option is the difficulty of imagining that anyone could expect to gain leverage from Paul's preconversion practice since it would be obvious to everyone that he had changed dramatically. Nor does it make good sense of the *still being persecuted*, since he was not persecuted in the preconversion period.

The more likely option is that something in Paul's ministry provided the basis for a claim that he was still preaching circumcision. The only such possibility we know about is his practice of circumcision for pragmatic reasons. An example of this is the circumcision of Timothy recorded in Acts 16:3. Furthermore, Paul apparently accepted circumcision for believers of Jewish background, though not on the basis of the Law's authority (see comments on 3:25). That Paul could indeed be flexible on circumcision, and on other things, is supported by the mission strategy he spells out in 1 Corinthians 9:19-22, becoming "all things to all people" as long as it does not violate the law of Christ. It is easy to understand that flexibility of this kind could be exploited by those with a more rigid position. Thus Paul's opponents were (wrongly) representing his action as active support (as *preaching* implies) of circumcision.

A possible criticism of this explanation is that Paul does not clarify his apparently inconsistent position. But Paul may not consider the accusation worthy of taking it seriously. Instead, he answers with rhetorical irony. He points to the irony of opponents trying to win points by citing his acceptance of (some) circumcision while also opposing Paul on the issue of circumcision.

Paul does not state what form of persecution he has in mind. We know from Acts that Paul experienced persecution by the Jews in his mission work. However, the present context implies persecution by fellow Jewish Christian opponents. This is consistent with the assertion Paul adds that, if he were still preaching circumcision, the offense or stumbling block of the cross would have been removed. Circumcision was the issue. If this is the persecution to which Paul is referring, it is not a *violent* persecution, but behavior that is disrespectful of Paul and undermining of his ministry (cf. 2:1-10).

The image of the stumbling block is found widely in the New Testament. Paul uses it to refer specifically to the cross in 1 Corinthians 1:23: the cross is a stumbling block to the Jews. That the Messiah was crucified is a scandal. But the sense required here in relation to circumcision is the scandal of understanding the cross as the death of one's relationship to the Law as a means of righteousness (see 2:21; 3:13; 4:5), with the result that circumcision is no longer essential. This is the scandal that Jewish Christians wanting to hold on to Law observance could not embrace. Paul refers to this explicitly in 6:12, when he accuses his opponents of promoting circumcision in order to avoid persecution (by the Jews). Thus Paul's statement in our verse contains an implied critique of his opponents.

I wish those who unsettle you would castrate themselves! (5:12). Paul is not finished with his surprises. With this coarse invective, he exhausts all rhetorical means of persuasion in his passionate appeal to the Galatians. We can imagine that this comment goes to the edge of propriety in his day as in ours. Clearly Paul is reaching for the greatest shock effect that he dare create to make his readers sense the depth of his frustration with the adversaries. In using the word *unsettle*, Paul describes his opponents' action with a stronger word than he uses in 1:7 and 5:10. The word translated *castrate* (NRSV) has the more general meaning of "cut off" and could well suggest that, beyond circumcision (removing the foreskin of the male organ), his opponents cut off the penis entirely.

But this is not just a bloody joke or the sarcastic and crude exclamation of a frustrated apostle. In some parts of the Jewish tradition, castration was grounds for exclusion from the worship assembly (Lev 21:20; Deut 23:1; but see also Isa 56:3b-5). And in the cult of Cybele, which had its home in the Galatian area, males who wanted to serve as priests in the cult castrated themselves as a show of solidarity to that mother goddess. Thus Paul's reference to castration elicits negative connotations for circumcision that are totally contrary to what the opponents intend or desire.

THE TEXT IN BIBLICAL CONTEXT

Freedom in Scripture

While Paul is its leading voice on the theme of freedom, the entire Bible is saturated with it. Indeed, God wants to liberate humanity and all of creation from their fallen condition. Bondage and enslavement express themselves on many personal, social, and cosmic levels. Likewise, God's acts of deliverance and redemption operate on all these levels. This constitutes biblical salvation in all of its breadth.

In the Old Testament the prime example of such liberation is the deliverance of Israel from Egyptian bondage in the exodus. This event serves as a paradigm (a basic model or type) for subsequent liberating acts of God, including Jesus' death and resurrection. Freedom describes the condition of those who have experienced God's deliverance. It follows that in a biblical sense, freedom is defined in terms of God's purpose, not mere human interest. Freedom is always *for God*, that is, for the service of God, and by extension for the neighbor. This explains why freedom and servanthood in Galatians are compatible. Moreover, in the Bible, freedom is achieved only by God's intervention.

The Old Testament portrays freedom primarily, but not exclusively, in terms of political freedom for Israel as a nation. The Psalms are full of petition and thanksgiving for deliverance from threats of all kinds to the individual and the community. Isaiah uses the exodus motif to describe Israel's liberation from exile. The coming of Jesus fulfills Isaiah's visions of a liberated people in an ideal world of peace and blessedness.

Luke and its sequel, Acts, highlight this fulfillment in Jesus' ministry and in the life of the early church. In his programmatic sermon at Nazareth in Luke 4:17-21, Jesus proclaims the fulfillment of Isaiah 61:1-2 with its strong language of release and liberation from economic, physical, and social bondage. Jesus' acts of healing and deliverance from evil spirits are prominent expressions of this releasing. In Greek, even the phrase "forgiveness of sins," which figures centrally in the Christian message in Luke-Acts, literally means release from sins, or freedom from sin. For Luke, liberation describes and encompasses the full range of the salvation Christ brings. Paul thus stands in a long biblical tradition in emphasizing the liberating power of the gospel (see also TLC on 4:8-11).

Indicative and Imperative

Students of Paul generally agree that the interplay of indicative and imperative verbs is a key to understanding Paul's ethics (Furnish: 9). Verbs in the indicative mood are often in the past tense and state an act or gift of God for believers. Verbs in the imperative mood call for the response of believers to God's prior act or gift. This feature of grammar discloses, in essence, how Paul relates ethics to the rest of his theology.

As noted in the Explanatory Notes, 5:1 contains a clear example of this typical Pauline language: *For freedom Christ has set us free. Stand fast, therefore, and do not submit again to a yoke of slavery.* The prior fact of Christ setting us free, which is in the indicative mood, affirms a given fact. The human response of standing firm in freedom and not submitting to slavery is expressed as an imperative, a command. The two parts are linked by *therefore*, emphasizing that the first part calls forth or motivates the second. Such use of *therefore* is found elsewhere in Paul. Notable is Romans 12:1, which marks a discernible transition between the two parts of the entire epistle, the first part being characterized by the indicative and the second part by the imperative. The effect of this is that God's action is the ground and impulse for the human action of response to that act.

Paul is not the originator of this approach, since the entire Bible bears witness to it. Conspicuous is the case of the Ten Commandments, which are the heart of the Mosaic covenant. Both in Exodus (20:2) and Deuteronomy (5:6), the commandments begin with a prologue that states God's act of deliverance from Egypt. Thus Israel is reminded that before God demands anything, God acts for the benefit of the people. God gives before God asks. The same indicative-imperative structure appears in other New Testament writings. For example, the first chapter of 1 Peter is so structured, with *therefore* in verse 13 marking the transition.

Several key implications follow from this structure of biblical understanding. First, God is always the initiator in the plan of salvation and blessing. The movement of redemption is from God to humans, not from humans to God. Second, God's action is the justification or ground for God's claim on humans. At the deepest level, the character and manner of God's action defines the nature of the human response. As God has treated us, so are we to treat our neighbor (Matt 5:44-45; Rom 15:2-3; Eph 4:32–5:2; 1 John 3:16). Third, the prior act of God supplies the resources by which weak humanity can fulfill the requirement of God.

This last point is more evident in Paul, and particularly in the Galatian letter. Without the action of God and the presence of the Spirit, there is no empowerment for godly living. This means that the indicative and imperative are not completely separate phases of Christian experience in temporal sequence. Rather, as Paul passionately asserts (3:3), the indicative of God's empowerment continuously undergirds the imperative of human response. In biblical thought, the will and action of God, expressed in God's saving purpose for the world, do not displace the will and action of the person. Rather, the former fully engages the human response and even depends on that for realizing God's purpose in human experience.

Grace and Perseverance

In this group of verses, another theme touches on the question of how divine will and action relate to human will and action. In 5:4, Paul speaks of the Galatians cutting themselves off from Christ and falling away from grace. This verse has played a prominent role in the debate about whether the Bible teaches that salvation is conditioned on human perseverance or whether it affirms that God's sovereign choice (election and predestination) makes salvation unconditioned on human faithfulness. Not surprisingly, those who defend the conditional view of grace and salvation cite this verse, concluding that salvation can be lost by disowning Christ or by (persistent and willful) disobedience.

What is clear enough in all of Scripture is the initiative of God in all aspects of becoming and being the children of God. Humans do not take the first step, nor do they provide the grounds for salvation and discipleship. God moves first with acts of saving and empowering grace (as noted in the preceding TBC section) on the indicative and the imperative. Equally clear is that humans are responsible for their actions and that consequences result from those actions.

A close reading of the biblical narrative discloses that the covenants and promises of God, however unconditional they may sound, are not absolute guarantees. God does not permit humans to claim a promise of God while violating the will of the God who made the promise. It is misleading to distinguish sharply between unconditional and conditional covenants in Scripture. The Bible itself bears witness that even covenants whose language sounds unconditional are, in fact, conditional. The promise of God to David that his throne would be forever is an example (2 Sam 7:12-16).

On the other hand, God, "the hound of heaven," as the poet Francis Thompson expressed it, does not simply abandon God's covenantal promises. God's covenants and promises reflect God's unchanging character and purpose. As a consequence, an earlier covenant and promise may reappear in a different form. The faithful saying of 2 Timothy 2:11-13 expresses this beautifully. In this passage, the author states God's response first as conditioned on human action, but then concludes that God will always be true to Godself, so that the faithfulness of God is not affected by human unfaithfulness. This subtle balance captures the spirit of Scripture well. It means that the relationship of God to humanity is dynamic and cannot be reduced to human logic and prediction. It also means that God is God, sovereign, and cannot therefore be held to account even by God's own promises (cf. Rom 9:15-29).

THE TEXT IN THE LIFE OF THE CHURCH

(See also "Freedom and Bondage," in TLC for 4:8-11.)

Servile and Filial Obedience

The concept of obeying the truth that Paul employs in this section raises the question of how to understand obedience in a Spirit-inspired and Spirit-empowered life. Doesn't obedience imply conformity to demand or requirement? Does obedience really fit into Paul's gospel? Paul obviously thinks it does. Although in Galatians the language of obedience is not pervasive, it is present in the key expression *obeying the truth* (5:7; cf. the inclusio of "obedience of faith" in Rom 1:5 and 16:26). The parallel statement in Galatians 2:14, where Paul condemns the practice of not walking in conformity to *the truth of the gospel*, indicates that for him, obedience is not so much conforming to a formulated pattern of behavior as it is consistently living out the basic character of the gospel through the transformed, Spirit-energized life in Christ (2:20; 5:5).

That Paul can contrast these forms of obedience with the image of slave versus child (4:7, 31) suggests another way of describing the different forms of obedience. Other writers throughout church history have adopted this imagery for that purpose. Michael Sattler, an early Anabaptist leader in the sixteenth century, reputedly authored a tract titled "Two Kinds of Obedience" (Yoder 1973: 121–25). In it, Sattler compares and contrasts the servile obedience of a servant or slave with the filial obedience of a child within the family. The servant is under external constraints and has no choice but to do what the master demands. The servant has no interest in doing more than what is required and is focused on reward for what is done. The relationship is marked by control and obligation. Sattler likens this to life under the Law of Moses.

On the other hand, the child lives in a relationship of mutual love and concern. An intrinsic bond between parent and child informs and motivates action that serves the relationship. Obedience is not an end in itself; it serves the family relationship and the family's good, not its own separate benefit. Theoretically, at least, the child obeys out of a sense of respect for the family ties, rather than out of mere obligation. Filial obedience is the way of the new covenant in Christ. Sattler reflects the emphasis of Paul in our present context when he characterizes filial obedience as attentive to the inner witness and the Spirit.

In the life of the church, the primary concern should be the cultivation of deep relationships with Christ and with other believers: in short, the formation of family identity. Out of living relationships spring the desire and the energy to conform one's behavior to the ideals of the family of God. This does not mean that the church cannot or should not occasionally define and prescribe some behavior for a given time and circumstance. However, the easy appeal to obligation or to sanctions fosters a superficial obedience that lacks authenticity and leads to legalism. That is servile obedience. Filial obedience does what we see Paul constantly doing in his writings; it connects expected behaviors with the fountainhead of spiritual reality, which is life in Christ. (See the comments on 4:5-7 and the discussion of the indicative and imperative in TBC above.)

Faith Working through Love

As stated in the Explanatory Notes, *faith working through love* (5:6) is a particularly happy phrasing of Paul's spiritual vision. While its brevity leaves room for various interpretations, the general thrust is clear enough. True Christian experience combines faith and love, which in turn result in godly living. In Paul the exclusive position of faith (faith *alone*) does not mean the gospel is restricted to faith as an inner attitude or vertical relationship with God. Faith and works are compatible. What is not acceptable is a view of works as based on grounds other than faith itself, such as on the Law (cf. Rom 14:23). Faith is itself a legitimate and authentic form of work, but only in response to the grace of God. Work grows out of the experience of faith in the flow of everyday life, when faith expresses its life-giving power. A life lived in constant dependence on God and trust in God is nourished by a relationship that motivates and empowers one's actions. This is consistent with Paul's claim, in the next section of the letter, that the Spirit of God empowers godly living. The faith of the believer and the Spirit of God complement each other in support of godly living.

This kind of living can be named and described, at least in general, by the word *love*. Just as faith is focused on relationship, so is love. The form of Christian life that Paul envisions originates in relationship with God (faith) and expresses itself in relationship with God and neighbor (love). Relationship is thus the key to authentic human existence. In relationship, we find our true place in the order of the universe, and relationship also provides the resources from which to draw the empowerment that we lack as individuals without God and neighbor. (For further comment on love, see on 5:13-14, 22.) In his commentary on this verse, Martin Luther captures the thrust well:

> That is to say, faith which is not feigned nor hypocritical, but true and lively. That is that faith which exercises and requires good works through love. It is as much to say as: He that will be a true Christian indeed, or one of Christ's kingdom, must be a true believer. Now he believes not truly, if works of charity follow not his faith (Luther: 465–66).

Galatians 5:13-24

Overcoming the Flesh by the Spirit

PREVIEW

Having dealt forcefully with the inadequacy of Law observance as a basis for justification, Paul now anticipates a reactive objection to his argument. Paul addresses the slippery-slope fears in the mind of his audience by theologically explaining the practical power of the Holy Spirit in daily life. The slippery-slope mentality comes from the fear that if the church should accept some particular practice, it will open the floodgates of evil and immorality. All constraint will be thrown off, and unchecked evil will reign. The slippery-slope fear of the Galatians that Paul is anticipating here is that without Law observance, what will guide faithful living? Won't the lack of direction and constraint provided by the Law leave us in a wasteland of moral chaos?

Paul's letters often move from a more theoretical or theological middle section to a more practical or ethical closing section. In the case of Galatians, that point of transition is often placed at 5:13, or even earlier, at 5:1 or 2. Unfortunately, some commentators see the latter part of Paul's letters as disconnected from the first and even of secondary importance to the first. In the case of Galatians, some think that Paul added the ethical section almost as an afterthought, a series of exhortations on matters unrelated to the main issue. Others think that here Paul is addressing a subgroup in Galatia that is leaning toward moral license rather than Law observance.

In point of fact, however, this section is closely connected to the earlier material around the theme of the Law, the Spirit, flesh, and freedom. Paul does transition from his rebuke section to his request section at 4:12, but attempts to divide this letter into theological and the practical sections fail to appreciate Paul's theological method. At 5:13 Paul takes up a major issue in the Galatian controversy: *how* (note well: *not* whether) the followers of Jesus shall pursue an upright and holy life. In that sense this material does, in fact, deal with practical matters, but does so within a strong theological framework that continues the central argument of the letter.

Paul's claim is that no one need fear a slippery slope in his argument. The ground for moral living in the gospel has even higher ethical aspirations and possibilities than the Law! His specific argument is that the keys to Christian morality are (1) the general guiding principle of love and (2) the enabling presence of the Holy Spirit. A believer whose life is continuously given over to the control of the Spirit receives the only source of power that *can* overcome the flesh and fulfill God's will in the believer and in the believing community.

OUTLINE

Conflict of Spirit and Flesh, 5:13-18
Works of the Flesh and Their Consequences, 5:19-21
Fruit of the Spirit, 5:22-23
Crucifixion of the Flesh, 5:24

EXPLANATORY NOTES

Conflict of Spirit and Flesh 5:13-18

For you were called to freedom, brothers and sisters; only do not use your freedom as an opportunity for self-indulgence, but through love become slaves to one another(5:13). The opening words pick up the theme of freedom from 5:1 and, like the earlier statement, take the form of a direct, unequivocal assertion. Paul's emphasis is on *you*, which contrasts nicely with the preceding references to the false teachers. God has called the Galatians into freedom. By now the theme of calling is familiar (1:6, 15; 5:8), pointing to the initiative of God. In Galatians, it is part of Paul's overarching emphasis on spiritual immediacy with God, based on living, dynamic relationships and expressed in acts of divine working in and among believers. Paul expects each believer to possess a full awareness of a personal call from God into the life of faith.

Paul is well aware of the distortion of freedom that comes from the human propensity to self-interest and self-gratification, what he will shortly call *desires of the flesh*. So he begins his discussion with the explicit warning that freedom is subject to abuse. He does not talk about a false form of freedom but of freedom as a good that can be exploited by evil (cf. Rom 7:8, where Paul says the same thing of the Law). The enemy of freedom is *the flesh* (lit. translated by NRSV as *self-indulgence*). The concept of *the flesh* first appeared at 3:3 in a key thematic paragraph of the letter (see discussion there). *Flesh* stands for our creaturely nature (which is not evil in itself) and, by extension, for that nature when, without the guidance and control of the Spirit, it is left to its own drives toward evil. Note how this definition anticipates the coming discussion of the Spirit.

To this statement of what true freedom is *not*, Paul adds a definition of what true freedom *is*: *through love become slaves of one another*. *Through love* is the same wording as in 5:6. That is, love is the means or instrument we use to serve each other (see the discussion of love in the next verse). This bringing together of freedom and service is striking because it contrasts directly with the selfish form of freedom native to our human nature outside of Christ.

The use of the image of slave may seem to be in tension with the argument in chapter 4, where the slave status is set as a negative over against the child-of-God status. But Paul has used it with a positive sense in 1:10: he is *a slave of Christ* (lit.). The one is a slavery that limits and dominates; the other is a slavery, voluntarily assumed by the free person, that embraces the tasks and burdens of the greatest cause on earth: God's people and their mission. It is significant that Paul defines true freedom in corporate rather than individualistic terms—in terms of relationship in community. This note anticipates a central feature of this section on the moral life. We will consider below why Paul is so focused on the ethics of community building and maintenance.

For the whole law is summed up in a single commandment, "You shall love your neighbor as yourself" (5:14). Paul used the expression *the whole law* in 5:3 (RSV), with slightly different vocabulary, in a negative sense to reflect the consuming obligation of the Law. Here Paul uses the same concept with a positive sense, in a different frame of reference. Now the focus is not on the details that make up the entire Law but on the intent of the Law as a whole. Paul says that *the entire Law is fulfilled* (lit.) in the *love* commandment. Not only is the Law summarized (cf. NRSV translation, *summed up*) by love of neighbor; the Law is also put into effect or carried out by that love.

In the expanded parallel passage in Romans 13:8-10, Paul uses a word with the precise meaning of *sum up*, along with the word in our text here that means *fulfill*. The distinction is important to Paul. In Galatians the emphasis is on the Law being brought to realization or being put into practice when we love our neighbor (as in Rom 8:4 where *fulfill* is also used).

Here the word *fulfill* may also refer to bringing something to a new stage of maturation. Paul's argument in Galatians is that God has fulfilled God's purposes in Christ and in the Spirit. This puts the Law in a new, subordinate position to Christ and a new complementary, but secondary, role in relation to the Spirit. (For the relation to Christ, see Gal 3; for the relation to the Spirit, see below.) Behind this section of the letter lies Paul's concern to demonstrate a new way of practical obedience to the will of God. This, Paul says, involves the Law, but in a new role.

The unmistakable implication of this text is that the Law faithfully reflects the will of God. To balance the sharply negative statements about the Law to this point in the letter, we must give full weight to this dimension of Paul's view. Paul's unspoken conviction here is that one can no longer approach the Law as a detailed code or standard based on human will and effort. The underlying spirit of the Law, which Paul names as *love*, must grasp the believer. This love is not just an external standard but instead is an inner virtue nurtured by the Spirit (5:22). Paul is not playing an intellectual game in formulating the least common denominator of the Law. He is trying to appropriate the Law through the lens of his dynamic and relational view of life in Christ and in the Spirit (cf. letter and Spirit in 2 Cor 3).

The practice of summarizing the Law in one succinct statement was common in late Second Temple Judaism. Jesus did it (see Mark 12:28-34 and parallels). Rabbi Hillel (Babylonian Talmud, *Shabbat* 31a) summarized the Law in the commandment: "What is hateful to you, do not do to your neighbor." Jesus' summary of the Law in Matthew 7:12 represents the same summary in positive form. Jesus also used this device as a way to establish relative priorities within the Law. In Mark 12:28-34, Jesus responds approvingly to a scribe's question about which of all the commandments is the most important. Paul's similar summary of the Law in Galatians 5:14 allows him to put to rest any fears of moral chaos arising from leaving Law observance behind while actually fulfilling the overall intent of the Law.

Love plays a key role in the view of ethics Paul is describing. Love provides the crucial bridge between the Law and life in Christ. The

Law defines the general contours of love. But love depends on the
living presence of the Spirit and has its final definition in the self-
sacrificial love of Christ for all people, including one's enemy (2:20;
cf. Luke 23:34; Matt 5:43-48). As Paul has been arguing throughout
the letter, this new configuration demands some redefinition of the
specifics of the Law (such as how the Gentiles are viewed). This
helps to explain why the early church and especially Paul emphasized love so much and why they were the first to use the Greek
word *agapē* to express that other-directed, deed-oriented, unconditional love that God in Christ has shown to them and that they, in
turn, practice toward others (cf. Rom 15:1-3; Eph 4:31–5:2).

*If, however, you bite and devour one another, take care that you are not
consumed by one another* (5:15). Paul rather abruptly applies his
teaching on love to the Galatians. This must reflect what Paul
understands to be taking place (or potentially taking place) in the
Galatian churches. Paul repeats this direct reference to conflict in
community life in 5:26. The lists of works of the flesh and fruit of the
Spirit are dominated by the vices or virtues of life experienced
together. The best explanation is that the theological debate precipitated by the teachers in the Galatian churches is causing (or
could cause) bitterness, factionalism, and division. Paul wants to
address this matter.

Paul's imagery is dramatic. His words evoke images of animals
of prey snapping at one another with the intent to kill and eat.
The rhetoric suggests that unloving infighting in human community is actually uncivil, mere animal existence. The potential
result in the community is mutual destruction. All are consumed,
the text says. Conflict in community can easily lead to the destruction of community—a loss for everyone, regardless of who is right
and who is wrong.

Walk in [NRSV, *Live by*] *the Spirit, I say, and you will most definitely
not gratify the desires of the flesh* (5:16 AT, cf. NIV). Love is the first key
component in Paul's moral vision. Life in the Holy Spirit is the other.
To that he now turns. Paul has introduced the concept of *the flesh* in
verse 13. Now Paul discusses it in more depth, contrasting it with
the Spirit, its antithesis. As in 5:2 (AT), Paul sets the stage for a solemn declaration with *I say*. The declaration begins with an imperative and ends with an affirmation (contrary to NRSV).

Paul uses several verbs to describe life in the Spirit in the larger
context (see 5:18, 25) and it is important to observe the distinctions.
In 5:16 Paul says, *Walk in*, or *by, the Spirit* (lit.). The idea of walking
in the Spirit suggests a constant presence. But the idea of the Spirit

as the helping agent (*by the Spirit*) is also present in the context (see comments on 5:5). The image of "walking with God" is the fundamental image of spirituality in the Old Testament, and early Christians naturally adopted it. The church was even known as "the Way," the path (of life) where one walks (Acts 9:2; 18:25; etc.). The expression emphasizes biblical faith as a total way of life. In adopting this language, Paul makes a novel move by making the Spirit the defining companion in that walk. This continues the point made in 3:1-5, where the Spirit defines faithful living rather than the Law.

Then, with an eye to his detractors who find no ethical power in his message, Paul affirms emphatically that the person who walks by the Spirit *will most definitely not gratify the desires of the flesh* (AT). The Greek could be rendered as an English imperative (as with the NRSV's prohibition *Do not gratify*) or an emphatic negation in the English indicative mood. In the context Paul's larger argument calls for reading it as an emphatic negation. Paul is certain that where the Spirit reigns, the flesh is without power. And where that condition exists, the will of God is sure to come to expression. Given the problem in Galatia, Paul wants to show that moral renewal is intrinsic to the life of those who have identified with Christ (2:20) and are indwelt by the Spirit (4:6).

Desire is a key word here and elsewhere in Pauline writings. Both the noun and the verb appear throughout the present section in 5:16, 17, 24. Like the word *flesh*, with which it is associated, it can be either morally neutral or negative. In the neutral sense it refers to any desire, appetite, or drive that characterizes human nature and that is essential to human survival and flourishing. In the negative sense it refers to that same desire when it is controlled by self-interest and/or evil powers rather than God. The negative sense applies in this passage.

The phrase *desire of the flesh* is equivalent to a Hebrew phrase (*yeṣer haraʿ*) that speaks of an impulse or inclination to evil (Gen 6:5; 8:21). Paul understood the expression to refer to the flesh characterized by its desiring and craving, without godly control and guidance. Such a condition becomes the opportunity for sin to fill the vacuum with its own influence (cf. Rom 7:5-6). Since Paul believes powers of evil (e.g., the *elements* in 4:1-11) can exploit the flesh and thus prompt sin, he can also depict flesh itself as a power with person-like qualities. That same viewpoint informs the present context, where Paul portrays the two powers of Spirit and flesh as being in conflict with each other.

For what the flesh desires is opposed to the Spirit, and what the Spirit desires is opposed to the flesh; for these are opposed to each other, to prevent you from doing what you want (5:17). The statement is fascinating for the way it opens windows into understanding human nature. It also is one of the more challenging passages for interpreters. The general picture it portrays is clear enough. The flesh and the Spirit are contrasting forces, whose struggle is played out in human experience. Here the verb form of the word *desire* appears. That the flesh is a desiring agent was already expressed in the previous verse. Now Paul presents the Spirit too as an agent, with its own desires and cravings. This demonstrates that desire is not inherently negative. In fact, this quality of the Spirit is what attracts Paul, since this quality gives the Spirit an energizing drive to assist the believer in moral achievement.

To the description of the opposing moral forces, Paul adds a clause (*to prevent*) that is more difficult. It could be read as expressing either purpose or result: (1) purpose, *in order that you might not do what you want*; or (2) result, *with the result that you don't do what you want*. Either reading could make sense. The purpose idea expresses intention, not inevitable result. It therefore leaves some room for the human choice implied in the imperative of verse 16, *Walk in the Spirit*; and in the human willing that is stated here, *what you want*. On other hand, it would be strange for Paul to imply that the opposition between Spirit and flesh itself has an intention. On this logic the sense of result seems preferable.

If we interpret it as a purpose clause, Paul would be saying that the opposing intentions of Spirit and flesh seek to influence the person in contrasting directions. If we take it as a result clause, Paul would not be saying that the conflict of flesh and Spirit completely determines the outcome apart from our will. Rather, these forces inevitably draw the human will into the conflict of flesh and Spirit. This seems to be the most likely meaning of this clause.

Either way, the real issue is how to understand the interaction of the three subjects involved—the Spirit, the flesh, and the personal subject (*you*). There are multiple conflicts: between the Spirit and the flesh, and between the will of the person and the Spirit, or between the will of the person and the flesh. The explanation that best fits the context and Paul's theology is this: as opposing forces, both the Spirit and the flesh desire to have their way in a person's life. Though this struggle is universal, Paul is clearly thinking about the Galatian believers, as the second-person pronoun shows (see further below). The striving of one or the other of these two forces is bound to clash with the will of the person. Whether a particular human desire is good or bad, this desire will find opposition from either the flesh or the Spirit, the flesh against the good and the Spirit against the bad.

In the present context, Paul may be responding to the earlier question (5:13) about whether freedom becomes the instrument of the flesh. If so, he is emphasizing here that in opposing the flesh, the Spirit is also in the believer and resisting any tendency to use freedom to abdicate to the flesh (see Barclay: 115). Stated positively, the Spirit assists the weak human will to oppose the desires of the flesh that would otherwise use freedom for unrighteousness. Whether this is Paul's specific thought or not, the general thrust of the larger passage is to show how believers can live in victory over sin while at the same time realistically facing their continuing vulnerability to temptation.

One can readily recognize a certain parallel to the picture of moral conflict in Romans 7 (esp. vv. 14-20). People generally have a certain moral sensitivity and desire to do right. Yet the flesh is powerless to resist sin (Rom 7:15, "I do not do what I want"). Galatians also speaks of this conflict and acknowledges that one does not do what one wants. While recognizing this parallel, we should also notice the differences between the conflict in Galatians 5 and that in Romans 7. The Spirit is not part of the description of the conflict in Romans 7:7-25 as the Spirit is here. In Romans 7 the conflict is two-way, between flesh and will. In Galatians the conflict is three-way, between the flesh, the will, and the Spirit. That supports the view that the Romans conflict is pre-Christian. That conflict is then overcome through Jesus Christ and the Spirit (Rom 7:25a; 8:1-17). In Galatians, however, the Spirit is part of the confrontation, and Christians are being addressed. Romans describes a condition of despair before a relationship with Christ and the Spirit; Galatians depicts a condition of hopefulness requiring commitment and perseverance in fellowship with the Spirit.

But is this struggle within the believer constant and unrelenting, with no resolution or attenuation? This could hardly be the final word if for no other reason than the fact that such a meaning would undermine Paul's purpose of showing the Galatians how his gospel assures right living. We do best to see this portrayal of struggle as a continuously potential one, not a necessary and continuously experienced one. The unbeliever normally does not have this conflict for the simple reason that the flesh is in control. But conflict can arise when a spiritual stirring or awakening takes place. Now something

of a parallel situation happens for the believer. Under ideal conditions the Spirit is in control and the flesh is overcome. The question
is not whether the Spirit is greater than the flesh (it is), but whether
the believer deliberately *walks by the Spirit* (5:16) and is *led by the
Spirit* (5:18). At the same time, the believer stills lives *in the flesh*
(2:20) and therefore remains vulnerable to the flesh through temptation, as 5:13 clearly implies. On those occasions, the struggle
between opposing forces flares up.

We must resist viewing Paul as consistently optimistic *or* pessi-
mistic. There are elements of both. Paul is realistic about the presence of sin in the world, from which the believer is not isolated, but
he is optimistic about the potential of victory over sin when the
Spirit is given full sway. For Paul, victory over sin is fully possible,
but not guaranteed. There is no place for indifference or presump-
tion (cf. 6:1!). The Christian life is a dynamic experience, in which
the believer must continually cultivate openness to the Spirit,
which alone assures one of victory. This is the implication of the
present-tense verbs for the imperatives and indicatives of this
entire section.

But if you are led by the Spirit, you are not subject to the law (5:18).
Here it may seem that the discussion has taken an abrupt turn. We
might have expected something like "If you are led by the Spirit, you
will not succumb to the desires of the flesh." Instead, the contrast
here is between the Spirit and the Law. Paul's return to a main
theme of the letter proves that he is still answering the same questions posed in the earlier parts of the letter: Do Christians need to
submit to the Law? Is Christ a servant of sin (2:17)? The answer
again is no.

Here, as elsewhere in the letter, Paul associates the Law with the
flesh (3:2-3). Controlled by sin, the flesh exploits the Law for its own
ends and brings death (2:19; Rom 7). Spirit-filled believers are no
longer under this enslaving power—that is, they are not under the
Law. Moreover, those led by the Spirit have no need of the Law for
moral control. It is not that the Spirit *frees* one from the Law; Christ
did that in the cross (3:13; 4:5). Rather, the Spirit removes the indispensability of the Law by simply being a new and better moral
guide. Note that this does not negate the Law's continuing value.
The presence of the Spirit in the believer replaces the Law as moral
guide (cf. Rom 7:6!). The Galatians, and all believers, are not under
the Law, *not subject to the Law.*

By using the verb *are led* (present tense, passive voice) in relation
to the Spirit's presence, Paul stresses the positive control of the

Spirit in the moment-to-moment life of the believer. This control is the key to victory in the struggle with the flesh—a control over the flesh that the Law simply cannot exercise (cf. Rom 8:3!). The Law can demand, but it cannot *desire*; that is, the Law is not like flesh and Spirit, which can motivate and energize its subordinates to achieve its ideals.

Notice the balance created by the active verb *walk* in verse 16 and the passive verb *are led* here. Paul wants to underscore the necessity of divine action in Christian experience, but not as a complete substitute for human action. Human action is inadequate in the battle with the flesh, but without the human actions of openness, availability, and cooperation with the Spirit, provided by faith, the Spirit is not free to act for us on our behalf.

Works of the Flesh and Their Consequences 5:19-21

Now the works of the flesh are obvious: fornication, impurity, licentiousness, idolatry, sorcery, enmities, strife, jealousy, anger, quarrels, dissensions, factions, envy, drunkenness, carousing, and things like these (5:19-21a). To the discussion of the conflict between flesh and Spirit, Paul now appends two lists that illustrate their influence. This shows that, despite Paul's emphasis on theological principle, he can be specific and concrete in his moral judgment. Even here, however, he protects himself from misunderstanding by leaving the list open-ended: *things such as these*. Neither evil nor good can be exhaustively and finally defined. These works are obvious. The point is not that all people recognize these as vices, since some likely are not self-evident to those who practice them. Rather, Paul's point is that the works of the flesh are clearly *visible*. They cannot be hidden.

The designation *works of the flesh* probably means that the works are the action of the flesh. Because the flesh is an agent of power that exercises its influence in persons, *works of the flesh* represents a contrasting parallel to *fruit of the Spirit* (5:22-23). Both the flesh and the Spirit are powers, active agents that produce outcomes (with the cooperation of persons). In speaking of *works* rather than *fruit*, Paul is perhaps suggesting a connection (though not an exact parallel) to works of the Law. In Paul's argument, both represent action based on human resource rather than God's.

Lists or catalogs of vices were common in both Jewish and Greco-Roman contexts. The specific items in the present list are by no means unique to Paul. The ancient world shared much of its moral vocabulary in common even though different groups had their distinctives. For instance, in our list the first three vices and the last two are common to many groups. But idolatry and sorcery reflect Jewish concerns. The group of eight vices in the middle of the list are closely related and less obvious evils. All the items in this group have to do with interpersonal relations, in keeping with the communal emphasis in this section of Galatians (5:13-15, 22-23, 26). These eight vices may reflect the Galatian situation. If so, Paul may have formulated this list for the occasion, which thus indicates Paul's sensitivity to his audience by including both what he can affirm and what they need to hear by way of admonition.

The first three vices are closely related (see the same grouping in 2 Cor 12:21). All three apparently refer to sexual practices. Such is definitely the case with *fornication*, which here may refer to illicit sexual intercourse. *Impurity* has both cultic and moral application. Here it most likely refers to moral impurity of a sexual nature. *Licentiousness*, or debauchery, connotes sexual indecency (Rom 13:13; 1 Pet 4:3; 2 Pet 2:7). Nothing illustrates the meaning of *desires of the flesh* (5:16-17) better than the sexual drive when it is its own master. *Idolatry*, of course, reflects concern for Judaism's strong monotheistic tradition. Paul explains the link between idolatry and moral decadence in Romans 1:21-27. *Sorcery* comes from a word meaning "pharmaceutical drug," but it came to stand for magic and witchcraft, since drugs were used in those practices. Paul's Jewish tradition rejected alternate ways of communicating with the supernatural realm, especially ways of communication that were manipulative.

Next comes the group of eight vices that are social in orientation. Their number and their emphasis on social vices may suggest that these carry special weight. We already suggested that Paul may be addressing the situation, whether actual or potential, in Galatia. In listing these vices, he may be addressing the divisive forces being triggered by the debate between a Pauline party and a circumcision party (5:15). The list includes attitudes, actions, and outcomes.

Enmities means feelings or actions of hostility. *Strife*, or discord, is clearly the consequence and result of enmity. *Jealousy* is related to the word *zeal* but here speaks of a negative passion that sets self-interest against that of others (cf. the similar *envy* later in the list and the selfish use of others in 4:17). Again we move from disposition to action; *anger* refers to fits of anger and rage. *Quarrels* suggests ambition of a selfish and disruptive kind. This vice leads on to *dissensions* and *factions*. These last two, especially the second, are not common elsewhere. *Faction* is often neutral, as in Acts, where the church is described as a faction within Judaism (24:5, 14; 28:22). Paul may be thinking of the factions in Judaism, with their bitter differences about the shape of faithfulness to the Law. He does not want factionalism to develop in the Galatian congregations (Dunn 1993: 305). Last of the social vices is *envy*, or malice, which is close to the earlier *jealousy*.

The list concludes with two vices from the common stock of moral opinion of the time. *Drunkenness* stems from the immoderate use of alcohol. *Carousing* could more aptly be translated as *revelries* or *excessive feasting* since the word originally had to do with a festival. These two vices are related since banquets and feasts were occasions of excessive drinking.

I am warning you, as I warned you before: those who do such things will not inherit the kingdom of God (5:21b). Paul connects his present teaching with what he has taught the Galatians on earlier occasions (cf. 1:9). Here Paul admonishes the Galatians about the dire consequences of a particular course of action; hence he gives them a warning. Those who practice the works of the flesh will have no part in the final reign of God. The verb suggests a lifestyle rather than an isolated, atypical act. Paul's reference to kingdom of God derives from the teaching of Jesus. Paul uses the term sparingly, preferring to speak of the work of Christ and the Spirit. The specific language of inheriting the kingdom appears first in Mark 10:17 on the lips of a rich Jewish man. Paul uses the expression in 1 Corinthians 6:9-10; 15:50; and Ephesians 5:5. *Inheriting the kingdom* refers to a future time and setting when God's purposes for creation and humanity are fully realized, when God's justice is fully established, as in 5:5. This connects well with the concept of inheritance in chapters 3–4 (see esp. 4:7).

Particularly significant is that Paul ties future salvation or condemnation to human deeds or works—in a letter so critical of human works! Paul also makes this point clearly and emphatically in Romans 2:1-11. For Paul, human action, while not itself the basis for right standing with God, is a necessary expression of life in the Spirit and an adequate basis for judging the validity of one's faith claims. Faith and morality are as inseparably linked in Paul's theology as tree is linked to fruit (Matt 7:15-20).

Fruit of the Spirit 5:22-23

By contrast, the fruit of the Spirit is love, joy, peace, patience, kindness, generosity, faithfulness, gentleness, and self-control. There is no law against such things (5:22-23). The NRSV phrase *by contrast* appropriately expresses the fundamental difference between the fruit of the Spirit and the works of the flesh in the preceding list. Paul is illustrating the practical expressions of the contrast between flesh and Spirit asserted in 5:17. The choice of *fruit* to describe the effects of the Spirit is consistent with Paul's larger perspective. The word parallels and yet also contrasts with *works of the flesh* (see on 5:19). The word *works* (though not the idea of good deeds) in Galatians is negative, so it is not surprising that Paul chooses a different word for the work of the Spirit. Moreover, the metaphor of the tree producing fruit appropriately expresses Paul's view of the moral life as something that springs naturally out of a faith relationship with God. What the Law lacks as a life-giving power (3:21), the Spirit possesses.

The fruit metaphor appears in secular writings of the time as well as biblical writings (Prov 1:31; Jer 17:10; Amos 6:12; Matt 3:8-10; John 15:1-8). Of particular significance are Jesus' teaching in Matthew 7:16-20 and Paul's use of the verb *bear fruit* in Romans 7:4-5. That Paul uses the single word *fruit* rather than the plural *works* is probably not significant. The word is always singular in the undisputed writings of Paul. As with English, the Greek is capable of using the singular of *fruit* with a collective sense. The following verse uses the plural (*such things*) to refer to the list.

As with vice lists, virtue lists appear widely in the ancient sources. The last three virtues in our list are especially prominent in Hellenistic writings. The first six are more characteristic of New Testament lists (2 Cor 6:6; 1 Tim 4:12; 6:11; 2 Tim 2:22; 2 Pet 1:5-7). It is significant that this list of Spirit fruit reflects the influence of Jesus' teaching (see the close parallel in the Beatitudes in the Sermon on the Mount; cf. Swartley: 411, citing Glen Stassen). Dunn (1993: 310) suggests that Paul sees his list as a "kind of 'character sketch' of Christ." Later Paul describes those who display these virtues as possessing a Christlike identity (5:24, reflecting 2:20) and as those who *fulfill the law of Christ* (6:2; see comments there). Not surprisingly, because most of these things describe God throughout Scripture, Paul sees Christian virtue as rooted in the character of God (cf. Matt 5:45; Eph 5:1; 1 Pet 1:17). We use the term *virtue* for this list in a general sense. Joy is more of a character trait, not normally thought of as a virtue. In keeping with the social character of most of the virtues in this list, Paul is speaking about the interpersonal peace that derives from a manner of life, rather than an inner psychological condition of the individual. Only *joy* and *self-control* seem primarily individual.

In Christian thought, virtue refers to both external practices and internal character traits. Biblical thought typically holds these together. As with the vices, the list of Spirit fruit is strongly, though not exclusively, oriented to social virtues, qualities that create and sustain community, or in the case of the vices, that destroy it.

That *love* stands at the top of the list is predictable. Love is the leading light in Paul's ethics. Indeed, love encompasses the entire list and summarizes all Christian virtue. This is clear from the two other passages where Paul mentions it in our letter: 5:6 and 13-14. Agape (*agapē*) love is Christlike (2:20; see 5:13-14). It is both distinctive to and characteristic of Christian virtue lists. In 1 Corinthians 13 Paul states that love is the greatest virtue. It is a particular gift of God's working in the believer by the Spirit, as stated in Romans 5:5, "Love has been poured into our hearts through the Holy Spirit."

Joy cannot be humanly contrived, but grows out of the interaction of factors internal and external to the person. Joy is characteristic of the new life in Christ (John 15:11; Acts 2:46-47; 1 Pet 1:8). Joy is associated with the uplifting sense of participation in God's new and final acts of salvation, represented especially in the Spirit's presence and work (Acts 2:46-47). Paul typically links joy with the Spirit (Rom 14:17; 15:13; 1 Thess 1:6).

Peace is commonly tied to joy, as in the passages just cited. As noted above, the Bible typically uses the term to refer to the health and wholeness of the individual in relationship, hence describing the well-being, or shalom, of the community. Here the context implies a form of peace that is not just inner serenity, but also one that leads to harmonious relationships with others. Peace is rooted in right relationship with God and is thus a fruit of right relationship with God (justification, as in Rom 5:1).

Patience is the capacity to endure or persevere under unfavorable circumstances or provocation. It is an important virtue for anyone who wants to maintain or build God's peaceable kingdom in a world of hate, violence, and evil. Without patience or long-suffering, one loses hope and falls back into compromises with the present evil state of affairs. God is the example of this virtue in Romans 2:4.

Kindness and *generosity* are closely related. Kindness is an attitude of goodwill toward others (also used of God in Rom 2:4). Generosity is the expression of kindness in concrete action. The word translated *generosity* is (lit.) *goodness* and could refer broadly to what conforms to the will of God (Rom 12:2), who alone is good (Mark 10:18). In the New Testament the word appears only in Paul's writings (Rom 15:14; Eph 5:9; 2 Thess 1:11). Most commentators see here the connotation of goodwill demonstrated to others (i.e., beneficence or generosity), and the context supports that meaning.

The presence of the word *faithfulness* (exactly the same word as *faith*) in the list may seem surprising. In Galatians, *faith* typically speaks of the receptivity to God's promise, which opens believers to the work of the Spirit. It is, therefore, a presupposition for the fruit of the Spirit. Here, however, faith is a *fruit* or result of the Spirit's work in the community. As 3:1-5 shows, faith as confidence in and reliance on God is a continuing essential to life in the Spirit (cf. 5:6). An example that parallels faith as a fruit of the Spirit is Paul's inclusion of faith in his list of the gifts of the Spirit in 1 Corinthians 12:9. The gift of faith empowers the one so gifted to minister in some unspecified sense to the needs of others in the church (e.g., through prophecy, as in Rom 12:6).

Since our word appears here in a trio of typical Greek virtues (the two that follow), it likely carries overtones of faithfulness and trustworthiness, as in Greek usage. This connotation is also present in the Old Testament view of faith. Paul uses the term this way in praising God's "faithfulness" (Rom 3:3). In the fruit of the Spirit, given Paul's emphasis on virtues of social relations, the word almost certainly refers primarily to human relationships. All the above suggests that *faith* has the broadest possible meaning of trust, being ourselves worthy of trust (faithful), and having trust and faith in others. On the idea of faith in others, compare 1 Corinthians 13:7, "Love has faith in all things" (AT). Trust or faith in God's trustworthiness or faithfulness inspires in us, as a work of the Spirit, a life of trustworthiness and faithfulness toward God and neighbor. This mutual fidelity, as in marriage, is essential to fruitful community.

The other two virtues in the last group of three are *gentleness* and *self-control*. In the biblical context, *gentleness* might well be translated as *meekness*. It means something like *humility*, with which it is often joined (Matt 11:29; 2 Cor 10:1; Eph 4:2; Col 3:12). The Psalms often describe the righteous person as gentle. This quality is closely associated with Christ and his teaching (Matt 5:5; 11:29; 21:5, citing Zech 9:9). In 2 Corinthians 10:1, Paul takes this virtue of Christ as the example for himself (cf. 1 Cor 4:21). Here we see Paul giving christological content to traditional virtues.

The other virtue, *self-control*, is more common to Greek ethical discourse than to the biblical writings. No equivalent appears in the Old Testament, though the concept is present in the wisdom tradition (cf. Prov 25:28, where NRSV uses *self-control*). In the New Testament it appears (as a noun, verb, or adjective) in Acts 24:25; 1 Corinthians 7:9; 9:25; Titus 1:8; and 2 Peter 1:6. This usage reflects the Hellenistic emphasis on control of the passions and moderation in general. Here, where Paul is speaking of the Spirit's assistance in controlling the desires of the flesh, it fits well. But control is not solely the responsibility of the human self, as implied in Greek thought. Paul sees the Spirit as the necessary and effective empowerment of the self.

Just as the vice list closed with a statement of consequence, so the virtue list concludes with a summary statement: *There is no law against such things* (5:23b). The statement is brief and cryptic, making it open to various interpretations despite its apparent significance to the letter's main theme of Law versus Spirit. The Greek grammar could allow the sense *There is no law against such people [who possess these virtues]*. But the parallel expression *such things* in 5:21 argues against that translation. Moreover, the fruit of the Spirit seems to emphasize virtues, not the persons possessing them, so no antecedent supports a reference to persons. The usual sense of the language, as reflected in the NRSV translation, is that no laws prohibit the fruit of the Spirit. Many interpreters find such a meaning obvious to the point of being trivial. They suggest the translation: *There is no law concerning such things*; that is, these matters lie beyond the realm of law. That is grammatically possible, though unlikely. Furthermore, such an interpretation appears to contradict the plain sense of 5:14, which cites a love command from the Law.

Paul may be directing this statement against the Galatian opposition in the form of an irony. If so, Paul is pointing out that since these virtues obviously are not contrary to the Law, it demonstrates that the life in the Spirit can be virtuous without recourse to the Law. The Greek philosopher Aristotle made a similar statement: "Against [certain virtuous persons] there is no law; they are a law to themselves" (cited in Bruce: 255; Witherington: 411). While the parallel is not exact, it illustrates the use of *against* not to mean something opposite and opposing, but to mean something unnecessary and irrelevant. The person of virtue does not need the law to make them virtuous. That sense fits our context better since Paul is trying to demonstrate that the believer in Christ under the Spirit does not need the Law to achieve holy living. The Law may well provide moral guidance (5:14), but it no longer has ultimate authority or power for achievement. More implicit is the thought that the will of God is bigger than any formulation of it, including the Mosaic Law. The Spirit, however, can speak at any time to any area of life about what conforms to the character of God as known in Jesus Christ.

Crucifixion of the Flesh 5:24

And those who belong to Christ Jesus have crucified the flesh with its pas-sions and desires (5:24). Paul has just completed a long exposition of the contrast and conflict between the flesh and the Spirit. Now, in the case of the true believer, he restates the outcome of that strug-gle. In 5:16 Paul has affirmed that life in the Spirit makes possible victory over the desires of the flesh. To the word *desires* in 5:16, Paul for emphasis adds *passions*, a near synonym. Now Paul states the basis of victory over the flesh in terms of identification with Christ in his crucifixion.

Paul's thought here is an extension of 2:20, where he describes the experience of dying with Christ (see extended comments there). However, Paul now emphasizes the negative impact and conse-quence of that identification with Christ's crucifixion. It means death to desires and passions. Paul makes a similar statement in 6:14 in relation to the world. In both cases, Paul means death to these things inasmuch as and to the extent that they are instruments of evil in life.

Throughout the letter, Paul has been moving back and forth between explaining the Law-free life as encounter with Christ and as life with the Spirit. In the present discussion of the moral life, Paul again reaffirms this dual basis in the work of the Spirit and of Christ. These are not separate stages or experiences, but two aspects of one reality. The work of Christ is both the ground for and the shape of new life. The work of the Spirit activates Christ's work in new life. Both aspects are crucial as divine action is made fully effec-tive in human experience.

Here Paul uses a verb tense for *crucified* that points exclusively to the moment of conversion, when a believer definitively commits to following Christ. That was the decisive moment when Christ's con-trol of one's life began, excluding all other controlling powers, including the flesh (cf. Rom 6:6). Here again, Paul's indicative (*cruci-fied*, an assertion of a past action of God) issues in an imperative (a call for implementing action by the believer; see TBC on 5:1-12). In our context, Paul states the imperative in terms of life in the Spirit (5:16, 25). An important implication of this indicative and impera-tive structure is that the crucifixion of the flesh does not assure the end of temptation and moral failure. The exhortations that follow in 5:25–6:1 make this abundantly clear. In 6:1, Paul says that even the spiritually mature are vulnerable to temptation.

THE TEXT IN BIBLICAL CONTEXT

Love as Ethical Norm

When Paul cites the love commandment from Leviticus 19:18 in Galatians 5:14, he points to a leading concept in both testaments as well as a central theme in his own writings. In the Old Testament, love reaches a high point in the context of the covenant that binds God and Israel. Love is covenantal. In that context, love expresses the commitment that sustains the relationship. But because relationships are not only legal and volitional, they also involve the feelings and passions that reach out for relationship and that sustain it. So God is said to love Israel (Deut 4:37), and Israel is to love God in return (Deut 6:5). Here the same sentiment that motivates us to human bonding in marriage and friendship describes the spiritual relationship. The book of Hosea is an extended application of the analogy of human marital love, as well as faithfulness and unfaithfulness, to the covenant between God and Israel.

Besides being covenantal, love in both testaments is characteristically communitarian. Love builds community. It does so first in the relationship between God and God's people. But then it builds and nourishes the relationship among God's people: "You shall love your neighbor as yourself" (Lev 19:18). In covenant love, the focus is not on sentiment itself, but on what love does in realizing the purposes of God. It is not an end in itself. What counts is the *fruit* of love—what it accomplishes. True love results in genuine fellowship with God and fruitful life in community. The epistle of 1 John (3:17-18) makes this point emphatically: love without concrete actions on behalf of the other is no love at all. But neither can the actions be separated from the inner wellspring of compassion and affection. Paul himself makes this clear in the great hymn to love: "If I give away all my possessions . . . but do not have love, I gain nothing (1 Cor 13:3).

In the New Testament love is also christological. Love is defined by the example of Jesus Christ. From the life of Jesus, we learn what love is and does. Christian love is not defined by observing natural human behavior. Without some specific definition, love cannot serve as a useful ethical guideline for the simple reason that it is subject to a range of meanings. In Galatians, Paul makes clear that Christian love is other-directed and is self-giving. The other-directed quality of love is stated in 5:13: *Through love become slaves to one another*. Paul clearly presents the self-giving quality of love in 2:20, where he links Christ's own love with his self-giving.

The clearest example of Paul portraying Christ's love as the model for the believer comes in Philippians 2:1-11. Here Christ in his incarnation is depicted as one who sacrificed his own interests even to the point of death on the cross. In this example Paul sees the kind of love (Phil 2:1-2) that leads believers to put the interests of others ahead of their own interests (Phil 2:3-4). We see the same point in Ephesians 5:2, 25; 1 Peter 2:21-23 (alongside 3:8-9); and 1 John 3:16. Throughout his letters, especially in 1 Corinthians, Paul often exhorts his readers to lay aside self-interest and rights in the interest of forming and preserving Christian community. Sacrificial love is unconditional love of the other, even the enemy. This kind of love redeems and restores human relationships because it overcomes evil with good (Rom 12:14-21; 13:10; 1 Pet 3:9; Matt 5:44-45; for a full study of Paul's view of love as self-sacrificial, see Gorman 2001).

Paul was likely drawn to the concept of love because of the way it joins together the dimensions of inner vitality and the outer life of conduct. It also connects with the pervasive concern in Galatians regarding the motivating force for godly living. Love is a driving passion that moves a person to action. It shares this quality with that other important concept in Paul, the desires of the flesh. The latter are the negative drives that are under the dominion of sin in the person not led by the Spirit. But love, which is also a desire or passion, is a positive drive, a fruit of the Spirit, that reflects the love Christ had for us (Gal 2:20) and builds up the community of believers (Gal 5:13-14). It is therefore no surprise that love is the central theme of Paul's ethical vision.

Love serves another purpose as well at this point in Galatians (5:13-14). From the teaching of Jesus, Paul takes the insight that the entire Law of Moses is embraced in the themes of love for God and love for neighbor (Mark 12:28-34 and parallels, quoting Deut 6:5 and Lev 19:18). This point serves Paul's argument about the place of the Law for Christians. Paul's focus on love respects the Law because the essence of the Law is taken up and preserved or fulfilled in love. On the other hand, love serves an ethical vision (see previous paragraph) that is consistent with the work of Christ (2:19-21), the inclusion of all nations in the church (3:8, 14), and the empowerment of the Spirit (3:14; 5:16)—all of which surpasses the former stage of the Law. In this sense believers are no longer under the Law (5:18).

Spirit, Flesh, and the Human Will

Use of the terms *Spirit* or *spirit* and *flesh* to describe the moral options in human experience is not widespread in Scripture. Outside of Paul's writings, it appears in the writings of John, where it plays a significant role. The one who is born from above is born from the

Spirit and consequently understands the things of the spirit or heavenly realm (John 3:5-8, 12; 1 John 3:24). Anyone else is born of the flesh and understands only from a natural or earthly point of view (John 3:5, 12; 1 John 2:16). It is the spirit that gives life; the flesh is useless (John 6:63).

Both Paul and John use the word *flesh* in both negative and positive ways. Negative uses are clear in Galatians and in the Johannine passages above. Positive meanings appear in Galatians 2:20 in reference to Paul's life in Christ and in 1 John 4:2, where true believers acknowledge that Christ came in the flesh. So these two leading voices in the New Testament agree that flesh is essentially good; but where it is controlled by evil, it can itself be described as evil. The latter is the condition of the earthbound person who is not alive to the Spirit. For Paul, this describes all humanity, since all are under the power of sin. Although Paul does not expressly state it this way, when the Spirit controls the life, the flesh becomes the good instrument by which the works of God are achieved. Such works are the fruit of the Spirit.

New Testament writers reflect the view of human nature presented in the Old Testament, but adapted to the Greek language in which they write. In the Old Testament *flesh* stands for humanity in its weakness. The word commonly and misleadingly translated as *soul* points to humanity (the whole person) in its hungers and desires. In the New Testament these two aspects appear together in the phrase, *desire of the flesh*, or *lusts of the flesh*. The human creature is a combination of strong drives and great weakness. The resulting vulnerability is readily and effectively exploited by evil powers.

In our present context the word *Spirit* refers to the Spirit of God, as it does in the Old Testament. In the New Testament it can also refer to an aspect of human nature, as in Galatians 6:18. When Paul speaks of conflict of Spirit and flesh over against the human will, we can ask which of these actors is external to the person and which is internal. Certainly the Spirit is external, a force outside the person. On the other side, the will (*what you want*, or will, in 5:17) is clearly part of the person.

For *flesh*, the situation is not so evident. Flesh is normally an aspect of human nature. On the other hand, Galatians 5:17 depicts it as a power over against human willing, which suggests something external to the person. The answer to this anomaly is that flesh in itself is part of the human person as a creature of desire, but when flesh becomes the point of access for sin (seen in Paul as a power), flesh becomes the servant of a power external to the person. This creates the situation where one aspect of the person (flesh) can oppose another aspect of the same person that is inclined toward God (cf. Rom 7; but see Explanatory Notes above on 5:17). Thus Paul sees a dynamic interaction of external and internal forces, whose influence on and interaction with the individual explains the complexity of human moral behavior.

As bringing hope for moving out of this impasse, Paul credits the work of the Spirit, who is capable of tipping the scales toward victorious, godly living. This is the same perspective Paul has in Romans 8:1-17, 23, where he adds the additional dimension that redemption from sin and its effects has both a present fulfillment and a future expectation. We are already living the reality of the Spirit's victory over the flesh, but in some respects we are not yet liberated from the struggle with sin and must await the final restoration of all creation for our own full redemption (Rom 8:23). Paul expresses this already-but-not-yet quality of Christian living in references to the present (genuine but incomplete) work of the Spirit as *first fruits* (Rom 8:23) and *pledge* (down payment and guarantee, as in 2 Cor 1:22; 5:5; Eph 1:14). With his emphasis on the Holy Spirit as a key element in the better things that Jesus Christ brings, Paul stands with Jesus himself (John 14:16-17) and the rest of the early church. They all saw in the outpouring of the Spirit the fulfillment of an Old Testament promise (Acts 2:16-21, citing Joel 2:28-32; cf. Ezek 36:26-27).

THE TEXT IN THE LIFE OF THE CHURCH

Virtues of Community Formation

The portion of Galatians we are considering strongly emphasizes life together in the church. The immediate context contains warnings against behaviors that damage life together (5:15, 26). This emphasis continues in the fruit of the Spirit, where the virtues that build community predominate. Even joy and self-control, which seem more personal, have implications for life together. The same general emphasis is present in the list of the works of the flesh.

Paul's emphasis on community is consistent with the central place of God's holy community in both testaments. Biblical faith is communal faith, but for all that, no less personal. It is a commonplace to decry the individualism of modern Western culture. This criticism applies also to the church in the West, and with substantial consequences. From ancient times up through the Middle Ages, the individual's interests were subordinated to the collective interests of society. Individual rights and benefits were sacrificed for the perceived good of society. In modern times, the reverse is true. With the reversal, we have made some important gains for the welfare of the individual, but we have also experienced loss when individual self-interest consistently overrides community welfare. In Western culture today, Christian community is under continual threat. Many of the moral dilemmas of our time (e.g., divorce) hinge on how we negotiate the conflicting interests of the community and the individual. This currently is a major challenge for the church.

Today some of the virtues of biblical faith are treated as suspect precisely because they may seem to threaten the good of the individual. As we noted above, *humility* is a near synonym of *gentleness* in the list of the fruit of the Spirit. From an individualistic perspective, humility can cultivate low self-esteem. Indeed, some Christians have understood humility in this way and, as a result, have a poor self-image and lack any holy ambition to use the gifts God has given to them.

However, if we understand humility in a communitarian frame of reference, the point is not how we view our self as an isolated self, but how we view ourselves in relation to others. In that case, a person with good self-esteem is sensitive to the needs of others and sets aside self-interest to advance the good of the community as a whole. In Scripture, humility is a community virtue. In Romans, Paul expresses this understanding by appealing for honest self-image, neither too high nor too low, in order to fill one's role in the body of Christ (Rom 12:3-8). In the believers church tradition, the emphasis on community has understandably been strong. Not surprisingly, the tradition has highly valued humility. The Anabaptists made much of the attitude of yieldedness (*Gelassenheit*), meaning not only surrender to God, but also surrender to the interests of the church as a whole (see also TBC on 5:25-6:10).

The Place of the Spirit in Christian Experience

Galatians, other writings of Paul, and the rest of the New Testament make clear that the Spirit was central to early church belief and experience. The work of the Spirit was visible in the display of divine power in personal and community life. Although this has not always been the case throughout church history, many periods of spiritual renewal have been marked by an emphasis on the Spirit and by unusual manifestations (signs and wonders). Early Anabaptism is a case in point. Yet much of church history lacks signs and wonders, and believers often fear the fanaticism that sometimes accompanies these renewal movements. What are we to make of this? What is the proper place and role of the Spirit in the faithful church?

Some believe that the time of the apostles was a unique period of intense Spirit activity. The Spirit needed to inspire new revelation of the gospel's meaning and prove the truth of the gospel in miracles. That time ceased, some claim, with the generation of the apostles. Others, such as those in the Pentecostal-charismatic movement, see in the New Testament, particularly in Acts, a blueprint for all times and places. The gifts of the Spirit, which prove authentic faith, have preeminent value.

Most likely the truth lies somewhere between these positions. On the one hand, the Spirit is too central to the distinctiveness of the gospel to be marginalized or limited to one period of time. If the voice of the Spirit is silenced, are we saying God no longer speaks in the present? We still need the guidance of the Spirit even though we have the Bible. In fact, we need the Spirit to rightly understand and apply the Bible, as well as to discern the truth in new questions of our time. Moreover, doesn't our witness to the gospel still need supportive evidence in acts that display the Spirit's powerful intervention? This does not mean that we should turn the picture of the Spirit's work in Acts into a rigid pattern that respects neither the Spirit's freedom nor the changing circumstances of the church in differing cultures and historical periods.

We need balance in appropriating the work of the Spirit. The New Testament presents a rich variety of ways that the Spirit blesses God's people. Renewal movements tend to focus on one aspect of the Spirit's ministry, an aspect seen as the crucial corrective needed for the moment. Because of their practical and sometimes spectacular character, the "gifts of the Spirit" tend to receive more attention. Indeed, they are important for enabling the ministry of the church within itself and to the world. Charismatic movements highlight this dimension of the Spirit's work.

Here in Galatians, Paul focuses on the moral empowerment of the Spirit, the *fruit of the Spirit.* Churches that emphasize discipleship and holiness of life find this aspect of the Spirit's work essential. Yet another major aspect features prominently in the gospel of John. In this writing the Spirit is called "the Spirit of truth" (e.g., John 14:17). So we can speak of the *truth of the Spirit*, the role of the Spirit in discernment. John explores the questions, What is the truth? Where is it found? The guidance of the Spirit is indispensable because moral darkness blinds us to the way things really are. So this has to do with how human beings can know what is true. It is a perennial issue in human experience and in the life of the church. In an age of skepticism, such as the present, we can find a renewed confidence in the promise that the Spirit will guide us into full truth (John 16:13). Where these three dimensions of the Spirit are taken seriously— truth, fruit, and gift—the church will prosper spiritually.

Galatians 5:25–6:10

Acting in Conformity to the Spirit

PREVIEW

So what does a Spirit-filled "body life" look like? People tend to think of the worship setting when considering the proofs or signs of Spirit empowerment. Here Paul describes what kind of difference the presence and power of the Holy Spirit make in the life of the church. In the previous section (5:13-24), Paul identified love and the Holy Spirit as the keys to moral living. In the present section (5:25–6:10), Paul shows how these same two elements, love and the Holy Spirit, prove to be the keys to life in the body of Christ as well.

Paul begins with a summary assertion (5:25) that relates what follows to the previous, general theme of the Spirit's empowerment for obedience. Because the transition is not abrupt, some prefer to make the division at 6:1. The section ends with a summary (6:7-10) of the entire request section from 4:12 onward, which contrasts the way of the flesh and its outcome with that of the Spirit. In fact, this summary serves well as a wrap-up of the entire letter if, as we have argued, the contrast of flesh and Spirit introduced in 3:1-5 is the key theme of the letter.

This section continues Paul's concern for community life. Paul wants his readers to exercise the fruit of the Spirit through love to build community up, rather than to tear it down. Although the vocabulary and concepts have parallels in non-Christian writings, Paul describes healthy body life through the lenses provided by the person and work of Christ and the power of the Spirit. He dares, in fact, to call the result *the law of Christ* (6:2). By doing so, he redeems the term *law*, which he has so heavily criticized throughout the letter.

OUTLINE

Virtues That Build the Faith Community, 5:25–6:6
A Summary Appeal, 6:7-10

EXPLANATORY NOTES

Virtues That Build the Faith Community 5:25–6:6

If we live by the Spirit, let us also be guided by the Spirit (5:25). In a conditional sentence, Paul states another of his general principles of life in the Spirit (see 5:16 and 18). Yet here he uses other vocabulary to bring out different nuances. The statement *live by the Spirit* has essentially the same meaning (but a different word) as *Live* [lit. *walk*] *by the Spirit* in 5:16 (NRSV translates them with the same word). The emphasis is on continuing and persisting in opening one's life to the leading of the Spirit. In the present statement, Paul introduces that truth as a presupposition: *If we live by the Spirit* (it could be translated as *since we live*).

Paul uses that assumption as the warrant for a new admonition in the imperative: *Be guided by the Spirit.* This is a most interesting verb. Clearly Paul has chosen it with care. He uses it twice in the final part of the letter (also 6:16). It is a verb related to the noun for *elements* in 4:3, 9. Paul may well want the reader to see the connection with that discussion. The word here means "stand in line" (as soldiers) or "keep in step." One can see in it the idea of conforming to a pattern or standard. This idea is especially clear in 6:16, which speaks of conforming one's life to a standard, the rule [of the gospel].

Paul is suggesting that the Christian should discern what specific shape of life is consistent with the mind of the Spirit (cf. Rom 12:2; Eph 5:10, 17; Phil 1:10). That shape of life will contrast with the shape of life (the *elements*) both in paganism and in Judaism under the Law. In one respect, Paul wants to guard against the idea that life in the Spirit is freewheeling and disorderly (cf. 5:13). In another respect, he wants the Galatians to know that the ordered moral life they think they want under the Law is better realized by Spirit-centered faith. So verse 25 serves well as the heading for this section, which lays out concrete examples of life ordered by the Spirit as Paul finds relevant for the occasion.

Let us not become conceited, competing against one another, envying one another (5:26). Before introducing the more positive advice in 6:1 and following, Paul counsels what to avoid. The language obviously deals with relationships in the Christian community. This is the only use of the adjective *conceited* in the New Testament (the noun appears only in Phil 2:3). It expresses an inflated sense of self, marked by arrogance and boasting, and contrasts with the gentleness (meekness) that is a fruit of the Spirit. The two dependent clauses that follow further define the term by expressing its consequences. Conceit leads to competition because the ego seeks status and prestige. Moreover, it breeds envy because it perceives the successes and glory of others as a threat to one's own importance.

My friends, if anyone is detected in a transgression, you who have received the Spirit should restore such a one in a spirit of gentleness. Take care that you yourselves are not tempted (6:1). As the preceding verse implied and this verse makes plain, Paul does not believe that the community of the Spirit has reached perfection. He knows there will continue to be moral imperfection, and the Christian community must be prepared to handle such situations. This is stated as the possibility that someone will be caught (i.e., detected) in a moral lapse or wrong step. What nuance might the idea of being caught by surprise have? (1) Does it refer to the fact that sin is not the natural thing in the Spirit-led life, and so moral lapses can happen only in moments of spiritual distraction, when sin entraps us? Or (2) does it imply that the offender was hiding the sin? Or (3) was the offender unaware that the action was wrong and was noticed by other believers (implied in the NRSV's *detect*)? Given the tenor of the larger context, the first option seems likely. However, Paul may have intentionally chosen a word open to more than one meaning.

What is striking is that Paul does not go outside the spiritual realm to find help for spiritual imperfections. It is precisely the qualities produced by the Spirit in believers that enable the community to attend to its weaknesses and failures. Here *gentleness* or meekness specifically illustrates the point, because it is a fruit of the Spirit (5:23). This virtue permits one to show empathy toward the person who has erred and hence show a spirit of openness to restoration. It creates the kind of atmosphere that makes confession and restoration less onerous to the offender.

Paul makes another connection to the Spirit by admonishing the spiritual ones (*you who have received the Spirit*) to take the initiative in remedial action. Most likely, Paul does not have in mind a particular group, but is saying that all who identify with his view of the

Spirit-filled community should engage in restorative action. The remarkable message here is that the presence and power of the Spirit both enable and require attention to church discipline! Both Paul (1 Cor 5:4-5) and other New Testament writers (cf. Matt 18:17) see discipline as the responsibility of the whole body of believers. But Paul wants the disciplinary response to reflect the godly attitudes that the Spirit desires to bring to fruition.

The kind of discipline Paul advises here is restorative, not punitive. He uses a word that means "to mend a wrong situation and restore to a former condition." In some instances Paul proposes a more punitive response, even when his ultimate concern is for restoration (4:30; 1 Cor 5:1-5). Paul may see these latter cases as persistent and intractable errors and sins, but those in our present text as more occasional lapses, which the person is ready to acknowledge and correct. (See the discussion of discipline in TBC and TLC on 4:12-31.)

Seeing the transgression of another member of the community should lead to introspection about one's own vulnerability to temptation by the appeal of the flesh. The idea is that of looking at something carefully and critically. This attitude is the opposite of the conceit Paul proscribed in 5:26. The ability to build and preserve community is proportional to the capacity for honest self-awareness and self-criticism, which allows one to interact constructively and harmoniously with others. Judgmentalism destroys the body of Christ as surely as does the failure to engage in loving church discipline at all.

Bear one another's burdens, and in this way you will fulfill the law of Christ (6:2). The building of strong, intentional community depends on the concrete commitment to a shared life expressed in the exchange of needs and resources. Fraternal exchange aims at a fair balance between abundance and need (2 Cor 8:13-14, based on Exod 16:18; cf. Gal 2:10). This is the fundamental idea in the counsel to bear each other's burdens.

The word *burden* is not precise, since it can cover a broad range of things. In about half of its occurrences in Paul's letters it refers to financial burdens. That could fit here, as the Corinthian ideal cited above would support. Some connect it to the burden of moral failure in the preceding verse. However, there is no connecting word between the two verses, which would be natural if Paul wanted to limit *burden* through its relationship with the previous verse. Therefore, it is better to take the word in a broadly inclusive sense to refer to moral, material, social, physical, and psychological burdens. However, the connective in the following clause should tell us something about its meaning: *in this way* fulfill the law of Christ (see below).

This brings us to one of the most striking and debated statements in the letter. What does Paul mean by *the law of Christ*? That Paul should use the word *law* in a positive sense within a document of polemic against law is surprising and noteworthy. Along with 5:14, this phrase serves to reconstruct a positive view of law. What is surprising is that Paul does not explain and defend this positive usage.

The phrase *law of Christ* clearly refers to a standard or pattern of life that reflects what Christ stands for and expects of his followers. The implication is that Christians can and should apply their faith to their way of life. This is the sense of the passage presenting the only close parallel in Paul's letters (1 Cor 9:21). There he says that, in his identification with Gentiles who are not under the Mosaic Law, he nevertheless is "not free from God's law but [is] under Christ's law." A moral standard, defined by Christ, always guides Paul, and this standard also represents the will of God.

Defining *the law of Christ* more precisely quickly becomes controversial and highly dependent on one's overall view of Paul's understanding of law (for the range of views, see Barclay: 127–31). Some take the term *law* as referring specifically to the Mosaic Law. The qualifying phrase *of Christ* means the Law as interpreted and applied by Jesus. This position gives the Mosaic Law an important position of continuing authority in Christian faith. Others take *law* as a direct reference to the standard of righteousness in Jesus' life and teaching. This standard, or law, builds on the Mosaic Law but goes beyond it and becomes the only authority for the church. In the light of our explanation of Paul's view in Galatians, the second position is preferable.

The *law of Christ* is the moral vision based on the example and teaching of Jesus in his life, death, and resurrection. That vision is fundamentally in harmony with the Old Testament Law (5:14), though it modifies it in accordance with the truly new dimensions that Christ has brought (4:4-7). At the same time, that vision sees the role of (any) law not as a complete and fixed code of behavior, but as a pattern (paradigm) that the Spirit of God re-creates as living virtue in the believer (5:16-23) and reapplies dynamically in the changing contexts of life (5:25). The latter point may help explain why Paul so rarely cites the tradition of Jesus' teaching. He wants to avoid the appearance of setting up a new law code to replace the

Mosaic Law. At the same time, the law of Christ gives some specific-
ity and definition to Christian morality, so that we do not confuse
the mind of the Spirit with our own human or even demonic ideas.

Here Paul probably has in mind the example of Christ, who sacrificially bears the burdens of others and is therefore the standard
for his followers in bearing one another's burdens. That meaning
fits well the present context of burden bearing. The cross is the central symbol of this self-giving (Gorman 2001: 174, 186). This example
of Christ is a typical emphasis in Paul (e.g., Phil 2:5-11; Rom 15:1-3)
and the dominant one in Galatians (1:4; 2:20; 3:13). Paul uses the
concept of love to carry this meaning. He sees love as the fulfillment
of the Mosaic Law. That love is marked by service to others (see
5:13-14 and discussion there). The law of Christ is synonymous with
love—the love that is defined by the example of the life of Jesus
Christ (Elias: 338).

The form of the verb *fulfill* suggests completeness in practicing
Christ's law. This is not fulfillment as replacement but as realization,
that is, putting it into effect. This could have the sense of putting the
law of Christ into practice in every way. Or it could mean that
Christ's own service is brought to completion through the service of
his followers, in the same way that Paul saw his sufferings as the
completion of Christ's suffering (Col 1:24, where the verb has a similar form). Both nuances may be intended. The latter idea is particularly appropriate here.

*For if those who are nothing think they are something, they deceive
themselves* (6:3). The focus shifts from corporate concerns in the
previous two verses (6:1-2, with the exception of 6:1b) to individual concerns in the following three verses (6:3-5). Paul is aware of
the interaction between the two and knows that both are crucial
for the formation of strong community. Strong individuals
strengthen community, and strong community strengthens individuals—with *strengthen* understood as growth in wholeness, health,
and growth in conforming to the character of Christ. This is what
Paul wants to clarify.

As already noted, the conceit of 5:26 is antithetical to community
and to realistic self-perception. The conjunction *for* indicates that
Paul is reemphasizing the connection between right self-
understanding and healthy community interdependence. Paul does
not mean that some persons have no worth. Rather, Paul is strongly
stating that one should not claim a strength one does not, in fact,
have. He is calling for a realistic assessment of oneself (cf. Rom 12:3).
Strength of personal character and of community life depends on it.

All must test their own work; then that work, rather than their neigh-bor's work, will become a cause of pride. For all must carry their own loads (6:4-5). The idea of testing as a significant activity at various levels of Christian experience features prominently in Paul (e.g., Rom 12:2; 2 Cor 13:5; 1 Thess 5:21). One puts something to the test to prove its real character. Interestingly, the object of the testing here is the *work* of the believer. Once again, *work* is not totally negative for Paul. The actions of a person are a good (the best?) way to know that person. True self-understanding cannot come from comparing one's own work with the work of others. In other words, one should not take credit for another's accomplishment. Furthermore, one should not assume that they share in the strengths that others have. Either way, wrong self-assessment does not develop the kind of person that contributes best to the community.

Paul's reference to *pride* (or *boasting*) as the result of proper self-assessment seems to contradict 5:26, which warns against conceit (cf. the negative use of *pride/boast* in 6:13). But in Hellenistic culture and in Paul's writing, pride (or boasting) can be an acceptable qual-ity (Rom 15:17; 1 Cor 9:15; 2 Cor 1:12; 10:8, 13-17; 11:10, 30; 12:5-6, 9; Phil 2:16). These passages show that Paul applied the principle in the present passage to himself. Second Corinthians 10:12-18 is a particu-larly close parallel. Paul is concerned to evaluate himself honestly and not to claim for himself the achievements of others. His distinc-tive perspective on boasting lies in the constant recognition that his accomplishments are possible only in the strength of the Lord and in sacrificial service for others (see 6:14!). Perhaps what Paul means comes close to what we express in the concept of self-esteem. Only a positive, healthy ego can usefully serve the alter ego of Christ-in-me (2:20) and interact fruitfully with the multiple egos of a community.

The final statement of balance between community and indi-vidual comes as Paul commands, *All must carry their own loads.* The future tense of *carry* is taken by some to refer to the final judgment, when each person will answer for themselves (cf. Rom 14:12). However, the context here does not suggest a future orientation. The statement stands in deliberate counterbalance with the earlier command, *Bear one another's burdens* (6:2).

Different words are used in these two places, as NRSV suggests with *burden* and *load.* The words can have the same meaning, but the present context calls for a difference in meaning. *Burden* in 6:2 prob-ably stands for the abnormal and unusual burdens of life (such as the spiritual and moral testing mentioned in 6:1), while *load* here in

6:5 stands for the normal and reasonable share of responsibility an individual should carry. Some burdens, unless they are shared, destroy us, making us unfit for community life. Other burdens are manageable, and we are responsible for them. Carrying them ourselves strengthens us, making us contributors to community rather than parasites of community. Only such a balance of mutual caring and personal responsibility can support a strong, viable, and intentional community like the church.

Mirrored in these exhortations about community, some have seen a veiled criticism of the false teachers, who are boasting on false grounds (6:13). Perhaps so. Throughout the letter, however, Paul appeals directly to the Galatians themselves, with the hope that they will act in a manner consistent with the gospel. He seems to believe that such a strategy will best close the door on the false teaching. This is the way we should take this paragraph. Paul is genuinely focused on helping the Galatians to see that his Christ- and Spirit-centered gospel creates a new order of things that touches all of life (cf. *new creation* in 6:15). Paul is fighting error by making the truth look more attractive.

Those who are taught the word must share in all good things with their teacher (6:6). A specific case comes to Paul's mind on the subject of burden bearing. The likely reference here is to the material support given to the teachers in the community of believers. This is an instance of the mutual aid Paul has been encouraging, but he may mention this particular case because of possible misunderstanding. Those who serve the church in a demanding leadership role, such as teaching, deserve appropriate compensation—something more than or other than simply the result of the equalizing that occurs in exchanging resources and needs.

This throws some light on the importance of the teaching role in early Christian congregations. The role was a major one because the process of nurturing new believers, especially Gentiles, into a radically new faith and life demanded much by way of preparation and implementation. That this teaching is characterized as *word* means that it involves the entire Christian worldview (belief and practice) in its verbal articulation.

The word used here for *sharing* was common in the early church in connection with material assistance (cf. "koinonia" and cognates). It is found among the first believers in Jerusalem (Acts 2:44-45; 4:32-34). Paul describes the collection he raised for the Jerusalem saints as a "sharing" (Rom 15:26-27; 2 Cor 8:4; 9:13). Romans 15:27 expresses the same principle of exchanging spiritual ministry and material support. In relation specifically to support for a person in Christian ministry, see Philippians 1:5 and 4:15, which uses words from the same root. Paul states the principle of support for ministering persons in 1 Corinthians 9:14, where he cites a saying of Jesus (Luke 10:7).

While the support Paul has in mind may well be financial, the language of *all good things* suggests a wider range of application. Many forms of assistance contribute to the good of a person (cf. 6:10.) Significant is the idea of mutual sharing in the case of teacher and learner. That relationship can be easily seen as a one-way exchange from teacher to learner in nonmaterial gifts, and a one-way exchange from learner to teacher in material gifts. However, for Paul the relationship must not be unilateral. He wants it to express his vision of the church as a community of mutuality.

A Summary Appeal 6:7-10

Do not be deceived; God is not mocked, for you reap whatever you sow. If you sow to your flesh, you will reap corruption from the flesh; but if you sow to the Spirit, you will reap eternal life from the Spirit (6:7-8). In wrapping up the argument of the main body of the letter, Paul turns to the powerful imagery of sowing and reaping. Strictly speaking, this is a summary appeal for the section from 5:13 onward, in which Paul applies the contrast of Spirit and flesh to the moral life. That same contrast reappears here. The image of sowing and reaping has broad usage in moral instruction. Yet this general maxim on sowing and reaping comes at the end of an entire letter stamped with the theme of Spirit versus flesh. So the reminder also serves well in concluding the argument of the entire letter (see below).

Do not be deceived is an imperative geared to capture the attention of the reader. *Mocking* means, literally, to turn up the nose. It is similar to the modern expression "thumb one's nose" at someone. The one who ridicules and makes light of God will ultimately be accountable to God. The idea of mocking God is not common in biblical writings (see Prov 1:30; Ezek 8:17), but the image of sowing and reaping as a metaphor for the consequences or rewards of human action is widespread. Paul uses it in another way in 2 Corinthians 9:6, and Jesus adopts it in his parable teaching, as in Matthew 13:3-9. Old Testament examples include Job 4:8; Proverbs 22:8; Jeremiah 12:13; Hosea 8:7.

Here Paul gives the proverbial statement of sowing and reaping a novel and creative application. Sowing to the flesh brings a harvest of corruption, but sowing to the Spirit brings a harvest of eternal life. Paul picks up the obvious fact that flesh, as the material substance of which living beings are made, is subject to corruption and decay; he applies that fact to the question of the resurrection body in 1 Corinthians 15:42-49 (the body must be transformed from a fleshly to a spiritual body). Here, however, he uses the moral, spiritual meaning of *flesh*: the body and its drives on its own without a spiritual control. And he concludes that this leads to moral and spiritual decay, and thus ruin.

In this way, Paul effectively points out the limitations of humans seen as material beings apart from God: decay is always the last word. In contrast, the Spirit produces that which lasts without end: eternal life. In this context, *eternal* is quantitative in that it emphasizes unending time. But as generally in Scripture the idea of eternal life also carries qualitative connotations (the fullness and abundance of life). Here Paul again evokes the parallel point with the resurrection body in 1 Corinthians 15:44. For another statement of the general principle, but without the sowing-reaping image, see Romans 8:13.

This truth lies at the root of all that Paul has been saying in the letter. The Galatians began their experience of the Spirit by depending on the divine power at work among them. But in turning toward the Law, they turned toward the principle of the flesh—materially in the act of circumcision, and spiritually in accepting an authority independent of life in Christ and the Spirit.

So let us not grow weary in doing what is right, for we will reap at harvest time, if we do not give up (6:9). The close tie to the preceding material is clear in Paul's reference to the harvest. The expression *doing what is right* connects with the concrete moral exhortations of 6:1-6. A more literal translation, *doing the good*, better emphasizes serving the good of one's fellow believers in community. Paul is aware of the challenge that vindication and reward are often deferred to the future. As a result, he warns against the tendency to become weary. Believers live the values of the kingdom before the kingdom has fully come. Thus some incompleteness and ambiguity in the present are inevitable. The temptation is to become weary and fainthearted (cf. 1 Thess 3:13). Only hope-filled faith and endurance can face this tension. Paul also uses *weariness* in relation to Christian ministry and the temptation to give up (2 Cor 4:1, 16).

But here the consequence of giving up is not just unfruitful ministry, but also eternal loss. The exhortation is sobering. That the harvest of corruption is in parallel contrast with eternal life in the previous verse means that *harvest time* here refers to the final judgment. It follows that *doing what is right* can only mean that one's eternal reward is linked to the moral quality of one's life. Paul does not believe that works are the ground of salvation, nor does he believe there is eternal blessing without them as the fruit of faith and the Spirit (see also 5:6 and 21). Now beyond all doubt it is clear that salvation and conduct are inseparable for Paul. In the argument of Galatians, the Spirit is what unifies them, resulting in adoption into the family of God (3:14; 4:5-6) and a life of godliness.

So then, whenever we have an opportunity, let us work for the good of all, and especially for those of the family of faith (6:10). Paul recognizes that the fruitfulness of one's service is dependent on the opportunities one has. He thus removes from the previous affirmation what might otherwise appear as an unfair demand. What is so insightful is the way Paul holds together the responsibility to the neighbor outside the church and the fellow believer within. He shows his high view of the church by recognizing its priority. But he also has a strong theology of creation, in which all people are God's concern. They therefore deserve the concern of the people of God as well. The people of God are here called the *family* (lit. *household*, KJV) *of faith*, a phrase reflecting the Old Testament image of Israel as a house. Paul has already evoked the image of family in Galatians 3:7, 26, 29; 4:5-6. In Mediterranean culture, the household represented the social unit to which one gave highest loyalty and service. For Paul's audience, it evokes solidarity and compassion and thus is particularly appropriate to reinforce the challenge to serve others both inside and outside the church.

This way of setting the priorities (*especially for the family of faith*) is not simply a matter of natural self-interest or realism about the limits of what the church as a minority group can do for *all*. It is consistent with the New Testament view of the church as a model of the *new creation* (6:15), the city of God built on a hill as a light to the nations (Matt 5:14; Isa 2:2-4). The church must tend to its own affairs in order to be a worthy example to the world. Here maintenance of the church's life and mission to the world are interdependent. The church begins its service to the world by being a model of the good that can and should be. For the church to be such an example requires that it give high priority to the quality of its internal life and practice.

In this text Paul's chief concern is that believers do concrete actions of *good* in their relationships with others. The word *good* is a fundamental word for ethics in Paul (see, e.g., Rom 2:6-11; 12:2, 9, 21). Here it appears in verses 6, 9, and 10 (as two synonyms in

Greek). Paul uses it as shorthand for what Christian living should look like. In the brief span of these verses, the concept of the good clearly focuses on concrete actions that benefit others.

However, the word *good* in itself is ambiguous. For Paul, it reflects the character of God and mutual love (Westerholm 2004b: 156–57). The principle of love for the neighbor is prominent in Galatians (5:6, 13-14, 22). Ultimately the exhortation to do good to all is rooted in love. Love defines the good, and the good is the concrete expression of love. And this love is not exclusive in its object. Christian love is inclusive, directing its reach to everyone without exception.

THE TEXT IN BIBLICAL CONTEXT

Individual and Community

One of the obvious features of both testaments of Scripture is the centrality of community, the people of God. Such an emphasis reflects the social world of antiquity in which the community is highly valued. But community is also a key component of the biblical vision. In choosing a people, God began with the family of Abraham and Sarah. Biblical faith is not just a private matter between God and the individual. The fullness of God's blessing comes only in community. A holy community is the goal of God's redeeming action. It is also God's primary instrument in redeeming the world.

The theme of the peoplehood of God is especially strong in the early Old Testament. In the exilic period, Ezekiel emphasized the individual's responsibility before God for their own actions. The exilic and postexilic psalms also highlight the individual before God, offering a more balanced view of the individual and community. This more balanced portrayal appears in the New Testament and Paul as well, as this part of Galatians shows.

Today's English reader is likely to read the New Testament with a bias toward the individual, given the conditioning of Western individualism. Furthermore, the English language disguises the corporate emphasis in the translation process. English does not distinguish between the singular and plural forms of the second-person pronoun *you*, although the Greek clearly does. The result is that the English reader misses Paul's pervasive use of the plural *you* in the texts, reflecting community life. Furthermore, verbs in the Greek language of the New Testament often use a prefix that means "with" (as in the English words *cooperate* and *collaborate*). All of this makes it easy for the modern reader to miss Paul's emphasis on communal experience and shared actions. *One another* (5:13, 15, 26; 6:2) also features prominently in New Testament texts and here underscores Paul's corporate point of view.

In this section of Galatians, Paul is keen to address both the community and the individual, emphasizing their interdependence (cf. the same balance in Rom 14). Community and individual do not displace one another; they live from each other. In New Testament thought, individual piety and church life are not alternatives between which one must choose. These support each other. Individuals build community, and the community builds individuals. Paul's aim is to strengthen both. Any view of the individual or of the community as destructive of the other is a distortion (see also TLC on 5:13-24).

Community of Equality and Mutuality

The same press toward equality that is discernible in 2:6, 15-17 and present in 3:28 (*all … are one in Christ Jesus*) is clearly operative in this section of the letter as well. Paul's vision of equality leads naturally to mutuality, the interchange of care and support that both expresses equality and promotes it. This vision is deeply rooted in the Old Testament ideals of the covenant community. The sabbatical year and the year of Jubilee provided for some equalization of economic and social status (release from debts and freeing of slaves) in the community after periods of free enterprise (Lev 25; Deut 15). The prophets continued and built on these early ideals (Isa 61:1-2; Jer 34:8-22). In the New Testament, Luke-Acts especially highlights these themes in the Magnificat (Luke 1:46-55), in Jesus' programmatic sermon at Nazareth (Luke 4:16-21), and in the early believers' economic sharing (Acts 2:44-45; 4:32-35). Paul stands squarely in this tradition when he promotes financial aid among the churches (2 Cor 8-9; cf. Gal 2:10), based on the exodus story of equal access to food supply (2 Cor 8:15, quoting Exod 16:18). See also James 2:15-16 and 1 John 3:16-17.

THE TEXT IN THE LIFE OF THE CHURCH

Mutual Aid and Benevolence

Mutual aid has marked the Christian church from its beginning. In the early centuries, outside observers were struck by the charitable actions of believers among themselves as well as toward nonbelievers. Christians readily cared for the ill and needy—even at risk to their own lives. Not surprisingly, the impulse to benevolence rises and falls with the spiritual tenor of the church. Times of spiritual renewal are times of compassionate love for others, both in one's own community and beyond.

The radical wing of the Reformation stood out for its commitment to mutual aid as an expression of Christian love. Among the early Anabaptists, it was common in baptism for new believers to pledge to share their possessions if other community members had need. Full community of goods has been practiced to the present time by the Hutterite subgroup of the movement. The spiritual progeny of the Anabaptists in both Mennonite and Brethren traditions have maintained a strong emphasis on mutual aid in a great variety of ways, both informal and organized, addressing the full range of life experience. The same groups have been active in benevolent ministries in the name of Christ, meeting needs of neighbors near and far. This charitable impulse is shared widely among Christian groups and has nourished a notable philanthropic spirit in societies with a strong Christian presence.

Galatians 6:11-18

Conclusion to the Letter

PREVIEW

Paul himself pens the conclusion of the letter to the Galatians. This means someone else actually wrote the rest of the letter for him, although Paul does not name that person. Paul wrote the last small section of Galatians in his own hand to authenticate the letter as truly his. It was the ancient equivalent of a signature. Paul even writes a summary of the letter's argument in order to verify and underscore his point of view. He casts this summary as a contrast between his own and the adversaries' convictions and character. This summary is important for its restatement of the primary concern of the letter. Finally, Paul closes with the customary blessing, inserting a last-minute request into the middle of his final benediction.

OUTLINE

Restatement of the Argument, 6:11-15
Final Request and Benediction, 6:16-18

EXPLANATORY NOTES

Restatement of the Argument 6:11-15

See what large letters I make when I am writing in my own hand! (6:11). Paul normally used a scribe (or amanuensis) to do the actual writing of his letters. The practice was common in his time. It was also customary for the author to add a personal note in their own hand. Paul does this in several of his other letters (1 Cor 16:21; 2 Thess 3:17; Col 4:18). Probably Paul wrote the final greeting in other letters without expressly saying so (the recipients of the original manuscript would easily have noticed the different handwriting), as implied in 2 Thessalonians 3:17 and here in Galatians 6:11.

The purpose of this practice was to validate the letter's source. A comparison with Paul's other letters shows, however, that it is unusual for him to add extensive commentary on the letter's theme as he does here. This indicates that Paul wanted to validate not only his authorship of the letter but also his stance on the issues. The fact that he writes in large letters, and draws attention to it, may add some credence to the suggestion that the physical ailment with which Paul struggled was poor eyesight (see above on 4:13-14). That, along with the word *see*, may indicate that Paul expected the document to be held up before the gathered congregation for visual examination (Dunn 1993: 335).

It is those who want to make a good showing in the flesh that try to compel you to be circumcised—only that they may not be persecuted for the cross of Christ (6:12). Paul's summation begins with a final critique of his opponents in Galatia. He accuses them of being concerned about appearances, the impression they make on others, their public image. In their behavior he sees their interest in social status. Paul made a similar criticism in 4:17. It is an attitude that Paul rejects for himself (1:10). To describe the action of the opponents as *in the flesh* is, at the heart, a charge that they are acting with an eye to this-worldly values and human interests. The following reference to avoiding persecution is an example of this fleshly perspective.

Such a fleshly perspective influences the full range of human experience. In this context, however, Paul is talking specifically about circumcision. According to Paul, the adversaries' motivation in promoting circumcision is to gain social approval (see below). Throughout the letter, circumcision is never far from Paul's thought when he speaks of *flesh*. The association of circumcision with matters of flesh is obvious and may partly explain why he uses the motif of flesh and Spirit in the letter. Paul may even intend some irony in the suggestion that the disfigurement of circumcision makes a pleasing appearance. His association of flesh and circumcision is even clearer in the next verse (6:13).

Galatians 6:12 is the clearest statement that the opponents were trying to convince the Galatian Gentile Christians to be circumcised (cf. 5:2). In recounting the Jerusalem meeting in 2:3 Paul used the word *compel* to describe the pressure that some were exerting on others to be circumcised. The NRSV translation *try to compel* implies that the teachers may not yet have succeeded in their com- pelling. This rendering of the Greek verb is possible, but a more straightforward translation would be *those who are compelling you to be circumcised*, without implying either success or lack of success in that effort.

Paul attributes the action of his opponents to their interest in avoiding persecution. Paul is likely not referring to persecution by Roman civil authorities. Since Jews had official recognition in the Roman Empire as a tolerated religion, there could be advantage for a Gentile Christian to be recognized as a Jew by circumcision. However, that is not the probable background here. In Galatians, Paul clearly has in mind a persecution by the Jewish community, as reflected in 4:29 and 5:11 (see there and 1:13). Such persecution focused on the offense of giving greater allegiance to a crucified Messiah (Christ) than to the Law (the stumbling block for Jews, as in 5:11 and with different focus in 1 Cor 1:23). If Paul's opponents were Jewish Christians, they likely wanted to be tolerated, if not respected, by the Jewish communities in Galatia and in Jerusalem. Paul states his interpretation of their motivation with probable rhetorical overstatement (*only*) for maximum effect.

Circumcision and *cross* are the key words of the conclusion. This supports the interpretation that circumcision was the particular issue behind the letter and that the cross served as the main theo- logical source for Paul's passionate argument. It is remarkable that the resurrection is practically absent in Galatians. It appears once in the introduction (1:1) and is assumed in 1:16 and 2:19-20. On the other hand, *cross* and the related words for crucifixion appear often. This reflects the indisputable fact that the suffering and death of Christ were key factors in Paul's thought. The cross put to death an old order of things and brought into being a new order of things (cf. the *new creation* in 6:15). This is why the Law can no longer be the defining authority for life (see 2:19-21). The cross of Christ is repli- cated in the personal experience of the believer in Christ. It also provides the believer with a readiness to suffer in the defense of the gospel of new creation rather than to compromise it.

Readiness to suffer is a test of fidelity to that gospel. The promi- nence of the cross in Paul's letters does not suggest that it has more theological weight than the resurrection (cf. 1 Cor 15!). The cross simply had more ethical and pastoral relevance to the specific prob- lems of Paul's churches. Then as now, the dominant human ten- dency is to shun the sacrifices implied in a following of Christ

—especially those that entail being crucified to self and to the present world (6:14).

Even the circumcised do not themselves obey the law, but they want you to be circumcised so that they may boast about your flesh (6:13). *The circumcised* here means *the ones being circumcised* (lit.). This might seem to refer to those in Galatia who were heeding the call of the opposing teachers to be circumcised. But the context calls for the same subject as the preceding verse; and the following clause, with its subject, *they*, has to refer to the teachers. Paul is therefore saying that the teachers *themselves do not obey the law*. This could mean either that they are not as strict as some parties of Judaism (not likely because it doesn't really help Paul's argument). More likely, Paul is suggesting that they are guilty of transgressing the Law in their pride and privilege as Jews (see next paragraph). In any case, Paul's point is that the opposing teachers are in some unspecified way failing to observe the Law. Perhaps they are even lax in it. They are interested in circumcision primarily for the political and social-status reasons Paul alludes to in the preceding verse and in the following clause (see also the comments on 5:3).

As in the previous verse, Paul judges that the motive of the opponents for wanting the circumcision of the Galatians is to be able *to boast about your flesh*. This boasting is not of a good kind (cf. 2 Cor 11:18; contrast Gal 6:4, 14). It probably is the kind of boasting named in a close parallel passage in Romans 2:17, 23. This is boasting in the Jewish ethnic identity and moral superiority (Dunn 1993: 339). To boast in the flesh of a convert to Judaism is best understood as pride in the fact that a Gentile has accepted circumcision (the likely allusion of the word *flesh*) and is now a part of the ethnically separate people as a natural, flesh-based category, contrary to the new *Israel of God* (6:16), which is open to all peoples. Paul senses a partisan spirit in the adversaries. They are promoting a particular group's way of life (Judaism) and seeking affirmation and status from that group. This implied group is apparently composed of Jewish Christians who want to identify with the larger Jewish family and is on friendly terms with it, thus avoiding persecution (6:12).

May I never boast of anything except the cross of our Lord Jesus Christ, by which the world has been crucified to me, and I to the world (6:14). Paul employs the full title *Lord Jesus Christ* here and in 6:18 (otherwise only 1:3), giving a more formal tone to the statement. To the false boasting of the opponents, Paul juxtaposes his boasting in the cross. His boasting is in God and in God's work for him and through him (cf. 6:4). The thought is found also in 1 Corinthians 1:31–2:2;

2 Corinthians 10:17 (cf. Phil 3:3). Notable here is the fact that Paul's boast is exclusively in the cross. This is a boasting in death to the self (2:19-20) and therefore is not self-serving. In contrast, the boasting of the opponents is self-centered and self-aggrandizing.

As noted in the comments on 6:12, Paul understood the cross as radically transforming life. It was a matter of life and death for Jesus the Messiah, but it is also a matter of life and death for Israel and Israel's Law, for every individual and indeed for the whole world. Here the word *world* suggests the total created order, including the world of people and nature, physical and spiritual. This world is marked by sin and rebellion against God. The previous order must die so that a new order can come into being. For Paul, nothing in all creation remains untouched by the cross and the change it brings.

Paul's reference to crucifixion picks up on 2:19, where he also testifies to having been *crucified with Christ*. Paul uses the same perfect tense in both contexts, expressing a past event with continuing effects. However, here Paul states the matter in terms of his own relation to the world. The world has been *crucified* to him and he to the world. The same reciprocal relationship appears in 2:19-20 (but to opposite effect): as Christ lives in me and I live in him, Paul declares, so likewise the world dies to me and I to the world. The first reference applies the crucifixion to the individual's inner self. The present reference extends crucifixion to the individual's larger social and cosmic context.

Nothing expresses more radically the polarity Paul sees between Christ and what he stands for, on the one hand, and the world and what it stands for, on the other. This is the world without God, which has created its own systems of belief and its own values that guide its way of living (cf. *the present evil age* in 1:4 and *the elements* of 4:1-11). Paul speaks of his death to this world. He also speaks of a death of the world to him.

Thus, while speaking of a change of relationship, Paul also points to a change in the agents themselves: Paul and the world. Just as Paul himself has been changed by the cross (2:19-20), so also the cross has in some sense changed things at a cosmic level (realm beyond the person; cf. 2 Cor 5:17). Paul's wider teaching confirms that the world external to the person has itself been affected by the cross as explained in Colossians 2:15: at the cross Christ "disarmed" the powers. For Paul and the rest of the New Testament, this new-creation reality (see the next verse) has begun in the work of Christ and the Spirit and awaits its final completion in the future (cf. 5:5).

For neither circumcision nor uncircumcision is anything; but a new creation is everything! (6:15). The presence of the conjunction *for* indicates that this statement further elaborates on the previous verse. It states the implications of the death of the relationship between Paul and the world. But the connection also extends back to verse 13, with its theme of circumcision. Now Paul affirms that one part of the world to which one dies with Christ is the Law-oriented world, which defines social reality in terms of who is circumcised and who is not. That reality is not a part of the new world established by the death of Christ. The expression *neither circumcision nor uncircumcision is anything* closely parallels 5:6 (see on 5:6; also 1 Cor 7:19; Rom 2:25-28). There the point was that neither circumcision nor uncircumcision has any strength to bring about true righteousness. Here the point is an all-encompassing negation: these things amount to nothing.

Paul now names the new world that replaces the world to which Paul has died (6:14): *new creation.* The term could also mean *new creature,* but since the term clearly contrasts with *the world* in the preceding sentence, the preferred translation is the more inclusive *new creation.* This includes both the individual human creature and the larger context (or world) in which the individual lives. God's death-dealing and life-giving act in Christ results in a whole new creation in and for the believer.

The expression also appears in 2 Corinthians 5:17: *So if anyone is in Christ, there is a new creation* (for related language, cf. Eph 4:24; Col 3:10). Paul clearly believes that the renewal of creation has begun in the work of Christ by the action of the Spirit. This renewal centers in the believer and the believing community. In the future, it will embrace all creation (Rom 8:18-23). God's purpose in salvation is as all-embracing as God's original creation. It restores the natural order, the social order, and the personal. Thus the mission of the church tends to the same range of concerns (see TBC, "Creation Old and New").

Final Request and Benediction 6:16-18

As for those who will follow this rule—peace be upon them, and mercy, and upon the Israel of God (6:16). This verse bridges the summary with the conclusion proper. *This rule* refers back to the preceding two verses, where Paul summarizes his own credo. However, since those verses summarize the entire letter, the *rule* includes, in effect, the letter's entire teaching. The word *rule* does not mean regulation or law, but standard of measurement. Paul may have chosen the word deliberately to avoid the connotation of law while preserving truth as a standard (cf. *the truth of the gospel* in 2:5, 14; and *truth* in 4:16; 5:7) that governs the church. The Greek word is literally *canōn*, which later came to designate the Christian Scriptures as the standard of truth, or rule, for the church.

Rule fits well with the accompanying verb, translated here as *follow*. The latter is the same verb found in 5:25 (see comments there) and has the sense of ordering one's life by some standard. Paul is not against the function of law in providing guidance or testing faith. Rather, he combats holding on to a standard (the Law) whose authority has given way to that of Jesus Christ. He opposes using that Law as an alternative to faith in Christ and the life-giving work of the Spirit (cf. *law of Christ* in 6:2).

Peace and mercy—with these words of benediction, Paul offers a traditional Jewish conclusion. *Peace* was used in the opening greeting (1:3). But instead of *grace* named there, Paul here uses *mercy*. The latter word is the most common Greek translation of *ḥesed*, the important Hebrew word for God's favor and faithfulness within the covenant relationship. Given these traditional Jewish concepts, it is not surprising to find another Jewish expression in the benediction: *the Israel of God*.

But what does this mean? The benediction begins with a blessing on those who conform to the rule of Paul's gospel. That is clear. But to what does the phrase *upon the Israel of God* refer? Does it mean ethnic Israel? If so, Paul is offering a gesture of goodwill to his Jewish opponents. Or is Paul referring to the Christians who conform to the Pauline rule? The latter is more likely. Paul appears to formulate a blessing on a particular individual or group by placing it in the context of blessing for the entire people of God, Israel—*on [such person/group] and on all Israel* (Buscemi: 627; Betz: 321). This meaning is consistent with the general thrust of the letter, which sees the gospel as fully continuous with and the true extension of Israel's heritage. It is also consistent with Paul's teaching in chapter 3 that the followers of Christ *are Abraham's offspring*, meaning *Israel* (3:29).

If this is the meaning here, Paul is emphasizing the continuity of the people of God throughout history with the newer Jewish and Gentile community of Jesus' followers. In fact, Paul likely formulated this benediction quite consciously to express his conviction that *Israel*, when true to the Abrahamic covenant, encompasses Jews and the nations (Gentiles), not the Jewish nation alone. If so, the language here includes both traditional Jewish Christians and Gentile Christians—on the condition that they follow the *new-creation* standard Paul has articulated in the letter.

From now on, let no one make trouble for me; for I carry the marks of Jesus branded on my body (6:17). With this interjection Paul breaks the flow of his formal concluding benediction, reminding us that the ending to this letter is different from Paul's usual practice. It lacks Paul's usual warmth. The first benediction even includes a condition. Paul does not bring greetings from other believers, nor does he offer any thanksgiving or doxology, as he often does in his letters. Instead, Paul offers a stern demand. Thus the ending of the letter carries much the same tone as the introduction.

The opening phrase could mean either *finally* or *from now on.* Either fits the context. The noun for *trouble* is a new one in the letter. It can connote striking and hitting, hard labor, and toil (2 Cor 11:27), or causing one to toil; hence, to trouble or bother (Luke 11:7; 18:5). The latter is likely the sense here, though Paul may be deliberately alluding to the physical marks of abuse in the next clause. The exact nuance of the verb is a command to stop the action, to cease the troublemaking already in progress.

Paul gives a reason why he should not be troubled. He bears *the marks of Jesus* on his body. The word for *marks* could connote the brand mark carried by a slave or the mark placed on the body to indicate dedication to a god. In the latter instance, the mark assures one of protection by the deity (Longenecker: 300). That could serve Paul's intention here, since by this comment he wants to deter malicious actions against him. Either option fits Paul's situation and self-understanding. The Greek word for *marks* has entered Christian vocabulary and history, in transliterated from, as stigmata. (See TLC, "Cross and Discipleship.")

By referring to the *marks of Jesus*, Paul is drawing attention once again to the cross and suffering of the human person, Jesus. And given Paul's emphasis in Galatians on his own identification with the suffering of the cross, Paul is using this vivid image to remind the Galatians of the persecution and hardships he has endured in his ministry for Jesus Christ. This is shorthand for the longer description of those experiences in 2 Corinthians 4:7-12, where Paul also uses the name *Jesus* (see also 1 Cor 4:11-12 and 2 Cor 11:23-27).

Paul bears on his body the evidence of a suffering, cross-bearing ministry like that of Jesus. This authenticates his ministry as one who is faithful. All should recognize and respect that Paul is a true apostle of Christ. If this is the sense, then the letter has come full circle. In the end, as in the beginning, Paul defends his apostleship (cf. 1:1; 1:10–2:14).

May the grace of our Lord Jesus Christ be with your spirit, brothers and sisters. Amen (6:18). The wording of the final blessing resembles that of other Pauline letters. Paul's mention of *grace* is particularly poignant since it has underlain his larger argument in the letter without being prominent (but see 1:6; 2:21; 5:4). And Paul's reference to the *Lord Jesus Christ* (note the full title) reflects the Christ-centered theological perspective that everywhere dominates Paul's way of thinking and reasoning. Even Paul's mention of *your spirit* (the only time in the letter *spirit* refers to the human spirit) is significant in a document that makes so much of the Spirit's work, since the human spirit is the point of contact for the Spirit of God (Rom 8:16).

For the last time in a long series throughout the letter, Paul uses the direct address *brothers and sisters* (see on 4:12). Through all the ins and outs of his argument and all the ups and downs of his feelings, Paul has spun a web of fraternal bonds to forestall the potential destruction of relationship represented by the present crisis. All that remains is for Paul to close with the conventional affirmation of *Amen*, that is, *may it be so*. Here it carries all of Paul's passionate concern that what he hopes for the Galatians will indeed come to pass.

THE TEXT IN BIBLICAL CONTEXT

The Significance of the Cross

The cross is a distinctly theological concept based on the unique event of the crucifixion of Jesus, though it draws on the suffering servant of Isaiah 53. The servant is a representative figure that suffers and dies on behalf of others. In so doing, he takes upon himself their sin and afflictions and imparts healing and peace. While New Testament writers do not often directly cite this passage, its imagery and language mark their writings. This is most obvious in the passion narratives and in passages like Acts 8:32-35 and 1 Peter 2:21-25.

The first Christians understood the cross as the first of a two-part transition (cross and resurrection) from a former age to a new age in God's dealing with the world. The cross puts to death the old order, which has been subjected to the powers of sin and death. The resurrection and the outpouring of the Spirit mark the beginning of the new order. The new lies at the end of the path through death. Jesus himself affirms this in his life example and in his call to take up the cross and follow him. The point is explicit in his teaching to the disciples on the Emmaus road: "Was it not necessary that the

Messiah should suffer these things and then enter into his glory [resurrection and exaltation]?" (Luke 24:26; cf. 24:46). The early confession in Philippians 2:6-11 is structured around these two stages, Christ's abasement and his exaltation. In time, the themes of death and resurrection pervaded the structure of early Christian thinking, shaping every aspect of belief and practice.

Paul's determination to measure all thought and action by the cross is fully in harmony with this essential conviction (1 Cor 2:2; see on Gal 2:21). That the cross has multiple levels of meaning and application is fully understandable. Christian belief and life are cross-shaped, cruciform. The cross is God's act of intervention in history to conquer evil powers and to make forgiveness of sin possible (salvation). It is also the norm for Christian existence in the world, following the example of Christ (discipleship).

First Peter 2:21-25 reflects this clearly in asserting that, by his suffering as he bore our sins on the cross, Christ set an example for believers to follow. Paul in Galatians claims the same role for the cross. He speaks of redemption from sin (1:4), of freedom from the bondage of the *present evil age* and from *the elements of the world* (1:4; 4:3-5 KJV; 6:14), and of conforming his entire being and existence to the cross of Christ (2:19-20). Only such a full view of the cross provides an adequate basis for God's mission to establish peace in the whole of creation.

Creation Old and New

The language of creation is rooted in the Old Testament belief in God as the Creator of heaven and earth. Israel's experience as the special object of God's redemption and blessing is but one part in the larger framework of God's ownership and blessing of the entire creation. Throughout the biblical story, we see the interaction of the particular and universal action of God played out. The Bible begins with the first creation and ends with the new creation in a new heaven and a new earth.

The biblical theology of creation forever closes the door to a separation of the spiritual and the material, in which eternal value is attached to the spiritual but not to the material. Even though the New Testament stresses the spiritual—that which relates to the Spirit—it, no less than the Old Testament, is interested in the material dimensions of present and future existence. The purposes of God encompass the total creation.

New-creation language is rooted in the prophecies of Isaiah (see ch. 65), which foresee a new heaven and earth. The apocalyptic thought world of late Second Temple Judaism typically contrasted this age and the renewed age to come. Some Jews used the language of new creation (or new birth) to describe conversion to Judaism. Paul, and other Christian writers, used this vocabulary (new birth, new creation, regeneration) for the profound transformation experienced in encountering Christ (Davies: 119–21).

However, these Jesus followers believed that the new reality was not just a future hope, but also truly a present reality even as we wait for its fullness in the future. That present reality is rooted in the work of Jesus Christ and the presence and power of the Holy Spirit. The resurrection of Christ and the outpouring of the Spirit bear witness to the new creation at work in historic events and in the personal experience of changed lives. Paul himself preferred the language of *new creation* over new birth (John 3:1-8; 1 Pet 1:3). This may reflect his concern to hold together the personal (new birth) and the broader contextual aspects included in the language of new creation.

THE TEXT IN THE LIFE OF THE CHURCH

Cross and Discipleship

If the cross is the mark of authentic Christian living, one might not recognize this truth in the longer history of the church. Life under the cross implies the maintenance of some contrast with the essentially unredeemed social order. This contrast, or holiness, was profoundly compromised when Christianity became the officially sanctioned religion of the Roman Empire. Even as much of Europe was converted to Christianity, Christianity itself was converted to conform to the purposes and ethics of state politics. With this close identification of church and state, known as Constantinianism, the church lost its contrast with the world. The cross lost its ability to point to the costly way of faithfulness to Christ. Instead, its symbolic value was redirected to inner spiritual struggles. In a strange reversal, bearing the cross is now the symbol not of suffering for the gospel but of military victory for the state. In this situation the concept of marks of Jesus, known as stigmata from Galatians 6:17, continued to be important in the church but came to have a different meaning. The stigmata were now not physical marks of persecution for the gospel, as in our text, but signs of a holy person whose body carried marks similar to the crucified Jesus and of supernatural origin.

Throughout subsequent church history, marginal, nonconforming groups and movements have rediscovered the New Testament understanding of the cross as the pattern for true Christian living. The Radical Reformation of the sixteenth century stands squarely in this tradition. Cross bearing in the name of Christ is an essential sign of true faith. Leonard Schiemer expressed it this way: "If the cross is not experienced, then we have the proof that we are false Christians, not yet adopted into the sonship of God" (quoted in Verduin: 261). Under these circumstances, bearing in one's body the marks of Jesus' suffering in persecution and martyrdom was, as for Paul, a powerful reality.

In the modern secular world, the church has an increasingly minority status, which prompts it to rediscover an understanding of the cross as a way of living as well as a means of salvation. In these circumstances, the values of God's kingdom clash with the values of earthly kingdoms. Standing for God's kingdom and promoting it will likely arouse opposition. It will be costly.

Where overt persecution is replaced by benign disdain and hostility, such as in a democratic society, the biblical understanding of the cross easily loses out. When Jesus calls his disciples to take up their cross and follow him (Mark 8:34 and parallels), he does not dwell on what kind of opposition the disciples will face. Rather, he wants them to understand that to join his cause and mission, one must be prepared to make great sacrifice, renounce the normal comforts and privileges of life, and give oneself sacrificially in support of the cause of the kingdom. It is not the kind or degree of opposition that counts, but the readiness to focus oneself and one's resources in one cause: the cause of God's mission in the world. One should expect opposition of some kind, since God's reign is opposed to evil and injustice. But opposition is certainly not the goal of Christian discipleship. The cross involves both Christ's sacrifice for us and the believer's sacrifice for Christ and the kingdom for which he stands.

Conversion and New Creation

The phrase *new creation*, which Paul uses, has not had a prominent place in the language of the church over the centuries. More popular have been related biblical terms such as "regeneration," "new birth," and "conversion." In a way parallel to the theme of cross-bearing (as discussed in the preceding TLC section), even these terms have had a mixed history in the experience of the church. Christendom, which blurs distinctions between church and non-believing society, tames the radical transformation of life implied in these biblical concepts by limiting it to the inner, spiritual level. One is thought to be born into Christendom rather than *reborn* into the family of God (Gal 4:5-7).

But in church groups where the distinction between general society and the church is strong, such as in the free church, and where voluntary, personal faith is crucial, such as in the believers church—conversion is significant. For Anabaptists in the Reformation, conversion and regeneration (new birth) were essential. Unchanged lives reveal only the lack of genuine faith. So Dirk Philips affirmed, "Here [John 3:3, 5] the kingdom of God is absolutely denied by the Lord himself to all who are not born again of God, and who are not created by Him anew in the inner being in his image" (Williams and Mergal: 234). The Anabaptists were distinctive in their emphasis on the ethical dimensions of conversion. Conversion is rooted in an inner spiritual encounter with God; it flowers and bears fruit in a changed life of obedience to the will of God. These are inseparable. In Christ, all of life is marked by likeness to Christ, both inwardly and outwardly (cf. Gal 2:20-21).

The full meaning of Paul's *new creation* has been obscured throughout the centuries. The *new creation* refers both to the transformative new birth of the individual (see the Dirk Philips quotation above) *and* to the transformative new life of the believing community, the renewed people of God. Furthermore, Paul links human and community renewal to the renewal of the whole creation, including the natural order. This aspect of God's renewing mission has often been neglected throughout church history. Paul and the New Testament treat the renewal of natural creation primarily as a future hope (Rom 8:21; Matt 19:28; Acts 3:21; Rev 21:1-8). However, as with biblical thought generally, the church's hope for the future also defines the church's mission in the present. Since we hope for a new heaven and new earth, it follows that care of the natural order falls also within our present mission. New creation is as all-embracing as God's original creation.

Outline of Galatians

Essays

THE FAITH OF JESUS CHRIST Over the last several decades, a lively debate has been taking place over the meaning of the phrase *faith of Christ* or *faith of Jesus Christ* in Paul's writings. The recent debate was triggered by Richard Hays's dissertation on Galatians 3. He took the position that the phrase refers to Christ's own faith or faithfulness rather than to the believer's faith in Christ, which has been common in English translations (Hays 2002). However, we should notice that in subsequent debate Hays has taken a moderate position, resisting the now fashionable trend to see this meaning in many other formulations of Pauline faith.

The *faith of Christ* is the literal translation of the Greek *pistis tou christou*. The expression appears in Galatians in 2:16 (twice); 2:20 (*Son of God*); and 3:22. It appears elsewhere in the undisputed letters of Paul in Romans 3:22, 26; and Philippians 3:9. The two principal ways this phrase is currently translated in the debate are *Jesus Christ's faith/faithfulness*, or, *faith in Jesus Christ*. Thus, the person named can be either the doer (the subject) or the receiver (the object) of the action implied by the other noun—*faith*, in this case.

The expression *baptism of the Spirit*, for example, can mean either the baptism done by the Spirit or the baptism in which the Spirit is given. In Greek grammar these options are known respectively as the subjective genitive or the objective genitive. Consequently, if we take our phrase in the subjective sense, the meaning is the faith or faithfulness that Jesus Christ displays, while the objective sense is expressed as faith directed to Jesus Christ. The Greek phrase can be used either way. In fact, there are more than two ways to understand it. This kind of ambiguity is common in language, and we depend on something in the context or our experience to determine the correct meaning. For instance, when Paul says, "The love of Christ compels us" in 2 Corinthians 5:14 (NIV), does he mean *our* love for *Christ* (objective genitive), or *Christ's* love for *us* (subjective genitive)? Either possibility exists in both the Greek and the English.

Martin Luther's translation is the first known instance where our phrase was rendered in a German equivalent to *faith in Jesus Christ*. Before that, translations tended to preserve the ambiguity by translating word for word. The history of English translations is interesting in this regard. The King James Version translated our phrase in its usual literal way as *faith of Jesus Christ*. How the common reader understood this is unclear, but the overwhelming number of commentators before the late twentieth century interpreted it in the sense of the believer's faith in Jesus Christ. Presumably that was the popular understanding as well. Later the translation *faith in Jesus Christ* became nearly universal. Only recently have translations begun to footnote the possible alternate reading of *the faith of Jesus Christ*. For this reason, modern English readers remain largely unaware of the ambiguity in Paul's expression.

Adding to our difficulty is the fact that *pistis*, the biblical word for faith, has a range of meanings. It can mean "trust, faith or faithfulness, fidelity, or beliefs" in the sense of the thing believed. Particularly relevant to the present question is the choice between placing trust in something or someone and being faithful or trustworthy. Is Paul emphasizing the disposition with which one relates to God (i.e., faith as trust), or with a behavior that displays fidelity toward God (as with faithfulness), or a combination of the two? If Paul means Jesus Christ's faith (subjective genitive), did Christ himself exercise trust in God (as do other believers), or did he demonstrate faithfulness to God in his life and work, or both?

One can also see why major questions of theology soon surface in this discussion. What is Paul trying to do? Is he emphasizing Jesus Christ's work in redemption by grounding it in Christ's own faith or faithfulness? Or is he accenting the fact that the believer is redeemed through the believer's faith, based on Jesus Christ's work? Moreover, is Paul focusing more directly on salvation (by faith) or on ethics (in faithfulness)? Or does Paul focus equally on both? If *faith* means the thing believed, is the question of who does the action beside the point, since the emphasis is on the character of the gospel rather than on someone's action, whether Jesus Christ's or the believer's? Such fundamental theological issues make this debate lively and lasting!

Despite the preceding ambiguities, most interpreters agree that none of the options in this debate fundamentally changes Paul's theology. Adequate evidence for his views exists in other parts of his writing. Nevertheless, accurate assessments of Paul's meaning in each context can help us weigh nuances and accents in his theology.

Many students of Paul find, in the concept of Christ's faith or faithfulness, a fresh way to understand Paul that opens new options for old problems in interpretation or that can reinforce established confessional views. For example, understanding faith as faithfulness can open up new ways to relate the saving benefit of Christ's death and his life as a model or example for Christian living. Relating salvation and ethics more closely makes Paul more congenial to Christian traditions, such as the one represented in the present commentary series, for which discipleship and holiness of life are central (see Toews on the Romans texts). However, the traditions that emphasize the sovereignty of God stress faith over faithfulness in the translation and are attracted to the strong accent on the divine action in faith: in Christ himself, God supplies the faith that saves (see Martyn on the Galatians texts). This helps explain why the translation *Christ's faith* or *faithfulness* has become popular across a wide theological spectrum.

In light of the recent trend just identified, it seems appropriate to test the strength of the translation as Christ's own faith or faithfulness. Despite the potential of this translation to stimulate new insights in Paul's thought, there is no claim that it introduces a totally new dimension. It supports the highlighting of other topics in Paul that have not always been given their due. Principal here is the concept of Christ's obedience, which closely parallels the idea of faithfulness. And identification with Christ makes the life example of Jesus Christ essential. Thus a theology of Christ's own faith is compatible with Paul's thought. It also indicates that how we understand our expression does not determine how we understand Paul's theology overall.

Whatever the strengths of understanding *pistis tou christou* as referring to Christ's own faith or faithfulness, there are weaknesses in attributing this meaning to Paul.

First, Paul nowhere gives an extended exposition of such an understanding, using this specific vocabulary. If it actually had the importance that proponents find in the phrase, it would be surprising that this phrase appears only this way in Paul's writing. Paul never uses either the noun *faith*, or the verb *believe*, or the adjective *faithful* for Christ apart from this expression. Paul never engages in an expanded discussion of such a concept. The fact that Paul never uses faith language unambiguously as an act of Jesus Christ himself, while he consistently uses the language of obedience in this sense (see Phil 2:1-11; Rom 5:19), makes it unlikely that our phrase refers to Jesus Christ's own faith.

Second, in both the Galatians and Romans contexts where our phrase appears, Paul uses Abraham as an example of faith in support of his argument. In Galatians 3, Paul shows that Abraham's faith exemplifies human response to the promise of God, or to the divine initiative of God. Note the large number of references in the chapter to *promise*, which has *faith* as its corollary. Attempts to make faithful Abraham a type of the faithful Christ (cf. Hays 2002; Gorman 2009) in support of the concept of Christ's faith or faithfulness in Galatians do not do justice to this context. Although Paul cites Christ as the seed of Abraham and thus shows that Christ stands in the tradition of the promises to Abraham (3:16), Paul's point is that God's *promise* is what endures to the present time and what characterizes the gospel of Christ—not the Law! Christ is not an exact parallel to Abraham; Christ is not said to have faith in divine promise in the way that Abraham did. To the contrary, in Galatians 3 Christ is presented as the fulfillment of promise, not as one who submits to promise. Furthermore, Paul's appeal to Abraham focuses on faith as trust and openness to God's promise, not on faithfulness or obedience. The same is true in Romans 4. This applies also to the allegory in Galatians 4. Not that one should contrast or even separate these two meanings in Paul's thought! But close attention to Paul's arguments in this context suggests that Paul is emphasizing *faith* more than *faithfulness*. *Faith* in Galatians refers predominantly to human receptivity to God's gift of redemption and to God's gift of the Spirit.

Third, Paul's view of faith was a matter of dispute in the earliest church. The letter of James reflects this debate. Interestingly, the debate in James centers on *faith* in relation to *works*—both of which are actions of the believer. Clearly the debate is not about faith as faithfulness; otherwise James would have had no reason to emphasize works. The idea of faithfulness does appear in Hebrews and Revelation, which refer to Christ as faithful. This fits the themes of those books, which call for the perseverance of believers under testing. But Galatians deals with a different issue.

Fourth, the earliest commentators of Paul, whose native Greek language was the same as Paul's, show no evidence of understanding the phrase as referring to Christ's own faith (Harrisville). This is a significant observation! Most of the occurrences of the expression in the Greek writers carry the same ambiguity as they do in Paul. But scholars generally agree that, in some instances, *faith* clearly refers to the response of the believer. No instance refers unambiguously to Christ's own faith or faithfulness.

Fifth, no interpretation of our phrase as Christ's own faith has been identified before the eighteenth century (Bird and Sprinkle: 15). It is rare until the twentieth century. Translations of the phrase into other languages from the early centuries to the King James Version use equivalents of *faith of Jesus Christ* without indicating how it was interpreted. Translators in premodern times translated as literally as possible out of reverence for the sacred text. How the expression was understood must be shown by commentaries, sermons, and explicit discussions of the interpretation. But so far, no case is known where the reference is to Christ's faith.

So although understanding *pistis tou christou* as a reference to Christ's own faith or faithfulness is grammatically and theologically possible and even attractive, no certain case exists of this sense, either in Paul, in his early interpreters who shared a common language, or in any interpreter before modern times.

Readers of the Toews volume on Romans in this same series will note that he understands the phrase to refer to Christ's faith. He gives four reasons for his view. The first two reasons are based on language usage. He states that the usage in Greek outside and inside the New Testament is overwhelmingly in support of his position. However, later study has not sustained this claim, and today the more typical view is that appeals to language usage cannot answer our question. Both subjective and objective meanings are possible in the Greek (for details, see Bird and Sprinkle: 16–26). Toews's third reason takes the earlier translations of our phrase as *faith of Jesus Christ* as evidence for his position. But this does not constitute solid evidence, as noted in point 5 above. The full evidence points in the opposite direction. His last reason is that taking the phrase in an objective sense would introduce a redundancy in many of the relevant

Pauline texts, with the human act of believing being stated twice in immediate succession. Not everyone sees the redundancy, but the position
defended below makes the question mute.

Now let us consider the traditional meaning of faith as that which the
believer directs to Christ and the divine promises centered in him (the
objective genitive)—*faith in Christ*. This reading assumes a more consistent
meaning in the literary settings where the phrase appears. All agree that
faith as an act of response to the gospel by the believer is prominent in
these contexts. Without clear evidence to the contrary, it is better to
assume that Paul is not mixing the meaning. As noted above, the trusting
response of the believer fits best both the theme of Galatians and the
example of Abraham that Paul invokes.

Two objections to this traditional understanding *appear* to carry serious weight. First, in Galatians and in Romans, the phrase *faith of Jesus
Christ* is immediately followed by a statement that clearly refers to a
human act of receiving (believing) the truth just affirmed in the phrase
faith of Jesus Christ. This creates the appearance of redundancy when the
latter phrase is translated *faith in Jesus Christ*. The objection has some justification, especially if our phrase is taken to emphasize the act of faith, or
believing, as the English translation suggests. However, if the phrase
stresses faith as the thing believed rather than the believing act itself, the
redundancy disappears. This is the viewpoint that is defended below.

Second, some offer a *theological* argument against the traditional
meaning. This has a negative and positive side. Negatively, some claim
that it places too much emphasis on the human contribution to redemption. In Paul's discussion, it may seem more worthy to contrast the works
of the Law, which imply human action and which Paul critiques, with the
faith of Jesus Christ as a divine action. Some have even suggested that the
objective meaning in effect makes faith a human work—the very thing
Paul is combating. But this last point is irrelevant. In Paul's understanding, faith is not a work, as Romans 4:5 expressly states. Positively, the
theological argument finds the idea of Christ's own faith (subjective genitive) useful and fruitful in rounding out Paul's view of the saving work of
Christ (see the discussion above). We will address this objection in what
follows.

One approach avoids focus on the word *faith* as a noun expressing
action. *Faith* can refer to the thing believed. This is common today when
we speak of the "Christian faith." This meaning is already present in
Galatians. In 1:23 Paul is said to be *proclaiming the faith he once tried to
destroy*, and in 6:10 the church is called the *household of faith* (KJV). Clearly
these refer to the gospel message in its entirety, with one part of the message standing for the whole (called "metonymy"). In Galatians 3:23 and 25,
Paul uses *faith* to refer to the historical event of Jesus' life: *faith came*. This
means that a third option exists for understanding the expression *faith of
Jesus Christ*. Here *Jesus Christ* refers neither to the one having faith nor the
one receiving faith. Rather, the name specifies or defines which faith is
meant. *Faith* is not just any faith; it is qualified or characterized in some
way by the person of Jesus Christ. This is commonly called the qualifying

genitive, though genitives of authorship, source, or possession all fit within this third option. In this case one may still ask who the "doer" of the faith is. However, such a question is not central to the phrase itself and is not the point Paul is making. The *substance* of faith is in view, not *who* exercises the faith.

It seems best to take our phrase primarily in this sense, recognizing that different contexts may support differing nuances. Although this is not a new proposal, it has not figured prominently in the discussion until recently. Such English translations as *Christ-faith* or *Christic faith* have been suggested, but they are awkward. Retaining the literal *faith of Jesus Christ* seems preferable. Since we have found reason to reject a Pauline idea of Christ's own faith or faithfulness, we can assume that *faith* in our phrase originates in the idea of the faith of the believer, with that idea lying in the background. However, in the present phrase, *faith* names that message whose character is defined essentially by the person of Jesus Christ. Therefore the phrase reflects both Paul's Christ-centered theology and his conviction that faith is the single means for appropriating God's provision in Christ.

The expression *faith of Jesus Christ* is thus Paul's shorthand way of defining the gospel he preaches in a form that evokes the fundamental concerns in his debates with believers who continue to observe the Law on circumcision and expect Gentile believers to do the same. This is exactly the way Paul uses our phrase in 2:16, where he contrasts it to the phrase *works of the Law*, a shorthand expression for the position he rejects. Both phrases express a larger theological perspective rather than a particular action.

This proposal has the strength not only of tersely capturing Paul's conviction that Christ is central to the gospel. It also has the advantage of overcoming the main objections to the traditional meaning as *faith in Christ*. It removes the appearance of redundancy in the Pauline contexts. Paul is not repeating a reference to the human response of believing. Rather, Paul is expressing the essence of the gospel. In what immediately follows, he refers to the act of the person who accepts that offer by believing. Another advantage of this proposal is that it reshapes the debate about whether the traditional translation places too much weight on the human side of salvation. In our solution, Paul defines the substance of the gospel exclusively in terms of the person of Jesus Christ. The expression does not draw attention to the human aspect of salvation, but rather to the divine provision that has come in and through the person and work of Jesus Christ.

In conclusion, this essay does not discount the legitimacy of Christ's personal faithfulness or its relevance for discipleship in Paul's theology. On the contrary, this emphasis is present in and crucial to Paul, but he makes this point with other language and concepts. That emphasis exists particularly in the theme of identification with Christ (2:20; 3:26-28; 4:19). Paul's language of faith makes a different point. (For further reading on the range of viewpoints in the debate see Hays 2002; Toews: 108–10; Bird and Sprinkle.)

JUDAISM IN THE TIME OF PAUL The term *Judaism* (1:13-14) is often used indiscriminately to describe the people of Israel since the second century before Christ. However, scholars today distinguish between the diverse and variegated "Early Judaism," which existed before the Romans destroyed the Second Temple in 70 CE, and the more monolithic Judaism that developed thereafter.

The term *Judaism* first appears in the time of the Maccabean revolt, in the years 167–164 BCE. However, Early Judaism shares important points of continuity with postexilic Israel. The monarchy, which was so important for the nation of Israel, disappeared with the exile. The Jewish people were without an independent national state until the century-long Hasmonean Dynasty, which began in the mid-second century BCE. The temple and its sacrificial system continued to be important through the Second Temple period. However, Israel's temporary loss of land in the exile contributed to an increased emphasis on the Mosaic Law as the basis for Jewish identity in exilic and postexilic Israel. The writing, gathering, and growing recognition of a body of religiously authoritative writings, focused primarily in the Pentateuch, or Torah, paralleled this trend and supported it. As already reflected in the book of Ezra, the reading and interpretation of the Law became central to the religious life of the Jews. As a result, the priestly and scribal roles came to the forefront in religious leadership. Recent scholarship sometimes refers to late Second Temple Judaism as "Early Judaism," the context in which Jesus and Paul, Jews by birth, lived and carried out their ministries.

Early Judaism was profoundly shaped by its encounter with the nations—foreign empires that often controlled them politically and pressured them culturally. These influencers included the Greek and Roman Empires. The complex of Greek language, religion, culture, known as Hellenism, pervaded the Eastern Mediterranean world. Antiochus IV Epiphanes took a particularly aggressive approach to hellenizing his Jewish subjects, effectively outlawing the practice of Judaism. The Jews' responses to Antiochus's aggressive hellenization were mixed. Some welcomed the new developments and discontinued their religious observances. Others responded with horror, advocating resistance against the hellenizers, some through nonviolent means (e.g., Daniel), others through violent means (e.g., 1–2 Maccabees).

The resisters vigorously defended their identity and remained committed to the Law of Moses. Increased zeal to defend the Law both contributed to and resulted from their defense of their heritage. This was precisely the zeal that motivated Paul in his days as a persecutor of the first followers of Jesus (Gal 1:13-14). Under these circumstances, features of Law observance that defined the boundary between Jew and non-Jew, such as circumcision, carried particular weight. This helps explain the intensity of the struggle within Judaism regarding the Jesus movement, which redefined the role of the Law in certain ways (cf. esp. Sabbath observance). Strategic differences over how to relate peacefully with fellow Jews were likely a factor in Peter's compromise in the Antioch incident recounted in Galatians 2.

Amid the internal and external struggles in Early Judaism was a great diversity of perspectives and parties. Readers of the New Testament are familiar with the principal parties of the time—the Pharisees, the Sadducees, and the Herodians. Another group, the Essenes, occupied the site of Qumran near the Dead Sea. Late Second Temple Judaism was quite diverse in the way it defined religious faithfulness and coped with foreign political and cultural forces. Purity wrestled with accommodation and survival.

Two features in the diversity of early Judaism are particularly important for understanding the emerging movement of Jesus' followers. During this time the Jews' desire for liberation from the oppressive occupying empires fed their hope for an end-time deliverer—an anointed one, a messiah—who would usher in God's final reign of peace and right. From time to time, messianic pretenders appeared and gained a following. Jesus also raised messianic hopes even as he taught a distinctive view of the kingdom of God.

A second feature of this time was the rise of an apocalyptic worldview in the postexilic era, which developed over the centuries. In the first century CE, apocalypticism characterized a good portion of Early Judaism, including Jesus and Paul themselves. When Israel returned from the exile, they soon discovered that their restoration was not quickly attaining the full flower of glory that Isaiah's prophecy promised. However, their confidence in Isaiah's vision remained solid, and their hope began to take on an apocalyptic character. Specifically, they saw the present as a time of evil, which would be fully overcome only when God establishes a more perfect future. Such a transformation will require a cataclysmic intervention of God to destroy the old age and establish the new. Paul's theology is built on an apocalyptic understanding of history. Apocalyptic thought provided a ready framework for understanding Jesus as God's end-time agent, the Messiah, who would restore all things. Thus Paul teaches that the promised new age has broken in with Jesus, in his ministry, death, and resurrection. With the coming of the Spirit as the power of the new age, a time of joy, hope, and optimism is possible.

This diversity of Judaism lasted until the rise of rabbinic Judaism, after the destruction of the temple in 70 CE. Within that diversity, however, there was a high degree of commonality around God's call for Israel to be a distinct and separate people, and God's covenant relationship with Israel was conditioned on observing God's Law. For all Jews, the Law was the center of Jewish identity. The differences of perspective had to do primarily with how to interpret and apply the Law. In this broad sense, Paul's fellow Jews were highly legal in their orientation. That is, they were oriented to Law. Through temple worship and sacrifice, they celebrated the works of God in Israel's past and provided for the restoration of right standing with God.

This dual emphasis on God's gracious provision for an elect people and compliance with the standards of God's holiness characterized late Second Temple Judaism, both within and without the newly developing Jesus movement. As we noted above, the Jewish Scriptures accent both

God's unconditional choice of Israel in promise and grace *and* the principle of moral retribution, with reward for the obedient and punishment for
the disobedient. The result is that the conditional and the unconditional
coexisted in late Second Temple Judaism. Most Jews in the first century CE
held both faith and obedience as important, including Jesus and Paul.

Although scholars readily document both perspectives in late Second
Temple Judaism, they differ in the relative weight they give to each and
hence differ in their characterization of Judaism in its various expressions. Understanding and describing fairly, accurately, and generously
the nature of the theological tensions within Judaism became much more
difficult after the parting of the ways, when Jews and Christians began to
define themselves over against the other. Some Christian interpreters of
Paul have found it all too easy to conclude that what Paul was arguing
against in Galatians was Judaism itself—or perhaps a Judaizing party—
when Paul himself would have been shocked at the suggestion.

So how *is* one to keep the grace of election together with covenant
obligations? This question is an old one that refuses to go away. Israel
was constantly failing by neglecting one side or the other. The prophets
focused their critique on this very thing. It should not surprise us that
Jesus and Paul, as prophetic figures, spoke to the failures of God's people in their day, failures to respect the proper relationship of these
fundamental elements of biblical faith. Nor is it surprising that a constant debate went on (and continues to this day) within the people of
God as to what the proper relationship ought to be. Galatians illustrates
that debate.

For our purposes in interpreting the apostle Paul, the recognition of
first importance is that the viewpoint with which he wrestled was not a
pure legalism that saw salvation as something to be earned by doing good
instead of evil. When Protestant theology, in debt to Martin Luther, read
the Judaism of Paul's day in this fashion, it projected onto Judaism the
lack of balance described in the preceding paragraph. When Jesus and his
first followers critiqued elements in the Jewish experience of their time,
they were not critiquing Judaism itself, but what they saw as an aberra-
tion of true Judaism. As with prophets in all ages, their critique often
addressed the fact that one's practice did not live up to one's profession.
But Jesus also interpreted the Law in ways that many saw as striking in his
day (cf., e.g., his views on Sabbath observance). The early Christian movement was distinctive among the Jewish parties in the first century CE in
the ways in which it rethought the role and purpose of the Law of Moses.
Of the voices we hear, Paul was the most radical of those rethinkers.

Given the diversity of perspectives both within Judaism more broadly
and within the Christian stream of Judaism more specifically, and given
the challenges of describing intra-Jewish debates accurately and fairly
from a perspective set after the parting of the ways, we will probably
never have a clear picture of the beliefs or actual practices across this
wide spectrum. We can say that Paul offers one of the more complete and
nuanced perspectives on the issues. And while we hear his defense of how
Law relates to grace, we do not garner much certain information on the

viewpoints he is challenging. We do know that Paul believes that the coming of Christ and of the Spirit constitute a decisive development in the flow of salvation history. Even more than his fellow Jewish Christian believers, he was committed to think through and live out consistently the implications of those events as he understood them. (See the essay on *Paul's View of the Law in Galatians, p. 316.*)

LITERARY AND RHETORICAL FEATURES OF GALATIANS According to David Aune (204), early Christian letters fall into two categories: circumstantial and general. The circumstantial letter is linked to a particular historical occasion. It captures one moment in a larger relationship and conversation between author and reader(s). The message is tailored to the particular situation of which the author is aware. This type of letter can be difficult for later readers because the writer can assume otherwise essential knowledge of previous contact and the current context. Galatians belongs to this type. The general letter is not tied to a particular historical situation. The content is not conditioned by a specific context. There is no two-way conversation between the author and reader(s). The author is not aware of the particular circumstances or is not interested in them. Although the general letter can be written to a single audience, it is often intended for a wider or general readership. Examples of general letters in the New Testament are Ephesians, 1 Peter, and James.

Further analysis of the New Testament Letters has taken two different lines. One identifies different types of letters on the basis of purpose: friendship, accusation, apology, recommendation, request, rebuke, consolation, thanksgiving, and so forth. The other differentiates types by means of the style of discourse or rhetoric. Here the emphasis is not on the content or purpose but on the way the author uses language to motivate response in the hearer. These rhetorical styles are of three types: the style used in court to accuse or defend (*judicial*); the style used to persuade or dissuade a course of action (*deliberative* or *exhortative*); and the style employed to praise or blame in the setting of entertainment or celebration (*epideictic*). Both of these approaches are based on descriptions found in Greek or Roman writers. They are compatible to a large extent. Accusation and apology are a form of judicial style; rebuke and request are examples of exhortation, in the deliberative style.

Hans D. Betz has argued that Galatians is an apologetic letter (1979: 14). Its purpose is apology or self-defense on the part of the apostle Paul. The style of discourse it employs is that of the courtroom (judicial). In Hellenistic society, such a defense had a fixed form and structure. First, the author introduced the basic issue in an exordium. There followed a narration of the events in the case (*narratio*). The author then offered a brief statement of the position to be defended (*propositio*). Next the author presented supporting evidence (*probatio*) and rebutted counterarguments (*refutatio*). Finally, the author delivered a summation of the case (*peroratio*).

This structure characterizes Galatians, yet with the important exception that Paul adds a large section of practical advice or exhortation

(*exhortatio*), and his rebuttal (*refutatio*) is not a separate section. Betz out-
lines Galatians as follows:

I.   Epistolary Prescript, 1:1-5

II. Exordium, 1:6-11

III. Narratio, 1:12–2:14

IV. Propositio, 2:15-21

V.   Probatio, 3:1–4:31

VI. Exhortatio, 5:1–6:10

VII. Epistolary Postscript, 6:11-18

     (Peroratio, 6:12-17)

Betz's proposal has been welcomed because it gives meaning to what
otherwise seems an arbitrary flow of argument. It is particularly helpful
in chapters 1–2, where Paul is defending his apostleship. Chapters 3–4 fit
the scheme somewhat less clearly. Betz's outline encounters a major
weakness, however, with the long section of exhortation (chapters 5–6),
which has no parallel in other apologetic forms. The offering of advice or
admonition does not fit the argument of legal defense.

The presence of exhortation in a speech or writing suggests the deliberative style of discourse (see above). For this reason and in light of the
problems with Betz's proposal, some students call Galatians *a deliberative
letter with some apologetic features* (Aune: 207; also Kennedy: 145–47; Hall:
277–82). Paul's primary concern is to correct the thinking and behavior of
the Galatians. His defense of his apostolic position and of his view of the
gospel serves to enhance his credibility. The narrative material in chapters 1–2 does not rehearse the past in order to clarify facts that determine
right or wrong behavior in a case of law. What it does is establish the
character and credentials of the writer. The importance of the speaker's
character or credibility (*ethos*) was a recognized feature of sound rhetoric
in the Greco-Roman world. Therefore, the apologetic (*judicial*) elements
serve the larger purpose of exhortation.

This conclusion finds additional support in certain stylistic features of
Galatians. A conventional feature of Greek letters is the formula of astonishment found at the beginning of the body of our letter: *I am astonished*
(Gal 1:6). This is a standard way to introduce a rebuke. The strong outburst at 3:1 (*You foolish Galatians!*) continues this mode of expression. The
first part of Galatians can be described as a rebuke. Beginning at 4:12,
however, another epistolary feature begins and predominates in the
remainder of the letter. This is the request formula, well illustrated in 4:12
by the words *Friends, I beg you*. The second part of Galatians can then be
seen as a request. Consistent with this pattern is the absence of imperatives before 4:12 (a possible exception is 3:7) and the presence of many
imperatives thereafter.

On the basis of these literary features in Greek letters, Galatians has been called a letter of rebuke and request (Longenecker: ciii; similarly Martyn: 24–27). Longenecker uses this for his structural analysis of the book:

Salutation, 1:1-5

Rebuke Section, 1:6–4:11

Request Section, 4:12–6:10

Subscription, 6:11-18

These two alternative ways of analyzing Galatians via style of discourse (deliberative) or via epistolary type (rebuke/request) are actually compatible. Rebuke and request are types of deliberative speech that characterize a category of Greek letters. From the point of view of its rhetorical style, Galatians is deliberative; from the perspective of its literary type, it is a letter of rebuke and request.

PAUL'S VIEW OF THE LAW IN GALATIANS The status of the Mosaic Law (hereafter, the Law) in Paul's letter to the Galatians is a complex question and, as a consequence, a highly debatable subject. On the one hand, Paul has a grand view of God's plan, in which the Law has a significant and positive place. On the other hand, Paul makes some sharp contrasts between Christ and the Law and presses his readers to choose between these options. There is a strong either-or tone in the argument of the letter. Is there consistency and coherence in Paul's view? Or, as some conclude, is his argument illogical and ultimately incoherent? Is Paul perhaps merely jostling for political advantage over the opposition that figures prominently in Galatians? If Paul's argument is coherent, how do we articulate it?

Contributing to the complexity of our question is the polemical style of the letter. Paul wants to persuade the readers in a certain direction. Understandably, he sharpens the terms of the choice that he wants them to make. Paul uses a wide range of rhetorical methods to help achieve that end. Thus he does not nuance every statement, nor does he deal with issues that might detract from his argument, even if we should consider them important from our perspective. Because Paul's less polemical letter to the Romans treats similar issues, we must also consult it in reconstructing Paul's theology, based on subtle clues as well as explicit claims.

Paul's view of the role of the Law after Jesus Christ is shaped by his conviction that nothing can challenge the all-sufficiency of God's action in Christ to save the Gentiles—not even the Law. Much of Paul's theology reflects his attempts to use the Law and the Prophets to support the truth of this revelation. The various parties in Judaism, including the first followers of Jesus of Nazareth, shared a high respect for the Law, even though they interpreted it differently. In trying to understand Paul, interpreters of the letter to the Galatians find themselves constantly asking what view Paul is countering. Here a range of possibilities presents itself. Paul himself was a Pharisee, and he remained a Pharisee as a believer (cf. Acts 23:6), even though his new convictions put him at odds with his fellow Pharisees. We have already noted the existence of Essenes, Sadducees, Herodians, and other groups within Judaism. We cannot assume a unified view of the Law within this range. This complexity contributes to the challenge of fully understanding Paul in his context.

We begin by identifying, in summary fashion, Paul's broader view of the Law, including some aspects to which he alludes in the letter but does not emphasize because of the letter's polemical purpose.

1. The Law is divine revelation. In Galatians 3, Paul speaks of the Law being given and added. The unspoken but clear subject for these actions is God. True, Paul mentions that the Law was ordained through angels (3:19). Paul thus acknowledges that the Law is supernatural in origin. At the same time, he implies that the mediated character of the Law by angels lacks the full agency of God. Galatians implies that only Jesus Christ expresses the full agency of God, and only the love commandment (5:14) reveals the true will of God.

2. The Law plays a significant role in the story of God's saving purpose. The Law was added because of transgressions (3:19). Whatever the exact meaning of this statement (see commentary), Paul affirms that a divine purpose stands behind the giving of the Law. That purpose was for the good of God's people. At the same time, the Law served its purpose within the more fundamental covenant of God's promise, accepted by faith. That covenant was with Abraham and came to full flower in Jesus Christ. The Law thus had a kind of parenthetical and temporary character. Its positive if secondary function in the service of God's purpose centered on promise and faith. It follows that the Law cannot serve as an autonomous instrument for building or sustaining relationship with God.

3. The Law is subservient to Christ. The coming of Christ represents the fulfillment of God's deepest intention reflected already in the promise to Abraham to bless Israel and the nations. For Paul, this means that Christ is the full authority for the church. The authority of the Law is now conditioned by the greater authority of Christ. The Law is neither superior to Christ nor is it equal to him.

4. The Law has a continuing function for the followers of Jesus Christ. This is a point that Paul makes by his example, not by his exposition. Nowhere in Galatians does he explain what role the Law can legitimately have for the believer in Christ or how it plays that role. In 5:14, Paul supports his exhortation that the Galatians serve one another in love by stating that such conduct fulfills the love commandment from the Law. He even calls this moral demand *the law of Christ* (6:2). This is not surprising since Paul believes that the Law originated with God. It should and does reveal the will of God. But there are caveats, to which we now turn.

The coming of Jesus Christ and the Spirit—and perhaps also his own experience with the Law—has revealed certain limitations in the Law, or weaknesses. Paul cites these weaknesses in his appeal to the Galatians not to submit to the Law without qualification.

1. The Law is not the latest and final stage of God's redemptive plan and action. This is the *salvation-historical* argument in relation to the Law. The Law was a central feature of the religious life of God's people and its final authority. Now for Paul and the early believers generally, Jesus is the Messiah (Christ), God's agent of revelation and salvation at the end of time (cf. the theme *fullness of time* in Gal 4:4). In contrast to many of his fellow Jewish believers, from this theme Paul drew the radical implication that Jesus is now the final authority, to which the authority of the Law is fully subordinate. The revelation of God's will in and around the person, teachings, life, and death of Jesus, and Paul's conviction that this good news must be preached to the Gentiles (including God's call on Paul's own life to do so)—all this called for a modified application of the Law and a change in its role. These changes are determined by the role of Jesus Christ in mediating our relationship with God, by the role of the Spirit in guiding and empowering the church, and the role of the church to be a light to all the nations. Paul does not allow that Christ is simply another chapter in the story of redemption that merely adds to or supplements the authority of the Law. Christ is the final authority, who is complete in himself, and to whom all preceding revelation must answer.

Particularly helpful in this regard is the concept of fulfillment. In the Sermon on the Mount, Matthew cites Jesus as saying that he has come not to abolish but to fulfill the Law and the prophets (Matt 5:17). Christ fulfills the Law. The word *fulfill* expresses well the general viewpoint of New Testament writers, including Paul. This word communicates both continuity and discontinuity between God's action in the past and God's action in Christ. Christ takes up the old and brings it to culmination. The old is not left behind but is enhanced and in some ways changed in the light of the character of the new. For Paul, there can be no returning to the old in the form that it was. Among the early followers of Christ, Paul was distinctive in seeing the radical implications of Christ as the unconditional center of faith.

2. The Law is not capable of giving full life in God. This is Paul's *soteriological* argument in relation to the Law. In 3:21, Paul explicitly acknowledges that righteousness would indeed come from the Law, *if* the Law could give life. But the Law, in fact, does *not* give life. In 2:19, similarly, Paul affirms that the Law itself caused him to die to the Law in order that he might live to God. Paul's relationship to the Law was marked by spiritual death (cf. Rom 7:4). That death opened the way to life in God. Paul immediately explains that he means life as the living presence of Christ within Paul (2:20). By identifying with Christ, Christ's life is active in the person of Paul. This further demonstrates that Paul understands the reference to life in the Habakkuk 2:4 proof text quoted in 3:11 to include this sense. Even though the Law defines true qualities of life with God, the Law does not have the ability to create the living relationship with God that is the heart of spirituality and the basis for godly living. This may appear to contradict the Old Testament claims that often associate true life with Law observance, such as those in Deuteronomy and the Psalms. But Deuteronomy observes that love for God, followed by obedience to the

Law, is the key to life (Deut 30:6-20). So even here the Law witnesses that, in itself, the Law does not give life. Given that point of agreement, for Paul, life in Christ reaches a new and unprecedented level of quality.

3. The Law cannot empower holy living. This is Paul's *ethical* argument. In Galatians, Paul thinks of life as both being alive to God relationally and living out the will of God in conduct. Certainly Paul's Jewish heritage and training would have offered him this perspective. The key factor here is that the Holy Spirit is a major topic of the letter. The Spirit is the agent of power and makes possible what God intends. The opening verses of chapter 3 highlight the Spirit as the basis for the Galatians' own spiritual breakthrough. The work of the Spirit did not result from works of the Law but from faith in what God offers in Christ. In this context, the evidence of the Spirit's work lies in the miracles that have taken place in the Galatian churches. The clear implication is that the Law does not have the power to realize what God intends and offers for believers.

Paul applies this contrast of Spirit and Law specifically to ethics in chapter 5. Here Paul describes the Christian life as living in the Spirit, walking in the Spirit, and being led by the Spirit. The Spirit brings to fruition the godly virtues in the believer (5:22-23). Thus the Spirit achieves what is in harmony with the Law (5:23b; cf. Rom 8:4). For this reason those who are *led by the Spirit* are *not subject to the Law* (Gal 5:18). The Spirit can contend with the flesh and its desires (5:17), but observance of the Law apart from the Spirit relies on the very flesh that weakens our ability to obey (see 3:2-3, which places works of the Law and flesh in parallel; cf. Rom 7!).

Paul does not, however, identify Law with flesh. He associates the two to make the point that Law observance is based on frail human resource (flesh), which sin so easily dominates. This is a formula for moral failure. Paul explains this point in Romans 7. Paul also implies that the Law is an *element of the world* (Gal 4:3, 9 KJV). As such it is *weak and beggarly* and represents more slavery than freedom. Here again, Paul does not see the Law as evil in itself. Rather, Paul is saying that even the Law, standing alone as a foundational principle for living, enslaves rather than frees.

4. The demand for Law observance negates the saving action of God in Christ in removing the divide between Jews and Gentiles. God's action in Christ saves all on the same basis, faith in Christ, thus forming a people of God from all nations. This is the *ecclesiological* argument. Weaving through Galatians 2–3 is Paul's concern that the Gentiles readers of his letter understand themselves as truly one with and equal to the Jewish believers in Christ. The classical statement is 3:28. Paul makes the point explicitly when he reminds Peter that their encounter with Christ has revealed themselves to be sinners, just as they, as Jews, had always viewed the Gentiles (2:15, 17). Paul vigorously defends the Gentiles' freedom within the Christian family (2:4-6). For him, the Jewish identity markers of circumcision and ritual purity compromise the unity of the new people of God. As identity markers, those practices create boundaries that separate Jewish and Gentile believers. If the Gentiles need to become full-fledged Jews by submitting to circumcision, they are no longer on equal terms. Both Jews and

Gentiles need to submit to a third party, namely, Jesus Christ. Paul's passionate defense of the universality of the church is the central issue in Galatians. Submission to the Law by the Gentile believers can only compromise the unity of the church by making them second-class kingdom citizens. Their freedom is at stake.

Paul's description of the Law in Galatians is conditioned by the situation in the Galatian churches as he understands it. One should thus avoid overreading the negative tone of the letter. Paul believes that the opposing teachers are moving from a faith- and Spirit-based stance to a works- and flesh-based one (see esp. 3:1-5). Their understanding and use of the Law effectively negates the Spirit and faith, replacing them with reliance on human resources (the flesh). As a result, the Law remains a complete and full authority in its own right. Here Paul does not discuss whether or how one can respect and use the Law in a way that does not negate the fundamental principles of Spirit and faith. Paul's appeal to the Law in 5:14, and throughout his letters, indicates that he does believe there is such a way. Paul does resist, however, any tendency to claim unconditional authority for the Law instead of or even alongside Christ. Paul will not allow the Law to compromise the great breakthroughs of God's action in Christ or the enablement of the Spirit.

Throughout much of church history, especially since the Reformation, Paul's position on the Law has been contrasted with a view—attributed to the Judaism of his time—that right standing with God is achieved by doing good works. Classic Protestant theology has typically held that Paul was arguing against "Judaism" in Galatians—a Judaism believing that salvation depends on keeping the Law: salvation by works. Paul's alternative gospel is salvation by faith. Over the last twenty-five years, initiated largely by the work of Krister Stendahl and E. P. Sanders, research has made clear that the Jews of Jesus' time and Paul's time did not believe in self-salvation. For them, as in the Old Testament texts, God's gracious election was a gift, the ground of salvation. Law observance *maintains* right standing, but it is not the *basis* for it. But if this is the standard view of Judaism, what is Paul opposing in his argument regarding the Law?

Paul's concern can be summarized in two broad categories. First, the revelation of Jesus as God's messianic agent at the end of time constitutes the very definition of God's will. God's revelation in Christ is in continuity and essential harmony with the Law. At the same time, Christ changes how the Law applies to today. God's revelation in Christ gives higher priority to some aspects of the Law that were present all along, but perhaps not central in the practice of it. An example central to Galatians is the mission to the Gentiles, which Paul sees in God's call to Abraham to be a blessing to the nations. This mission is hindered by a requirement like circumcision, which creates a barrier between Jew and Gentile and compromises the vision of a people of God inclusive of all nations. In other ways, the earliest Christians saw Christ as replacing a feature of the older covenant. For example, the death of Jesus terminates the system of animal sacrifice. Weighing the implications of Christ's finality has continued in church history, often with controversy. The historic peace churches understand Jesus' command to love one's enemies (Matt 5:44-47) to suggest that the Old Testament examples of war do not justify war in this era. In Galatians, Paul is concerned that believers not compromise either the gospel or their freedom by embracing the Law in a way that negates or diminishes the greater authority of Christ.

Paul asserts that the coming of the Spirit enables righteous, Christlike living. That living is readily compromised by a wrong use of the Law. Paul seems to imply that the Spirit can guide believers in ways that go beyond the Law, though not in a way that is fundamentally contrary to it (5:23b). His central point is that the Law, while true in its substance, has to rely on a source outside of itself for achievement. The source of that empowerment is either the human will and effort (i.e., the *flesh*) or the Spirit. The flesh is inadequate because its passions and desires are controlled by sin rather than godliness (5:16-17). Only the Spirit can overcome the weakness of the flesh and enable righteousness. Thus Paul is not critical of anything in the Law itself. He is, however, deeply concerned that the teachers' focus on the Law is shifting the Galatians' attention away from the Spirit to the Law. And since the Law is vulnerable to the weakness of the flesh, the Galatians will likewise be vulnerable to it.

As Paul himself admits, there is nothing inherently incompatible between Law and Spirit. Paul himself appeals to the Law (5:14) and to standards (laws or regulations) in general (cf. "the law of Christ" in 6:2 and 1 Cor 9:21). So how might we explain Paul? Apparently Paul shares the perspective of Israel's prophets (cf. 1:16) and of Jesus himself, who saw around them the hypocrisy of external conformity without genuine love for God. In the perspective of Paul as prophet, Israel is once again in danger of lapsing into a nominal adherence to the formal requirements and practices of the Law. In Galatians, Paul does not explicitly indict his fellow Jews with this charge, though he may imply it in his critique of justification by works of the Law.

In contrast to classical Protestantism, we have learned not to characterize the Judaism of Paul's day as a religion of salvation by works. However, Paul did see in his fellow Jewish Christians a tendency to give more weight to the formal observance of the Law than he considered appropriate. Like Jesus, Paul saw the people of God in his day as lacking in practice what they professed in word. The writer of 2 Timothy (3:5) eloquently describes this condition as "holding to the outward form of godliness but denying its power." To combat this tendency, Paul passionately promotes genuine relationship with God, a reality made possible now, in the age of the Spirit, when one can and must aspire to a deeper and more fruitful life with God in Christ.

In short, Paul sees the Law itself as "good" (cf. Rom 7:12). The problem arises, however, (1) when one takes the Law as *final* authority without submitting to the fullness of truth in Jesus Christ, (2) when the Law's authority is taken as independent of the divine empowerment that comes from the Spirit of Christ, and (3) when Law observance maintains the boundary markers that distinguish Jew from Gentile.

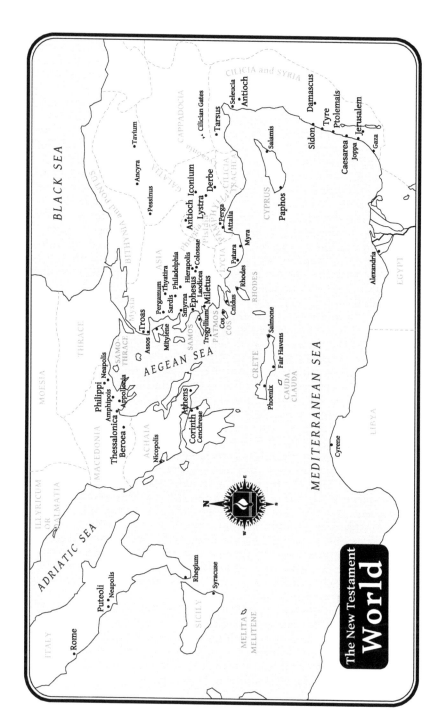

Bibliography

Aune, David E.
  1987   *The New Testament in Its Literary Environment*. Philadelphia: Westminster.
Barclay, John M. G.
  1991   *Obeying the Truth: Paul's Ethics in Galatians*. Minneapolis: Fortress.
Betz, Hans Dieter
  1979   *Galatians: A Commentary on Paul's Letter to the Churches in Galatia*. Hermeneia. Philadelphia: Fortress.
Bird, Michael, and Preston Sprinkle, eds.
  2009   *The Faith of Jesus Christ: Exegetical, Biblical, and Theological Studies*. Peabody, MA: Hendrickson.
Bruce, Frederick Fyvie
  1982   *The Epistle to the Galatians: A Commentary on the Greek Text*. New International Greek Testament Commentary. Grand Rapids: Eerdmans.
Burton, Ernest DeWitt
  1921   *A Critical and Exegetical Commentary on the Epistle to the Galatians*. International Critical Commentary. Edinburgh: T & T Clark.
Buscemi, Alfio Marcello
  2004   *Lettera ai Galati: Commentario esegetico*. Jerusalem: Franciscan Printing Press.
Campbell, Constantine
  2012   *Paul and Union with Christ: An Exegetical and Theological Study*. Grand Rapids: Zondervan.
Cosgrove, Charles H.
  1988   *The Cross and the Spirit: A Study in the Argument and Theology of Galatians*. Macon, GA: Mercer University Press.
Davies, W. D.
  1980   *Paul and Rabbinic Judaism*. 4th ed. New York: Harper & Row.
Dunn, James D. G.
  1990   *Jesus, Paul, and the Law: Studies in Mark and Galatians*. Louisville, KY: Westminster John Knox.
  1993   *The Epistle to the Galatians*. Black's New Testament Commentary. Peabody, MA: Hendrickson.

1998   *The Theology of the Apostle.* Grand Rapids: Eerdmans.
Elias, Jacob W.
2006   *Remember the Future: The Pastoral Theology of Paul the Apostle.* Scottdale, PA: Herald Press.
Furnish, Victor Paul
2009   *Theology and Ethics in Paul.* Louisville, KY: Westminster John Knox.
Gorman, Michael J.
2001   *Cruciformity: Paul's Narrative Spirituality of the Cross.* Grand Rapids: Eerdmans.
2009   *Inhabiting the Cruciform God: Kenosis, Justification, and Theosis in Paul's Narrative Soteriology.* Grand Rapids: Eerdmans.
Hall, Robert G.
1987   "The Rhetorical Outline of Galatians: A Reconsideration." *Journal of Biblical Literature* 106:277–87.
Hansen, G. Walter
1989   *Abraham in Galatians: Epistolary and Rhetorical Contexts.* Sheffield: Sheffield Academic Press.
Harrisville, Roy A.
1994   "*Pistis Christou*: Witness of the Fathers." *Novum Testamentum* 36:233–41.
Hays, Richard B.
2000   "The Letter to the Galatians." *The New Interpreter's Bible,* 11:181–348. Nashville: Abingdon.
2002   *The Faith of Jesus Christ: The Narrative Substructure of Galatians 3:1–4:11.* 2nd ed. Grand Rapids: Eerdmans.
Kennedy, George A.
1984   *New Testament Interpretation through Rhetorical Criticism.* Chapel Hill, NC: University of North Carolina Press.
Kenneson, Philip D.
1999   *Life on the Vine: Cultivating the Fruit of the Spirit in Christian Community.* Downers Grove, IL: InterVarsity.
Koperski, Veronica
2001   *What Are They Saying about Paul and the Law?* Mahwah, NJ: Paulist Press.
Kuiper, Frits
1947   *De ware vrijheid.* Haarlem, Netherlands: H. D. Tjeenk Willink & Zoon.
Lightfoot, J. B.
1986   *Saint Paul's Epistle to the Galatians.* Reprint of 10th ed., 1890. London: Macmillan.
Longenecker, Richard N.
1990   *Galatians.* Word Biblical Commentary 41. Dallas: Word Books.
Luther, Martin
1953   *A Commentary on St. Paul's Epistle to the Galatians.* Westwood, NJ: Fleming Revell.
Martin, Troy
2003   "The Covenant of Circumcision (Genesis 17:9-14) and the Situational Antitheses in Galatians 3:28." *Journal of Biblical Literature* 122:111–25.
Martyn, J. Louis
1997   *Galatians.* Anchor Bible. New York: Doubleday.

Sanders, E. P.
  1983   *Paul, the Law, and the Jewish People*. Philadelphia: Fortress.
Riches, John
  2008   *Galatians through the Centuries*. Oxford: Blackwell.
Swartley, Willard M.
  2006   *Covenant of Peace: The Missing Piece in New Testament Theology and Ethics*. Grand Rapids: Eerdmans.
Toews, John E.
  2004   *Romans*. Believers Church Bible Commentary. Scottdale, PA: Herald Press.
Verduin, Leonard
  1964   *The Reformers and Their Step-Children*. Grand Rapids: Eerdmans.
Westerholm, Stephen
  2004a   *Perspectives Old and New on Paul: The "Lutheran" Paul and His Critics*. Grand Rapids: Eerdmans.
  2004b   *Understanding Paul: The Early Christian Worldview of the Letter to the Romans*. 2nd ed. Grand Rapids: Baker Academic.
Williams, George, and Angel Mergal
  1957   *Spiritual and Anabaptist Writers*. Library of Christian Classics 25. Philadelphia: Westminster.
Witherington III, Ben
  1998   *Grace in Galatia: A Commentary on Paul's Letter to the Galatians*. Grand Rapids: Eerdmans.
Wright, N. Thomas
  1991   *The Climax of the Covenant: Christ and Law in Pauline Theology*. Edinburgh: T&T Clark.
  1997   *What Saint Paul Really Said*. Grand Rapids: Eerdmans.
  2013   *Paul and the Faithfulness of God*. Vols. 1–2. Minneapolis: Fortress Press.
Yoder, John H.
  1973   *The Legacy of Michael Sattler*. Classics of the Reformation. Scottdale, PA: Herald Press.
  2009   "The Apostle's Apology Revisited." In *To Hear the Word*, 3–24. 2nd ed. Eugene, OR: Cascade Books.
Young, Norman
  1998   "Who's Cursed—and Why? (Galatians 3:10-14)." *Journal of Biblical Literature* 117:79–92.

Selected Resources

Dunn, James D. G. *The Epistle to the Galatians*. Black's New Testament Commentary. Peabody, MA: Hendrickson, 1993. An accessible commentary from a leading New Testament scholar, promoting what he was the first to identify as the New Perspective on Paul.

———. *The Theology of Paul the Apostle*. Grand Rapids: Eerdmans, 1998. A comprehensive treatment of Paul's theology across his writings, organized for easy use as a reference work on particular aspects of Paul's thought.

Gorman, Michael J. *Cruciformity: Paul's Narrative Spirituality of the Cross*. Grand Rapids: Eerdmans, 2001. Highlights the theme of Christ's crucifixion in its salvific, spiritual, and ethical implications, a theme crucial in the letter to the Galatians. Makes Paul's perspective deeply compatible with the discipleship concerns of the believers church tradition.

———. *Reading Paul*. Cascade Companions. Eugene, OR: Cascade Books, 2008. A compact and readable summary of Paul's understanding of the gospel, reflecting contemporary discussion about the issues. Of particular interest is Gorman's emphasis on peace and nonviolence in Paul.

Longenecker, Richard N. *Galatians*. Word Biblical Commentary 41. Dallas, TX: Word Books, 1990. A thorough and masterful treatment by an evangelical scholar of Paul's letter to the Galatians, giving attention to its historical and literary aspects as well as its theological claims. Based directly on the Greek text but usable for all readers.

Martyn, J. Louis. *Galatians.* Anchor Bible 33A. New York: Doubleday, 1997. An advanced-level commentary, offering a detailed reconstruction of the conflict in Galatia. The commentary accents the apocalyptic viewpoint of the letter, characterizing the event of Jesus Christ as an intervention of God that creates a pronounced break with the time of the Law. The traditional Protestant emphasis on salvation by grace alone is vigorously defended.

Wright, N. Thomas. *Paul and the Faithfulness of God.* 2 vols. Minneapolis: Fortress, 2013. This massive and masterful work on Paul's theology is currently the touchstone with which to assent or dissent in the study of Paul. Although challenging for its wordiness, the style makes for interesting reading. As the title suggests, Wright makes the faithfulness of God the organizing theme of Paul's thought, seeing in the life and work of Jesus Christ an extension of that faithfulness.

Index of Ancient Sources

The Author

George R. Brunk III is dean emeritus and professor emeritus of New Testament at Eastern Mennonite Seminary (EMS) in Harrisonburg, Virginia. He served as dean of EMS for twenty-two years and as interim president of Anabaptist Mennonite Biblical Seminary in 2009. Brunk has also served as moderator of the Mennonite Church general assembly and a member of the general board of the Mennonite Church. He worked as missionary pastor and field administrator with Virginia Mennonite Board of Missions in Palermo, Sicily, for six years.

Brunk, who was born in Newport News, Virginia, is a graduate of Eastern Mennonite University, Eastern Mennonite Seminary, and Union Theological Seminary of Virginia. His articles have appeared in numerous publications.

A resident of Harrisonburg, Virginia, Brunk is a member of Lindale Mennonite Church, where he has served as chair of the board of elders. He was married to Erma Hess for forty-one years and has two children. After Erma's death, Brunk married Ruthann Miller, and together they have eleven grandchildren.

Galatians

"Brunk offers new insights that challenge the common understanding of this early Christian letter. Utilizing insights from many years of teaching, this commentary challenges traditional Protestant understanding of justification by faith alone to a more holistic understanding of Christ-centered faith and life in the Holy Spirit. I highly recommend it." —*Paul M. Zehr, professor emeritus of New Testament, Eastern Mennonite Seminary*

"Brunk's Galatians—notable for its clarity—is the gift of a seasoned teacher. It highlights Paul's bold defense of the gospel against false so-called apostles, treating at length the relation of law and gospel. Brunk's contribution to the much debated translational issue of 'faith of Jesus Christ' or 'faith in Jesus Christ' is a stimulating complement to John Toews' treatment of the same in his Romans commentary." —*Willard Swartley, professor emeritus, Anabaptist Mennonite Biblical Seminary*

"Here is first-order exegesis for the church. This commentary masterfully elucidates Paul's 'revolutionary manifesto,' locates Paul's argument within the wider Pauline and New Testament contexts, and assesses Paul's message for the twenty-first-century church." —*Dorothy Jean Weaver, professor of New Testament, Eastern Mennonite Seminary*

"Brunk offers a compelling tool for reconnecting Christ-centered faith and Christ-centered living at the heart of Paul's gospel. He points to a living encounter with Jesus that is personally transformative and socially disruptive in the best sense. In Galatians, Christ invites everyone to the familial table for a feast of grace." —*Meghan L. Good, pastor, Albany Mennonite Church*

"Brunk gives a lucid, erudite interpretation of Galatians by illuminating its first-century context, following its rebuke-request literary structure, and applying its themes with keen discernment to the twenty-first-century church. I am especially encouraged by his clear vision of equality for all in Christ and liberty for all by the Spirit." —*G. Walter Hansen, retired associate professor of New Testament, Fuller Theological Seminary*

Ingram Content Group UK Ltd.
Milton Keynes UK
UKHW021258260523
422400UK00023B/654